The Re-Enchantment of the West

Volume I

The Re-Enchantment of the West

Volume I

Alternative Spiritualities, Sacralization, Popular Culture, and Occulture

Christopher Partridge

T & T CLARK INTERNATIONAL
A Continuum imprint
LONDON • NEW YORK

Copyright © 2004 T&T Clark International
A Continuum imprint

Published by T&T Clark International
The Tower Building, 11 York Road, London SE1 7NX
15 East 26th Street, Suite 1703, New York, NY 10010

www.tandtclark.com

British Library Cataloguing-in-Publication Data
A catalogue record for this book is available from the British Library

Library of Congress Cataloging-in-Publication Data
A catalogue record for this book is available from the Library of Congress

ISBN   0-567-08269-5 (hardback)
          0-567-08408-6 (paperback)

Typeset by CA Typesetting, www.sheffieldtypesetting.com
Printed on acid-free paper in Great Britain by CPI Bath

For Sarah

CONTENTS

Part I
THE DISENCHANTMENT AND THE RE-ENCHANTMENT OF THE WEST

Part II
THE SIGNIFICANCE OF OCCULTURE

ACKNOWLEDGEMENTS

I began writing this book several years ago. In fact, to be honest, I began writing another book several years ago. The book I initially began writing was about contemporary Western Paganism. For encouraging me to write this abandoned book I am enormously grateful to Janet Joyce, who was then with Cassell. By the time Cassell became an imprint of Continuum my research had broadened. It had done so for several reasons. First, it became increasingly apparent that some fundamental sociological and cultural questions about the emergence and growth of contemporary Paganism in the West needed to be addressed. Secondly, I was also aware of literature which claimed that Paganism was a manifestation of a fairly superficial contemporary religious phenomenon and, indeed, may even be interpreted as part of the secularization process. Although initially persuaded by such arguments, it became increasingly clear to me that they needed to be challenged and that this could only be done satisfactorily by broadening the scope of my research to examine the milieu to which Paganism belonged. Finally, several excellent studies of Paganism were quickly filling the gap I had initially identified when I began thinking about the book in the mid-1990s. Although I had already read some superb treatments such as Tanya Luhrmann's *Persuasions of the Witch's Craft: Ritual Magic in Contemporary England* (1989), in 1997 two significant textbooks were published: Graham Harvey's *Listening People, Speaking Earth* and Lynne Hume's *Witchcraft and Paganism in Australia*. However, the book that finally settled the matter for me and led me to apply my efforts elsewhere was Ronald Hutton's seminal historical study, *The Triumph of the Moon: A History of Modern Pagan Witchcraft* (1999). That year also saw Helen Berger's fine sociological study, *A Community of Witches: Contemporary Neo-Paganism and Witchcraft in the United States*. Since then the flow of worthwhile monographs, such as Sarah Pike's *Earthly Bodies, Magical Selves: Contemporary Pagans and the Search for Community* (2001) and Jone Salomonsen's *Enchanted Feminism: The Reclaiming Witches of San Francisco* (2002), as well as several important collections of essays, has increased. Although there is still much interesting work to be done in the area (such as the growing phenomenon of teen witchcraft – to which I know scholars, particularly Hannah Sanders, have turned their attention), and although I would like, at some point, to look at Paganism from a theological and philosophical perspective (particularly with reference to pantheism, panentheism and Pagan ethics), I am glad that I left that particular area of study when I did – and have since enjoyed reading the work of those with more specialist expertise than I. When I discussed this shift of focus with Janet Joyce she was, as ever, very encouraging and urged me to follow my interests and continue my wider explorations. As both the project and the publisher grew, my much larger book transferred to Continuum's T&T Clark International imprint. As it did Philip Law became my main point of editorial contact. Again, I feel enormously fortunate, in that he too has been both helpful and encouraging, as have Lydia Newhouse and Slav Todorov at Continuum. I have also been fortunate to have T.W. Bartel as the copy-editor for this volume. I am indebted to his careful attention to detail and to his overall competence.

Over the years of the project I have, of course, benefited from the ideas of those with whom I have had the pleasure of working. I am particularly indebted to the many kindnesses of those who agreed to talk with me and put up with my unimaginative questions about their beliefs, as well as to the minds of scholars with whom I have chatted over the years. The latter certainly include those who have so willingly contributed excellent essays and articles to books I have edited in the area, especially *UFO Religions* (2003) and *The Encyclopedia of New Religions* (2004). A big thank you also to the following who have, as a result of conversations or correspondence over the years, unwittingly contributed to my thinking in this area (in alphabetical order): Ruth Bradby, Eric Christianson, George Chryssides, Andrew Dawson, Celia Deane-Drummond, Joan Evans, Theodore Gabriel, Ron Geaves, Andreas Grünschloß, Graham Harvey, Paul Heelas, Steve Knowles, James Lewis, Gill McCulloch, Jo McRitchie, Séan O'Callaghan, Mikael Rothstein, Graham St John, Hannah Sanders, Bron Szerszynski, and Dan Wojcik. I also want to acknowledge my gratitude to *all* my colleagues in the Department of Theology and Religious Studies who make University College Chester such an enjoyable place to work.

Last, but by all means first, my wonderful family and close friends (you know who you are – I hope!) make it all worthwhile. One family member deserves a particular mention, my partner Sarah, to whom I happily dedicate this book. Likewise, one friend, Rick Crookes, deserves particular mention for producing such an excellent cover for the book.

Small portions of this book have appeared in the *Journal of Contemporary Religion* and *Culture and Religion*.

INTRODUCTION

This book is about the alternative spiritual milieu in the contemporary Western world. It is about the way spirituality is explored, why it is explored, and who explores it. It is about the variety of ways increasing numbers of Westerners are discovering and articulating spiritual meaning in their lives. It is not about organized Christianity (or, indeed, any of the 'world religions'), about which there are more than enough books. If this had been the form of religion under discussion, the book might have been entitled *The Disenchantment of the West* (thereby suggesting the usual, narrow premise of such texts). But it is not. It is about the re-enchanting of what many assume to be an increasingly disenchanted part of the world. It is about new ways of believing in societies in which the old ways are inhibited and declining.[1]

To a large extent this book reflects my own development and interests, both spiritual and cultural: the happy hedonism of my teenage years, which were characterized by close friendships, music, psychedelic experiences, and an openness to paranormal ideas (I remember being particularly inspired by the writings of Carlos Castaneda); my idealistic early twenties, which included a year travelling East, living on a kibbutz, sleeping on beaches, and chatting with fellow travellers about Hinduism and Buddhism; my late twenties and early thirties, which were largely devoted to Christian theology and the study of religion, first at theological college and then at university. Now in my forties, having taught for some years, I find myself as a scholar of contemporary religion and culture, tooled up with critical baggage, reflecting on the work of fellow academics who are persuaded that the world 'out there' (and it does seem to be 'out there' for some of them) is quickly sliding into spiritual superficiality and secularity. I'm not convinced. Maybe I'm wrong (it wouldn't be the first time), but this supposedly secularized West looks very different from where I'm standing. After more than a few years reflecting on these issues, several years of talking with those treading alternative spiritual paths, and most of my life gratefully consuming (both critically and uncritically) popular culture, this book (along with a further volume) is the result. Although it is a typically academic work (for which I apologize), I hope it is also of interest to and accessible to all those fascinated by the pursuit of spiritual meaning and the significance of alternative ways of believing in the contemporary Western world.

I should say at the outset (although it will quickly become apparent) that, unlike some I have spoken to and whose books I have read, I am not working with the assumptions that just because spiritual reflection is entwined with popular culture and urban myths it is therefore superficial; that just because an alternative spirituality *may* not require its adherents to sit in pews and believe systematic theologies that it is, compared to mainstream religious belief, insignificant in the life of the believer; that just because new ways of believing are not allied to the state or located in large buildings next to the village green they are therefore socially insignificant.

Another point worth mentioning is that, to some extent, the shelf life of this book is, more than most, limited. Please keep this in mind *if*, as you read these words, the year on the calendar is 2008 or beyond. While I feel confident that my overall thesis and its principal components will still be relevant for some years to come – indeed, increasingly so – as those who have studied popular cultures and alternative spiritualities will know, it is all too easy to slip into the reification of ideas in an attempt to analyse and categorize. It is not unusual to find recently published academic discussions of 'current' trends looking outdated and out of step with the contemporary milieu. An example of this within the study of alternative spirituality is the way scholars (including myself) have happily seized on the term 'New Age' to define a particular network of ideas and beliefs. The problem is that some of those we talk to who are supposed to be 'New Agers' do not use or even like the term. Again, in popular cultural studies, we have seized upon the term 'rave' to define a particular form of music and culture. We use it indiscriminately of contemporary dance culture, when within large sections of that culture it has now largely lost currency. When it is used by certain subcultures, it is in a relatively specialized sense, sometimes not recognized by scholars. The point is that, if we are to keep our fingers on the pulse of contemporary religion and culture, we must make sure that the body of evidence we are testing is alive and kicking, not some dead cadaver that few outside the cosy halls of academia would recognize.

I have sought (probably not as successfully as I like to think) to check the spiritual health of the West by utilizing studies and methods developed in religious studies, cultural studies, and the sociology of religion. I have done this, not because I am pretending to have any particular expertise outside the study of religion, but because I am firmly of the opinion that interdisciplinarity is the way forward in the study of religion and culture. As one who has spent several years reading 'cultural studies' (and teaching a little in the area), I am deeply grateful for the tools that discipline has made available to me and which, no doubt, I so inadequately use. Again, although this analysis of spirituality in the West does not claim to be a detailed sociological analysis, the concepts and studies presented obviously and necessarily engage with and use ideas developed by sociologists of religion. I have been particularly interested in the debates and issues raised by theorists of secularization. From a fairly early stage in this book's evolution it became clear that, because of the obvious decline of organized religion (particularly Christianity in Europe, Scandinavia, Australia and to a lesser extent America), which is well documented and widely discussed,[2] some engagement with secularization theories could not be avoided. This was especially true of those theories which predict widespread secularization beyond the traditional religiosity of the pews. Hence, in the final analysis, I decided that, before chasing some of the alternative spiritual rabbits which are happily reproducing on the Western cultural landscape, I needed to begin with some discussion of the claims that any such rabbits are small, scarce, malnourished, and impotent. I attempt this in the opening chapter, which discusses theories of disenchantment.

Chapter 2 begins laying the foundations for a discussion of re-enchantment. In particular, it outlines theories of sect and cult development in the West, paying special attention to those which claim that such developments should not significantly alter our estimation of the demise of religion. Although these initial two chapters are perhaps a little more heavy going than the rest of the volume, they are necessary for completeness and as a protection against misunderstanding. That said, I sympathize with those readers who can't be bothered to wade through these theoretical swamps and want instead to join the discussion at Chapter 3. For it is here that we properly begin to survey the re-enchanted Western landscape. That is to say, in Chapter 3 I turn to analyse work which suggests that the new and alternative spiritual milieu is, in fact, more significant than some scholars have suggested. Commenting on the growing realization that certain assumptions by Western scholars regarding the culture of modernity may be erroneous and misleading, I suggest a model of re-enchantment.

The model of re-enchantment I suggest is, needless to say, not one of Christian revivalist optimism. Although, for good sociological, and psychological reasons, certain streams of experience-based, charismatic Christianity (and, possibly, some streams of 'liberal' Christianity) may continue to hold their own (in, I suspect, transformed ways),[3] we will *not* see the large-scale revivals that were witnessed, for example, during the eighteenth and early nineteenth centuries. Hence, although one might want to qualify some aspects of secularization theory, its fundamental premises concerning the decline of institutional Christianity, certainly in Europe, cannot seriously be questioned. There is simply not the required sociological, psychological and spiritual soil needed for such Christian seeds to take root.[4] Whereas pre-industrial Europe was fundamentally religious, and principally Christian,[5] this is not the case today. That Christianity now flourishes in, for example, Latin America and Africa is testimony to the very different histories and the distinctive social and cultural conditions of those areas of the world.[6] Certainly I am aware of no evidence at all to support Gerald Coates's claim that the West is 'in the middle of a colossal revival' or R.T. Kendall's insistence that Britain stands on the brink of a Christian revival 'greater than anything heretofore seen'[7] – unless increasingly widespread apathy and lack of interest in church attendance constitute such evidence. As Peter Brierley puts it, Britain 'is full of people who used to go to church but no longer do'.[8] Although, of course, there may be sporadic eruptions, such as the Toronto Blessing, which began at the Airport Vineyard Church in Canada in the early 1990s and petered out by the end of the decade,[9] and although there are undoubtedly many who, as Grace Davie argues, *believe* without *belonging* to a church,[10] any large-scale, socially significant 'awakenings' are very unlikely in the foreseeable future of the contemporary West. Even if one were to understand Christian revival less spectacularly as simply the slow reversal of secularization, this too seems unlikely.[11] Christianity is just too marginal in lives of most Westerners, particularly in Europe, and many of its thought-forms and ideas too alien to those of the majority. The popular Christian milieu, which was so important for the Christian revivals of the past, has collapsed. However, that it has collapsed does not mean that the West has become fundamentally secular. Another religio-cultural milieu has taken its place.

One of the principal theses developed in the pages that follow concerns this new religio-cultural milieu. Although, because the most conspicuous streams of religion are drying up it may look as though the West is experiencing creeping secularization, this, in fact, is not the whole story. What we are witnessing in the West is a confluence of secularization and sacralization. Spiritualities are emerging that are not only quite different from the dying forms of religion, but are often defined over against them, and are articulated in ways that do not carry the baggage of traditional religion. Unlike those forms of religion which are in serious decline, the new spiritual awakening makes use of thought-forms, ideas and practices which are not at all alien to the majority of Westerners. They emerge from an essentially non-Christian religio-cultural milieu, a milieu that both re-sources and is resourced by popular culture – the 'occult milieu', what I refer to as 'occulture'.

Part II of the book examines Western 'occulture' – the existence of which is one of the more important points made in the volume. Building on work done in particular by Ernst Troeltsch and Colin Campbell, I seek to develop their theories of mystical religion and the occult milieu. I expand the narrow, technical defini-tion of the term 'occult' to include a vast spectrum of beliefs and practices sourced by Eastern spirituality, Paganism, Spiritualism, Theosophy, alternative science and medicine, popular psychology, and a range of beliefs emanating out of a general interest in the paranormal. What A.D. Duncan said of occultism *per se* is equally true of 'occulture': it 'is not so much a religion or a system as a "general heading" under which a huge variety of speculation flourishes, a good deal of it directly contradictory'.[12] Occulture is the new spiritual environment in the West; the reservoir feeding new spiritual springs; the soil in which new spiritualities are growing. Things have changed. Spiritualities are not what they used to be – that's why they're flourishing.

The following three chapters in Part II examine several important streams that have both fed into and flowed from the occultural reservoir. Generally speaking, I will examine the Easternization thesis, assess the contribution of the 1960s, investigate the significance of popular culture, and explore certain alternative spiritual themes within literature, film and music.

Concerning popular culture, which is constantly referred to in Part II of the book, I want to demonstrate to the reader that it is a key component of an occul-tural cycle, in that it feeds ideas into the occultural reservoir and also develops, mixes and disseminates those ideas. This is important because, more generally, popular culture is also a key element in shaping the way we think about the world. To some extent this resonates with the thinking of the Frankfurt School, which developed a critical variant of Marxism. For example, we will see that Theodor Adorno argued that the visual arts, music, etc. manipulate the way their consumers perceive the world. Popular culture has a profound impact on perception, belief, and ultimately on how humans behave. For Adorno, of course, the impact is negative. Hence, concerning popular music, particularly jazz, he argued that it is fundamentally standardized, the end product being the production of standardized reactions and an affirmation of one's current existence – opium for the people.[13] As Chris Barker puts it, 'This is a matter not just of overt meanings, but of the structuring of the human psyche into conformist ways.'[14] Indeed, Adorno argues that 'the total effect of the culture industry is one of anti-enlightenment, in which ... enlightenment, progressive technical domination, becomes mass deception and is turned into a means of fettering consciousness.' Consequently, 'it impedes the development of autonomous, independent individuals who judge and decide consciously for themselves ... while obstructing the emancipation for which human beings are as ripe as the productive forces of the epoch permit.'[15] Whether we agree or disagree with Adorno's assessment of the *negative* dynamics of popular culture, his thesis concerning its transformative effect does need to be heeded. Again, Walter Benjamin – whose work was not entirely representative of the Frankfurt School and who was far more positive than Adorno – reached similar conclusions concerning the impact of popular culture. In his seminal 1936 essay, 'The Work of Art in the Age of Mechanical Reproduction',[16] he argues that the reproduction of art, in particular by photography and film, is a good thing for society, in that, although art is thereby divested of its 'aura' – the authority and uniqueness belonging to the original – it is made available to the masses, and innumerable people are encouraged to think differently about the world, seeing things they might otherwise never have realized existed. Film especially captures reality in a particular way and asks its many viewers to consider what has been captured. In other words, unlike Adorno, Benjamin stresses the participatory and democratic role of popular culture, rather than its darker repressive, conditioning potential. However, again, the point I am seeking to make is that popular culture has a significant formative effect on society. Popular *occulture* has a significant sacralizing effect.

Of course, others, from their own particular perspectives, will decide how successful I have been in demonstrating occultural re-enchantment. However, regardless of how well I have managed to carry out the task I set myself, I hope my discussion is sufficiently convincing to persuade others that this area, or at least the interface between contemporary spirituality and popular culture, needs to be explored much more thoroughly than it has been thus far. I have no doubts that there are better people than I who can set their hands to the task and I genuinely look forward to reading their efforts.

Part I

THE DISENCHANTMENT AND THE RE-ENCHANTMENT OF THE WEST

Chapter 1

THE DISENCHANTMENT OF THE WEST

What follows is not a wide-ranging introduction to the debated themes and history of secularization. The aim of this chapter is simply to introduce readers to key aspects of the general thesis. Whilst this discussion makes use of several accounts of secularization, one in particular should be noted, namely that of Steve Bruce, particularly as discussed in his recent book *God is Dead*.[1] Bruce's work is important because (1) it is persuasive, (2) over the past decade it has increasingly raised the principal issues with which this chapter is concerned, and (3) it has most clearly articulated the interpretations of alternative religion in the West with which I have come to disagree.

Types of Secularization

Linda Woodhead and Paul Heelas have provided a useful fourfold typology of secularization theories:[2] the disappearance thesis; the differentiation thesis; the de-intensification theory; and the co-existence theory. The former two are the dominant models, the latter two are less common. The *disappearance thesis*, which reflects nineteenth-century theories, claims that religious understandings of the world will effectively disappear in the West. The *differentiation thesis* is more cautious in that it argues that religion will become privatized and socially insignificant: 'religion gets pushed out of social domains whilst remaining (of some) significance in private life'.[3] The *de-intensification theory* claims that religion will remain in society, but only in a de-intensified, weak and insubstantial form. The *co-existence theory* is more positive in that, 'whilst secularization takes place in particular circumstances, in other contexts religions retain their vitality, even grow'.[4] Whatever the merits or demerits of this typology it does highlight the fact that there is no one model of secularization, just as, we will see, there is no one theory of the processes involved.

Max Weber and the Disenchantment of the World

Max Weber's (1864–1920) influential theory of 'the disenchantment of the world' (*die Entzauberung der Welt* – a phrase which he borrowed from Friedrich Schiller) describes a network of social and intellectual forces, the origins of which can be traced back to the Protestant Reformation. Weber's thought, which has its roots in Enlightenment rationalism, claims – as does, arguably, much subsequent secularization theorizing – that disenchantment is a progressive unilinear process – not unlike Friedrich Nietzsche's pessimistic narrative of the West, which begins with primal myth and ends with the 'death of God'.[5] As Gerth and Mills have argued, 'Weber's view of "disenchantment" embodies an element of liberalism and of the enlightenment philosophy that construed man's history as a unilinear "progress" towards moral perfection (sublimation), or towards cumulative technological rationalization.'[6] That said, as we will see, whilst some theorists might welcome the projected outcome, Weber did not. (Indeed, although Nietzsche looked forward to a world in which *Übermenschen* will overcome their 'human all too human' selves, celebrate 'life', create values, and live happily in a godless world, he too was concerned about how people would cope in the disenchanted world toward which the West was inevitably heading.) The driving force of rationalization – the dominance of bureaucracy which underlies the declining significance of religion in the modern world – is famously described by Weber as an 'iron cage'.

Again, although I do not intend to provide an overview of the various histories posited by secularization theorists,[7] it is worth noting that, while the Reformation is an important historical watershed for understanding secularization, and was of course absolutely central to Weber's thought,[8] Weber, Peter Berger, Alan Gilbert and others have traced the roots of the process back to the emergence of Jewish monotheism. In Gilbert's words,

> the seeds of secularization were implanted at the very genesis of the Judaeo-Christian tradition. Christianity inherited the radical theological and cosmological insights of an ancient Semitic people, a people with a grand yet precarious vision of a monotheistic universe. Monotheism was a potent, creative cultural force, but its impact on religious consciousness was two-sided. The sublime religiosity it produced, enriched first Hebrew and later Christian consciousness; but by setting up a dichotomy between 'sacred' and 'profane' aspects of reality it established an intellectual framework within which secularization was almost bound to occur. A dialectical tension between 'religious' and 'secular' modes of thought became a fundamental of Judaism and, through it, of Christianity.[9]

Unlike ancient polytheisms, the Judaic monotheistic God is transcendent, is not subject to natural forces, cannot be manipulated by magic, is not capricious, and requires obedience. For Weber, this had important implications. Instead of worrying about a host of competing, capricious deities, spirits and entities, because the worshipper was concerned with obeying only one God, the ethical was rationalized and the scope of the sacred shrunk as the mysterious, the miraculous and the magical were expunged from the world. That is to say, a single system of religious ethics evolved, humanity was liberated from a dependence on magic, and the natural world, evacuated of spirits and magic, became simply the physical arena in which one obeyed God. The natural world was the creation of a good and loving God, but it was not itself divine. Consequently, bearing in mind that secularization is only possible in societies in which there is a clear distinction between the religious and the non-religious, that the spheres of the sacred and the secular were thus demarcated is very significant – the seeds of disenchantment were sown:

As Hellenic philosophical and scientific notions intruded into the Jewish world of the
pre-Christian era, 'secular' elements became increasingly evident in Jewish culture. And
wherever this cultural synthesis occurred, the rationalizing implications of monotheism
left the residual polytheism of Hellenic culture with very little 'religious' plausibility
indeed.[10]

Consequently, as Gilbert has noted, as heir to both the Jewish and the Graeco-
Roman worlds, Christianity, from its beginnings, carried within it the dialectical
tension between the sacred and the secular.

That said, 'many of the most pronounced secularizing tendencies carried
over from the ancient world were either eliminated or suppressed'[11] in Christianity. This was particularly evident during the medieval period. To quote Gilbert
again:

The dialectic could work in two directions, not one. If secularization could occur, it could
also be reversed; and during more than a millennium of Christian history this is exactly
what happened. The history of the west from the collapse of Rome to the fall of
Constantinople involved, in the famous words of Edward Gibbon, 'the triumph of
Barbarism and religion' ... After the Roman Empire had disintegrated, secularization
had not simply been retarded, it had been effectively reversed.

The dominance of the Catholic Church in medieval Europe, while hardly producing the cosmologies of indigenous paganisms, nevertheless ensured that the
world was interpreted almost entirely theologically. Theology was the queen of
the sciences and the Church pervaded the institutional life of Western Europe.
Religious values had a shaping effect on medieval society and culture: 'at all
levels of social life and human need the Christian religion acquired immense and
ubiquitous *utility* in the minds of medieval men. At the level of popular consciousness, for example, it functioned as "a vast reservoir of magical power,
capable of being deployed for a variety of secular purposes".'[12] That medieval
enchantment inhibited 'secular' thought is clearly evident in Karen Jolly's study
of elf charms and popular religion in medieval England:

invisible powers associated with the Devil afflicted people with physical as well as
spiritual ailments; hence Christian words of power made herbal medicine handed down
through classical and Germanic lore efficacious against these forces ... All of the
remedies show the conjunction of good forces against evil forces without a necessary
distinction between physical and spiritual, natural and supernatural ... Any material
phenomenon had a potential spiritual meaning, whether it be a demonic illness or
temptation testing the resistance of a Christian or a weakness of body designed to
demonstrate God's miraculous power.[13]

While secular cosmologies within this spiritual milieu were not unheard of,
their sphere of influence was very small. The dominant worldview of medieval
England was religious and predominantly Christian. Keith Thomas likewise
provides evidence for the widespread supernaturalism of the medieval period:

The medieval Church ... found itself saddled with the tradition that the working of
miracles was the most efficacious means of demonstrating its monopoly of the truth. By
the twelfth and thirteenth centuries the *Lives* of the Saints had assumed a stereotyped
pattern. They related the miraculous achievements of holy men, and stressed how they

could prophesy the future, control the weather, provide protection against fire and flood, magically transport heavy objects, and bring relief to the sick.[14]

Whilst ideas such as these continued into the modern period, Thomas's work argues that, beginning with the decline of magic, the supernaturalistic worldview started experiencing erosion. Although the erosion began during the periods of the Renaissance and Reformation, from the time of the industrial revolution it had significantly picked up momentum.

The general process of secularization, of course, is deceptively complex. However, the essential idea informing secularization theory is relatively straightforward. In the words of Berger, 'Modernization necessarily leads to a decline of religion, both in society and in the minds of individuals.'[15] More bluntly, Bruce comments that 'The basic proposition is that modernization creates problems for religion.'[16] Again, Bryan Wilson defines secularization as follows: 'Secularization is the process in which religion loses its social significance.'[17] For Weber, of course, the disenchantment of the world is the process whereby magic and spiritual mystery are driven from the world, nature is managed rather than enchanted, the spiritual loses 'social significance',[18] and institutions and laws do not depend on religion for their legitimation. And certainly, looking back over the past couple of centuries, it would seem to be overwhelmingly evident that religious beliefs, practices, and symbols are gradually being abandoned at all levels of modern society.[19]

What Secularization Is Not

A helpful way into the analysis of recent treatments of secularization is Bruce's discussion of certain misunderstandings of what secularization theorists claim. First, the theory does not claim that secularization is universal:

> Anyone who had actually read Weber, Troeltsch, Niebuhr, Wilson, Berger or Martin … would appreciate that they did not see themselves as discovering universal laws comparable to the basic findings of natural science. Like Weber's Protestant Ethic thesis, the secularization story is an attempt to explain a historically and geographically specific cluster of changes. It is an account of what has happened to religion in western Europe (and its North American and Australasian offshoots) since the Reformation.[20]

Hence, that there is a resurgence of fundamentalism in some areas of the world, or that some Islamic countries are not secularized, does not count against the thesis.

Secondly, the secularization thesis is a model that identifies general trends rather than predicting inevitable decline:

> it does seem reasonable to see some social changes accumulating in a 'value added process' … so that, once they have occurred, it is very difficult to see how their effects can be reversed in any circumstances that are at all likely … [It] is difficult to see how a religiously diverse liberal democracy can again become religiously homogeneous while religion retains much of its substance … We are claiming irreversibility, rather than inevitability.[21]

That said, I cannot help feeling that Bruce at least suspects that there is a certain inevitability about secularization. More bluntly, his distinction between irreversibility and inevitability seems a little disingenuous, in that he is not describing a state, but a process. In other words, the secularization of the West is not static, it is an *irreversible process*. Consequently, whilst he does not claim it to have an 'even trajectory', he does believe it to be in motion and, since it is irreversible, it can only move in one direction. Therefore, in what sense is secularization not inevitable?

Thirdly, there is, Bruce says, 'no reason to suppose the decline of religion to be linear':[22] 'It does not require or expect that all indices of religious vitality will decline at the same speed or evenly. The process is bound to be lumpy because the world is complex.'[23] Clearly, this is an important, if obvious, point to make. Whether as a result of migration, or as a result of tragic events such as the terrorist attacks on the World Trade Center (11 September 2001), societies periodically become more or less religious. However, although Bruce describes his model of secularization as 'cyclical', the metanarrative is actually strikingly linear. For example, the metaphor he uses to describe his cyclical theory is that of a wheel travelling down a hill:

> the changes which accompany modernization and which create problems for religion are often described in ways which allow them to be seen as evenly *progressive* (or regressive!), but the more nuanced accounts include elements that repeat and mutations that run against the *overall direction*. Perhaps a suitable metaphor is that of the progress of any point on the circumference of a wheel on a vehicle running *downhill*. As the wheel turns the point rises and falls, but on each turn the high point is *lower than it was before.*[24]

The wheel travels in a line, in one direction (down) and, whilst the point on the wheel moves up and down (indicating the unevenness of secularization), its dominant trajectory is one of descent. Indeed, he goes on to relate the metaphor specifically to the religious life of Europe from the Reformation to the present, arguing that modernization led to the gradual demise of the religious and the domination of the secular.[25] (This is, of course, not so very different from Weber's equally linear thesis.) Moreover, to return to the above point, if this descent, this demise of religion, this gradual domination of the secular is irreversible, as Bruce claims it is, not only is it *not* a fundamentally cyclic process, but, again, it is difficult to see how it can be described as anything other than *inevitable*. (With John Milbank's general critique of social theory in mind,[26] I cannot but feel that this is an example of a thesis driven by a secular ideology – a suggestion which we will see Bruce vigorously reject.)

Fourthly, mapping the decline of religion is different from predicting a rise in explicit atheism. Individuals in a secularized society may simply have no interest in even thinking about religion, let alone arguing against religious worldviews and defending atheism *à la* Nietzsche.[27] They may simply be indifferent to religion *per se*. Indeed, in a sense, explicit atheism, in the form of an argued rejection of religion, testifies to the continuing significance of religion. If religion becomes truly insignificant in society, people will simply lack the knowledge and interest to discuss it, let alone oppose it. However, the point is that most secularization theorists claim not to expect the widespread emergence of atheism or the absolute demise of religion. (Moreover, again, it should also be noted that, like Weber, secularization theorists do not necessarily welcome the demise of religion. While many are neutral regarding secularization, some are pessimistic about the possibility of a secular future. As Bruce says of Wilson, he believes that 'the erosion of shared values will make life decidedly less pleasant'.[28])

Finally, it is important to understand that, generally speaking, unlike Auguste Comte, who argued that secularization is the inevitable result of human maturation,[29] or Sigmund Freud, who believed it to be the demise of a primitive illusion in an age of scientific enquiry,[30] contemporary theorists do not claim that secularization is simply due to a better-educated and more sophisticated public. Bruce in particular is very keen to refute the idea that he is bolstering an implicit ideology of progress: 'Increasing knowledge and maturity cannot explain declining religion. There are too many examples of modern people believing the most dreadful nonsense to suppose that people change from one set of beliefs to another just because the second lot are better ideas.'[31] Whatever 'dreadful nonsense' Bruce has in mind, it is certainly true that sophistication and intelligence do not necessarily lead to a secular worldview. Some of the most intelligent and sophisticated people I know are also some of the most conservative and committed Christians I know. Rather, as we will see, secularization is the product of a range of social, political, and, arguably, psychological processes.[32]

Rationalization and Pluralism

Having looked at what one sociologist claims secularization is not, we now need to look at what it might be. As we have seen, 'rationalization', which is central to the process of secularization in modern societies, is a concept that lies at the heart of Weber's theorizing. As Gerth and Mills opine,

> The principle of rationalization is the most general element in Weber's philosophy of history. For the rise and fall of institutional structures, the ups and downs of classes, parties, and rulers implement the general drift of secular rationalization. In thinking of the change of human attitudes and mentalities that this process occasions, Weber liked to quote Friedrich Schiller's phrase, the 'disenchantment of the world.' The extent and direction of 'rationalization' is thus measured negatively in terms of the degree to which magical elements of thought are displaced, or positively by the extent to which ideas gain in systematic and naturalistic consistency.[33]

'Rationalization' is essentially the 'concern with routines and procedures, with predictability and order, with a search for ever-increasing efficiency'.[34] It has therefore led both to increased bureaucracy and to an emphasis on process and organization. Everything can and should be done better, faster, cheaper, and more efficiently. Consequently, religious beliefs such as, for example, the value of petitionary prayer and divine providence are at odds with a culture that values predictability, order, routine, and immediate quantifiable returns. Many Westerners, including those with religious convictions, will implicitly or explicitly accept that there are more practically effective ways of getting through life than the traditionally religious ways. As such, secularization theorists point out that there seems to be relatively little left in the world for God to do. For example, in pre-modern societies immediate spiritual and moral connections would be made with tragic physical events, such as crop failure, and prayers of contrition would be offered. In the modern, industrial world, individuals instinctively seek a physical cause for a physical effect and, consequently, initially turn to physical remedies. Christians may pray for relief from a migraine, but few will not first avail themselves of the appropriate medication. Similarly, we can no longer accept that psychiatric disorders such as epilepsy and schizophrenia are the result of de-monic possession. We know there are physical causes which can be very effec-tively controlled by the careful use of scientifically researched chemicals.

Central to modernization and a product of 'rationalization' is the differentia-tion and specialization of social units. Bruce, for example, draws attention to structural and functional differentiation, that is 'the fragmentation of social life as specialized roles and institutions are created to handle specific features and func-tions previously carried out by one role or institution'.[35] The family ceased to be a unit of production as industrialization rationalized the process. Commerce and industrialization led to the division of labour and introduced values determined by rationalization. Small, closely knit, family-based communities with the Church at the centre, living under a protective 'sacred canopy' (Berger), have been fun-damentally eroded. Gradually, education, economic production, health care, and a host of other activities have shifted from ecclesiastical control to specialized secular institutions. In short, over the past few centuries religious authorities have lost their grip on the reigns of economic power as the world of employment has been increasingly motivated by its own values. Consequently, Christian influence is gradually weakened to the point at which it is all but absent. Even when the Church is involved in education, health or welfare, it is more often than not nomi-nally involved. For example, 'the Church of England provides various forms of residential social care, but its social workers are tested in secular expertise, not piety, and they are answerable to state- rather than church-determined standards. Spiritual values may inspire the Church's involvement in social work but there is very little in the expression of that inspiration that distinguishes it from secular provision.'[36]

Similarly, central to Karel Dobbelaere's strong secularization thesis is the proc-ess of *laicization*. This process, first, highlights the distinction between institu-tional religion and the modern administrative state, and, secondly, identifies a shift of responsibility from the former to the latter.[37] No longer, for example, does the provision of welfare come under the aegis of religious organizations, which was once the case in the West, but rather there has been a shift of control to gov-ernment bureaucracies. This shift has, of course, also led to the emergence of experts and centres of expertise (doctors, social workers, teachers, schools, hos-pitals, departments of social services etc.). In modern societies, health, welfare and education are no longer primarily the concerns of ecclesiastical authorities. Consequently, laicization has meant that ecclesiastical concern is now limited to pastoral care and 'spiritual matters'.

Another key interrelated process that has contributed significantly to the secularization of the West is pluralization. As Robert Hefner has commented, 'Kinship, politics, education, and employment all separate from an original unity and assume a dizzying variety of specialized forms. In the process, human society is transformed from a simple, homogeneous collectivity into the pluralistic entities we know today.'[38] Communities in which people operated with a shared religious worldview, a shared morality, and a shared identity, and within which an individual's material, intellectual, and spiritual sustenance was provided, are rapidly disappearing. Berger in particular has drawn attention to the fact that, unlike pre-modern communities in which a single religious worldview was dominant and permeated all areas of community life, in modern societies there are few shared values to which one can appeal and the beliefs an individual does hold cannot be taken for granted: 'The pluralistic situation multiplies the number of plausibility structures competing with each other. *Ipso facto*, it relativizes their religious contents. More specifically, the religious contents are "de-objectivated", that is, deprived of their status as taken-for-granted, objective reality in consciousness.'[39] Consequently, to quote Berger again, 'the fundamental problem of the religious institutions is how to keep going in a milieu that no longer takes for granted their definitions of reality'.[40] Related to all this of course is the fact that individual believers are constantly aware that their faith is a *chosen* worldview from a spectrum of worldviews on offer. This situation, Berger has argued, leads to a crisis of credibility in religion: 'secularization has resulted in a widespread collapse of the plausibility of traditional religious definitions of reality'.[41] In other words, there is a relationship between the 'subjective secularization' of an individual's consciousness and the 'objective secularization' at the social-structural level: 'Subjectively, the man in the street tends to be uncertain about religious matters. Objectively, the man in the street is confronted with a wide variety of religious and other reality-defining agencies that compete for his allegiance or at least attention, and none of which is in a position to coerce him into allegiance. In other words, the phenomenon called "pluralism" is a social-structural correlate of the secularization of consciousness.'[42]

Popular relativism and the revision of traditional concepts of deity are of course encouraged by contemporary consumer-centric cultures that are driven by an insistence on variety and individual choice. Hence, 'by forcing people to do religion as a matter of personal choice rather than as fate, pluralism universalizes "heresy". A chosen religion is weaker than a religion of fate because we are aware that we chose the gods rather than the gods choosing us.'[43] As a consequence, religion is increasingly a private rather than a public matter. It is not that religion disappears, but rather that it is relegated from the social to the private sphere. A palpable consequence of the overall secularizing, relativizing shift in modern democracies, which has seen the demise of the Church as a monopoly regulating thought and action, has been a series of laws that have repealed certain sanctions in order to ensure the equality of most forms of religious expression.[44] Hence, in Britain, the 1951 repeal of the 1735 Witchcraft Act was not an attempt to promote witchcraft, but rather a logical step in a modern, secular democracy.

There is no longer an acceptable rationale for defending the rights of one religious belief system over another. Since religion is simply a matter of personal preference, and since concepts of religious truth have been relativized (there being little empirical evidence to establish the validity of one choice over against another, or indeed to establish the validity of any of the choices), there are few reasons to limit choice. As Bruce comments, 'Modern society seeks to assimilate all citizens into the mass culture of free-wheeling choice where community commitments are notoriously difficult to maintain.'[45]

Concluding Comments

This then, according to many, is the disenchanted world in which we live. The decline of the community, the proliferation of large, impersonal conurbations, the increasing fragmentation of modern life, the impact of multicultural and religiously plural societies, the growth of bureaucracy, the creeping rationalization, and the influence of scientific worldviews have together led to a situation in which religion is privatized, far less socially important, and far less plausible than it was in pre-modern communities. Certainly, a large question mark has been placed over the notion that there exists a single religious and ethical worldview which alone is true and to which all good and reasonable people should therefore assent – as was the case with Christianity in the medieval period.

Chapter 2

UNDERSTANDING NEW RELIGIONS AND ALTERNATIVE SPIRITUALITIES

Having provided some indication of the general thrust of the secularization thesis, I want now to turn to some of the theoretical discussions about the nature and emergence of new religions, sects, and alternative spiritualities. This will equip us with a few key terms, concepts and theories which will assist analysis later in this and the following volume. Moreover, some grasp of these processes is necessary for understanding the nature of contemporary alternative spiritualities, how and why they might have emerged in the West, and why some secularization theorists believe their significance to be limited.

Max Weber on Sectarianism and Charisma

The pioneer theorist in the sociological study of sectarianism was undoubtedly Ernst Troeltsch (1865–1923). However, because his thesis is essentially a development of Max Weber's, some discussion of the latter's distinction between the sect and the Church is perhaps a good place to begin.

For Weber, traditionally the Church is not a voluntary organization, but rather a community into which one is born. Hence, theoretically at least, membership is compulsory. The sect, on the other hand, is voluntary and does not, generally speaking, seek to regulate the lives of those who *do not* explicitly wish to become members. Those who *do* wish to become members must, however, satisfy certain membership criteria in order to demonstrate their religious and ethical commitment to the organization. In his important essay 'The Protestant Sects and the Spirit of Capitalism', Weber provides accounts of inquisitive Germans encountering sectarian attitudes in America. One such account relates a conversation following a baptism in a pond:

> When I asked him after the ceremony, 'Why did you anticipate the baptism of that man?' he answered, 'Because he wants to open a bank in M.' 'Are there so many Baptists around that he can make a living?' 'Not at all, but once being baptised he will get patronage of the whole region and he will outcompete everybody.' Further questions of 'why' and 'by what means' led to the conclusion: Admission to the local Baptist congregation follows only upon the most careful 'probation' and after the closest inquiries into conduct going back to early childhood (Disorderly conduct? Frequenting taverns? Dance? Theatre? Card playing? Untimely meeting of liability? Other frivolities?) ... Admission to the congregation is recognized as an absolute guarantee of the moral qualities of a gentleman, especially of those qualities required in business matters.[1]

This, we have seen, is quite different from how he understands a Church to operate:

> It is crucial that sect membership meant a certificate of moral qualification and especially of business morals for the individual. This stands in contrast to membership in a 'church' into which one is 'born' and which lets grace shine over the righteous and the unrighteous alike. Indeed, a church is a corporation which organizes grace and administers religious gifts of grace, like an endowed foundation. Affiliation with the church is, in principle, obligatory and hence proves nothing with regard to the member's qualities. A sect, however, is a voluntary association of only those who, according to the principle, are religiously and morally qualified.[2]

Hence, for Weber, the church/sect distinction focuses on membership, the church being inclusive, the sect exclusive.

It is important to understand, however, that Weber goes on to observe that this is not a static distinction, in that successful sects tend to evolve into churches. On the one hand, the size of a sect has an impact on the internal dynamics of the movement, in that the more people that are involved, the more likely it is to progress towards an ecclesiastical institution. On the other hand, and more importantly, Weber observes the 'routinization of charisma'. The following passage from his essay 'The Meaning of Discipline' gives us a sense of this process:

> Charisma as a creative power, recedes in the face of domination, which hardens into lasting institutions, and becomes efficacious only in short-lived mass emotions of incalculable effects ... Genuine charisma ... does not appeal to an enacted or traditional order, nor does it base its claims upon acquired rights. Genuine charisma *rests on the legitimation of personal heroism or personal revelation*. Yet precisely this quality of charisma as an *extraordinary, supernatural, divine power* transforms it, after its routinization, into a suitable source for the legitimate acquisition of sovereign power by the successors of the charismatic hero. Routinized charisma thus continues to work in favour of all those whose power and possession is guaranteed by that sovereign power, and who thus depend on the continued existence of such power.[3]

A sect's charisma is usually located in a founder, an individual religious hero, the recipient of personal revelation. As the sect continues, particularly after the death of the founder, the charisma may be relocated in an office, such as that of priest or bishop. Successors, as they are inducted into their official position within the organization, inherit the charisma of the founder in much the same way as it is believed that the charisma of Jesus Christ was communicated through Peter to the papal office and to the priesthood. The following statement from the First Vatican Council illustrates this understanding of charismatic authority:

> the Roman Pontiff, when he speaks *ex cathedra*, that is, when in discharge of the office of pastor and doctor of all Christians, he defines a doctrine regarding faith or morals to be held by the universal Church, by the divine assistance promised to him in blessed Peter, is possessed of that infallibility with which the divine Redeemer willed that His Church should be endowed for defining doctrine regarding faith or morals, and that such definitions of the Roman Pontiffs are irreformable, of themselves and not by the consent of the Church.[4]

Charisma is located in the Church's teaching office, which culminates in the Pope and can be traced back to Christ. In this case, that has led to an institutional understanding of *ex cathedra* papal pronouncements (i.e. spoken by one invested with the charisma of that office) as infallible. This then is essentially what Weber means when he speaks of the routinization of charisma. As bureaucracies emerge, charisma becomes located in social/religious structures, regulated by systems of doctrines and ethics.

Hence, churches and sects can be distinguished, not simply by the principle of membership, but also by the nature of charisma – whereas in a sect it is original, attached to a leader, in a church it is routinized, attached to an office or offices.

It is also worth noting at this stage that Weber began using the term 'charisma' when discussing what he (like many at the beginning of the twentieth century) understood to be the most elementary forms of religious belief and behaviour, namely indigenous religion. As in early anthropological discourse (e.g. James Frazer's massive and impressive *The Golden Bough*[5]), Weber draws a distinction between magic and religion. Essentially, magic is understood to be the direct manipulation of power. This power is often located in particular objects, places or persons. Again, in accordance with much early evolutionary anthropology, Weber understood magic to evolve into religion when this power, this charisma (which tended to be volatile and capricious), came to be located in some transcendent being or entity, rather than in objects and places. Once charisma is located in this transcendent realm and not in amulets, sacred groves or shamanistic individuals, it becomes less capricious and less a matter of the direct manipulation of power and more a matter of prayer to and propitiation of the divine source of power. This leads to a process of rationalization in which priestly and other structures are established to deal with the divine being(s) and in which, again, charisma is routinized.

Although the evolutionary thesis has been abandoned by many, aspects of Weber's basic model have been helpfully used to interpret certain dynamics within contemporary new religious movements. For example, while some such movements may struggle and die following the death of their charismatic leader, others, such as Scientology[6] and, as Diana Tumminia has shown, the UFO religion Unarius, have managed to continue through the process of charismatic routinization.[7]

Ernst Troeltsch on Churches, Sects and Mysticism

As noted above, Weber had a significant influence on Troeltsch. Indeed, following a trip together to a St Louis congress in 1904, their friendship became so close that in 1910 they began living in the same house, Ziegelhäuser Landstrasse, 17 – Weber and his wife living on the first floor and the Troeltsch family on the second floor. In his obituary of Weber, Troeltsch writes: 'Of myself I will only say that for years I experienced the infinitely stimulating power of this man in daily converse.'[8] At the end of the first volume of Troeltsch's seminal work *The Social Teachings of the Christian Churches*[9] (arguably his most important and certainly his favourite book[10]), which he understood to be the sociological parallel to Adolf von Harnack's equally significant *History of Dogma* (1886–9), he employs Weber's church/sect distinction as a key tool of interpretation.[11] The influence of Weber can be clearly seen in the following definitions:

> The Church is that type of organization which is overwhelmingly conservative, which to a certain extent accepts the secular order, and dominates the masses; in principle, therefore, it is universal, i.e. it desires to cover the whole life of humanity. The sects, on the other hand, are comparatively small groups; they aspire after personal inward perfection, and they aim at a direct personal fellowship between the members of each group. From the very beginning therefore, they are forced to organize themselves in small groups, and to renounce the idea of dominating the world.[12]

Focusing, unlike Weber, solely on Christianity, and in critical dialogue with Albrecht Ritschl's thought, Troeltsch examines the teaching of Jesus and the formation of the early Christian church, after which he provides a detailed socio-logical analysis of medieval Christianity. Following his discussion of the medie-val church, at the end of the first volume he turns specifically to the development of the church/sect typology. Although much is taken from Weber, Troeltsch differed significantly from him in several respects, the two principal differences being that he identified particular attitudes to 'the world' as a key distinguishing feature and, in a short and ambiguous discussion, he added to sect and church a third type, namely 'mysticism'.

Troeltsch's types can be summarized as follows. The *Church type* is open to the world and, to some degree, will accept the secular order. As Weber observed, its principle is universal in that it seeks to include the whole of humanity. It is inclusivist, rather than exclusivist. The Church makes use of the secular order and even becomes part of it. 'The fully developed Church,' he says, 'utilizes the State and the ruling classes, and weaves these elements into her own life; she then becomes an integral part of the existing social order; from this standpoint, then, the Church both stabilizes and determines the social order; in so doing, however, she becomes dependent upon the upper classes, and upon their develop-ment.'[13] Ascetic and monastic movements are incorporated as elements of reli-gious achievement, in that such paths to virtue usually require the repression of normal appetites. The Church type is, for Troeltsch, most obviously represented by medieval Catholicism, though it can also be seen in the later development of mainstream Protestant Christianity.

The *sect type* of Christianity is found in relatively small voluntary groups which tend to separate themselves from church-type institutions. Moreover, Christian sects are, he argues, 'connected with the lower classes, or at least with those elements in Society which are opposed to the State and to Society; they work upwards from below, and not downwards from above'.[14] Asceticism in this context is understood differently as 'merely the simple principle of detachment from the world, and is expressed in the refusal to use the law, or to swear in a court of justice, to own property, to exercise dominion over others, or to take part in war'.[15]

Mysticism is, strictly speaking, not a type of social organization (and indeed transcends fixed organizations), but rather an emphasis on direct interior and individualist experience of the divine. It is his discussion of mysticism that so presciently and helpfully describes emergent spirituality in the West. Indeed, it is very difficult to read Troeltsch's comments on mysticism without at the same time thinking of the 'self' religiosity of the 'New Age':

> The popular religious movements of the later Middle Ages ... presuppose a loosening of the ties of objective ecclesiasticism. Through all these movements, however, a sociological type of Christian thought was being developed, which was not the same as that of the sect type; it was, in fact, a new type – the radical religious individualism of mysticism. This type had no desire for organized fellowship; all it cared for was freedom for interchange of ideas, a pure fellowship of thought, which indeed only became possible after the invention of printing ... The isolated individual, and psychological abstraction and analysis become everything.[16]

Whilst, on the one hand, mysticism's universality links it with Church-type Christianity, on the other hand, its emphasis on the individual's personal experience locates it within the sect type. Having said that, it cannot be considered sectarian, because of its lack of association with religious groupings. For Troeltsch, 'the view of individuality which finds expression in the mystical type has a parallel to or comes close to modern thought. The advantage of mysticism lies in the possibility of taking up elements of freedom and leaving room for the autonomous formation and bond of the conscience. The weakness of mysticism lies in its lack of organization.'[17]

Troeltsch's work is important, not only because it demonstrates that the history of Christianity cannot be understood as a unilinear development, but also because it established the significance of sectarian and mystical religion in that history. To summarize, the Church type of organization has dominated the history of Christianity, embodying the ideal for a universal worldview which will shape society and culture. The Church must be 'the great educator of the nations', 'compelling all members of Society to come under its sphere and influence'.[18] However, in order to achieve this end, it has necessarily had to seek accommodation with the secular order. The problem for the Church is that, as soon as it becomes established as the sole provider of 'the saving energies of grace',[19] the sectarian impulse surfaces. Sectarianism is motivated by a refusal to accept domination in the sphere of the sacred and accommodation in the sphere of the secular. There is a turn to the personal, to the experiential, and to the relational. Hence, sectarianism is fundamentally a movement of protest. Finally (and this is particularly noticeable in the contemporary West), the mystical impulse emerges, driven by an internalization of religion. Interior personal experience replaces exterior doctrine and ethics. Fellowships or networks of 'experiencers' form to share ideas, but they lack the organization and structure of the worship-oriented sect. Indeed, Troeltsch indicates that, because of the lack of centralized structure, such mystical religion becomes eclectic, incorporating new ideas, and a luxury principally available to, and appealing to, the educated middle classes.[20] Again, this epistemological individualism, of course, comes very close to what we would now describe as 'New Age' spirituality.[21]

H. Richard Niebuhr on Sectarianism

A particularly important development of Troeltsch's work was soon provided by H. Richard Niebuhr (1894–1962) in *The Social Sources of Denominationalism* (1929).[22] Directly influenced by both Weber and Troeltsch, Niebuhr argued that a further type should be added to the church/sect model, namely the 'denomination'. While he followed Troeltsch's church/sect typology, he argued that 'by its very nature the sectarian type of organization is valid only for one generation'.[23] Sects evolve towards churches as the sectarian impulse is diluted and as they too increasingly accommodate the secular order:

> The children born to the voluntary members of the first generation begin to make the sect a church long before they have arrived at the years of discretion. For with their coming the sect must take on the character of an educational and disciplinary institution, with the purpose of bringing the new generation into conformity with ideals and customs which have become traditional. Rarely does a second generation hold the convictions it has inherited with a fervour equal to that of its fathers, who fashioned these convictions in the heat of conflict and at the risk of martyrdom. As generation succeeds generation, the isolation of the community from the world becomes more difficult.[24]

Again, he writes, 'Christendom has often achieved apparent success by ignoring the precepts of its founder. The church as an organization interested in self-preservation and the gain of power, has sometimes found the counsel of the Cross quite as inexpedient as have national and economic groups.'[25] The point is that, as John Wesley noticed in the Methodist societies he formed, over time there is a tendency to submit to external pressures, to become socialized and to lose enthusiasm. Moreover, it is important to understand that, for Niebuhr, this process is fundamentally related to socio-economic circumstances, in that, in some respects, it seems to reflect the Weberian Protestant ethic.[26] That is to say, the work ethic of sectarians can lead to secular success, in that their diligent labour, their frugal living, and their deferral of gratification to the next life can lead to economic prosperity. This prosperity leads to a growing social respectability, to upward social mobility, and to a distance from the poor. Again, Methodism is a good example, in that it rose from being 'a church of the poor to a middle-class church, which, with its new outlook, abandoned the approach to religion which made it an effective agency of salvation to the lower classes in the century of its founding'.[27] Generally speaking, those who joined Methodist societies worked harder, stopped spending money in a way that would have been considered frivolous, saved earnings, maybe invested in worthy business enterprises, and thus, by the next generation, moved up the social ladder – the Methodist Church becoming, according to Niebuhr, a fundamentally middle-class organization. Moreover, whilst Methodist children continued in the faith, they were not as religiously zealous as their parents had been. Again, the general point is that, after the first generation's zeal has cooled, a sect becomes settled and denominational. The cooling of religious enthusiasm is simply part of the process – rather than being, for example, a general indicator of long-term decline.

Indeed, this cooling, in turn, leads to the surfacing of new forms of sectarianism among those who are zealous for the original teachings and unhappy with comfortable denominational religion:

> One phase in the history of denominationalism reveals itself as the story of the religiously neglected poor, who fashion a new type of Christianity which corresponds to their distinctive needs, who rise in the economic scale under the influence of religious discipline, and who, in the midst of a freshly acquired cultural respectability, neglect the new poor succeeding them on the lower plane. This pattern recurs with remarkable regularity in the history of Christianity. Anabaptists, Quakers, Methodists, Salvation Army, and more recent sects of like type illustrate the rise and progress of the churches of the disinherited.[28]

Following Weber and Troeltsch, Niebuhr also drew attention to the fact that, in the face of numerical and geographical expansion, effective organization becomes necessary. Forms of government thus replace inspirational leadership. In other words, there is a routinization of charisma and a growing bureaucratization in the form of professional ministerial structures.

Niebuhr's hypothesis is an important one, which has been fruitfully developed and modified by a range of scholars from Bryan Wilson to Rodney Stark. However, it is limited. For example, not only is the typology principally determined by American Christianity, but also it does not account for the facts that (1) some sects are not motivated by a work ethic and do not experience significant upward social mobility, (2) some sects, because of their deliberate isolation, as in the case of the Amish communities, or insulation, as in the case of the Jehovah's Witnesses, do not become socially integrated, and (3) some sects are resistant to denominationalism because the original sectarian enthusiasm is continued by second-generation converts. Nevertheless, Niebuhr's hypothesis does help us to understand some of the processes involved in the emeregence and decline of new forms of religion.

Bryan Wilson on Sectarianism

An interesting refinement of the Niebuhr model has been provided by Bryan Wilson, who distinguishes four sub-types of Christian sects: conversionist, Adventist/revolutionist, introversionist/pietist, and Gnostic. Sect types are determined by 'the response of the sect to the values and relationships prevailing in society':

> The *Conversionist* sects seek to alter men, and thereby to alter the world; the response is free-will optimism. The *Adventist* sects predict drastic alteration of the world, and seek to prepare for the new dispensation – a pessimistic determinism. The *Introversionists* reject the world's values and replace them with higher inner values, for the realization of which inner resources are cultivated. The *Gnostic* sects accept in large measure the world's goals but seek a new and esoteric means to achieve these ends – a wishful mysticism.[29]

As to Wilson's definition of a sect *per se* (which is, again, indebted to that of Weber and Troeltsch), this is, it seems to me, far more useful.[30] Essentially, although there are, of course, many aspects to sectarianism (historical, social, doctrinal etc.), Wilson seems to draw out their particularist epistemologies and their notions of purity and pollution. More specifically, sects can be identified by their understandings of truth and authority and by their notions of separateness and distinctiveness as sacred communities.

> A sect is a self-consciously and deliberately separated religious minority which espouses a faith divergent from that of other religious bodies ... Typically, the sect claims to provide better access to salvation than is elsewhere available, and does so by virtue of a monopoly of truth, commitment to, and belief in which are normally indispensable conditions ... Whatever specific terms it employs, the sect is always an agency of salvation.[31]

They are voluntary organizations that require members to fulfil certain criteria (e.g. tangible evidence of conversion, and acceptance of particular doctrines and codes of ethics) and to achieve levels of commitment well beyond those found in non-sectarian religion. In other words, they have a strong sense of self-identity with clear insider/outsider boundaries. This is supported by an exclusivist theology and an elitist understanding of the sect as the sole possessor of religious truth. Consequently the sect is separated from both 'the world' (wider secular society) and also the prevailing orthodoxy. Failure to fulfil doctrinal and ethical requirements can lead to shunning and even expulsion.[32] Finally, sects have no distinct or professional ministry. We will return to some of these points later, but the important characteristics of sectarian religion to note are those of commitment, strong self-identity, doctrine, morality, and what might be understood as purity-pollution issues.

Towards a Typology of the New Religious Life

Bearing in mind the limited usefulness of all typologies (which are, after all, only blunt tools to assist understanding), perhaps the most adequate to be developed in recent years, to which several contemporary sociologists are indebted, are those provided by Roy Wallis in his important studies *The Road to Total Freedom*[33] and *The Elementary Forms of the New Religious Life*.[34] In the former, drawing, again, on the work of Weber and Troeltsch, as well as that of David Martin[35] and particularly Roland Robertson,[36] he develops a typology which very helpfully examines religious groupings from two angles: interior and exterior (see Table 1). It is, in other terms, an *emic-etic* model: *emic* being the perspective of the insider, *etic* that of the outsider. In constructing the typology, several key questions are asked. On the one hand, what is the self-understanding of insiders? In particular, do they understand their organization to be *uniquely legitimate*? In other words, is the organization understood to be the sole repository of truth and the only path to salvation? Or is it *pluralistically legitimate*? That is to say, although a particular faith, such as Christianity, may be understood to be uniquely legitimate, particular denominations within that faith, whether Methodist, Baptist, or Pentecostal, do not consider other Christian denominations to be illegitimate – they thus understand themselves to one of several legitimate paths to salvation. On the other hand, what conception of the organization do *outsiders* have? Specifically, is it generally understood to be a *respectable* or a *deviant* organization? The answers to these questions allow the scholar to locate organizations in one of four categories (see Table 1).

Table 1. The Wallis typology, 1976. *Source*: Roy Wallis, *The Road to Total Freedom*, 13.

	Outsiders	
Insiders	Respectable	Deviant
Uniquely legitimate	CHURCH	SECT
Pluralistically legitimate	DENOMINATION	CULT

One of the most important features of this typology is that it is socio-culturally sensitive. Account needs to be taken of, not simply *emic* perceptions, but also *etic* perceptions, since respectability and deviance are socially conferred. Indeed, social contexts are important for a variety of reasons, some of which go beyond social attitudes to material advantages such as charitable status. Hence, for example, there are very good reasons why organizations seek respectability within a particular social context. Moreover, some movements are understood to be less sectarian in one local context and more sectarian in others. Christian Science, for example, has a more sectarian identity in the UK than it does in the USA. Again, although the Church of Jesus Christ of Latter-day Saints (Mormons) may be considered sectarian in the UK and also in certain parts of the United States, in Utah it is the dominant religious tradition.[37] The point is that Wallis's model allows one, indeed encourages one, to take account of local socio-cultural contexts when studying new religious movements and alternative spiritualities. Hence, for example, we will be raising questions later in the book about whether beliefs such as astrology, reincarnation, and *feng shui* should be considered deviant or respectable in the contemporary West. Whereas they would certainly have been considered exotic and deviant a hundred, or even fifty years ago, there is evidence to suggest that this is not the case today.

Particularly noticeable about Wallis's typology is its inclusion of another category into which religious organizations can be placed, namely 'cults' (a category which was initially introduced by Howard Becker in 1932,[38] and then influentially developed by J. Milton Yinger in 1957[39]). 'Cult', as defined by Wallis, has similarities with both Becker's and Yinger's definitions, and can be interpreted in terms of a development of Troeltsch's mystical religion. Wallis understands the cult to be, *like* the sect, deviant, in that it exists in some tension with the dominant culture, but, *unlike* the sect, is not epistemologically exclusivist. (This is a type that Bruce has found particularly useful in his analysis of New Age belief and practice.[40]) It is, in Wallis's terminology, 'epistemologically individualistic' rather than 'epistemologically authoritarian'.[41] The locus of authority is within the individual.[42] *Charisma is internalized.*

Cults, therefore, allow far looser organization, shaped as they are by the individuals themselves, who decide what they will or will not believe. As with denominationalism, cultic religiosity does not claim unique access to truth. Sectarian religiosity, on the other hand, is top-down epistemological authoritarianism, which understands there to be a particular interpretation of religious knowledge to which the believer must assent. (It is important to understand that when the terms 'cult' and 'cultic' are used in this book, they are specifically used in *this sense* and *not* in the popular, broad and derogatory sense often used by, for example, journalists and the Christian counter-cult movement.[43] Not only will 'cult' not be used as a term of opprobrium, but the discussion will seek, as far as possible, to be objective and non-judgemental.)

Wallis's work, which we have seen is sensitive to social contexts, also allows for the fact that the process is not always schismatic (i.e. smaller groups breaking away from larger groups), but may also be evolutionary. For example, in his *The Road to Freedom* he maps Scientology's development from Dianetics[44] – a relatively non-authoritarian version of what Stark and Bainbridge have since referred to as a 'client cult'[45] – into a sect with an authoritarian epistemology, expelling those who challenge its central teachings and particularly the authority of L. Ron Hubbard, the founder and leader. As Wallis makes very clear in his discussion of the Dianetics–Scientology transition,

> Hubbard sought to exert control over practitioners and other followers in the field, he also tightened control over his central organization, dismissing officers who failed to perform precisely in accordance with his requirements ... [He] progressively gained complete control over Scientology, its membership, ideology, practices and organizations. He was not prepared to accept the attempts by some British Dianetics leaders to limit his authority.[46]

The point is that here we see a clear transition from the cult to the hierarchical, authoritarian sect. Hence, there are problems with the definition of 'sect' provided by such as Stark and Bainbridge, which claims that cults are distinct from sects because they are not schismatic: that is to say, 'sects have a prior tie with another religious organization. To be a sect, a religious movement must have been founded by persons who left another religious body for the purpose of founding the sect.'[47] That said, they are right to argue that cults 'do not have a prior tie with another established religious body in the society in question. The cult may represent an alien (external) religion, or it may have originated in the host society, but through innovation, not fission.'[48]

Furthermore, whilst Stark and Bainbridge's definition of sectarianism has weaknesses, their typology of cults is helpful and can be used to refine Wallis's understanding of cults. They identify three forms of cult depending on how organized they are. That said, whilst this is very helpful, their general definition of cult (see the previous paragraph) applies comfortably only to one of these forms, namely 'cult movements'. The other two forms of cult, audience cults and client cults, are much closer to Wallis's definition of cult. Having said that, on the one hand, client cults are essentially therapy-based, structured around the individual relationship between a client/consumer and a therapist/teacher/provider: 'Since Freud ... cults increasingly have specialized in personal adjustment. Thus, today one can "get it" at *est*, get "cleared" through Scientology, store up orgone and seek the monumental orgasm through the Reich Foundation, get rolfed, actualized, sensitised, or psychoanalysed.'[49] Audience cults, on the other hand, are loosely organized, epistemologically individualist networks: 'there are virtually no aspects of formal organization ... and membership remains at most a consumer activity. Indeed, cult audiences often do not gather physically but consume cult doctrines entirely through magazines, books, newspapers, radio, and television.'[50]

A further influential classification worth mentioning briefly is that developed by Wallis in his *The Elementary Forms of the New Religious Life*. Here he distinguishes three ideal types of new religion: world-rejecting, world-affirming, and world-accommodating:

> The typology I wish to present requires the construction of a *conceptual space*. This conceptual space is formed by the components of a logical trichotomy, the elements of which constitute an exhaustive set of ways in which a new religious movement may orient itself to the social world in which it emerges. A new movement may embrace that world, affirming its normatively approved goals and values; it may reject the world, denigrating those things held dear within it; or it may remain as far as possible indifferent to the world in terms of its religious practice, accommodating to it otherwise, and exhibiting only mild acquiescence to, or disapprobation of, the ways of the world.[51]

World-rejecting movements include those groups that are popularly referred to as 'cults' (i.e. those the Christian counter-cult movement would describe as brainwashing movements deserving only of censure). Examples would be, says Wallis, the Children of God (now known as the Family) and the Family Federation for World Peace and Unification (popularly known as the Moonies).[52] Epistemologically authoritarian, these organizations stress boundaries between God and humanity, the world and God, and the community and the world. The community of believers is the ark of salvation floating in a sea of profanity. Salvation, it is believed, is found only within the organization. Needless to say, this leads to a strong emphasis on the maintenance of purity (e.g. dietary codes), self-denial (sometimes asceticism), and uncritical obedience. It is also not unusual for such movements to have apocalyptic eschatologies. For example, in answer to the question why a holy and pure God who is very willing to judge the wicked allows such a profane society to continue, it is simply argued that he will not. God will soon break into the existing world order, violently judge it, and replace it with a new world order.[53]

World-affirming new religions are situated at the opposite end of Wallis's spectrum and 'lack most of the features traditionally associated with religion. [They] may have no "church", no collective ritual or worship, [they] may lack any developed theology or ethics (in the sense of general, prescriptive principles of human behaviour and intention ...).'[54] Finding much to value in the world, the world-affirming new religion draws no sharp distinctions between God and humanity, the world and God, and the organization and the world. Indeed, although it will have a concept of the sacred, and usually a belief in the divine, such a religion or spirituality may not even require belief in a personal God. Transcendental Meditation, for example, is a technique which, whilst initially developed by Maharishi Mahesh Yogi within a Hindu religious framework, can be practised by anyone within any or no faith tradition. As Peter Russell comments from his *emic* perspective, 'Meditation, [Maharishi] said, could be easy; it did not require effort or control; anyone could meditate whatever their disposition or life-style. He was turning most of the traditional teachings upside down: yet he seemed to make a lot more sense than many of the other teachers I had come across.'[55] More importantly, 'Unlike some other forms of meditation the TM program does not advocate any renunciation of worldly affairs. The actual practice of meditation, it is true, does involve a temporary withdrawal from activity, but it is a withdrawal in order that one may return to activity that much more effectively.'[56] The emphasis is not on *collective liberation from* the world, but *individual liberation within* the world. As is the case within Human Potential organizations, the focus is placed very pointedly on the individual and the realization of the individual's inner potential. Such movements are epistemologically individualist, the devotional focus being the sacred self, the divine within, internalized authority. 'By epistemological individualism,' says Wallis, 'I mean to suggest that the cult has no clear locus of final authority beyond the individual member. Unlike the sect, the ideal-typical cult lacks any source of legitimate attributions of heresy.'[57] Again, charisma is internalized.

World-accommodating religion, which is less socially significant than world-rejecting and world-affirming religion, 'draws a distinction between the spiritual and the worldly in a way quite uncharacteristic of the other two types. Religion is not construed as a primary social matter; rather it provides solace or stimulation to personal, interior life.'[58] This is, it seems to me, more of a miscellaneous category situated somewhere between the other two poles on Wallis's spectrum. Indeed, on the one hand, much of what he defines as 'world-accommodating' would apply to the world-affirming beliefs of Transcendental Meditation. On the other hand, charismatic Christianity and the Aetherius Society, which he regards as typical of world-accommodating religions, whilst less extreme and less ghetto-ized than what he describes as world-rejecting religion, are both world-rejecting to some extent (sometimes a significant extent). Indeed, it should be noted that often these movements are critical of established religions precisely because their lukewarm approach tends toward accommodation with the world, rather than distinction from it. That said, whilst problematic in certain respects, his identification of a separate category for moderate developments that protest against petrified and lukewarm religion within institutional organizations is useful.

Finally, it is worth noting a recent classification of religion in 'modern times'[59] posited by Linda Woodhead and Paul Heelas which, although having similarities with other typologies discussed above, is more fluid (at least as I understand it). Their three types of religion are (1) religions of difference, (2) religions of humanity and (3) spiritualities of life. All of these, they point out, co-exist in the contemporary world 'on a global, national, local and personal level'.[60] These, they argue,

> can be thought of as three points on a spectrum of understandings of the relationship between the divine, the human, and the natural order. At one end of the spectrum,

religions of difference distinguish sharply between God and the human and natural. At
the other, spiritualities of life adopt a 'holistic' perspective and stress the fundamental
identity between the divine, the human and the natural. And in the middle of the
spectrum, religions of humanity attempt to keep the three elements in balance, resisting
a subordination of the human to the divine or the natural.[61]

That is to say, in much the same way as other typologies, the emphasis can, as I
have already pointed out, be understood in terms of sacred/profane boundaries.
(Indeed, although Mircea Eliade is rarely, if ever, mentioned in these sociologi-
cally oriented treatments, there is still a great deal that can be learned from his
analyses of the sacred and the profane in religion.[62]) At one end of the spectrum
there is religion which stresses boundaries between a transcendent God and a
sinful humanity and between the fallen natural order and holy deity. This, we
have seen, is characteristic of epistemologically authoritarian sectarian belief and
what Wallis identified as world-rejecting religion. At the other end of the
spectrum is an immanentist type of religion, in which the boundaries between the
sacred and the profane are blurred. Such religion is essentially cultic, mystical (in
the sense in which Troeltsch understands that term), and epistemologically
individualist. What Woodhead and Heelas describe as 'religions of humanity'
simply make up the ground between the theologically left-wing and right-wing
types. It is the religion of those who are unwilling to turn to the left or to the
right, or who have not made up their minds to do so. Overall, compared with
Wallis's world-accommodating religiosity, this is a more satisfactory attempt to
classify the middle ground. Indeed, by identifying *experiential* religion in both
'religions of difference' and 'religions of humanity', Woodhead and Heelas,
unlike Wallis, are able correctly to locate movements such as charismatic Christianity in the former. As noted above, although experience is central to charismatic
Christianity, it should be understood as a variant of world-rejecting religion – the
logical corollary of it being a 'highly differentiated' religion (or, I suggest, more
accurately, a religion of 'discontinuity' – 'de-differentiated' religions being
religions of 'continuity').

Secularization and New Age Spiritualities

Having briefly introduced secularization (in the previous chapter) and theories
concerning typologies of sects, new religions and alternative spiritualities, we
now need to begin pulling the discussions together. In particular, we might ask
whether the emergence of such new forms of religion is not a rather large fly in
the secularization ointment, in that their proliferation is hardly a ringing endorsement of the demise of religion in the West. It should come as little surprise to
learn that a complex and flexible theory such as the secularization thesis, which
seems able to accommodate an enormous range of variables, is able to account
for the widespread emergence of religious phenomena such as the New Age.
That said, it is able to do this principally by arguing that such phenomena are not
as significant as they might first appear to the casual observer. As Bruce asserts
(without, it has to be said, much ethnographic evidence): 'For the vast majority
of people interested in the New Age milieu, participation is shallow. They read a

book or two and attend a few meetings. They do not become committed adher-ents to particular cults; they do not regularly engage in time-consuming rituals or therapies; they do not radically alter their lives.' He continues, 'Even for the small numbers of people who are deeply committed to various forms of new religion or new psychology, the impact may be limited. Or to be more precise, the changes that result from such involvement may be largely perceptual and rhetorical.'[63] Moreover, he makes the forceful point that the numbers involved in new religions hardly inspire belief in the resurgence of religion.[64] For example, concerning sec-tarian religion in Britain, 'the new religious movements of the 1970s are numeri-cally all but irrelevant. One of the most generous estimates … can find only 14,515 members. Knowing that the Unification Church has fewer than 400 members puts the contribution of the new religious movements in its proper context.'[65] Again, whilst it is difficult to assess the numbers involved in *cultic* religion, Bruce nevertheless notes that they appear to be relatively insignificant. For example, 'Even if the number who have stayed at Findhorn for any length of time reached ten thousand (and it might be some way short of that), this would be less than the membership of Ian Paisley's Free Presbyterian Church of Ulster and far less than the number of people lost to the Christian churches in Scotland in a decade.'[66] Hence, to return to Bruce's analogy, although new forms of religion may be lo-cated at a relatively high point on the rim of the religious wheel rolling downhill in a secular direction, they do not alter the fact that the overall trajectory of the wheel is consistently one of descent. With reference to Wallis's typology, he sum-marizes his understanding as follows:

> Modernization entails structural and social differentiation and geographical and social mobility. Leaving aside the cases where ethnic, national or international conflict cause social solidarity to remain the primary imperative, these social forces typically bring cultural diversity and egalitarianism, which in turn make the church form of religion impossible. The sect can survive where, and to the extent that, the social structure permits the creation of subsocieties. That leaves the denomination and the cult. Because they have at their heart an individualistic epistemology, both types are sociologically precarious.[67]

Moreover, 'the individual autonomy at the heart of the New Age will prevent this new form of religion gaining the presence or influence of the denominational, sectarian and churchly forms it replaces'.[68]

Wilson likewise locates new religiosity within the general flow of seculariza-tion. For example, in an interesting analysis of Scientology he focuses on Hub-bard's claim to have rationalized the path to salvation: 'in Scientology there was a standardized, routinized procedure and increasing predictability of soteriologi-cal results. In this claim, we see the full influence of secularization: there is an attempt to discipline, regulate, and routinize access to the supernatural sphere. Scientology provides technical devices by which to increase the production of salvation: to reduce mystery to formulae.'[69] Whilst Wilson clearly understands the Church of Scientology to be a religion,[70] his claim is that it is a secularized, this-worldly religion, concerned with life enhancement,[71] which rationalizes belief and, in contrast with traditional Christianity, 'has much closer affinity with the ethos of the late 20th century, an ethos of permissive hedonism, emphasizing human happiness and encouragement for people to realize their full potential'.[72] Scientology appears 'altogether congruous to the secularized world in which it operates and from which it draws so much of its organizational structure and therapeutic preoccupations'.[73]

It is interesting to note that, just as Wilson understands such religiosity, no matter how distinct from traditional religious systems, to be essentially 'religious',[74] so Bruce understands diffuse New Age spiritualities to be truly 'religion'. The reason this needs to be noted is that some have argued that Bruce and others do not really believe this to be the case, defining 'religion' solely in terms of the epistemologically authoritarian beliefs of the church and the sect. Hence, it is claimed that what he has interpreted as decline is actually a shift from this form of religion (which is undoubtedly declining) to diffuse systems of belief (which, his critics argue, are growing). This, Bruce insists, is not the case. Indeed, he makes no such judgement. His principal concern is not to define what *is* and what *is not* 'truly religious', but rather to assess the significance of movements, which, as a sociologist, he does principally by looking at the countable numbers of people involved and the impact of their beliefs on society as a whole. 'I have,' he says, 'no difficulty accepting that cultic religion is indeed a form of religion. My case is that, like the denomination in its most liberal form, cultic religion lacks the *social significance* of the church and the sect.'[75] This is an important point. In criticizing secularization, scholars also need to attend to the social significance of religion – even if they do not accept Bruce's or Wilson's understanding of what is and what is not socially significant.

As well as claiming that cultic religion lacks social significance, Bruce argues that it is also 'a form of religion that is particularly difficult to sustain and promote. Hence, the number of adherents (if that is not too strong a term for the consumers of cultic religion) will decline.'[76] (Incidentally, to press the point a little, whilst he may define the cultic as technically 'religion', we have seen that Bruce also seems to understand it to be superficial, trivial and shallow.[77] One therefore has to ask questions about the criteria used to make such judgements. Why is this trivial religion? What makes religious belief shallow? What constitutes an 'adherent'? We will return to these issues in the following chapter.) Bruce's overall point is that cultic religion's lack of social significance and its diffuse nature hinders its effective promotion and maintenance, which, in turn, means that it is 'unlikely to stem secularization'.

Hence, in the final analysis, cultic spirituality is, at best, a manifestation of what William Swatos has termed 'pseudo-enchantment'.[78] Indeed, as noted above, it is argued that, rather than being evidence of the resurgence of religion, new religions are actually evidence of secularization.[79] They should not be regarded as revivals of a tradition, but rather, says Wilson,

> they are more accurately regarded as adaptations of religion to new social circumstances. None of them is capable, given the radical nature of social change, of recreating the dying religions of the past. In their style and in their specific appeal they represent an accommodation to new conditions, and they incorporate many of the assumptions and facilities encouraged in the increasingly rationalized secular sphere. Thus it is that many new movements are themselves testimonies to secularization: they often utilize highly

secular methods in evangelism, financing, publicity and mobilization of adherents. Very commonly, the traditional symbolism, liturgy and aesthetic concern of traditional religion are abandoned for much more pragmatic attitudes and for systems of control, propaganda and even doctrinal consent which are closer to styles of secular enterprise than to traditional religious concerns.[80]

Similarly, Bruce argues that the New Age, which is in many ways 'emblematic of religion in our culture',[81] mirrors the assumptions and values of the contemporary West.[82] This is established in an analysis of six key themes in New Age religion.

1. New Age belief systems teach that, in some sense, the self is divine or that the self can, by some means or other, become divine. To use the terminology I introduced earlier, this is a religion of divine–human *continuity* presupposing the innate goodness of humanity, not a religion of divine–human *discontinuity*, supported by a doctrine of sin. Again, in the terms suggested by Woodhead and Heelas, the New Age is not a 'religion of difference', but a 'spirituality of life'. Hence, true religion is located within, not without; one focuses on the good self *per se*, rather than the self over against the Good (i.e. God).

2. The problem with this form of religiosity is that it leads to epistemological individualism. There is no higher authority than the self. Personal experience is the final arbiter of truth.[83] (This, it will be recalled, is very close to what Troeltsch so presciently had in mind when he wrote of the turn to the 'mystical'.)

3. Epistemological individualism leads, in turn, to eclecticism. As their own priests and spiritual directors, individuals prescribe what they feel best meets their spiritual needs: 'As we differ in class, in gender, in age, in regional background, in culture we will have different notions of what works for us and this is reflected in the enormous cafeteria of cultural products from which New Agers select.'[84] Hence the popular jibe that New Age spirituality is supermarket spirituality – individuals are encouraged to peruse and select from a bewildering array of spiritual products from crop circles and dolphins to Buddhism and Celtic Christianity. For example, currently lying on my desk as I type these words is the *Alternatives* newsletter (Spring/Summer 2002) with a photograph of a crop circle on the cover. As I turn the pages, I am encouraged to attend a range of workshops and talks. For example, there are details of a session exploring 'the fundamental questions of life' by the great-nephew of the thirteenth Dalai Lama – followed by Philip Glass playing the piano for twenty minutes. Again, I am invited to attend talks by psychic Natalie O'Sullivan on 'Awakening Your Psychic Powers' and Geho and Sarita, who encourage the use of Tantra to 'explore our own inner universe'. If these are not to my taste, perhaps I should try a session with Donald Engstrom, an American witch, who teaches 'Spirit Mapping', or a workshop with Serge Kahili King, a shaman and healer 'in the Huna tradition', who will introduce me to 'techniques that [I] can use in [my] daily life', or even Ken Page, who offers guidance in the 'Third Eye of Horus Mystery School Teachings'.[85] No impression is given that any one of these is more effective or more authoritative than the next. They are simply offered as useful paths to explore. The Alternatives organization, based at St James's Church, London, simply 'seeks to inspire new visions for living through holistic

education and connection to the sacred dimension of life. Our programme of talks and workshops is offered in a spirit of service, integrity, and exploration.'[86] Essentially, that is the heart of the New Age, the nomadic, spiritual quest of the autonomous 'self'.

4. As indicated in the quotations from *Alternatives* literature, New Age spirituality emphasizes holism. It rejects what it perceives to be the reductionism of modern scientific worldviews. It bemoans modern medicine's treatment of people as a collection of parts, rather than as whole persons, and the separation of the spiritual and the material. Hence, themes of connectedness pervade New Age worldviews.

5. Epistemological individualism and eclecticism necessarily lead to relativism. Truth claims are relativized or, more likely, the implications of them are simply not noticed. The general claim is often the essentialist/perennialist one that no path is better than another, all generally leading in the same direction, and there is a unifying cosmic something behind the apparent diversity.

6. The *goal* of much New Age spirituality is health and happiness, rather than health and happiness being a potential *by-product* of the religious life. That is to say, whilst we have seen that some Christians may become wealthy as a result of the Protestant work ethic, health and happiness are not their goals. Indeed, suffering, poverty and the lack of worldly success are invested with spiritual significance. Arguably, even 'prosperity Christianity', which does prize health and wealth, only does so because such material gains are viewed as evidence of God's pleasure with a life lived faithfully. The aim is obedience to God. Material benefits are secondary. This is not the case in the New Age. For example, in another newsletter, *Inspiration*, therapist Nick Williams is interviewed about his new book, significantly entitled *Unconditional Success*. 'What is Unconditional Success?' he is asked. He replies, 'Being happy and fulfilled!' 'What does unconditional success mean to you?' 'For me it is knowing and being in tune with my own soul, being inspired, growing, becoming kinder, healing and making a difference. I love the outer material rewards, but at the expanse of, not expense of, my own soul… It is also about integration and balance – love and money, work and joy, our inner and outer worlds.'[87] Whilst spirituality is clearly important, it is inextricably allied to health, wealth and happiness as important goals.

The point is that Bruce argues that 'New Age' themes such as these provide evidence (as, indeed, they do) that the 'New Age' strongly resonates with the culture of contemporary Western societies. Essentially his point is that consumerist and pluralist democracies encourage the turn toward essentialism, relativism, and epistemological individualism. For example, as we have seen, one way of dealing with cultural fragmentation and the diversity of religious and ethical expression is to assert the equal value of most, if not all, worldviews and a common essence uniting them all. What Woodhead has referred to as 'the flight from deference'[88] (although that seems to overstate the point) is also significant. The decline in deference to expertise, stimulated by, for example, frequently uninformed media critiques of 'the experts' and the rising levels of education in the West generally, again lead to a shift towards the authority of individual perspectives. Bruce identifies three stages in the progressive rejection of authority:

Once culture was defined by experts. Now we accept the freedom of personal taste: I may not know much about art but I know what I like. In the late 1960s claims for personal autonomy moved to a second stage of matters of personal behaviour: I may not know much about ethics and morals but I know what I like to do and I claim my right to do it. In the third stage the same attitude is applied to areas of expert knowledge: I may not know much about the nervous system but I know what I like to believe in and I believe in chakras and Shiatsu massage and acupuncture.[89]

Again, relativism prevents the emergence of social conflict by allowing people to view the world from whatever perspective they desire and to adopt whatever worldview they want. There is no one way to be religious, there is no orthodoxy. This trend was carefully unpacked over twenty years ago by Peter Berger in his significantly entitled *The Heretical Imperative*:

In the premodern situation there is a world of religious certainty, occasionally ruptured by heretical deviations. By contrast, the modern situation is a world of religious uncertainty, occasionally staved off by more or less precarious constructions of reli-gious affirmation. Indeed, one could put this change even more sharply: *For premodern man, heresy is a possibility – usually a rather remote one; for modern man, heresy typically becomes a necessity.* Or again, *modernity creates a new situation in which picking and choosing becomes an imperative.*[90]

Add to this the emphasis on choice and the commodification of spirituality and it becomes clear that New Age religion is indeed well-suited to the modern world. Not only does the New Age encourage the individual to choose on the grounds of preference and presumed personal need, but it also encourages individuals to become consumers. Religious objects, books, courses, and retreats are for sale. Such items then become one's possessions to be used as one desires. Hence, whereas in traditional Christianity one purchases a Bible to study before God in accordance with the prevailing orthodoxy, in the New Age one might purchase a Bible to read alongside the Upanishads, *A Course in Miracles*, or channelled messages from extraterrestrials. That is to say, as with other consumer items bought and used, religious ideas and artefacts are simply incorporated into indi-vidual lifestyles and used according to individual preferences.

That the New Age is based on such a culturally adapted epistemology is, of course, central to any popularity it has in the contemporary West. However, for the same reasons, this type of religion, which Bruce terms 'diffuse religion', is also fundamentally precarious. This is because it does not submit to a central authority and therefore, unlike traditional hierarchical religions, is difficult to order socially. This, in turn, leads to several related problems.

1. As we have just seen, because 'the consumer is king', once-powerful religious hierarchies have become commodities to be chosen in accordance with individual likes and dislikes. In other words, because power is invested in the individual consumer, rather than in a particular religious organization, there is little commitment to particular organizational belief systems. Individuals choose the path that suits their spiritual journey, rather than being committed to a preordained route. More specifically, because there is no central control over the lives of individuals, no coercion can be applied and thus no consensus can be

achieved concerning orthodoxy and orthopraxis. And without coercion and consensus, Bruce maintains, it is difficult for a belief system to survive.

2. This lack of commitment is fundamentally related to a lack of cohesion. The sense of community which binds individuals together and enables the construction of orthodoxies is very weak in diffuse religion. Hence, in the New Age there is no community pressure and, whilst devotees may generally agree about certain abstract notions such as individual autonomy, reincarnation, and the value of the natural world, there is often little agreement about how such concepts should be understood or applied. Hence, again, doctrinal and ethical cohesion is impossible to maintain. 'Diffuse religion cannot sustain a distinctive way of life. When there is no power beyond the individual to decide what should be the behavioural consequences of any set of spiritual beliefs, then it is very unlikely that a group will come to agree on how the righteous should behave.'[91]

3. Regardless of the claims of New Age devotees to be both countercultural and also critical of many aspects of modernity, in reality their spiritual individualism has little social impact: 'Although a very few New Agers have become active in environmental protests, in anti-capitalist rallies, or in developing alternative technologies, the impact has at best been slight.'[92] For example, Bruce usefully contrasts what he understands to be the meagre achievements of New Agers with the massive social impact of Victorian Evangelicals, who transformed British society at all levels. However, the latter could do this because they 'were able to unite around very specific goals and devoted vast amounts of time and money to promote them. Their value-consensus meant that the movement organizations they formed exerted influence beyond that of their number as individuals.'[93] New Agers, on the other hand, whilst they are likewise critical of aspects of contemporary society, 'make little or no effort to change it and such efforts as they do make are not amplified by being concerted. Or, to put it rhetorically, where are the New Age schools, nurseries, communes, colleges, ecological housing associations, subsistence farming centres, criminal resettlement houses, women's refuges, practical anti-racism projects and urban renewal programmes?'[94]

4. 'Where we most clearly see the impotence of the New Age is in the shallowness of much of the rhetoric about taking control of one's own life, being the person you want to be and such like.'[95] Not only does New Age spirituality have little impact upon the world, it also has a negligible affect on the lives of the individual believers. It may absorb spiritual exercises and monastic disciplines from the world's religions, but it trivializes these. It reduces the ascetic to the aesthetic. In Bruce's words, 'It allows novices to become adepts without the difficult bits in between ... What is advertised as spiritual transformation is little more than acquiring a new vocabulary.'[96] Unlike Methodism, which transformed the lives of individuals who then went on to transform the societies in which they lived, the New Age does neither.

5. Because the emphasis is on individuals choosing their own spiritual paths, there is little incentive to evangelize: 'coherent ideologies can be transmitted intact but diffuse ideologies must always be reinvented. In essence there are two

problems: the transmission of diffuse beliefs is unnecessary and it is impossible.'[97] Whilst there is a general New Age assumption that people do need to change (e.g. to become more right-brained and less left-brained, or more spiritual and less materialist), there is no particular path that should be chosen and thus no need for a missiology. 'In the final analysis the injunction to be true to yourself subverts the possibility of effectively asserting that *these* people would be better if they became like *those* people.'[98] Moreover, Bruce seems to argue that, whilst New Agers provide numerous events (e.g. the Mind–Body–Spirit festivals), organize various retreats and workshops for the promotion of New Age ideas, and run introductory evening classes and the like, because they present a variety of approaches and spiritualities such events lack the force of effective evangelism. Sectarian or ecclesiastical evangelistic events, on the other hand, are usually based on a particular theology/missiology, rather than a range of abstract ideas. Billy Graham, for example, presents a simple, cohesive message, based on a clear Evangelical christology and soteriology, the principal details of which all those involved in his mission agree with. The lack of such cohesion is a problem for many alternative spiritualities: 'Cultists cannot add momentum to their persuasive efforts because their diffuse beliefs prevent them from agreeing in sufficient detail on what is to be promoted.'[99]

6. Furthermore, Bruce claims that, because the New Age is essentially commodified religion which thrives on novelty, like all fashion and consumer items, there is a need to present something *new and fashionable* for each season: 'Of course, more conventional religions are also affected by short fashion waves… but, because those fashions operate within a solid consensus of essential beliefs, they do not do much to hinder the consolidation of commitment. The New Age lacks that solid base and thus constantly has to market itself anew.'[100]

7. Finally, as we have seen, the result of the above is a vulnerability to dilution and trivialization: 'Unless one constantly works to preserve a body of doctrine, the ideas will gradually accommodate to the cultural norms. Deliberate social control is required to preserve a distinctive body of ideas and practices and the associate sense of shared identity.'[101] Again, Bruce is simply noting the asceticism-to-aestheticism process which I identified earlier. Doctrines and practices from the world religions are, as Heelas and others have observed, detraditionalized.[102] They are taken out of their original systematic theological contexts and have their original meaning diluted, in order to serve personal whims and desires. Ayurvedic remedies are used to promote beauty products, *feng shui* becomes the latest trend in interior design, and ancient meditation techniques developed over many centuries can be learned in an hour.

To conclude, alternative spiritualities provide eclectic, individualized religion for disenchanted Westerners who want to hang on to the remnants of belief without inconveniencing themselves too much. Such religion does not claim absolute truth, does not require devotion to one religious leader, does not insist on the authority of a single set of sacred writings, but rather encourages exploration, eclecticism, an understanding of the self as divine, and, consequently, often a belief in the final authority only of the self.[103] Mystical, cultic, epistemologically individualistic spiritual beliefs are quite distinct from 'church' religion, in that they lack ideological weight – 'because they are not embedded in large organizations or sustained by a long history... many elements of the New Age are vulnerable to being co-opted by the cultural mainstream and trivialized by the mass media.'[104] Unlike the church and sectarian forms of religion, such cultic spiritualities thus tend to be diffuse and precarious, lacking religious salience and functioning as weak, insubstantial substitutes for their dying predecessors. Hence, says Bruce, 'while I see every possibility that some sections of the population will continue to be interested in spirituality, I cannot see how a shared faith can be created from a low-salience world of pick-and-mix religion. Furthermore, I suspect that the New Age, weak as it always has been, will weaken further as the children of the New Age prove indifferent to the spiritual questing of their parents.'[105] Indeed, whilst not literally inconsequential, in the final analysis such diffuse religion, rather than being evidence of re-enchantment, is simply a symptom of modern capitalism: 'Rather than see the New Age as an antidote to secularization, it makes more sense to see it as a style and form of religion well-suited to the secular world.'[106] Indeed, he predicts that, not only will 'the cultic religion of New Age spirituality... become ever more diffuse and less significant', but 'the New Age as an organized movement will die out as it fails to recruit the next generation'.[107]

Chapter 3

THE RE-ENCHANTMENT OF THE WEST

In the previous chapters I introduced the process of disenchantment, typologies of the new religious life, especially cultic/mystical/epistemologically individualist religion, and the relationship between disenchantment and alternative forms of spirituality – often simply referred to as 'New Age' religion. We saw that, instead of understanding new forms of religion in terms of evidence against progressive disenchantment, some secularization theorists argue that the opposite is the case: there is nothing to get excited about; the general decline of religion has not been interrupted; new forms of spirituality are weak, contextualized substitutes for traditional religion; indeed, they are what one would expect in a late-modern, capitalist, secular culture, in that they mirror that culture. However, as I have indicated, whilst disenchantment theory cannot be dismissed, it is by no means the whole story. There is some evidence to suggest that 'a rising tide of spirituality ... is producing a re-enchantment of the world'.[1] Hence, what this chapter aims to do is simply introduce the re-enchantment thesis and broadly indicate my own reasons for supporting it, reasons which will be supplemented and further explored in Part II.

Disenchantment as the Precursor to Re-Enchantment

There is, as I hope I have indicated, much to commend the assessments of the nature of the contemporary religious milieu posited by Bruce, Wilson and others. However, I have also suggested that there are problems. More significance needs to be accorded to the fact that, in line with the global trend of a gradual upsurge of religion, and along with streams of 'fundamentalist' religion[2] (in particular, we might think of the increasing numbers of young Asians and Africans attracted to conservative forms of Islam, or the challenges made by Hindu 'fundamentalists' to secularism in India, or indeed, the emergence of conservative Christianity in Latin America and sub-Saharan Africa[3]), there seems to be a gradual, yet ubiquitous growth of 'spirituality' in the West. For example, a recent survey carried out for the BBC by Opinion Research Business found that, although traditional Christian belief is declining, the percentage of people in Britain who claim to have 'a non-everyday awareness' of 'the presence of God' rose from 27 per cent in April 1987 to 38 per cent in May 2000. Similarly, the percentage of people who claim to have 'a non-everyday awareness' that they are receiving help in answer to 'prayer' rose from 25 per cent in April 1987 to 37 per cent in May 2000.[4]

In a recent revision of his secularization thesis, Berger, after predicting that the world of the twenty-first century will be no less religious than it is today, asserts that 'the religious impulse, the quest for meaning that transcends the restricted space of empirical existence in this world, has been a perennial feature of humanity... It would require something close to a mutation of the species to extinguish this impulse for good.'[5] Even in thoroughly modern societies, such as Japan, religion has not only *not* been dissipated, but is flourishing.

Is Europe, therefore, an exception? Indeed, do Bruce, Wilson and many other academics also stand out as exceptions in an increasingly re-enchanted world? Although 'the world today is massively religious, is *anything but* the secularized world that had been predicted... by analysts of modernity', there are, says Berger, 'two exceptions to this proposition', namely 'Europe west of what used to be called the Iron Curtain', and, more ambiguously, 'an international subculture composed of people with a Western-type higher education, especially in the humanities and social sciences'.[6] This subculture, he claims, although 'thin on the ground', is very influential, mainly because its members 'control the institutions that provide the "official" definitions of reality, notably the educational system, the media of mass communication, and the higher reaches of the legal system... I cannot speculate here as to why people with this type of education should be so prone to secularization. I can only point out that what we have here is a globalized *elite* culture.'[7] One of the arguments in this book is that the theories posited by this globalized elite are being challenged by emergent, detraditionalized forms of popular spirituality. The religious situation in Western Europe is becoming less ambiguous year on year. This, of course, as Berger notes, will not be recognized by those academics who spend too much time listening to and writing for other members of the elite subculture who presume that their view of reality is the only valid one: 'Picture a secular intellectual from Western Europe socializing with colleagues at the faculty club of the University of Texas. He may think he is back home. But then picture him trying to drive through the traffic jam on Sunday morning in downtown Austin – or, heaven help him, turning on his car radio! What happens then is a severe jolt of what anthropologists call cultural shock.'[8] As we will see, and as Berger suggests, the situation may be less one of secularization and more one of the relocation of religion. In other words, we will conclude that, as mainstream religion loses authority, new forms of significant religion will evolve to compensate. Consequently, in the final analysis, any apparent disappearance of religion is illusory.[9]

To accept this general position, of course, does not require the wholesale rejection of secularization. (As noted at the beginning of Chapter 1, we may, for example, develop a version of the 'de-intensification theory' or the 'co-existence theory', as outlined in the typology by Woodhead and Heelas.) Stark and Bainbridge, for example, do not deny the existence of secularization, but rather understand it differently as part of a recurring process. The following statement is important and can be supported by my earlier discussion of sectarianism and denominationalism:

secularization is nothing new…it is occurring constantly in all religious economies. Through secularization, sects are tamed and transformed into churches. Their initial otherworldliness is reduced and worldliness is accommodated. Secularization also eventually leads to the collapse of religious organizations as their extreme worldliness – their weak and vague conceptions of the supernatural – leaves them without the means to satisfy even the universal dimension of religious commitment. Thus, we regard secularization as the primary dynamic of religious economies, a self-limiting process that engenders revival (sect formation) and innovation (cult formation).[10]

The point is that, unlike those secularization theorists who regard new religions and alternative spiritualities as evidence of the ultimate demise of religion in the modern world, this understanding of secularization views it as a stage in a larger process, a stage which will be followed by the increasing significance of new forms of religion. As we have seen, the process could be briefly described as follows. Churches/large religious institutions become ever more secular, liberal, dilute and indistinct from their 'worldly' contexts; consequently, they fail to meet the moral and spiritual needs/desires of their followers; revived breakaway groups (sects) or new, innovative forms of religion (cults) emerge; these then grow larger and more established (e.g. cultic religion may become sectarian – as was the case with, for example, Dianetics, which became Scientology – and sects may become denominations – as was the case with, for example, Methodism and Pentecostalism); they then, through rationalization, routinization, and socialization, may also become gradually more secularized. However, the key point to note is that, according to this general thesis, religious decline is only apparent or temporary, for dying churches seed new sects and cults.

More specifically, I would argue that the deteriorating/secularized Christian culture is being replaced by a cultic milieu, which is not shaped like sectarian, denominational or ecclesiastical religion. Nor is it principally determined by that 'international subculture' identified by Berger, which is 'composed of people with a Western-type higher education'.[11] Increasingly, 'official' definitions of reality are being challenged by a new subculture of dissent and opposition.[12] In a sense, we are witnessing a return to a form of magical culture – what I will call 'occulture'. Although it is perhaps a little silly to speak of an occultural reformation or revolution, there is nevertheless a significant religio-cultural shift happening in the 'real world'. Hence, to some extent, I would agree with Wouter Hanegraaff's analysis of the 'profound *transformation* of religion' in the West, away from traditional Christianity and towards what he describes as 'magic'. However, I cannot agree with his interpretation of this transformation in terms of secularization. Indeed, as far as I'm concerned, the following statement contains a basic contradiction: 'Far from involving anything like a disappearance or marginalization of religion, secularization can be understood as referring to a profound *transformation* of religion.'[13] No, it cannot. If a society as a whole is undergoing a process which does not involve anything like 'a disappearance or marginalization of religion', it has to be described in terms other than 'secularization'. If it is not, one is led into a thicket of terminological and theological problems. This is why Hanegraaff is forced to account for the prevalence of magic in the modern world with 'a paradox' – 'disenchanted magic': 'Ideas and practices popularly classed as "magic" may adapt with various degrees of success to the new circumstances of a secularized society, but in the process of doing so they themselves undergo qualitative changes. The result is a survival of magic in a disenchanted world, but the crucial point is *that this will no longer be the same magic* that could be found in periods prior to the process of disenchantment. It will be a disenchanted magic.'[14] Although his learned and fascinating comparison of pre-Enlightenment and post-Enlightenment magic is enormously helpful in demonstrating the significant and inevitable shifts that have taken place in the practice of magic, in the final analysis he is able convincingly to show only that modern magic is different, but *not* that it is secularized. It may be modern, in that it may be interpreted with reference to, for example, contemporary metaphors and psychology, but it is still 'magic'. For example, drawing on Tanya Luhrmann's excellent study,[15] he makes much of the fact that modern magicians believe in the existence of two worlds (or planes) – the everyday world and a separate magical world. Hanegraaff, however, overemphasizes the separateness of these worlds in order to argue that that modern, secularized occultists can distance the magical world from the disenchanted reality of their everyday lives. Luhrmann, on the other hand, accurately describes the relationship between the two worlds as 'separate-but-connected'. Work on the magical plane, as Hanegraaff agrees, is believed to have a direct impact on the everyday world. That this is so places a large question mark against his claim that occultists are able to keep the two worlds separate. Indeed, apart from anything else, it would be enormously psychologically demanding to operate with such a fundamentally fractured worldview. In fact, regardless of the updated metaphors, explanations, and interpretations, occultists, like most religious believers, have a single magical worldview. And one only has to read the works of contemporary magicians such as Pat Zalewski[16] to realize that the world they inhabit *is* enchanted. Spirit entities, the communications of the Elizabethan occultist John Dee, and much else that is explicitly magical/spiritual is firmly accepted as part of an integrated worldview. As Luhrmann comments, although magicians do not always agree about the nature of reality, 'the idea that spirits exist is not contested'.[17] Indeed, she later makes the point that what is believed and practiced by modern magicians can be understood as fundamentally religious – even 'magicians themselves come to use the term "religion" because they feel comfortable calling the feelings elicited in some meditations and rituals "spiritual" ... One might imagine that merely having a spiritual response to a ritual should not commit one to any theory about divine existence or magical force ... But people often find the distinction hard to handle: they tend to accept the magical or theological ideas because the involvement ... becomes so central to their lives.'[18] Again, while it cannot be denied that, as a result of the Enlightenment, significant changes have occurred in understandings of the nature of magic, its legitimacy and efficacy, the argument that contemporary systems of belief contitute 'disenchanted magic' is flawed.

The process of returning to a form of magical culture was discussed by the sociologist Colin Campbell in the 1970s: 'the contemporary transformation of religion is best viewed as a transition from "church religion" to "spiritual and mystic religion" and … such a change is intimately related to the processes of "secularization" that are occurring in the modern world'.[19] His argument is as follows:

> Secularization has commonly been measured by criteria that are largely irrelevant to spiritual and mystic religion… Hence data which suggest a decline of religion according to these criteria do not give ground for assuming that spiritual and mystic religion is in decline … However, the data on secularization have a broader significance, beyond the fact that they do not establish that there has been a decline in the fortunes of mystic religion. For the data are also consistent with the changes which would accompany an upsurge in this form of religion. A decline in formal, churchly religion and its con-comitants may well be taken as evidence of secularization, but it is important to note that it is also not inconsistent with the thesis that there is an expansion in the extent and influence of spiritual and mystic religion. For such an expansion would, almost certainly, be at the expense of churchly religion.[20]

There are important points here to which we will need to return. However, the principal point to grasp at this stage is the relationship between the secularization of 'church religion' and the expansion of alternative, mystic spirituality.

The compensation thesis of Stark and Bainbridge can be used to unpack the argument posited by Campbell. In response to the claim that, relentlessly driven by modernization, secularization is a one-way process, accelerated and made all the more virulent and corrosive by the modern scientific worldview, they again insist that religion will emerge as a dominant socio-cultural force simply because science and secular worldviews in general are not able to satisfy fundamental human desires. More particularly, their argument is that naturalistic worldviews cannot offer the much-desired, large-scale rewards and 'compensators' that religions offer (e.g. immortality/eternal life). Hence, for Stark and Bainbridge, while religion cannot offer such rewards directly, it does offer attractive 'compensators' which, although second-best in comparison to direct rewards, are nevertheless very appealing:[21]

> *A compensator is the belief that a reward will only be obtained in the distant future or in some other context which cannot be immediately verified* … When we examine human desires, we see that people often seek rewards of such magnitude and apparent unavailability that *only by assuming the existence of an active supernatural can credible compensators be created* … Some common human desires are so beyond direct, this-worldly satisfaction that only the gods can provide them … So long as humans seek certain rewards of great magnitude that remain unavailable through direct actions, they will obtain credible compensators only from sources predicated on the supernatural. In this market, no purely naturalistic ideologies can compete. Systems of thought that reject the supernatural lack all means to credibly promise such rewards as eternal life in any fashion. Similarly, naturalistic philosophies can argue that statements such as 'What is the meaning of life?' or 'What is the purpose of the universe?' are meaningless utterances. But they cannot provide answers to these questions in the terms in which they are asked.[22]

Indeed, as we will see in the next chapter, this coheres well with Troeltsch's thesis regarding mystical religion, which arises as a reaction against the pragmatism, ethical laxity and internal secularization of church religion. It compensates for the dry formalism and disenchanted nature of much institutional religion. In other words, compensation is a good way of understanding the overall point I am seeking to draw attention to, namely that secularization and re-enchantment run together. To quote Campbell again, 'secularization and the rise of new religiosity are … simply two aspects of the same process, i.e. the change-over from church religion to spiritual and mystic religion; a fundamental process of social and cultural change in which identical forces can be seen to be responsible for the decline of the one and the emergence of the other.'[23] More specifically, 'the evidence of a turning away from churchly religion could be given a very different meaning from that presented by the proponents of the secularization thesis. Indeed, it would seem to imply its very denial.'[24]

Moreover, it is important to understand that, whilst there is a reactive element to this shift, generally speaking it is not only a reaction to the secularizing forces of rationalization, bureaucratization and technological domination, but also, as Stark and Bainbridge suggest, a more positive striving for the spiritual and the supernatural. There will always be dissatisfaction with, and departure from, secularized worldviews and from religions that dilute supernaturalism and thereby allow themselves to become internally secularized. 'The bracing world of modernity', says Vernon White, 'with its own priests of rationality, liberated us from superstition. But it also left us a dull, one-dimensional, unconvincing world.'[25] Such a world will always be fertile soil for re-enchantment. Hence, as Theodor Adorno observed, regardless of the progress of the rational in the modern world, the authority of the irrational seems to be a perennial feature of human societies. For example, that people still do live their lives according to astrological charts in a world in which astrophysics is a developed science and astrology is 'utterly anachronistic' suggests, argues Adorno, 'very strong instinctual demands'.[26] The point is that, bearing in mind such 'very strong instinctual demands', internally secularized religions and secular worldviews which are unable to provide credible compensators will decline and be replaced by new groups and spiritualities which either revive traditional compensators (sectarian religion) or develop new compensators (cultic religion). This is why secularization is a 'self-limiting process'. Because the religious appetite, it would seem, is irremovable, secularization will always be accompanied by the formation of sects or, increasingly, cultic networks of individuals (perhaps meeting only in the chat rooms of cyberspace) and small localized groups which are, in turn, the beginnings of new forms of supernaturalistic religion. Disenchantment is the precursor to re-enchantment.[27]

Although the current state of religion in the West is complicated and difficult to map accurately, it would seem that, alongside traditional forms of institutional religion that have been seriously damaged, cracks are appearing in the disenchanted landscape and new forms of *significant* spiritual life are emerging.[28] As Martin Marty pointed out in 1970, 'the occult establishment' suggests 'one more instance in which the claims of analysts, both theological and historical, that the world is becoming mainly or utterly secular should be called into question'.[29] Similarly, Daniel Bell speaks of 'the return of the sacred'. The big existential questions of life are beginning to be answered by new religions and alternative spiritualities.[30]

To reiterate the point, emergent religion may look very different to previous forms of religion, it may operate in new ways, but that should not be interpreted as indicative of a lack of substance and social significance. As with all life, new conditions require evolution. Religion in the thin atmosphere of the modern West will necessarily evolve away from what we have become used to calling 'religion'. Moreover, as future generations of alternative spiritualities become established, rooted and increasingly mainstream, they may prove to be more hardy and resistant to the disenchanting forces their antecedents were ill equipped to deal with. (Of course, that is not to say that there will not be new antagonistic forces as yet unpredicted.) As Cheris Shun-Ching Chan persuasively argues in her study of the Hong Kong group Lingsu Exo-Esoterics, Western re-enchantment may be characterized by new hybrid forms of religion which are the result of a dialectical process of the re-enchantment of the secular and the secularization of the sacred.[31] Hence, again, perhaps the first characteristic of contemporary re-enchantment to note is that it is *not* a return to previous ways of being religious, but rather the emergence of new ways of being religious, ways which meet the new wants and needs of new Western people. For example, Robert Wuthnow makes the following interesting observation:

> At the start of the twentieth century, virtually all Americans practiced their faith within a Christian or Jewish framework. They were cradle-to-grave members of their particular traditions, and their spirituality prompted them to attend and to believe in the teachings of their churches and synagogues. Organized religion dominated their experience of spirituality, especially when it was reinforced by ethnic loyalties and when it was expressed in family rituals. Even at mid-century, when the religious revival of the 1950s brought millions of new members to local congregations, many of these patterns prevailed. Now, at the end of the twentieth century, growing numbers of Americans piece together their faith like a patchwork quilt. Spirituality has become a vastly complex quest in which each person seeks his or her own way.[32]

Wuthnow goes on to map a shift in American religion from 'a traditional spirituality of inhabiting sacred places' or 'a spirituality of dwelling' to 'a new spirituality of seeking'.[33] This shift is increasingly being noticed, not only by sociologists and scholars of religion, but also by clerics and laypeople. For example, Michael Green, an advisor to the Archbishops of Canterbury and York, summarizes the state of religion in the West as follows:

> the numbers attending church are in massive decline, and in many churches no children and young people are to be seen … The remarkable fact is that there is a spiritual quest among many people today that we have not seen for many a long decade. It may be crystals and channellers, Transcendental Meditation or a little mild Buddhism. It may be Stonehenge on midsummer morn, or Wicca dances by moonlight. But there is an undeniable spiritual quest in the air. New Age, the new Paganism and the cults have an enormous fascination for [those] who have found that materialism does not satisfy. But it has to be said that their quest for authentic spiritual experience rarely takes them to a church.[34]

Indeed, even some of those who still attend church have turned from a spirituality of dwelling to one of seeking. Not only have I personally met many Christians who are experimenting with a range of alternative spiritualities, but I was particularly struck by a recent book written by Rob Frost, a respected British Evangelical Methodist. 'To be frank', he confesses, 'I am deeply disillusioned with what the church is offering Sunday by Sunday. There is a deadness in the ritual, a dryness in the formality, and a growing irrelevance in the institution... I find a genuine hunger for spiritual things in the New Age community, an openness to try new ideas, and a deep respect for the beliefs of others... I share the hunger for the fulfilling kind of spirituality which is driving this New Age movement into the mainstream of our culture.'[35] Hence, he has become a 'spiritual searcher' and invites his fellow Christians to follow him as he wanders 'around the supermarket of ideas of New Age culture, [in order to] see what they can teach [him] about [his] own quest for deep spirituality'.[36] As he says, 'I am becoming a New Age Christian, and I am not alone. Many committed Christians are looking for something deeper in their everyday life and faith.'[37]

This shift from 'dwelling' to 'seeking' need not be as traumatic as secularization theorists such as Bruce suggest. Although, as both Bruce and Peter Berger have argued, pluralism in Western societies tends to undermine taken-for-granted certainties, as Berger notes, 'it is possible to hold beliefs and live by them even if they no longer hold the status of taken-for-granted verities'.[38] Indeed, this, it would seem, is one of the strengths of these hardy new forms of spirituality. This should not come as a surprise. Why would a form of spirituality that has recently evolved in the West, and which necessarily functions quite differently from an older form of religion which evolved in a different society, be vulnerable to the same forces? New alternative spiritualities serve the needs of a different people. The reason they are flourishing is because they function in a very different way, having adapted to a new environment.

Unfortunately, surveys and discussions of trends in contemporary religion in the West have focused on traditional institutional religion, particularly Christianity. Typical is Peter Brierley's general discussion of 'Religion'.[39] Although he notes that the percentage of occult books sold has more than doubled since 1930, and although the percentage of people who believe in paranormal phenomena has, again, more than doubled since the 1940s, and although the percentage of people who believe in God as spirit has risen since the 1940s (unlike those who believe in God as personal, which has dramatically dropped),[40] there is no significant analysis of the implications of such beliefs, the focus of his discussion principally being declining theistic religion. Alternative spiritualities and occult worldviews are simply mentioned as interesting asides in a discussion of the overall downturn of traditional Christian belief and practice.

From a slightly different perspective, my point is well made by the historian Callum Brown:

> The social-scientific study of religion has been one of the great projects of Enlightenment modernity. From the late-eighteenth century to the present religion has been defined, measured and 'understood' through 'empirical' evidence spawned by the supposed 'neutrality' of social science. Social science has privileged a 'rationalist' approach to religion which assigns importance to 'formal religion' and which denigrates or ignores 'folk religion', 'superstition' and acts of personal faith not endorsed by the churches. It privileges numbers, counting religion by measures of members or wor-

shippers, and ignores the unquantifiable in argument and methodology. It makes religion an institutional 'thing' of society, in the form of the churches, religious organizations, the acts of going to church, the act of stating a belief in God and so on. In doing so, social science dichotomises people: into churchgoers and non-churchgoers, into believers and unbelievers, those who pray and those who don't, into 'the religious' and 'the non-religious'. It is reductionist to bipolarities ... [This] social-science method obliterates whole realms of religiosity which cannot be counted. More than that ... the definitions of religiosity used by today's Christian churches rely on the social-science method initiated by evangelical churchmen of the 1790s and 1800s. Seduced by Enlightenment rationality, it was they who gave us the definitions of religion with which we today are still obsessed.[41]

Hence, those who study contemporary religion in the West may need to reassess their methodologies, their definitions of religion, and the criteria used when assessing 'social significance'. It is too easy to survey the religious landscape and, using inappropriate criteria, either fail to notice some central features or else misinterpret them as temporary outcrops or minor seasonal variations. As David Lyon has argued, 'secularization may be used to refer to the declining strength of some traditional religious group in a specific cultural milieu, but at the same time says nothing of the spiritualities or faiths that may be growing in popularity and influence. If we view religion in typically modern, institutional fashion, other religious realities may be missed.'[42]

Spiritual, But Not Religious: Non-Traditional Religious Vitality

In a recent article in *Vogue*, Jenny Dyson reflected on the increased penchant for and commitment to alternative spirituality displayed by many of her contemporaries and peers:

> In uptown Manhattan, a twentysomething fashion PR straight out of *Sex in the City* is 'smudging' her apartment with a bundle of smouldering sage leaves (a Native American ritual thought to rid spaces of 'dead energy'). In Paris, a model is thoughtfully carving a wish onto a candle before lighting it and watching it burn. In Auckland, a successful television producer is addressing a letter to the angels of real estate, requesting…the specific dimensions of a new home she is hoping for. In London, pop stars and career girls are having their tarot cards read at Mysteries, the capital's best known New Age store. *As if by magic, magic is becoming mainstream.*[43]

Evidence that these are not isolated cases and that the resurgence of spirituality in the West is taking a new trajectory is not difficult to find. For example, Michael York's recent study of alternative spirituality in Amsterdam, Aups and Bath found that,

> Whilst the numbers involved with new forms of religiosity remain hard to identify precisely, we can at least recognize the ubiquity and growth of the diffuse religious consumer supermarket which demonstrates an increasingly vital presence in both urban Holland and rural France. These areas are witness to the spiritual ferment which is either a product of, or concomitant with, the decline of traditionally Western forms of religion and the growth of secularization as the acceptable form of public life. Change occurs against a background of ubiquitous experimentation and innovation with regard to spiritual practice – one which eschews dogma, conformity and belief and emphasizes both individual autonomy and direct experience.[44]

This emphasis on non-traditional religious vitality within a secularized context is important, in that re-enchantment is taking place as 'either a product of, or concomitant with', secularization. Even in popular writing and the media this non-traditional religious vitality is acknowledged. For example, a recent sympathetic article on Wicca in America in a British teenagers' magazine makes the following interesting (if slightly exaggerated) points: 'Witchcraft, or Wicca, is the fastest growing "religion" in the USA today. It is estimated that around a million and a half teenage Americans, often as young as thirteen, are practising Wiccans. Television programmes such as *Sabrina the Teenage Witch* and films like *The Craft* have sparked continent-wide interest in Witchcraft and awarded it the official Hollywood stamp of "cool".'[45] Other, more conservative reports indicate that there are 200,000 members of Wiccan organizations in America[46] (though, of course, many younger practitioners may not be 'members' of groups – some I have spoken to simply purchase books and practise alone or meet informally with like-minded friends). Again, a recent study has found that, 'whilst the earliest scholarly reports suggested that American witches predominantly were teenagers or very young adults, subsequent studies found that most of them were young to more middle-aged adults... Our question about age produced the following results: 15.2 per cent were 18 to 25; 26.7 per cent were 26 to 33; 25 per cent were 34-41; 20.1 per cent were 42-48; 12 per cent were 48 or older.'[47] It has also been claimed that Paganism is 'one of the fastest-growing set of religions in the Western world', and that 'Britain alone has around 10,000 Wiccans, and their influence is increasing almost as fast as that of the established church is declining... Not bad going, in the 21st century, for a religion which... was invented only 50 years ago.'[48] Again, Kelly Burke notes that 'the last census proved that nature religions, and primarily Wicca... were the fastest growing in Australia'. Burke continues, 'the Melbourne-based Christian Research Association (CRA) has carried out the first in-depth analysis of the religious group that accounts for more than 24,000 Australians. According to that study, the profile of the modern Australian Pagan is a female Melbournian under the age of 35, Australian-born ...with a university degree.'[49]

This interest in alternative religiosity, of course, is not a new phenomenon. Non-traditional re-enchantment has been a long time coming. In particular, over the past forty years or so there has been a sharp rise in, not merely those tolerant of, but those taking a keen interest in, new forms of spirituality and in what might loosely be termed 'the occult'. For example, the fact that, as noted above, the percentage of 'occult' books published since 1930 has more than doubled,[50] and, according to a report in *The Economist* in 2001, 'sales of books about yoga and reiki...have exploded in the past 18 months',[51] is indicative of the steady increase of popular interest in alternative religiosity.[52] Similarly, Heelas points out that not only have, for example, 'New Age holidays...expanded rapidly during the last ten or so years', but 'there is no reason to suppose that...spiritual economics will not continue to prosper. Since the 1960s, we have witnessed a clear pattern of growth.'[53] Hence, he quite rightly notes that whilst 'it would be misleading in the extreme to conclude that everything going on beyond the frame of institutionalized worship is of great "religious" (or spiritual, paranormal etc.) significance ... *many* more people are (somehow) "religious" without going to church on anything approaching a regular basis than are attendees'.[54] In other words, not only has 'religious belief beyond church and chapel ... become progressively more significant relative to numbers going to traditional institutions', but 'it is possible to draw on statistics to argue that the numbers of those who have some kind of "religion" without being involved in institutional worship has actually been increasing'.[55]

Bearing the above in mind, it is no surprise to discover that, according to recent polls, whilst the numbers of people claiming belief in God or in heaven and hell are decreasing, once questions are asked about non-Judaeo-Christian beliefs, or framed in a non-Judaeo-Christian way, a different picture emerges, one which shows that growing numbers of people are becoming interested in 'spirituality'. Indeed, it is clear that while some people would not regard themselves as being 'religious' (almost certainly because of the baggage that term carries), they do understand themselves to be 'spiritual': '31 per cent describe themselves as "spiritual", compared with only 27 per cent who say they are "religious"'.[56] As Kate Hunt found in her research, 'Over the past 30 years, the word "spiritual" has gone from being a technical word within Christianity to being part of everyday parlance. Spirituality is now used as a concept in education circles, in health care, even in the commercial world.' She continues, 'Spiritual people are seen as open-minded, something that is highly prized in our society. By contrast, religious people are often considered narrow-minded; allegedly, they only believe what they are taught to believe.' This is important, for, as she notes, 'In a society where children are encouraged to question from an early age, the idea of believing in a rigid set of doctrines is seen as immature.' Indeed, it is interesting to note that she observed a value judgement being made about *religious* people, namely, that they 'do not think *deeply* about life'.[57] *Spirituality*, on the other hand, is understood by those outside church to be a *deep* pursuit. Hence, contemporary Westerners may not be 'religious', but neither are many secular; they are 'spiritual'. Douglas Rushkoff, for example, although clearly interested in 'spirituality', displays a sensitivity to the term 'religion' in his Foreword to a recent collection of studies on *Rave Culture and Religion*: 'I may have some problems with the word religion,' he says, 'because it sounds so organized and institutional, while rave has always been such a spontaneous and emergent phenomenon.' Although he is appreciative of the book, it would seem, reading between the lines, that he is a little unhappy with the title. Note, for example, his use of the two words in the following sentence: 'If it really is *religion*, then I suppose rave is over in some respects. For once it can be catalogued and comprehended is it still a *spiritual experience* capable of breaking the boundaries between self and everything else? Perhaps not.'[58] Spirituality is vital and subversive. Spirituality breaks boundaries. Spirituality is the life-enhancing. Religion is about cataloguing. Religion is about comprehending experience (rather than, I suppose, simply *experiencing*). Religion belongs to the past. Religion is lifeless collections of words. Religion is the end of vitality. If this is how these terms are understood it is no wonder that the 1994 Tarrance Group Report on religion in America found that an increasing number of Americans claimed that they were 'spiritual' but not 'religious', and that whilst the impact of religion on their lives was decreasing, their personal spirituality was growing.[59]

Having said that, I was interested to read the findings of Catherine Cornbleth's research into the self-understanding of young people in America: 'After race/ethnicity/culture, the identity markers most frequently mentioned by the young people we interviewed were religion, age, and gender. No other descriptors were used by at least one-quarter of the interviewees. Given the richness of some students' racial/ethnic/cultural and religious self-descriptions, most of their comments about age and gender seemed relatively thin.'[60] Thirty-eight per cent 'mentioned religion as part of who they were', and for 70 per cent of this group 'religion was an important part of their lives'. Moreover, 'of the students who said that religion was an important part of their life or who they are, half... credited religion with providing guidelines for right or good behavior'. She concludes, 'clearly, religion has had a major impact on these students' lives'.[61] Although, interestingly, much of this belief seems to be traditionally theistic and principally Christian, Cornbleth's following comment is significant: 'specific doctrine was less evident in their discourse than guidance toward "right" behavior and avoiding the temptations of "wrong" or destructive actions'.[62] This lack of concern with doctrine indicates some continuity with the general shift from 'religion' to 'spirituality'. Indeed, some of the interviewees' comments are particularly telling in this respect: 'I don't think anyone should be classified by their religion... I don't like to belong to any affiliation at all. We don't go to church. It's a, an individual kind of thing. Like if I wanted to, I could, but I, I don't choose to.'[63]

The shift from religion to spirituality, however, is far more conspicuous in other studies of contemporary youth culture in the United States. For example, Julia Winden Fey, who has carried out research into Goth culture, relates a not-untypical interview with one Goth:

> Monique has...developed a belief system of her own out of the hodgepodge of religious and secular ideas she has encountered over the years. Identifying herself as 'spiritual' rather than 'religious', she says, 'I'm interested in religions from around the world, but for me, spirituality is more of a personal sense of connection with the universe ...' She builds her 'personal sense of connection' by selecting from among the beliefs of the various faiths she has experienced or at least read about, ultimately creating her own, unique spiritual collage.[64]

Again, whilst the 1994 *British Social Attitudes* survey reports 48 per cent agreeing that too often people believe in science and not enough in feelings and faith, in 1998 this had risen slightly to 50 per cent. Similarly, whilst the numbers believing in 'God as personal' are falling, those believing in 'God as spirit', 'universal spirit' or 'life force' are rising.[65] Hence, it is unsurprising that the type of institutional religion that is experiencing significant growth is usually non-traditional. For example, even in the face of negative press coverage, the membership of the Church of Scientology has risen from 30,000 in 1980 to 144,400 in

2000.[66] (Indeed, even in Germany, where Scientology has experienced significant government opposition, the number of books sold by the organization has risen sharply in recent years.) Understandably, such figures have led to reports claiming that 'beyond the empty pews there is a spiritual revival ... Although the British are undoubtedly staying away from church, they are not abandoning spirituality.'[67] The point I am making here is simply that, when exploring the contemporary alternative religious landscape in the West, more account needs to be taken of those who may not belong to new religious movements (NRMs). As Eileen Barker points out, 'There are people who might be horrified at the thought they could be in any way connected with a "cult", but who are, none the less, "recipients", even carriers, of ideas and practices that are borne by, if not always born in, NRMs.'[68] Some may even carry recognizably 'spiritual' ideas and practices that are not borne by or born in NRMs, but, as I will argue, simply cultivated and circulated within a general occulture. It is important to think of new religion/spirituality (and the amorphous term 'spirituality' has perhaps found a worthwhile, distinct use in this context[69]) apart from NRMs.[70] Indeed, this, it seems to me, is one of the weaknesses of analyses such as Bruce's. The focus is on the numbers involved in, usually, groups and movements which, on the one hand, are relatively easy to estimate, and, on the other, traditionally look like 'religion'. Anything more amorphous and diffuse seems to be trivialized. Regardless of what scholars claim about their willingness to accept such diffuse and eclectic spirituality as 'serious religion', I suspect that many presuppose that spirituality which does not look and behave like religion traditionally has done is less important. However, as we will see, that it does not look and behave like 'religion' and that it is often diffuse does not therefore mean that it is individually and socially insignificant. As Hunt's recent research amongst 'non-churchgoers' demonstrated, 'Spirituality has depth. It is a serious aspect of life, and those who are not spiritual are often considered to be shallow and superficial by the people we spoke with.'[71]

De-Exotification and Contextualization

Interestingly, one of the main news stories in Britain just prior to the terrorist attacks of 11 September 2001 concerned comments made by the Roman Catholic Archbishop of Westminster, Cardinal Murphy-O'Connor. He proclaimed to a conference of priests on 5 September 2001 that 'Christianity was being pushed to the margins of society by New Age beliefs, the environmental movement, the occult and the free-market economy.'[72] The reporting of his comments was equally interesting. For example, Martin Wainwright of the *Guardian* wrote the following:

> On three counts, the cardinal's analysis was refreshingly blunt. First, he is right to claim that Christianity no longer has any impact on the majority of British people's lives and the moral decisions they make. Second, Christianity's influence on modern culture and intellectual life is non-existent. Third, a growing number of people now gain their 'glimpses of the transcendent' from the loosely labelled New Age ... Cardinal Murphy-

O'Connor is right. And he shows greater understanding than many of his fellow faith leaders in not equating this dramatic social development with secularization or 'tacit atheism', as the Archbishop of Canterbury [George Carey] described it last year. In fact...while we may no longer believe in eternal life, we do (curiously) believe in rein-carnation. In the place of the church or synagogue, people are putting together their own patchwork of beliefs, practices and rituals which provide the meaning, consolation and experiences of the transcendent. This DIY spirituality gains inspiration from Eastern traditions (from Buddhism and yoga to Sufism) and psychotherapy, but *it is now in the mainstream, no longer the preserve of New Age groupies.*[73]

Although this is not written by an academic analyst, and whilst, as Beckford has rightly warned, one should treat media reports of new religions with some caution,[74] this is actually a perceptive, common-sense summary of the contemporary religious milieu by an intelligent observer with, as far as I'm aware, no particular axe to grind. Indeed, it is an assessment broadly supported by Colin Campbell's recent analysis of British Gallup Poll data:

apparently straightforward evidence for secularization disguises the fact that this decline has been entirely at the expense of a Judaeo-Christian personal God. For when the question concerning belief 'in a personal God' is distinguished from belief in 'some sort of spirit or life-force', then virtually all of the falling off in belief in God over this period is accounted for by the fewer people who are prepared to state that they believe in a personal God. Such people now represent only about one-third of the population when, not so long ago, they constituted over half. By contrast that proportion prepared to admit belief in 'some sort of spirit or life-force' has actually increased slightly in recent years. [Concerning the afterlife] that proportion of the population prepared to say that they believe in standard Christian beliefs concerning heaven and hell has declined considerably (so much so that both are now minority beliefs very much on a par with belief in the Loch Ness Monster or flying saucers). However, belief in reincarnation...has actually been going up. About one-fifth of Britons subscribe to this belief, which is even more marked among the young.[75]

Not only has belief in flying saucers and even alien abductions (much of which is invested with religious significance) increased in recent years,[76] but the relative popularity of the non-Christian belief in reincarnation[77] is, as Wainwright and Campbell have observed, particularly worthy of note.[78] Since the proportion of Hindus, Sikhs and Buddhists in the West is relatively low (around 2 per cent in Britain), it is significant, as Tony Walter points out, that surveys consistently discover that 'around 20 per cent of the population of Western countries answer "Yes" to the question "Do you believe in reincarnation?" '[79] Indeed, some surveys indicate that a quarter of Europeans and North Americans believe in reincarnation.[80] Quite simply, there has been a substantial increase 'since the middle of the twentieth century when British surveys found figures of 4 per cent and 5 per cent'.[81] Moreover, although it may be tempting simply to categorize Western believers in reincarnation as 'New Agers', Helen Waterhouse has demonstrated that, whilst this may be true of some, many in fact operate within the mainstream of society and 'appear to have derived their belief in reincarnation from outside the *cultic milieu* in which New Age religion operates and they hold their belief in reincarnation alongside more conventional and mainstream attitudes'.[82] Consequently, it would seem that the claim that DIY spirituality is now in the mainstream, whilst perhaps a little exaggerated, is essentially sound. Spirituality, in some form or another, is alive and well outside traditional and new religions in mainstream Western society. Indeed, strictly speaking, it is simply oxymoronic to speak of such DIY spirituality as *alternative* or, indeed, *deviant*.

Taking this line of thought a little further, an example of what I would under-stand to be 're-enchantment' is the way a typically modern, science-based profession such as medicine is now witnessing a rise of interest in what used to be called 'New Age healing'. Manuals such as the *Nurse's Handbook of Alternative and Complementary Therapies* (produced by medical professionals) are being published and alternative, holistic approaches to illness and 'the spiritual' are increasingly being explored and utilized within mainstream medicine. This is not surprising bearing in mind the general public's rising levels of interest.[83] For example, in his now-famous study, David Eisenberg of the Harvard Medical School found that ordinary Americans were annually spending more than $13 billion on alternative therapies and that 'an estimated one in three persons in the U.S. adult population used unconventional therapy in 1990'.[84] The figures for the UK in 2000 are similar: 39 per cent of the population had tried alternative medicines; 32 per cent had tried aromatherapy; 22 per cent had tried meditation.[85] This trend has been noted in a recent project focusing on the English Lakeland town of Kendal, led by Paul Heelas and Linda Woodhead of Lancaster University:

> The number of complementary therapists working in the area had increased exponen-tially over the past 20 years, and the majority of these say that there is a spiritual dimension to their practice. CancerCare in Kendal receives referrals from Macmillan nurses and employs several complementary practitioners on part- and full-time bases, and the Lakeland College of Homeopathy, which was founded in 1993, has enjoyed rapid growth. One of its founders, Ian Watson, said in interview: 'The spiritual side of homeopathy has waxed. I'm pretty sure about that. It now attracts more students than ever ...'.[86]

As the *Nurse's Handbook* notes, 'Andrew Weil and Deepak Chopra have become household names, and their books espousing the benefits of natural and Ayurvedic remedies sell by the millions.'[87] Although it would obviously be misleading to claim that all consumers of complementary medicine hold alternative spiritual worldviews, there is at least evidence of a general ambient spirituality. That is to say, it is significant that, even in the areas of medicine and health, there seems to be a trend away from trusting *only* the conventional to experimentation with or trust in therapies and medicines which are not only unconventional, but are often supported by spiritual terminology and non-rational explanations. Many of the therapies, for example, have their roots in Eastern religious systems. As the *Nurse's Handbook* points out (in a way which suggests ancient and Eastern origins are some verification of their value – which is in itself significant[88]), 'Many alternative therapies practiced today have been used since ancient times and come from the traditional healing practices of many cultures, primarily those of China and India... The Indian principles of Ayurvedic medicine stem from the Vedas, the essential religious texts of Hinduism.'[89] And, as one might expect in such a book, there are references, not simply to exercises and herbal remedies, but also to spiritual concepts and belief systems such as *qi* (or *chi*), *qigong*, *prana*, meridians, *chakras*, shamanism, prayer, healing touch, and *yin* and *yang*. All this and more in a nurse's handbook!

This suggests that previously unusual spiritual beliefs and practices are being appreciated by and gradually absorbed into mainstream Western society. As Walter states regarding the belief in reincarnation, it is 'not an exotic, fringe belief, but an idea that is being explored by a significant minority of otherwise conventional people'.[90] This 'de-exotification' (if I can introduce another ugly term[91]) of previously obscure and exotic beliefs is fundamental to and symptomatic of the process of re-enchantment. Although many of the particular new religions and alternative spiritualities may still be considered fringe concerns, increasingly their ideas and beliefs are becoming accepted as normal and incorporated into Western plausibility structures. Again, it is important to understand that I am not saying that the West is vibrantly and explicitly religious in a way reminiscent of sacralized medieval society. It is not and one would not expect it to be. What I am saying is that the religious worldview has not collapsed. It is still operative at ambient levels and is gradually beginning to surface, permeate, and shape Western society and culture.

Although re-enchantment is beginning to scent all areas of society, it is interesting that, as Troeltsch foresaw, it is particularly aromatic amongst the middle and educated classes. For example, Stuart Rose's survey of those involved in the New Age movement established that 'participants are, in the main, middle-class ... and very few individuals (3 per cent) report occupations which could be classified as working class'.[92] As to the occupations of those involved in this form of spirituality, 'it was found that many of the professions are represented – including teaching and health care – as well as managers, administrators and sales personnel in commerce and industry... As to income levels, the income reported by a large minority of participants tends to be generally higher than the average for the national population.'[93] The point is that, as Troeltsch suggests, 'mystical religion' seems both to thrive in a modern, educated, materially comfortable world and to be less vulnerable to the forces of secularization.

Furthermore, we will see that 'mystical religion'/self-spirituality dovetails neatly with the beliefs and values of modernity.[94] As Campbell notes,

> it can be said that the new religiosity was 'riding on the back' of contemporary humanist and secular criticisms of established religion for, being predicated on the rejection of the dogma and doctrine that characterize an objective, historical, religious faith, it could wholeheartedly support such criticisms. Thus the whole thrust of Enlightenment secularism, in opposition to dualism, to dogma and revealed religion can be considered to have acted in such a way as to prepare the ground for spiritual and mystical religion.[95]

Hence, if one were asked to design a religion which took account of the shift from objective revelation to subjective experience, from exclusivism to pluralism and relativism, and from the historical particularism of 'revealed' religion to epistemological individualism, it would be difficult to find a more fitting model than Troeltsch's mystical religion: 'the characteristics which give mystical religion its adaptive advantage' in a scientific, secular culture are 'its monism, relativism, tolerance, syncretism, and above all, its individualism'.[96] Individualism is, of course, 'highly congenial to the ethos of contemporary society, which is marked by an extraordinarily high degree of individualism, especially among the educated classes'.[97]

Secularization theory, as James Richardson has pointed out, 'generally implies that religion is something of an anachronism in our differentiated and complex modern world. Anyone who believes is basically not "with it" in the modern age ... Rationality marches on and there is something odd about those who do not get in step, even if those discussing this inexorable process lament what they are describing.'[98] However, we have seen that, in fact, the opposite is increasingly becoming the case. The gap between religious 'deviance' and 'respectability' has considerably narrowed in recent years. Whether one thinks of spiritually informed environmentalism, the celebration of supposedly ancient traditions such as 'Celtic Christianity',[99] New Age retreats and holidays, the variety of religiously informed remedies and procedures, or spiritualities and practices from astrology to *feng shui*, these increasingly fail to raise eyebrows in the contemporary West. It is not simply that there is a lack of consensus about what is deviant, but that beliefs once considered exotic and deviant are now de-exotified and acceptable, even respectable. Consequently, those who do view such ideas as deviant and raise a wary eyebrow are viewed as outdated, out of touch, not 'with it'. In this sense the occult is, as I have already suggested, becoming less deviant and more respectable. This, of course, indicates the limits of a typology such as Wallis's, in that it leaves no room for respectable cultic religion. Yet this is exactly what is coming into being. As Campbell observes, the ideas of organizations which were 'clearly "fringe" or "cultic" groups in the years immediately following the Second World War', the response to which was 'typically one of incredulity or ridicule', are today 'commonplace, having entered the mainstream of cultural thought and debate'. He continues, 'It is this shift which is significant; not so much the appearance of new beliefs, but rather the widespread acceptance of ones which formerly had been confined to a minority; a shift which, it appears, really dates from the 1960s, when they were espoused by that significant and influential minority who comprised the counter-culture.'[100] Similarly, Heelas notes that, 'adding up all the evidence, it is fair to say that the 1960s saw the emphasis shift from older, professionally well-established spiritual seekers to the more youthful, the campus-based and, of course, the countercultural'.[101]

One form of spirituality worth mentioning very briefly at this point is contemporary ecological spirituality (which will be discussed at length in Volume II). Not only is there an apparent scepticism regarding aspects of the scientific worldview, but, as Bron Taylor argues, 'earth- and nature-based spirituality is proliferating globally', and, whilst those involved in countercultural environmentalist movements may be uncomfortable with the label 'religion' (though, I have found, not with the label 'spirituality'), in actual fact, some of the movements, such as, for example, Earth First!,[102] are essentially religious.[103] This has been noted by Peter Hay in his wide-ranging study of environmental thought:

'the hostility many environmentalists hold towards science and rationality often takes the form of a search for a new cosmological/spiritual/religious basis for human life and the interspecies relationships. And some look to a differently founded science, one seen to have much in common with certain religious ideas and promising an end to the long divorce between scientific and religious ways of ascertaining truth.'[104] Again, whilst the 1994 *British Social Attitudes* survey reports that 60 per cent agreed or strongly agreed that humans should respect nature because it was created by God (broadly defined), in 1998 this figure had arisen to 62 per cent (in Germany the 1998 figure was 74 per cent, in Italy 84 per cent, and in Ireland 90 per cent).[105] Whether one thinks of the increasingly popular 'creation spiritualities', the spiritual interpretations of the Gaia hypothesis,[106] ecofeminism,[107] or deep ecology's shift from anthropocentrism to biocentrism, there has been a noticeable re-enchantment of environmental concern.[108]

Finally, it should also be noted that, as Walter and Waterhouse have shown regarding reincarnation, Westerners tend to have detraditionalized, individualized understandings of the doctrine. In other words, the doctrine is inculturated.[109] Thought, of course, is always culturally and linguistically determined – being interpreted and shaped by particular contexts, it is always in process. Hence, when, for example, Wilson comments that new spiritualities are 'adaptations of religion to new social circumstances', or that 'they often utilize highly secular methods in evangelism, financing, publicity and mobilization of adherents', or that 'very commonly, the traditional symbolism, liturgy and aesthetic concern of traditional religion are abandoned for much more pragmatic attitudes and for systems of control, propaganda and even doctrinal consent which are closer to styles of secular enterprise than to traditional religious concerns',[110] he is doing little more than noting the strengths of what one would expect of an evolving spiritual milieu inculturated in a Western context. One can go back through religious history and show how religion has always adapted to new social and intellectual circumstances. In Christianity, for example, whether we think of the emergence of the parish system, or the scholastic theology of the Middle Ages and why it was fundamentally indebted to Aristotle rather than Plato, or the reasons for the emergence and popularity of Methodism in Britain, or the rise of modern theology during and following the Enlightenment, or the significance of liberation theology in Latin America, one cannot avoid the fact that religion has always engaged with and been shaped by the 'secular' social and intellectual world. Such contextualization is, of course, essential for the continued vitality and relevance of a faith. Indeed, that it is able and flexible enough to do this effectively is an indication of life, not death.

The problems with Wilson's line of argument become clearly evident, it seems to me, in Conrad Ostwalt's recent book, *Secular Steeples: Popular Culture and the Religious Imagination*. Basically, his argument is that, in 'the postmodern era...the increased visibility of religion' indicates secularization:

> Contemporary American culture witnesses secularization occurring in two directions: 1) the churches and religious organizations are becoming increasingly more attuned to the secular environment, particularly to popular culture, and are in some cases trying to

emulate it in the effort to remain relevant; 2) popular cultural forms, including literature, film, and music, are becoming increasingly more visible vehicles of religious images, symbols, and categories. These two directions of secularization demonstrate the blurred or malleable boundaries between religion and culture – the sacred and the secular – that define the relationship of religion and culture in the postmodern era.[111]

Where I and others find indications of sacralization, Ostwalt and Wilson find evidence of secularization. Of course, Ostwalt is correct to the extent that religious imagery can be used in secular ways – crucifixes can be worn simply as jewellery, rather than as statements of religious conviction (even then, it is perhaps of some significance that people choose to wear religious symbols as jewellery). However, there is also much evidence of this process being reversed. A small but moving example of this is, to my mind, Depeche Mode's song 'Personal Jesus'.[112] The words, as sung by Depeche Mode, are tongue in cheek and betray a strongly critical attitude to Christianity. However, the late Johnny Cash, a deeply Christian artist, provided a cover version of this song, using exactly the same tune and words.[113] In so doing, the secular and the critical became sacred and devotional. So yes, the boundaries between the sacred and the secular may be blurred. My point is simply that this shouldn't automatically be interpreted as an indication of secularization. Indeed, many of the cases Ostwalt cites as indications of religion becoming 'worldly' I would understand to be Johnny Cash-like indications of sacralization – conversions of the secular. To interpret the increased visibility of the sacred in society as an indication of secularization is, it seems to me, overly cynical. To argue, as Ostwalt does, that even popular music *per se* is 'secular' by nature (whether the lyrics and the inten-tion are religious or not) is to invest musical notes and genres (as fundamentalists do) with a significance they do not possess.[114]

This problem is especially evident in his discussion of the Monastery of Christ in the Desert in Chama River Canyon, New Mexico, which, he claims, provides 'no better illustration' of secularization. Why? Because the monks have acquired computers and are now connected to the Internet! 'On the one hand,' he says, 'like ancient monasteries, this one is no different in providing the monks retreat from the secular world and materialism. On the other hand, the monks are not afraid to use secular technology as a tool to remain relevant and to prosper.'[115] On the one hand, this seems a rather patronizing comment, which assumes that the monastery is a less sacred place because it has sought to keep up with the modern world. On the other hand, what is '*secular* technology'? Is driving a car an indi-cation of secularization? Is eating food cooked in a microwave a secular act? What might constitute a *sacred* artefact? Ostwalt responds to this question, in effect, by describing a scene in which monks are, by the light of a candle, busily scratching words on parchment with quills. Such artefacts are 'sacred objects' as opposed to 'the worldly technology' of the computer. 'Monks hunched over keyboards instead of over manuscripts, and rather than faithfully reproducing sacred words, they...provide information about their order through their own Website.'[116] Can one not faithfully reproduce sacred words on a website? Why is one artefact less sacred than the other? Am I missing something here, or is parchment really more sacred than a monitor, a quill more sacred than a keyboard, and a candle more sacred than an electric light?

Furthermore, as with many such declarations of secularization, Ostwalt's discussion focuses principally on Christianity (which he argues is becoming progressively 'worldly' as it seeks to meet the needs of its church attendees[117]) and lacks any significant analysis of new religions and alternative spiritualities. That is to say, because his discussion is not so much of 'religion' in America as of Christianity in America, it is less a discussion of secularization and more a discussion of shifts in Christian belief and practice. However, many new religions and spiritualities (and, indeed, some forms of Christianity) very effectively incarnate their theologies in contemporary Western culture, thereby purposely sacralizing the secular. That they do so does not mean that they therefore trivialize religion and transform it into that which lacks depth and significance for its devotees. My own discussions with contemporary Pagans and other alternative spiritual seekers suggest very much the opposite. The point is that, as supernaturalistic religions evolve, not only do they move away from parchment and pews, but they also move away from older, more dogmatic forms of religiosity which appear to offer little to those seeking an authentic spirituality. I fully agree with Jo Pearson's argument that softer, non-dogmatic, more syncretic forms of spirituality, including certain expressions of Christianity,[118] *will*, for that very reason, remain: 'the antithesis to institutional dogma is wholly in line with the *Zeitgeist* which has allowed Wicca and Paganism to proliferate'.[119] There may even be something to the argument that we should speak, not of the demise of Christianity in Europe, as Bruce does,[120] but, again, of the transformation of Christianity.

New forms of spirituality address concerns current in the cultures in which they are evolving. This may lead to the absorption of myths which are popular in those cultures (UFOs, Gaia consciousness, etc.), the utilizing of new practices, beliefs, ideas, and terms which are understood to meet spiritual needs more adequately (Eastern ideas, environmental thought, etc.), the expressing of these new beliefs and practices in challenging and culturally appropriate ways (popular music, film, and, in some cases, self-sacrificial political direct action), and the promotion of these in effective new ways informed by their contexts. Hence, terms and ideas such as Gaia, reincarnation, *feng shui*, *chakra*, karma, *prana*, *chi*, *yin*, *yang*, and *tao* are not only entering mainstream Western thinking,[121] but are being reinterpreted and owned by Westerners seeking to develop their own spiritualities. Whatever is going on here, it is not secularization.

Concluding Comments

While disenchantment is part of an accurate interpretation of the Western landscape, and for many years has been the dominant interpretation, it is time to move on and recognize the emergence of new realities. As Walter Truett Anderson puts it:

> Some people really believed that the modern era was going to bring an end to religion, the final triumph of reason over superstition: God is dead, remember? Instead we seem

> to be in a world with more religion than there has ever been before ... Opinion surveyors
> occasionally explore the beliefs of contemporary people, their views of the cosmos, their
> religious convictions and superstitions. And the findings are an amazing revelation to
> anyone who really believes we are living in a secular-humanist society. It turns out that
> beneath the rational surface of the more-or-less secular 'realism' that is supposed to be
> our official worldview – and not too far beneath, either – lurks a seething cauldron of
> cults and faiths of all descriptions. Surprisingly large numbers of people profess a
> surprisingly wide range of belief...[122]

Again, I would also concur with Linda Woodhead, who notes that 'the twentieth century has both confirmed and confounded the ideas of scholars who predicted widespread secularization. Although it is true that some forms of traditional religion have declined, it is also true that the late modern West has witnessed the spread of a "luxuriant undergrowth" of religiosity.'[123]

The point of this chapter – and, indeed, Part I – has simply been to suggest that, although it cannot be denied that disenchantment has reshaped Western societies, it seems myopic not to recognize the significance of the gradual and uneven emergence of personally and socially consequential alternative spiritualities.[124] It seems clear that religion/spirituality is able to sustain itself outside traditional institutions and indeed to thrive within a postmodern, Western consumer climate. This idea, of course, has been summed up by the British sociologist Grace Davie as 'believing without belonging'.[125] Focusing particularly on younger people, she makes the point that 'religious values are not so much disappearing...as being redirected'.[126] Indeed, she argues that most people will identify to some degree with some of the beliefs and experiences involved in what she calls 'common religion': 'The content of common religion may well, at one end of the spectrum, have some link to Christian teaching.[127] At the other end, it is enormously diverse, ranging through a wide range of heterodox ideas: for example...the paranormal, fortune telling, fate and destiny, life after death, ghosts, spiritual experiences...'[128] That this is so is supported by the research of scholars such as, for example, David Hay, Ulf Sjödin, and Wayne Spencer. In 1976 Hay discovered that roughly a third of his respondents had had some form of spiritual experience or encounter with the supernatural (although not all would describe it as an experience of God)[129] and that in 1986 this had risen to nearly half of those questioned.[130] This trajectory is affirmed by Spencer, who begins his study by noting that

> Opinion polls and other surveys routinely find that substantial proportions of the general
> public of western Europe and North America express belief in various 'paranormal'
> phenomena. Indeed, a Gallup poll of American adults conducted in June 1990 found that
> 93 per cent of respondents said they believed in at least one of a list of 18 paranormal
> claims, and almost one-half accepted the reality of five or more. Similarly, in a poll of a
> representative sample of residents in Reading, England, 88 per cent of respondents said
> they thought at least one of a series of propositions was definitely true, and 68 per cent
> definitely assented to at least three.[131]

Sjödin's work reaches similar conclusions about Sweden, arguably 'the most secularized country in Europe'.[132] He notes that, although church attendance has declined significantly (but, interestingly, not church membership[133]), 'empirical studies show beliefs in the paranormal to be widespread among Swedes. Although these beliefs turn out to be somewhat more common among the young, they are common among the population as a whole… Even if beliefs in the paranormal are not new, it may still be said that such beliefs are much more tolerated and accepted today than 20 or 30 years ago. The *Zeitgeist* seems to have changed.'[134]

Again, we will see in this and the following volume that the mere fact that religion is being reshaped and relocated (and, consequently, needs to be redefined – possibly as 'spirituality') does not mean that it is thereby trivialized. New forms of spirituality in which the tensions between the sacred and the secular, the spiritual and the rational, the divine and the mundane, the body and the soul are greatly reduced have taken root in the West. As Lyon comments: 'religious relationships and movements… are of increasing importance in today's modern world. Much secularization theory produced earlier in the twentieth century mistook the deregulation of religion for the decline of religion.'[135] Whether one considers the increasing significance of 'green spiritualities', the importance of virtual communities and the symbolic, or the re-enchantment of popular culture, just as we are witnessing a revolution in the way twenty-first-century religion/ spirituality is lived, so there will need to be a revolution in the way it is studied and understood.

Part II

THE SIGNIFICANCE OF OCCULTURE

Chapter 4

OCCULTURE

In this chapter we pursue some of the principal lines of thought raised by the re-enchantment thesis. Beginning with further reflections on the concept of 'cult', with particular reference to the idea of a 'mystic collectivity', the discussion will turn to the notion of a 'cultic milieu', and finally will develop these ideas and suggest the existence of an 'occulture'.

The Cultic Milieu and Mystical Religion

As I have already indicated, whilst my own general understanding of 'cultic religion' roughly accords with that of Wallis, it is also significantly indebted to Troeltsch's understanding of mystical religion, the type of religion which 'had no desire for organized fellowship; all it cared for was freedom for interchange of ideas, a pure fellowship of thought, which indeed only became possible after the invention of printing... The isolated individual, and psychological abstraction and analysis become everything.'[1] Cultic spirituality, we have seen, is self-oriented, eclectic and epistemologically individualistic – religious authority is internalized.[2] That said, on the other hand, whilst epistemological individualism is a dominant feature of cultic spirituality,[3] it is also important to recognize the significance of cultic organization. Troeltsch argued that such religiosity, in its *ideal form*, 'has *no* external organization' and '*only* emerges as a foreshadowing of coming developments'.[4] Contemporary cultic religiosity, however, often goes beyond such pure mystical religion and merely foreshadowing developments and actually becomes organized into cultic groups[5] (which, we will see, then feed ideas and inspiration into the cultic milieu). Indeed, there seems to be a strong tendency for even diffuse cultic spiritualities to coalesce into networks and organizations (usually around a charismatic figure), some of which have a short lifespan (e.g. Ishvara/Lifewave[6]) and others of which become established as cultic networks (e.g. *A Course in Miracles* and *The Celestine Prophecy*[7]) or evolve into sectarian religion (e.g. Scientology[8]).

An interesting discussion which seeks to give some clarity to the definition of what is an essentially diffuse phenomenon is Campbell's 1977 essay, 'Clarifying the Cult'.[9] (That said, bearing in mind Wallis's discussion of the previous year in *The Road to Total Freedom*, the problem of clarification was not as acute as Campbell thought it was.[10] Nevertheless, his particular perspective and his development of Troeltsch's ideas about mystical religion are helpful.[11]) Provoked by an unhappiness with what he understands to be 'vague and unsatisfactory' definitions which simply identify the cult as a 'non-group' and fail to distinguish it from the surrounding cultic milieu, he seeks to give the notion of cult more shape and substance. In what sense, he asks, is this ephemeral, amorphous, loosely structured, transitory phenomenon, for which 'the term "structure" is almost a misnomer',[12] a social group? With some justification (at the time), he claimed that the 'consensus is largely an agreement over what the cult is not, rather than what it is. The cult is described as a community which one does *not* join, which is *not* permanent and enduring, which is *not* exclusive, and which does *not* have clearly articulated beliefs.'[13] Membership, shared core beliefs, and much else that is essential to a social group seem to be absent. Hence, the understandings of cultic religion in the 1970s were founded on 'a double negativity': 'First of all, it is based upon the view that the cult is that form of religious organization which is *not* a sect, church, or denomination as these are conventionally understood, and secondly, that the cult is that form of social phenomenon which comes closest to resembling a *non*-group. Such a group is little more than a residual category.'[14]

Underlying this lack of clarity has been a failure to focus on the content of belief, a failure borne of the conviction that cultic religion shares no common beliefs to focus on – it is a term denoting little more than fragmented, individualistic religious phenomena. Campbell challenges this perception. Like sectarian or church religion, he argues, there are unifying beliefs within cultic religiosity. Following Troeltsch, he seeks to demonstrate that cultic religion is a particular mystical form of religion. It is not simply a diffuse religiosity that has mystical experience as one of its many characteristics, or even a form of religion that stresses mystical experience, as some theorists have claimed, but rather it is a mystical form of religion, a complex of mysticism-oriented beliefs. Quoting Troeltsch, he argues that 'the religion of mysticism…arises when mysticism becomes "independent in principle, contrasted with concrete religion" and seeks to take the place of established religion'.[15] Again, the point is that mysticism is not merely one ingredient in a type of religion, but rather a competing form of religion – the mystical path becomes the true salvific path, the ordinary way to union with the divine. Although a great variety of beliefs are tolerated, mystical teachings 'emphasize the truths obtained through mystic and spiritual experience, [and] are regarded as representing the "purest" form of religion'.[16]

As to the doctrinal content of mystical religion, according to Troeltsch (who, it must be remembered, was speaking principally of the Christian tradition), 'it feels independent of all institutional religion, and possesses an entire inward certainty, which makes it indifferent towards every kind of religious fellowship… Henceforward union with God, deification, self-annihilation, become the real and the only subject of religion.'[17] More specifically, the basic and distinct beliefs of mystical religion are the goal of union with the divine, a divine ground of being underlying all being, and spiritual evolution:

> A central belief is that all finite beings have their existence within God, who is the ground of the soul, the 'seed' or 'spark' of all creatures. Some form of union with God

(or more properly re-union) is thus the goal of this form of religion; a goal that can only be realized by the development of the divine seed into a power capable of overcoming the world. There is, thus, a belief in a 'scale of spirituality' which marks the progression of the soul's relationship with the divine, a conception which is necessarily emanationist and denies dualism in favour of a spiritual monism. There is no belief in a fundamental opposition of 'flesh' and 'spirit'...but merely in differences in the degree to which the finite is separated from the divine. Consequently an ascetic temper is excluded though there is an opposition to the selfishness and materialism of 'the world'. Indeed, secular concerns are regarded as unimportant and the placing of religion above ethics leads to Antinomianism and Libertarianism.[18]

Related to this basic thesis that there is a single divine reality behind the plurality of religions is a relativist philosophy and, in most cases, an eclectic syncretism which recognizes the validity of most religious belief and expression. Put simply, religious belief, wherever it is found, is grounded in an experience of the same divine reality. Hence, it makes sense for the spiritual traveller to explore as much of the religious landscape as possible, for in so doing she is gaining a breadth of insight denied to the person who does not stray outside a single religious tradition. (It is perhaps worth noting at this point that such mysticism-based perennialism is not uncommon in modern religious history. Whether one thinks of the American philosopher William Hocking,[19] Frithjof Schuon,[20] or Aldous Huxley,[21] the notion of a mystical unity of religions has consistently proved attractive.[22])

To reiterate what has been argued in Chapter 2, it should be noted that, following Troeltsch, because mystical religion is a type of religion, it is just as much a challenge to church religion as sectarian religion. As Campbell puts it: 'Of course, as long as religious organization alone is the focus of attention only sect and church are considered, but if all three are regarded as forms of religion, as indeed Troeltsch intended, then mystic religion can be viewed as just as much in conflict with church religion as is sectarianism.'[23] We have seen that Troeltsch argues that mystical religion arises as a reaction against the pragmatism, ethical laxity and internal secularization of church religion. It compensates for the dry formalism and increasingly disenchanted nature of much institutional religion. Secularization and re-enchantment run together. As Campbell claims, 'secularization and the rise of new religiosity are...simply two aspects of the same process, i.e. the change-over from church religion to spiritual and mystic religion; a fundamental process of social and cultural change in which identical forces can be seen to be responsible for the decline of the one and the emergence of the other'.[24]

Hence, whilst cultic religion may be, as Wallis argued, individualistic, deviant and pluralistically legitimate, when one examines its dominant beliefs it becomes apparent that there is in fact a coherent mystical form of religion in the background. For example, the very individualism of cultic religion is itself a doctrinal theme within a particular mystical worldview: 'The individualism that is so much a feature of the religion of mysticism stems from the statement of its primary aim as personal holiness, perfection or deification, and the consequent concentration upon inwardness and fulfilment of the individual's spiritual potential.'[25] In other words, individualism, rather than simply indicating social fragmentation and diffuseness, actually has its roots in a unifying system of belief. Hence, whilst the logic of such mysticism works against the construction of institutional religion, groups and networks do form around the shared common beliefs of the individuals involved.

Developing this line of thought a little, Campbell suggests that the social phenomenon corresponding to mystical religion is not 'the cult', as traditionally conceived, but rather 'the mystic collectivity'. Mystical religion 'does have definite sociological consequences and, although it does not lead to the formation of groups and organizations, it does lead to the existence of social collectivities'.[26] Such collectivities can be understood in terms of (to use the Augustinian concept utilized by Troeltsch) 'the invisible Church':

> the purely spiritual fellowship, known to God alone, about which man does not need to concern himself at all, but which invisibly rules all believers, without external signs or other means. The conception of a purely spiritual fellowship is the background of this sentiment, and in this the individual is therefore relieved of all obligation to organize and evangelise, and from all connection with ecclesiastical and sectarian organization.[27]

Hence, again, whilst mystical religionists are individualistic, they are aware that they belong to a wider community of like-minded religious individualists, the mystic collectivity: 'those people who have a sense of solidarity by virtue of shared common values and who have also acquired an attendant sense of moral obligation to fulfil common role-expectations'.[28] Moreover, I would argue that those belonging to the mystic collectivity often feel a sense of duty to serve that spiritual community through, for example, fairs, publications, or workshops, thereby leading, on the one hand, to a greater sense of fellowship and, on the other hand, often to the establishment of external organizations, centres and groups. For example, the Findhorn community, an internationally known spiritual community in north-east Scotland, is typical of the kind of service organization that encourages a sense of connectedness and a sharing of ideas within the mystic collectivity. Since 1962, it has 'hosted three generations of religious individualists engaged in the exploration of alternative spiritualities, psychophysical therapies, craftwork and gardening'.[29] Again, the Festival of Mind–Body–Spirit held annually in London and Manchester is an important source of ideas and practices:

> visitors to the Festival for Mind–Body–Spirit listen to lectures, attend workshops, watch performances and demonstrations, pick up literature and leaflets and purchase commodities and services from exhibitors. They accept many, all, or none of the ideas presented to them as they see fit and are 'interested in' and often willing to try out any new idea, therapy or technique to be found in the general milieu of the alternative sub-culture. The Festival might be described as the annual convention of New Age Britain.[30]

Certainly, my own experience of the festival bears this out. I have encountered a wide range of beliefs and practices from crystal healing to Native American shamanism, from Kirlian photography to psychic art, from angels to past-life therapy, from Theosophy to UFO religion,[31] and from New Age music to the vegetarianism of Suma Ching Hai.[32]

That the mystic collectivity is regularly made manifest in this way and that it regularly coalesces into identifiable groups and networks is significant, in that, to some extent, it undermines Troeltsch's thesis that it is simply a 'foreshadowing of coming developments'. That is to say, cultic/mystical religion is never purely diffuse, with 'no external organization'. It is a complex mixture of diffuse spirituality, amorphous networks, and structured groups and organizations. Indeed, it is continually in the process of coalescence. Despite the anti-organizational bias of mystical religion, the shared values and ideas, the consequent sense of community, the sense of belonging, even duty, that many 'mystics' feel towards that community, mean that the mystic collectivity is fertile ground for the formation of spiritual groups. The advent of the Internet in particular, which can encourage a sense of community,[33] has facilitated and accelerated the emergence of mystical networks and organizations.

All this has a direct relationship to Campbell's earlier thesis that cultic/mystical organizations arise out of a general cultural ethos, a 'cultic milieu'. 'The cultic milieu,' he wrote in 1972, 'can be regarded as the cultural underground of society. Much broader, deeper and historically based than the contemporary movement known as *the* underground, it includes all deviant belief-systems and their associated practices. Unorthodox science, alien and heretical religion, deviant medicine, all comprise elements of such an underground.'[34] The cultic milieu includes networks and seedbeds of ideas as well as various authoritative sources and particular groups. As Jeffrey Kaplan and Heléne Lööw comment, it is a 'zone in which proscribed and/or forbidden knowledge is the coin of the realm, a place in which ideas, theories and speculations are to be found, exchanged, modified and, eventually, adopted or rejected by adherents of countless, primarily ephemeral groups'.[35] Again, to reiterate the point I made above, there are established individuals, organizations, and traditions feeding ideas into this constantly growing and changing milieu, as well as emergent individuals, organizations, and traditions becoming established and influential. In Campbell's words, the cultic milieu

> includes the collectivities, institutions, individuals and media of communication associated with these beliefs. Substantively it includes the worlds of the occult and the magical, of spiritualism and psychic phenomena, of mysticism and new thought, of alien intelligences and lost civilizations, of faith healing and nature cure. This heterogeneous assortment can be regarded, despite its apparent diversity, as constituting a single entity – the entity of the cultic milieu.[36]

Occulture

The concept of the cultic milieu is an extremely helpful one for understanding contemporary alternative spirituality in the West. However, for purposes of clarification I want to argue that when one draws the above lines of thought together and identifies key themes within the milieu, the term 'occultic' suggests itself as a slightly more precise adjective than 'cultic'. This is certainly the case if, as Campbell tends to do, 'cultic' is interpreted primarily in terms of the 'mystical'.

We have seen Campbell argue that many of the central ideas within the milieu which lead to the formation of cults are 'mystical', in the sense that there is an emphasis both on immediate religious experience and also on particular monistic cosmologies, anthropologies and theologies (e.g. divine–human unity). However, whilst the milieu has elements which are both 'mystical' and 'cultic' (in the senses used above), the term 'occult' describes the mélange of beliefs, practices, traditions and organizations more accurately. Although the term 'mystical' describes some fundamental aspects of the milieu, it does not cover the breadth of religious belief and expression listed by Campbell as constituting the 'cultic milieu'.[37] Moreover, the term itself is problematic in that, as contemporary theologians and students of religion will be aware, 'mysticism' carries a lot of well-established baggage that could lead to misinterpretation.[38] For example, whilst some within the milieu might draw inspiration from the Christian mystical tradition, because the ideas are extracted from a Christian theological context and reinterpreted within an occult context, they are often understood quite differently than they are by Christian thinkers. (Indeed, although kept within a Christian context, even Troeltsch's use of the term 'mysticism' is distinctly idiosyncratic.) That is to say, many Christian mystics were devout, often exclusivist Christians who understood the Church to be 'uniquely legitimate'. They identified the divine with the God of Jesus Christ and, as Grace Jantzen has noted, they distinguished, as many new religionists fail to do, between '*experiences* of God (specific visions, voices, moments of intense emotion or ecstasy) and *experience* of God in a much broader, on-going sense'.[39] They emphasized 'not... intense moments, significant though they may be, but rather... the long term union of their *wills* with the will of the God of justice and love',[40] the aim being the transformation of their lives in accordance with that will.

The overall point I am making is threefold: (1) whilst the term 'mystical' can be used of some aspects of religious belief within the milieu, it can only be used of *some* aspects – it is not a good umbrella term; (2) because the term already has a history in theology and religious studies, it too easily leads to misinterpretation; and (3) ideas drawn from other mystical traditions are reinterpreted in terms of an occult milieu. Quite simply, the term 'occult' most accurately describes the contemporary alternative religious milieu in the West. As Stark and Bainbridge argue, 'the occult can be characterized as a true subculture – a distinctive set of cultural elements that flourish as the property of a distinctive social group'.[41] Although Stark and Bainbridge make no reference to Campbell's work, this is essentially what Campbell had argued of the mystical/cultic milieu. However, whilst the research of both support the notion of a distinct community, collectivity, or subculture, Stark and Bainbridge are right to identify its essential nature as occultic. Although 'occult interests may reflect a... superficial phenomenon', being a 'transitory and relatively private amusement that is not supported by significant social relations', it can also be 'a true subculture'.[42] Indeed, this is, to some extent, what I am suggesting. That said, I would not use the word 'subculture', in that what I am suggesting transcends subcultures. What we are witnessing is the emergence of an 'occulture'.

The term 'occulture' was suggested to me by George McKay in his excellent study of cultures of resistance, *Senseless Acts of Beauty*. However, I am fairly sure that the term is not originally McKay's. For example, in 2000 a one-day music and esoterica festival simply entitled 'Occulture' was established at Brighton, England,[43] in order, so Justin Hankinson (one of the organizers) told me, 'to protect the rights and interests of people working in the esoteric domain'. When I asked Hankinson, who was unaware of McKay's work, about the origin of the term, he suggested that it was originally coined by punk/electronica musician and occultist Genesis P-Orridge. Although McKay, as a former punk who has written authoritatively on the subculture, should certainly be aware of Genesis P-Orridge, he makes no reference to him in this respect. However, there is little doubt in my mind that Hankinson is right. Genesis P-Orridge's creative work in both the arts (he is, for example, the founder of Throbbing Gristle, Psychic TV, and Thee Majesty) and the occult (in 1981 he founded Thee Temple ov Psychick Youth), do suggest that, although McKay may have independently come up with the term, Genesis P-Orridge actually coined it.[44] (Indeed, we will see in Chapter 7 that 'occulture' has become a central term within Thee Temple ov Psychick Youth (TOPY) and related groups.)

Concerning McKay's usage, he makes the following point in commenting on an article in the *Guardian*:[45]

> Pat Kane identifies 'a much wider and deeper culture of the irrational: a culture which we often dignify with the term "New Age", but which should properly be called occult'. I'm not sure how far *New Age* can be called a term of dignity (any more), but possibly we should indeed be making greater use of the term *occult*, in its original sense of *hidden (from sight), concealed*. In this sense, occult groups and events are those this book revolves around: hidden or marginal figures or narratives. Though their etymologies are in fact entirely different, occult sounds like it ought to be connected to *culture*, too, even *counterculture*. Occulture as a term for the New Age's culture of resistance?[46]

However, McKay does not develop the idea and seems not to be particularly interested in contemporary spirituality. Indeed, my own use of 'occulture' is significantly broader than both his 'New Age' understanding and also TOPY's more specialized usage. Furthermore, I am defining the term 'occult' far more broadly than the technical esotericist understanding, though it is fundamentally related to it. Very briefly, occulture includes those often *hidden, rejected* and *oppositional* beliefs and practices[47] associated with esotericism,[48] theosophy, mysticism, New Age, Paganism, and a range of other subcultural beliefs and practices, many of which are identified by Campbell as belonging to the cultic/mystical milieu and by Stark and Bainbridge as belonging to the occult subculture.

The Occult

Before continuing our discussion of the nature of contemporary occulture, a brief etymological discussion will be helpful. What is meant when we speak of the 'occult'? Historically, the term 'occult' can be traced back several centuries and concerns that which is hidden or concealed. Jean-Pierre Laurant notes that, in English, the words 'occult' and 'occultism' first appear, according to the *Oxford English Dictionary*, in 1545 and that, in French, *occulte* first appears much earlier in 1120 in the *Psautier d'Oxford*.[49] In 1633 it is enriched with new meaning related to ancient knowledge and the secrets of antiquity.[50] Hence, in developing this enriched meaning of the term, from a religio-cultural perspective, 'occult' became a broad, multi-faceted concept referring to arcane and restricted knowledge. It has been specifically applied to what some identify as the 'Western Mystery/Esoteric Tradition' stretching back many centuries to Gnosticism, Stoicism, Hermeticism, neo-Pythagoreanism and in particular to a body of theological-philosophical texts written in late antiquity known as the *Corpus Hermeticum*.[51] Having said that, the roots of the modern religio-philosophical understanding of 'occult' with which the term has become principally associated, and which has had considerable impact on contemporary 'occulture', can be traced back a little further on to the Renaissance and particularly to Henry Cornelius Agrippa's *De occulta philosophia* (1533) and to the thought of Giordano Bruno (1548–1600). Subsequent occultism, particularly since the nineteenth century, can be described as a subculture of various secret societies and 'enlightened' teachers involved in disciplines concerned with the acquisition of arcane, salvific knowledge (*gnosis* and *theosophia*), the experience of 'illumination', the understanding of esoteric symbolism (often related to occult interpretations of the Kabbalah[52]), the practice of secret rituals and initiatory rites, and particularly the quest for a *prisca theologia, philosophia occulta* or *philosophia perennis* – a tradition of divine *gnosis* communicated, it is believed, through a line of significant individuals, including Moses, Zoroaster (Zarathustra), Hermes Trismegistus (the mythical author of the *Hermetica*), Plato, Orpheus, and the Sibyls.

Much time is invested by numerous individuals and groups in interpreting the 'true' meaning of occult material (e.g. the Enochian system famously communicated to the Elizabethan magician John Dee[53]) in order to gain access to, it is believed, profound and powerful natural and supernatural knowledge. In short, such occultism is concerned with the understanding of *gnosis* concealed within a system of complex symbolism and enigmatic alchemical formulae. As Robert Gilbert comments,

> Understanding the concealed, inner meaning requires keys presented in the form of pictorial symbols, systems of numerical analysis, and the clear statement of the need for the reader to follow specific initiatory processes – accessible within the confines of one or another secret fraternity. Such processes usually involve both commonly known practices (astrology and natural magic), and secret techniques such as those of 'spiritual' alchemy and theurgy (the invocation of angels).[54]

Interest in direct experience of the divine, in secret gnosis, in alchemy, in theurgy, in a *philosophia perennis*, and in ancient religious and mythical figures, texts and civilizations are all evident in contemporary occulture. Although particular occult organizations such as AMORC (Ancient Mystical Order of the Rosy Cross) or Servants of the Light function within this milieu, and indeed are sources for some of its ideas and practices, many individuals do not belong to such organizations.[55] While enormously influential, such occultism is only one of several broad strands within what I am identifying as 'occulture'.

When thinking of 'occulture', the above narrow, foundational understanding of the occult should be broadened to include a vast spectrum of beliefs and practices sourced by Eastern spirituality, Paganism, Spiritualism, theosophy, alternative science and medicine, popular psychology (usually Jungian[56]), and a range of beliefs emanating out of the general cultural interest in the paranormal. Indeed, to some extent, what A.D. Duncan said of occultism *per se* is equally true of 'occulture' generally: it 'is not so much a religion or a system as a "general heading" under which a huge variety of speculation flourishes, a good deal of it directly contradictory'.[57] Similarly, Peter Clarke's definition of the occult indicates something of the nature of occulture: 'The fact that the occult is a multi-dimensional concept makes it difficult to define. It is more of an umbrella term for a variety of kinds of thinking, not all of which is supernatural, and practice, than a unitary concept.'[58] This last comment is important – we are not dealing with a unitary concept. Western occulture includes a range of 'deviant' ideas and practices (although it is debatable as to whether some beliefs are socially deviant or, indeed, 'hidden', bearing in mind their massive and rising popularity), including magick (as devised by Aleister Crowley),[59] extreme right-wing religio-politics,[60] radical environmentalism and deep ecology,[61] angels,[62] spirit guides and channelled messages,[63] astral projection,[64] crystals,[65] dream therapy,[66] human potential spiritualities,[67] the spiritual significance of ancient and mythical civilizations,[68] astrology,[69] healing,[70] earth mysteries, tarot,[71] numerology,[72] Kabbalah,[73] *feng shui*,[74] prophecies (e.g. Nostradamus),[75] Arthurian legends,[76] the Holy Grail,[77] Druidry,[78] Wicca,[79] Heathenism,[80] palmistry,[81] shamanism,[82] goddess spirituality,[83] Gaia spirituality and eco-spirituality,[84] alternative science,[85] esoteric Christianity,[86] UFOs, alien abduction,[87] and so on.[88]

    Two very popular series of books introducing a broad range of such subjects – 'Principles of…' (published by Thorsons/HarperCollins) and 'Elements of…' (published by Element) – constitute a general introduction to what might be called 'right-hand path occulture' (a large area of the more 'respectable' occultural beliefs and practices) and are themselves good examples of the way such fungible ideas are utilized, understood, and disseminated. Although some of the books, such as *Principles of Numerology*, *Principles of Wicca*, *Principles of Tarot*, and *Principles of Your Psychic Potential*, are clearly 'occultic' in the sense outlined above, others, such as *Principles of Buddhism* and *Principles of Colonic Irrigation*, are not 'occultic' in themselves, but have nevertheless become occultural ingredients. Just as potatoes need not be part of a stew, and may be eaten on their own, unaffected by a stew, they can also be very effectively added to a stew. When they are thus added they become permeated by the aromas, flavours and contents of the stew, which are themselves transformed to some degree by the various other ingredients added. In other words, within occulture, it is not Buddhism *per se* that people are interested in, but rather the *principles* or *elements* of Buddhism – and as such 'Buddhism' becomes a fungible, detraditionalized concept. That is to say, some participants in occulture are not particularly interested in becoming devout Buddhists, but rather want simply to acquaint themselves with elements of Buddhist belief and practice, which can then be merged with elements from other systems in the service of the self. It is not the whole Buddhist dish that people want, but rather some tasty ingredients

which can then be stirred into the occultural stew with other appetizing ingredients, the aim being to create one's own occultic dish according to one's own
occultic tastes. This accounts for the enormous plurality within occulture, in
which continuities can exist between profoundly discontinuous belief systems.
The left-wing, peace-loving environmentalist may share certain basic beliefs with
neo-Nazi Satanists.[89]

The same is also true of other traditions, particularly mystical traditions.
Hence, although there is an emphasis on direct experience of the divine and
certain core mystical beliefs, and although we will see that Eastern mysticism in
particular is a central strand within occulture, many people do not want to be
mystics *within* a particular religious tradition, and with all that such a path of
devotion entails. If they do (as some eventually do), they may learn to distance
themselves from the eclecticism of occulture – as such, the occultural *bricoleur*
becomes a *Western* Hindu, Buddhist, Taoist, Sufi, or devotee of one of the numerous new religions. (In a conversation with one teacher of Buddhist spirituality,
I was told that, while happy to instruct any who came to his centre seeking
knowledge of Buddhist belief and practice, he was regularly frustrated by those
who wanted only to absorb *elements* of Buddhism into their own spirituality and
were unhappy with any commitment to Buddhism as a way of life. That said, as
noted above, there were those who moved from an eclectic spirituality to a more
exclusively Western Buddhist path.)

The Significance of the Self

Another broad band of beliefs and practices, sometimes understood as synonymous with the occult (or cultic) milieu,[90] might be identified as 'New Age'. Of
course, as scholars working in the area will be well aware, not only is the term
'New Age' notoriously slippery, but its enormous constellation of spiritualities
and therapies include much that is broadly mystical and much that is directly
influenced by Eastern and Western esotericism. Although not quite as flexible as
'occulture', in that, for example, it could not be used of narrowly esoteric
systems or some Pagan traditions,[91] it is a broad term that covers a great deal.

In academic treatments of the New Age *per se*, as opposed to discussions of
particular groups or individuals, it has become something of a convention to
begin by noting that (1) it is eclectic, (2) it has no founder, no central prophet, no
binding creed, and no headquarters, and (3) it is far broader and more amorphous
than what we normally understand to be '*a* religion'. In the words of the New
Age spokesperson David Spangler, whilst 'Christianity is like a great cathedral
rising around a central spiritual and architectural theme', the New Age is 'more
like a flea market or country fair, a collection of differently coloured and
designed booths spread around a meadow, with the edges of the fair dissolving
into the forested wilderness beyond. Where the cathedral may be a place of worship, the fair is a place of play and discovery'.[92] Although eclecticism, pluralism
and a lack of homogeneity would seem to undermine any attempt to discern a
particular New Age religiosity without being Procrustean and therefore failing to

represent many New Agers, a broad indication can be given because, as with occultural spiritualities generally, New Age spiritualities do connect at certain points. Indeed, there are some common themes running through New Age thinking which do tend to give its otherwise amorphous character some shape.[93] There are, in other words, several significant characteristics of New Age thought which operate as principal unifying occultural metanarratives. Two of the most important are eclecticism, which has already been mentioned, and the sacralization of the self. In particular, the sacralization of the self is fundamental to an understanding of the New Age, it being a point of attraction which is able to draw to it and unite an enormous range of beliefs and practices from across the religious and cultural spectrum. That said, whilst the particular eclectic constructions are relatively novel, there is, of course, nothing new in self-religiosity *per se*. It is, as Heelas notes, 'as ancient as the Upanishads, for instance; or, to take an example from the West, can be found in the millennarian movements of the Middle Ages'.[94] More significantly, a conspicuous Western emphasis on the self can be found in the modern period in Romantic thought.[95] Those familiar with the thought of, for example, Friedrich Schleiermacher, Samuel Taylor Coleridge, or William Wordsworth will be struck by the similarity of some of their emphases and concerns to those of contemporary New Agers. Opposed to the idea that reality can be known simply by the application of human reason, Romanticism argued that there needed to be a complementary emphasis on human intuition and imagination. There are things in the universe that reason cannot grasp. Reason may be a useful tool, but it is limited in its abilities – hence, for example, Wordsworth's and Coleridge's appeal to the imagination as a faculty capable of transcending the limitations of human reason. Individuals can, in other words, intuitively or by the use of imagination access the infinite through the finite, discover the metaphysical within the physical, see the spiritual flowing through the material. As in the New Age, the universe was understood to be, not simply a dry, inert, mathematical collection of rationally quantifiable matter, but rather a living, creative entity permeated with a spiritual 'presence' that cannot be discerned by the simple application of logic and reason. The point is that there was a great confidence in the individual's ability to know the truth about the nature of reality without recourse to divinely revealed or sanctioned authorities. Whereas Enlightenment rationalism emphasized the abilities of unaided human reason in this respect, Romanticism, still focusing on the autonomy of the individual, stressed feeling, intuition and imagination. Similarly for the New Age, whilst reason *per se* is not wholly rejected, it is distrusted and there is a stress on intuition, feeling and imagination.

As to why there is this turn to the self in the New Age, the answer is of course to be found in its particularly high view of the self. Whereas, for example, Schleiermacher still thought of the divine as distinct from the self, as 'the Other' on which the self absolutely depends,[96] the New Age, influenced by certain elements of Indian thought, thinks more in terms which indicate a sacralization or even divinization of the self. The 'pious self-consciousness' of Schleiermacher is, in the New Age, not a consciousness of the self as determined by God, an apprehension which leaves a person with an absolute sense of contingency; it is *self*-consciousness – which often includes consciousness of one's 'Higher Self'.[97] Hence, for New Age epistemology the self becomes supremely significant, in that not only is the self able to discover religious truth apart from divine revelation *from without* or the aid of some other external authority, but the truth it seeks is *within*. Hence, for example, Jesus' words have been used with reference to the self: 'I am the way, the truth and the life.'[98] Similarly, in her discussion of 'Super-consciousness and the Higher Self', Shirley MacLaine declares that

> self-realization is God-realization. Knowing more of your Higher Self really means knowing more of God. That inner knowledge is radiant with life, light and love … When I go within I look for communication and guidance … I like to ask questions, check my perceptions as to my opinions, my progress … When we go within and come into alignment with our spiritual power, we come into connection with that spark of Divinity…which I call the Higher Self. Some call it the Divine Oversoul, the Divine Center, the God within, the personal interface with God…whatever one calls it, it is the personalization of the God Source within us. When I first made contact with my Higher Self I was aware that I could, from then on, better touch my purpose on Earth and have it fit in with everyone else's.[99]

However, this emphasis on the self does not necessarily mean that the epistemological individualism of the New Age stops at the boundaries of the *individual* self, believing that there is nothing greater than the individual's own truth and authority. Although we will see that some do understand the Higher Self to be none other than a deeper level of the individual self, it is clear that there is, in much New Age thought, a sense of something greater than the individual self. Hence, operating, though not always very clearly, with a form of pantheism, MacLaine speaks of the 'Divine spark' as a *part* of God, a part of a truth and authority greater than the self, a part of 'the universal energy…which…has always existed'.[100] It is in this pantheistic sense that we need to understand MacLaine's oft-quoted declaration, 'I am God. I am God. I am God.' As she says, 'the basic principle of the New Age' can be summed up in the following words: 'Begin with the self; recognize the God within, and the result will be the recognition, with tolerance and love, that everyone else possesses God within as well. In other words, we are each *part of* God experiencing the adventure of life.'[101] And according to Marilyn Ferguson – who, like many within occulture, betrays an indebtedness to an understanding (or misunderstanding) of the Upanishadic doctrine of *brahman-atman* identification – 'All souls are one. Each is a spark from the original soul, and this soul is inherent in all souls… You are joined to a great Self… And because that Self is inclusive, you are joined to all others.'[102] Similarly, George Trevelyan writes, 'Look into the eyes of another human being… Just gaze into the human eye, thinking that God in me is looking at the God spark in you. But it is the same God, looking at Himself… If I look at you in this way I experience that we are both parts of the same vast being that is the totality of humanity.'[103]

This, of course, can be understood in terms of that type of 'cultic thought' that both Troeltsch and Campbell identify as 'mystical', and which Campbell later identifies as part of an Easternized *Weltanschauung*.[104] Although the Absolute is not *other than* the self, as in Schleiermacher's thought, there is that which is *greater than* the self, and of which the self is a small part. Although one can logically refer to the self's divinity, this is generally understood within a larger pantheistic context. Indeed, there is, in many cases, a sense of the transcendent. Whether one calls it 'the Spirit', 'God', 'the Life Force', 'the Source' or 'the Higher Self', it is an absolute with which all humanity should seek to live in harmony. That this is so is particularly clear in some forms of channelling – a practice central to much occultural spirituality. In the words of Geoff Boltwood, a channeller based in Glastonbury, ' "Channelling" involves achieving an ex-panded state of consciousness that allows for the transmission of information from higher, some say "divine", intelligence.'[105] Boltwood, for example, is 'a focus of energy for the Source known as "Tareth"… the centre of infinite creation and potential'.[106] And in a channelled message, Tareth communicates the following:

> I am Tareth of the source of creation, of the present and of the future … The Tareth has been here a long time and has returned in this era with the name Tareth … The Source of Creation is calling all those now who are ready to take upon themselves the role of becoming doorways to new dimensions, to heal and to teach others: no one is exempt. Anyone can become part of this.[107]

Clearly Boltwood makes a subtle distinction between the individual self and the Source/Tareth who addresses and appeals to that self. Interestingly, here, as with much occultural channelling, we are dealing with a doctrine of revelation, in which the Source communicates information to the self. Indeed, the theosophical proto-New Ager Annie Besant explicitly affirms the revelatory value of chan-nelling as 'communication from a Being superior to humanity of facts known to Himself but unknown to those to whom he makes the revelation – facts which they cannot reach by the exercise of the powers they have so far evolved'.[108]

Subtly distinct from these understandings, there are other New Age spirituali-ties within occulture which come close to narcissistic subjectivism. For example, recalling his own experience of enlightenment, Werner Erhard, the founder of *est*, states the following:

> after I realized that I knew nothing – I realized that I knew everything … I realized that I was not my emotions or thoughts. I was not my ideas, my intellect, my perceptions, my beliefs. I was not what I did or accomplished or achieved … I was simply the space, the creator, the source of all that stuff. I experienced Self *as* Self in a direct and unmediated way. I didn't just experience Self; *I became Self…* It was an unmistakable recognition that I was, am, and always will be the source of my experience … I was whole and complete as I was and now I could accept the whole truth about myself. For, I was its source. I found enlightenment, truth, true self all at once. I had reached the end.[109]

The point is that Boltwood's and certainly Besant's understandings of the divine, the Source of truth and authority, is distinct from that of Erhard, for whom there seems to be no understanding of a greater authority than one's self (in this sense, we might speak of Erhard's 'Self'). Certainly Erhard could not meaningfully work with a doctrine of revelation as understood by Besant. Having said that, there are channellers who do work with an understanding of the self similar to Erhard's. For example, whereas Eileen Caddy of the Findhorn community initially understood her channelled revelations to come from God, later she came to believe that it was simply guidance from her self: 'There is no separation between ourselves and God, there is only "I am". I am the guidance. It took me so many years to realize this.'[110] Although there is discussion of God *and* the self, it is clear the two are ultimately identified: *Homo autonomous*. Again, this aspect of the New Age, which has roots in the Indian religious tradition, is a key feature of occulture.

Perhaps the distinction between these different understandings of the self's relation to 'the Divine' can be best understood as a distinction between (1) pantheism, (2) polytheism and (3) panentheism. (1) For some within occulture, humans are, in the words of Trevelyan, 'parts of the same vast being'. (2) For others, humans are, in the final analysis, individual gods, in the sense that there is, in effect, no greater divinity than the individual self. Hence, there are as many divine beings as there are individual selves: polytheism. (3) Others, like Boltwood, Besant and many of those working from within the Christian tradition, such as Matthew Fox and Peter Spink, have developed a thesis which can best be described as panentheistic.[111] Although immanence is stressed, there is a fundamental theistic reluctance to identify God and the world. In the words of Fox,

> panentheism is not pantheism. Pantheism, which is a declared heresy because it robs God of transcendence, states that 'everything is God, and God is everything'. Panentheism, on the other hand, is altogether orthodox and very fit for orthopraxis as well, for it slips in the little Greek word *en* and thus means, 'God is in everything and everything is in God.' This experience of the presence of God in our depth… is a mystical understanding of God… Panentheism is a mature doctrine about the presence of God, about the deep with-ness of God.[112]

The Priority of Experience and a Hermeneutic of Suspicion

The New Age's emphasis on the self and the Higher Self is not simply a result of a sacralizing anthropology. Self-authority is also linked to a particular epistemology of experience which, again, significantly overlaps with Troeltsch's understanding of mysticism. Only personal experience, it is argued, can provide immediate and uncontaminated access to truth, particularly truth in the sphere of the spiritual/transpersonal. This is explicit in the work of Gabrielle Roth: 'The first shamanic task is to free the body to experience the power of being.' She continues,

> It is first in that it is both where we must begin and what is most fundamental. Your body is the ground metaphor of your life, the expression of your existence. It is your Bible, your encyclopedia, your life story. Everything that happens to you is stored in your body. Your body knows; your body tells. The relationship of your self to your body is indivisible, inescapable, unavoidable. In the marriage of flesh and spirit, divorce is impossible…[113]

Mediated knowledge communicated by sacred texts, by the Church, by society cannot be trusted. That is not to say that they contain no truth, but only that, to use Paul Ricœur's terminology, a 'hermeneutic of suspicion' must be pressed into use. 'New Agers' often make much of the fact that objective thinking is an *ignis fatuus*, and that observation and communication are always informed by one's interests and presuppositions. Truths cannot be communicated without being in some way interpreted and therefore 'contaminated'. Hence, the immediacy of personal experience is understood as epistemologically crucial. External truths should only be accepted if, in the words of George Trevelyan, they 'ring true to your own Inner Self'.[114] As Heelas comments, 'voices of authority emanating from experts, charismatic leaders and established traditions [are] mediated by way of inner experience. [E]ven New Age teachers (typically) do not expect their adepts to simply *listen* to what they have to say.'[115] 'The highest source of guidance for anyone,' says Corinne McLaughlin, 'is always within each person – the voice of the soul, the inner Divinity.'[116] To quote some sampled words on Ultramarine's 'Stella' (which, if I'm not mistaken, are the voice and words of Gabrielle Roth): ' ... dogmas and theories are just holding me back, and holding me down, and turning me into somebody that I'm not... Truth... I wanted it now; I wanted it in this body; in this lifetime; not some other day; not some other time; I wanted it now.'[117]

Taking this experiential emphasis a step further, because it is often claimed that we have worldviews which are permeated by left-brain rationalism and intellectualism, many of those who draw from and/or contribute to occulture have been led to a radical questioning of the presuppositions and understandings of truth in which they have been educated. Particularly in some of the more structured new religious groupings it is taught that only by purging the mind can one embark on the path to truth. For example, to quote the words of Bhagwan Shree Rajneesh (a.k.a. Osho), 'Only if you are ready to drop the ego, your judgements, and your rationality, your intellect – only if you are ready to allow me to cut off your head – will you be able to understand what is going on here.'[118] Indeed, Rajneesh did not, as such, want his followers to *understand* at all. What he aimed at was not an *understanding* of truth *per se*, but rather an *experience* of truth: 'Authentic religious life... must be approached by discarding the intellect. Bhagwan's utterances are those of the mystic, unable to do more than hint at the truth. His aim is to conjure up that which cannot be intellectually understood. His utterances are not to be taken literally, for they are aimed at evoking that *totality* of experience which goes beyond words.'[119] To quote Rajneesh, 'Once you become dependent on borrowed light, you are lost. Knowing is good, but knowledge is not good. Knowing is yours, knowledge is others.'[120]

Hence, in the light of this emphasis on inner experience, it is not surprising that Christian New Ager Peter Spink argues that the Church's insistence on the propagation of intellectual truth 'makes understanding impossible'. The Church should move away from insisting on the authority of 'borrowed light', of mediated truth, and rather help seekers to *experience* truth for themselves: 'Because of a quickening of perception at this deeper level, many who are travelling a spiritual path find unacceptable the idea of submission to either a biblical or an ecclesiastical authority without reference to an inner resonance.

Submission to the truth in this sense is felt to be a denial of integrity and something divorced from spiritual awakening.'[121] Again, 'the new consciousness … is to know that belief patterns and words, concepts and ideas, theological definitions, dogmas and doctrine are all articulations of the truth. They do not in themselves constitute the truth. Truth is the experience of reality in the present moment.'[122]

This is why, in occulture, 'religion, as normally understood in the west, has been replaced by teachers whose primary job is to set up "contexts" to enable participants to experience their spirituality and authority'.[123] Although an individual may turn to channelling, to a guru, to a sacred text, or to astrology, these, it is argued, are not to be understood as external authorities – rather, detraditionalized, they should be understood as aids to assist us on our experiential journey within.

Romanticizing the Premodern

Many of those within the occult milieu are convinced that the contemporary world has much to learn from premodern and primal cultures and that, to some extent, the modern period has seen a regression rather than a progression of human understanding of the nature of reality. Whether drawing on Eastern spirituality or Gnosticism, there is broad occultural agreement that the key to vibrant, authentic contemporary spirituality is the resurgence of ancient traditions. Whether one worships the Goddess, studies the rites of ancient orders, charts the stars, channels messages from those who once walked the streets of Atlantis, explores the secrets of the Mayan civilization, or even attempts to translate the ancient Enochian angelic tongue revealed during the crystal-gazing experiments of the Elizabethan occultists John Dee and Edward Kelley, there is a sense of continuity with the ancients.[124] Occulture has a strong sentimental attachment to the past (which is often a mythical past). Our ancestors, some believe, used to live in a harmonious, symbiotic relationship with Gaia, or they had privileged access to profound spiritual power and wisdom, or they were the architects of vast, advanced civilizations informed, perhaps, by extraterrestrial technology. Rather than suffering what Starhawk calls the contemporary person's state of 'estrangement',[125] the ancients were in touch with nature, themselves, each other and the sacred.

Although many are seeking to provide more realistic understandings of ancient societies it still seems to be the case that the 'ancient wisdom' of these cultures is understood to be the uncorrupted wisdom of a humanity unrepressed by the external dogma, rationalism and authority of later institutionalized religion and culture. They are therefore treated as spiritual and cultural paradigms. This, of course, is equally true of contemporary indigenous cultures which, it is believed, still retain their ancient wisdom and live in a symbiotic relationship with the environment. As Ray Castle and Mark Turner insist, 'Aboriginal people have a primordial oneness with the earth at ground level and have a direct relationship with the rocks, minerals, insects, animals and plants. The western world can learn much from these sacred people.'[126] Consequently, for many, the quest for truth, spirituality and a new way of life needs to take account of the wisdom imparted by the 'sacred people' of ancient and indigenous cultures.[127] Indeed, these cultures often carry the same sort of authority and inspire the same degree of blind faith that western science has inspired during the modern era. That is to say, an occultural matter can be settled by a simple appeal to some premodern belief or practice – hence the almost ubiquitous reference to a continuity with the premodern in occultural literature. For example, within occulture, the promotion of practices and philosophies usually includes references to premodern cultures; what may appear to be simply a bit of interesting information added to a leaflet, is actually a guarantee of its truth and authority.[128] Indeed, the feeling of authenticity and truth seems to be enhanced if promotional literature is adorned with symbols and illustrations which, if not ancient, have the look of antiquity.

Of course, sanitised, romantic understandings of the past and hagiographical representations of founders and leaders within a particular sacred history are not limited to new traditions and spiritualities. Similar developments and understandings can be seen in all religions.

Pagan Occulture

Principally because of the eclectic and inclusive nature of occulture, the occultural stream which might be described as broadly 'New Age' merges with another significant stream, namely contemporary Pagan occulture.

That said, it is important to begin by noting the distinctiveness of the two streams. Indeed, Pagans in particular reject any Pagan–New Age identification, arguing that, generally speaking, any apparent similarities are superficial:

> There are similarities between Paganism and New Age – but no more than there are (different ones) between Christianity and New Age … Pagans frequently associate New Age with a 'fluffy bunnies' vision of the world: their cosmos is a generous, self-sacrificing and loving place, 'all sweetness and light, the lions don't bite and the thorns don't scratch.' … Ability to meet the exorbitant and prohibitive cost of New Age events enables its beneficiaries the degree of leisure necessary to indulge in continual self-absorption.[129]

Essentially, the point is that the New Age tends to be a 'predominantly white, middle-class phenomenon in which health and wealth are prime indicators of spirituality'.[130] Again, 'Channelling of alleged wisdom from exalted masters, angels, devas, and others is typical of New Age and causes considerable cynicism among Pagans, who feel that if New Agers faced their darkness honestly they could admit that the "airy-fairy, wishy-washy" messages about being nicer people with more positive thoughts come from their own egos.'[131]

Although it is difficult to generalize about such diverse and eclectic spiritualities as the New Age and Paganism and whilst some Pagan perceptions of the New Age are no doubt caricatured, on the whole it is true to say that Pagans are right to question an easy identification of the two. The following broad points might be cited to support this conclusion:

1. Pagans reject what they understand to be the New Age's overly sanguine, saccharine, light-emphasizing view of reality. Paganism emphasizes both the beauty of nature and the fact that it is 'red in tooth and claw'. Inspired by the polarities of the natural world, Pagan thinking incorporates spring and autumn, life and death, light and darkness – the dark being understood, not as evil, but, like the winter and the night, simply a necessary feature of the natural world.

2. As is evident in particular in Wiccan rituals and rites of initiation, on the whole it draws much more heavily than the New Age on Western esotericism.

3. Hence, Paganism tends to be more ritualistic than the New Age. That is to say, it often has a priesthood, it works with particular rites and symbols, and has a religious calendar of festivals[132] (which is sometimes followed by New Agers).

4. Regarding the local group to which a person belongs (e.g. one's coven in the Wicca tradition), often the initiation process and the high level of commitment required is quite distinct from what would normally be found in the New Age and sometimes reflects sectarianism. Indeed, contemporary Paganism contributes significant centres of religious coalescence to occulture (i.e. groups and organizations with a developed social structure).

5. Generally speaking, whereas we have seen that much in the New Age is explicitly epistemologically individualistic, focusing on enabling the individual to 'go within' and to discover the 'Higher Self', in Paganism there is a greater emphasis on the other, on that which is external to the self: the planet, the deities and the community. Many Pagans, for example, are polytheists who will look to gods and goddesses for help and guidance. Although there are solitary practitioners, generally speaking the Pagan community is valued by individual Pagans as a source of spiritual guidance and support.

6. There is a great emphasis on one's responsibility towards other creatures (human and non-human) and the environment.

7. As Graham Harvey (quoting Margot Adler) points out: 'There is a funny saying in the Pagan movement: "the difference between Pagan and 'new age' is one decimal point." In other words, a two-day workshop in meditation by a "new age" practitioner might cost $300, while the same course given by a Pagan might cost $30.'[133] Again, this is indicative of the white, middle-class, consumerist nature of much New Age spirituality.[134] (Although this is not always true of what might be considered New Age workshops and events, having attended both Pagan and New Age gatherings, generally speaking my bank account prefers the former.)

That said, although New Age and Pagan spiritualities are distinguishable, that people do confuse them is of some significance in that it suggests that both New Agers and Pagans are drinking from the same conceptual pool. Certainly, as Douglas Ezzy has shown, it is not difficult to find New Age elements within 'popularized' Paganism.[135] Indeed, often what makes a spirituality New Age or Pagan are the emphases placed on certain occultural beliefs, the particular mix of ideas, and the context into which the ideas are absorbed. That is to say, if my general background interest relates to Wicca and Western esotericism, my understanding of, for example, faeries will be different than if my general background interest relates to the Church Universal and Triumphant or some other New Age organization. A quick comparison of the discussions of faeries/devas/

nature spirits by Doreen Valiente in *An ABC of Witchcraft Past and Present* and
Dorothy Maclean in *The Findhorn Garden* reveals the difference clearly.[136]
Maclean understands the Earth to be populated by numerous intelligent beings,
for which she uses the term 'deva' (Sanskrit 'shining one'). There is, she believes,
'a whole hierarchy of beings, from the earthiest gnome to the highest archangel'.[137] Moreover, 'the devas hold the archetypal pattern and plan for all forms
around us, and they direct the energy needed for materialising them. The physical
bodies of minerals, vegetables, animals and humans are all energy brought into
form through the work of the devic kingdom. Sometimes we call that work
natural law, but it is the devas who carry out that law, ceaselessly and joy-
fully.'[138] As to what these beings look like, 'the devas have no particular form.
But in attempting to establish communication and cooperation with humans,
members of the devic realms have made themselves visible in a form intelligible
to humans. These forms reflect their functions. For instance, a dwarf is usually
depicted with a pick-axe, denoting our human interpretation of his work with the
mineral world.'[139] Essentially, says Maclean, 'the devas are energy, they are life
force. (We humans are as well, only in our own unique way.) I was told in
guidance, *You are simply surrounded by life. You are a life force moving along
with other life forces. As you recognize this, you open up and draw near to these
others, becoming more and more one with them, working together for My
purposes.*'[140] Valiente, on the other hand, interprets them quite differently. She
understands the current belief in faeries to be 'a composite of several factors:
actual spirits of nature whose presence can sometimes be perceived, but who
usually share this world invisibly with humans', 'souls of the pagan dead', and
'folk memories of aboriginal races, now mostly vanished'.[141] Concerning the last
of these, she is thinking of Margaret Murray's thesis that faeries were actually
the aboriginal people of the British Isles:

> These small, dark people, displaced by the waves of incoming Celtic settlers from the
> Continent, took refuge in remote places. They lived in huts roofed over with green turf,
> an effective form of camouflage which made their dwellings seem at a distance like little
> hills. They feared the iron weapons of their conquerors, and would flee at the sight of
> them. But they had subtle and deadly weapons of their own; small, sharp arrowheads of
> flint, poisoned so that even a slight wound from one of them could be fatal; and, even
> more dreaded than their 'elf bolts', the powers of heathen magic, the uncanny and
> unholy glamourie that their conquerors feared.[142]

'People are', she continues, 'thoroughly afraid of the fairies, and propitiate them
by calling them the "Good Neighbours", the "Good Folk", or the "People of
Peace"'.[143]

The point is that from Maclean's New Age perspective faeries are manifestations of the life force or energy; they are, in a sense, one with us, they are
benevolent, they are angelic. Within Wicca, faeries are understood in terms of the
spirits of the Pagan dead or, indeed, a distinct race of beings who need to be
propitiated. Although drinking from the same occultural pool in that both work
with ideas of faeries/nature spirits, the particular interpretations are quite distinct.
Although there may be similar and overlapping elements and themes within
Pagan and New Age spiritualities, the understandings of the elements and themes

are often different – sometimes subtly so, sometimes clearly and obviously so. Again, Harvey makes the point well:

> The two broad movements appear similar because they celebrate similar festivals, name some similar other-than-human beings (e.g. elves and faeries), use visualization and meditation, eclectically draw on South Asian, Native American and Shamanic ideas and technology (e.g. chakras and sweat lodges) and read widely in astrology, geomancy, anthropology and Celtic mythology. But the exact mix of these elements produces atmospheres and actions which are distinguishable.[144]

The same point can be made regarding a further occultural misidentification Pagans are keen to refute, namely the Pagan–Satanist confusion. A confusion which probably stretches back to the Christian denunciation of Pagans as Devil worshippers, it has been exacerbated in recent years by films, horror novels and popular books dealing with 'the occult'. Most contemporary Pagans will insist that, because Satan does not feature in the Pagan worldview, and because Satanists work with a perverted understanding of the Christian worldview, Satanists are not Pagans, but rather Christian heretics: 'Paganism is not Satanism, it has no place for a devil, or for belief in ontological evil. Its cosmology has no room for a battle between forces of "good" and "evil" fought over the "souls" of humans who might be enticed towards heaven or hell.'[145] Hence, many Pagans will actively distance themselves from Satanists and Satanism.[146]

Apart from public and Christian perceptions, there are, however, good religious reasons for this confusion, the principal being, yet again, that both Satanists and Pagans live, breathe and have their being within Western occulture. For example: (1) the same deities appear in both systems (e.g. Hecate, Kali, Lilith, Pan and Set);[147] (2) there is considerable overlap between 'left-hand path' Paganism and Satanism – e.g. the emphasis on self-development, on the importance of carnal desire, and (following Aleister Crowley – who has significantly contributed to the occultural pool) on the significance of 'the will'; (3) some Satanists, because they operate with similar occultural ideas, do consider themselves to be Pagan; (4) there has even been some debate within Paganism over whether the figure of Satan can be divested of its Christian content and usefully used in a Pagan context;[148] (5) both celebrate the bodily and the sexual (e.g. in sex magick the energies sex arouses are utilized – again, Crowley is influential here);[149] (6) as is the case for many within the occult milieu, there is a shared distrust of, and sometimes open hostility to, Christianity.

Having said that, it is true that there is much about Satanism that distinguishes it from Paganism, especially if we understand Paganism to be, to use Charlotte Hardman's definition, 'a religion based on Nature worship and ancient indigenous traditions'.[150] Furthermore, some forms of Satanism are further distinguished from Paganism in that they are essentially manifestations of 'self-religion' which encourage egocentricity and personal development – in this sense they are closer to New Age and human potential thinking. According to perhaps the most influential Satanist, Anton Szandor LaVey,[151] 'Most Satanists do not accept Satan as an anthropomorphic being with cloven hooves, a barbed tail, and horns. He merely represents a force of nature – the powers of darkness which have been named just that because no religion has taken these forces *out* of the darkness.'[152] Again, he writes, 'My brand of Satanism is the ultimate conscious alternative to herd mentality and institutionalized thought. It is a studied and contrived set of principles and exercises designed to liberate individuals from a contagion of mindlessness that destroys innovation. I have termed it "Satanism" because it is most stimulating under that name. Self-discipline and motivation are effected more easily under stimulating conditions. Satanism means "the opposition" and epitomizes all symbols of nonconformity.'[153] Hence, Satan is understood more in terms of a useful icon which encourages self-interest and individualism, and promotes opposition to institutional religion and the dominant culture. Again, in this sense, Satanism is essentially a self-religion or human potential spirituality which utilizes the rebellious, offensive, and provocative symbolism the figure of Satan provides. This understanding seems evident in the clearly hedonistic 'Nine Satanic Statements' of the Church of Satan, eight of which begin with 'Satan represents' and none of which requires believing in the existence of a diabolical supernatural entity:

1. Satan represents indulgence, instead of abstinence!
2. Satan represents vital existence, instead of spiritual pipe dreams!
3. Satan represents undefiled wisdom, instead of hypocritical self-deceit!
4. Satan represents kindness to those who deserve it, instead of love wasted on ingrates!
5. Satan represents vengeance, instead of turning the other cheek!
6. Satan represents responsibility to the responsible, instead of concern for psychic vampires!
7. Satan represents man as just another animal, sometimes better, more often worse than those that walk on all fours, who, because of his 'divine spiritual and intellectual development', has become the most vicious animal of all!
8. Satan represents all of the so-called sins, as they all lead to physical, mental, or emotional gratification!
9. Satan has been the best friend the church has ever had, as he has kept it in business all these years![154]

However, there clearly are forms of 'traditional Satanism' or 'theistic Satanism'[155] in which Satan or Set is venerated as a deity (e.g. the First Church of Satan, the Temple of Set, the Church of Lucifer, the Children of the Black Rose, and the Brood[156]) as opposed to LaVey's arguably 'atheistic Satanism'. This mixture of understandings of Satan and Satanism appears in the results of a 1995 survey conducted by Harvey. For example, concerning the figure of Satan/Set, 'Some say that Set is a "real being", "an incorporeal entity", "a metaphysical reality"... "Lord of this world"... Others consider Set to be "the archetypal rebel", "the ultimate male principle", "a figure representing pride, self-interest, and self-gratification"... "the driving force in human evolution".'[157] That said, although some view Set/Satan as being a rebellious, self-serving being, rather paradoxically they rarely view him in the sinister way that Christians do, believing him to be a deity who can be "approached as a friend" and who (sometimes with reference to the serpent in Genesis 3) dispenses knowledge ('the black flame') to those who strive for it.

Again, some forms of Paganism, such as left-hand path magick and chaos magick, overlap more with Satanism than other forms, such as Druidry (the rituals of which some Christians attend). The point, however, is that, as with Paganism and the New Age, whilst Paganism and Satanism are distinct forms of religion, there is, as some Pagans recognize, areas of significant convergence. This, of course, is because both are fundamentally occultural.

As for Paganism's contributions to occulture, these include, perhaps most significantly, the importance of traditional and indigenous beliefs and practices. For example, Paganism has stimulated great occultural interest in traditional methods of divination.[158] One of the best known (used in particular by Pagans belonging to Heathenism/the Northern Tradition[159]) is the use of runes – a form of divination which has also been popularized by New Agers. These are important because they are both ancient (the importance of which has been noted above) and also because they are understood to have been developed by 'a people living in close harmony with the environment, the ancestors, the seasonal and stellar cycles and the deities'[160] (again, the importance of which has been noted above). Runes are symbols (often painted on small, smooth stones) which, for Heathens, are more than simply tools for 'fortune-telling' in the modern sense of that term. That is to say, using the runes is more about spiritual guidance, achieving wholeness, communicating with non-human beings and listening to the deities, and less about finding out what a person's future might hold:

> If you have come to the realization that you have forgotten the reason for your presence on Earth, the Runes can be used to restore that memory. By using the Runes as gateways, you descend to the underworld to regain lost knowledge and find the spiritual tools that will enable you to carry out the task that you remember ... Runes can ... help us towards achieving wholeness and act as a mouthpiece for the gods, goddesses, ancestors and non-human beings who will help us with the task of environmental regeneration.[161]

This quotation touches on several other important aspects of occulture which Paganism is helping to shape and promote, the most important of which are the emphases on the ancients, the Goddess, the environment and 'other-than-human persons'.[162] Indeed, of the various reasons that could be posited for the growth of Paganism in the contemporary West, most relate to these emphases – all of which can be found within occulture generally. For example:

1. Although there are always exceptions to the rule, generally speaking, contemporary Paganism eschews masculine images of power and authority. It rejects patriarchal monotheisms and the depiction of God as solely male. Although there is an explicit attempt to seek balance, in that Paganism often teaches that the God and the Goddess are of equal importance, the emphasis is often placed very firmly on 'the Great Goddess' and the feminine. Many contemporary Westerners have found this emphasis on the priestess, the Goddess, and the feminine *per se* to be liberating and enlightened. Often, those considering some form of Pagan spirituality will cite this aspect of Paganism as a welcome alternative to the attitudes of the principal monotheistic faiths, particularly Christianity.

2. Not only is Paganism feminist, it is also 'eco-feminist'. Paganism is an ecological faith tradition, a nature-centric spirituality that seeks to break down hierarchies. As such, in the contemporary Western world, its attitudes to non-

humans and to the Earth is felt by many to be healthy. In an eco-conscious culture an eco-conscious spirituality is understandably attractive. Indeed, some Pagans are essentially pantheistic, in that the divine is believed, in some sense, to be identical with nature. The Goddess/God is the force which animates all living things. Frederic Lamond, for example, calls for 'a return to' what he calls 'the pantheist polytheist religious paradigm of our ancestors, which recognizes the divine as *imminent* in all human beings, women as well as men, animals and plants; and recognizes the feminine quality of Being and loving as equally divine as the masculine quality of doing'.[163] This point is interesting, in that, as with much Pagan thought, it should perhaps be defined more accurately as panentheist. That is to say, strictly speaking, the divine and the universe are, conceptually at least, distinct. Although the divine indwells nature, is immanent within nature, is inseparable from nature, there is also a sense in which the Goddess/God transcends, guides and cares for the natural world.

3. Regardless of whether this is always the case or not (and sometimes it is not[164]), Paganism certainly advertises itself as being non-dogmatic. In a culture which is uncomfortable with exclusive truth-claims, such as those made by Christianity, it is not difficult to see the attraction of a religion which demands only a reverence for 'the life-force', an honouring of 'the divine' (however that might be understood) and, often, the single ethical injunction, 'if it harms none, do what thou wilt' – note again the preference for antique language.[165]

4. As we will see later in the book, it is a matter of observable fact that the Pagan worldview is both consciously and unconsciously promoted by popular fantasy literature, contemporary rock and dance music, films, and computer games. For example, the cosmology of J.R.R. Tolkien's wonderful stories about Middle Earth and strange other-than-human beings and powers is not entirely different from contemporary Heathen cosmology. Indeed, it seems clear that, for a variety of cultural, philosophical, and social reasons, areas of contemporary Western popular culture have been moulded by and also helped to mould the Pagan worldview.

5. Thinking in particular of the Western esotericism which has influenced much occultural thought, the appeal of ancient, occult knowledge, power and ritual is perennial.

6. In individualistic and essentially selfish Western societies which engender feelings of powerlessness and insignificance, the attraction of a small, closely knit group of people who claim to have access to such ancient power and knowledge is hard to underestimate.

Concluding Comments

We have seen that occulture itself is not a worldview, but rather a resource on which people draw, a reservoir of ideas, beliefs, practices, and symbols. Consumers of occulture may be witting or unwitting; they may engage with it at a relatively superficial level or they may have strong religious commitments; they may themselves contribute to the pool of occultural knowledge or they may simply drink from it. Occulture is the spiritual *bricoleur*'s Internet from which to download whatever appeals or inspires; it is the sacralizing air that many of our contemporaries breathe; it is the well from which the serious occultist draws; it is the varied landscape the New Age nomad explores; it is the cluttered warehouse frequently plundered by producers of popular culture searching for ideas, images and symbols.

The amorphous, constantly evolving nature of occulture is often reified and misunderstood. For example, although Adam Possamaï recognizes the eclectic nature of what he calls 'perennism', he is wrong to claim that those involved in the occultic milieu are 'involved in what could be called McDonaldised Occult Culture'.[166] Although it is popular today to apply George Ritzer's term 'McDonaldization' to almost every area of Western life, occulture is not, in itself, McDonaldized. While, as Possamaï notes, McDonaldization is 'the process by which the principles of the fast food restaurant are coming to dominate more and more sectors of American society as well as the world',[167] the problem is that Ritzer understands this principally in Weberian terms as bureaucratization and rationalization, including, for example, the development of scientific management.[168] This is not characteristic of occulture.

That said, I am not saying that bureaucratization and rationalization are not involved in the production, management and consumption of occulture. As we will see in the next volume, they have been involved. The arrival of the postmodern *bricoleur* certainly does not mean the collapse of modernity and the deconstruction of consumer capitalism. Possamaï is, therefore, right to conclude that 'it becomes almost an oxymoron to describe these spiritualities as "alternative", as they appear to be part of the dominant culture of today's society; that is part of the cultural logic of late capitalism. Their involvement in multinational capitalism and their "pastiche" to spirituality or religion makes them both a significant feature of the postmodern *zeitgeist*, and a new spiritual way of life in this phase of later capitalism.'[169] The problem with Possamaï's analysis (and he is not alone) is a failure to distinguish between the broad, amorphous nature of occulture *per se* and the particular ways it is used by cultural and spiritual *bricoleurs*. Occulture is not merely the standardized burger and chips of the Western religio-cultural milieu; rather it is the much less standardized and unpredictable raw materials – the animals and vegetables of the process. Possamaï's failure to make this distinction is evident in his notion of 'perennism', which, being far too narrow, becomes Procrustean in its interpretation of the occult milieu. Perennism is essentially a 'syncretic spirituality' with three defining characteristics, namely, monism (which includes the rejection of all dualisms), a human potential ethic (what has been described above as self-spirituality), and the quest for spiritual knowledge.[170] While occulture is certainly conducive to spiritual seekership, and while spiritual seekers are most frequently operating with what is best described as a form of 'self-spirituality', they need not be monists. Indeed, there is much within occulture, drawn from Western esotericism, that is fundamentally dualist. For example, we will see in the discussion of dark occulture and the emergence of new demonologies in the second volume that many of the ideas, drawing heavily on Christian thought, are fundamentally dualistic. The point is simply that contemporary alternative spiritualities need to be understood far more in terms of their relationship with a much broader and more nebulous occulture.

Chapter 5

EASTERNIZATION?

Oh, East is East, and West is West, And never the twain shall meet ...
(Rudyard Kipling)

We have seen that much current alternative re-enchantment in the West can be traced back, very broadly speaking, to Romanticism, mystical traditions, Western esotericism,[1] Spiritualism, and the modern revival of interest in nature religion. Added to these interrelated strands of Western thought and culture, the influence of the East, it would appear, has been peculiarly significant. Although this general observation is not entirely new, in the latter half of the twentieth century theorizing about this influence began to coalesce. Sociologists, psychologists, and scholars of religion, whether focusing on particular traditions or providing overviews of general religio-cultural patterns, have drawn attention to the Eastern turn.[2]

Turning East

Harvey Cox's *Turning East* makes much of the idea that young people in particular who are looking for both 'warmth, affection and close ties of feeling' and also a profound, life-changing religious experience have found a spiritual home in Eastern traditions.[3] 'Many people told us,' says Cox, 'they were looking for a kind of *immediacy* they had not been able to find elsewhere.' He continues: 'I do not refer here to those who were looking for experience merely for its own sake ... Here I refer to those persons who seemed to want a real personal encounter with God or the Holy, or simply with life, nature and other people. It also includes those who needed to find an inner peace and had not found it anywhere else.'[4] In their search, such people were led away from a tired, authoritarian, patriarchal, sermonizing Christianity to forms of faith which are perceived to be more vital, experience-centred, and Eastern.[5] Of course, this search led far more Westerners to *turn* east, rather than actually to *go* east:

> The people I am talking about here have not moved to India to live in an ashram. They have not left home to go to the Orient to dwell in a Tibetan temple or a Zen monastery, at least not permanently. They still live in Texas, Ohio, or New York, or somewhere else in the USA ... Their interest comes in widely varying degrees of seriousness and persistence. It extends from those who sneak a glance at a paperback edition of the *I Ching* or try some yoga postures to those who find, as I did, that one of the Eastern practices becomes important to them and to those who leave everything behind and sleep on mats

in an American Hare Krishna temple. It includes serious seekers and frivolous dilet-
tantes, converts and fellow travellers. But the fact is that large numbers of people are
involved, not just a fringe group, and the extent of interest has no precedent in American
religious history.[6]

Again, it is important to understand that central to this *turning* East is the turn
towards the experiencing self and away from external authorities. There is a shift
away from doctrine to techniques, to the facilitation of experience, and to the
growth of the self. As Cox points out,

almost all the neo-Oriental movements include instruction in some form of spiritual
discipline. Leaders in the neo-Oriental movements show initiates the primary techniques
of prayer, contemplation and meditation. Inquirers learn to breathe or dance or chant.
They use archery or swordplay or acupuncture or massage. Teachers do not rely entirely
on words but move inquirers quickly to the actual techniques ... for inducing the desired
forms of consciousness. Unlike many of the currently available Western religious
options, which stress beliefs or codes of ethics sometimes at the expense of a primary
encounter of the person with reality, most of the neo-Oriental groups begin right away at
the level of practice.[7]

John Dunne's now little-known book *The Way of All the Earth* takes the
reader through this process. In it he speaks of 'passing over' from one form of
faith to another: 'Is a religion coming to birth in our time? It could be. What
seems to be occurring is a phenomenon we might call "passing over", passing
from one culture to another, from one religion to another. Passing over is the
shifting of standpoint, a going over to the standpoint of another culture, another
way of life, another religion.'[8] Although, for Dunne, this also meant 'coming
back' with new insights to one's own culture, the process he describes is essentially one of turning east.

The principal point, however, is that, from the 1960s on, there has been a
sharp rise of interest in all things Eastern and, as Daniel Bell has noted (rather
dismissively), the emergence of a 'multiplicity of exotic consciousness-raising
movements – the Zen, yoga, tantra, *I Ching*, and Swami movements – which
have spread so quickly among the *culturati*'.[9] Numerous surveys support this
assessment. For example, if we go back to 1977, one Gallup Poll recorded that
'4 per cent of the population [of the USA] said they currently practiced Transcendental Meditation, 3 per cent practiced yoga, 2 per cent said they were
involved in mysticism, and 1 per cent claimed membership of an Eastern religion.' However, the figures for those under the age of thirty, including college
graduates, 'were approximately twice as high as in the population as a whole'.[10]
Since then there has been a steady increase in those believing in, for example,
karma and reincarnation. We have seen that recent surveys consistently discover
that 'around 20 per cent of the population of Western countries answer "Yes" to
the question "Do you believe in reincarnation?"'[11] We have also noted that some
surveys indicate that a quarter of Europeans and North Americans believe in
reincarnation.[12] Quite simply, there has been a substantial increase 'since the
middle of the twentieth century when British surveys found figures of 4 per cent
and 5 per cent'.[13]

It is arguable, therefore, that it is not simply a case of Western youth and *culturati* turning east, but, more radically, a case of the West undergoing a massive cultural, religious, and intellectual 'passing over' from Western to Eastern ways of being. This is essentially the 'Easternization thesis' advanced by Colin Campbell. His argument is that 'the traditional Western cultural paradigm no longer dominates in so-called "Western" societies, but that it has been replaced by an "Eastern"one. This fundamental change may have been assisted by the introduction of obviously Eastern ideas and influences into the West, but equally important have been internal indigenous developments within that system, developments which have precipitated this "paradigm shift".'[14]

This chapter discusses both the general turn east and also the Easternization thesis in particular. We will see that, on the one hand, Kipling's claim at the head of the chapter is, on several levels, simply wrong, and yet, on the other hand, the Easternization thesis, whilst valid in a limited sense, is also flawed. Rather, what we are witnessing in the West is not a general process of Easternization, but rather the emergence of neo-Romanticism, an aspect of which is mysticization, partly characterized by the turn east. This, again, can be understood in terms of occulture.

East Meets West

For centuries, of course, there has been contact between East and West. Whilst much of this interest was limited to trade, travel writing, and missionary endeavour, it eventually led to the beginnings of a 'scientific religious' interest in Eastern religions and cultures.[15] Towards the end of the eighteenth century, scholars such as Sir William Jones and Thomas Colebrooke began the study of Sanskrit. Indeed, as early as 1785 Charles Wilkens completed his translation of the *Bhagavadgita*, the first full-length translation of a Sanskrit text into a Western language. In 1808 Friedrich Schlegel published his *Language and Wisdom of the Hindus*, 'a book whose influence on the Romantic Movement in Germany is said to have been profound and far-reaching'.[16] A decade later, in 1818, Schlegel became the first Professor of Sanskrit at the University of Bonn, followed in 1832 by H.H. Wilson, the first Boden Professor of Sanskrit at the University of Oxford. That said, a 'scientific religious' interest in the East is very different from '*turning east*', in that Westerners can be academically interested in Eastern faith and culture without thinking that the East might have anything of value to offer to them. Hence, although several notable eighteenth- and nineteenth-century philosophers, including Schelling, Herder, and Hegel, were attracted to Eastern philosophies, particularly Vedanta, they seemed to treat them as inspirational articulations of *their own* ideas. That is to say, they were, perhaps, not directly influenced by Eastern ideas, but rather simply interpreted them as exotic parallels to their own. For example, because Hegel's 'absolute idealist' concept of 'Spirit' or 'Mind' in *The Phenomenology of Spirit*[17] is quite distinct from a Western, Christian notion of God who stands over against the created order, being far closer to Eastern monistic philosophies, he referred to the Vedanta as 'exalted idealism'. Rather than turning east, he discovered Western idealism in the East. Again, in a way not dissimilar to Hegel's early thought, Schelling, who understood God to develop in the successive ideas that humans form of the divine, argued that knowledge of God should be sought throughout the history of religions. However – although we see similar, but explicitly Eastern theses being developed at the end of the nineteenth century by the Theosophical Society, Vivekananda, and Dharmapala – the origins of Schelling's thought are to be found, not in the East, but, again, in Western idealism and its antecedents.

Having said that, there are nineteenth-century thinkers who can be described as, in some limited sense, turning east. There is, for example, more than a little support for Radhakrishnan's claim that 'Schopenhauer was greatly influenced by Buddhist ideals'.[18] Again, as Wilhelm Halbfass says, in his radical critique of fundamental themes in Judaeo-Christian theologies, Schopenhauer 'showed an unprecedented readiness to integrate Indian ideas into his own, European thinking and self-understanding, and utilize them for the illustration, articulation and clarification of his own teachings and problems'.[19] That said, although he may have addressed his followers as 'we Buddhists', as Gananath Obeyesekere notes,[20] he was 'interested in Vedanta and Buddhism equally'.[21] Indeed, it is even arguable that the principal Eastern influence on Schopenhauer's thought did not come from Buddhist texts, but rather from Anquetil du Perron's Latin translation of the Upanishads. As Nicol MacNicol has commented, 'These utterances of the Indian spirit seem to have so affected him as to determine from thenceforward the direction and tone of his teaching. He has himself described how profoundly he was affected when this new planet swam into his ken, even though those voices of the Indian sages reached him as a dim echo in a version that was twice translated, first from the original Sanskrit into Persian and then from Persian into Latin.'[22] That said, again, even with Schopenhauer, MacNicol notes that 'his sense of the unreality of the whole context of time and history as a creation of *maya*' may not have 'actually derived from that [Upanshadic] source', but was rather 'confirmed by what he found there'.[23] Indeed, certain key ideas within Schopenhauer's thought can be traced back to Schelling, the principal philosopher of the Romantic circle. Nevertheless, it is certainly true that Schopenhauer's study of Indian thought was an important moment in the West's reception of the East. 'German transcendentalism,' notes Radhakrishnan, 'was affected by Indian thought through Schopenhauer',[24] as well as later through Hartmann and Nietzsche. Indeed, Richard Wagner, having encountered Buddhism in the writings of Schopenhauer, later claimed to have 'unconsciously become a Buddhist'.[25] Of course, it should again be noted that much of what was passed on to German transcendentalism was far less Indian than it was Romantic and Western.

A more significant and concrete example of the West turning east came at the end of the nineteeth century with the founding, in 1875, of the Theosophical Society, which combined and introduced to the West Buddhist and Hindu spirituality in particular,[26] and, in turn, informed subsequent generations of alternative religionists.[27] That said, it should be noted that even Theosophy is fundamentally Western. That is to say, Theosophy is not Eastern thought in the

West, but Western thought with an Eastern flavour. For example, with reference to reincarnation, Wouter Hanegraaff is quite right to insist that

> progressive spiritual evolutionism was far more central than the belief in reincarnation *per se*. [Blavatsky] certainly did not adopt evolutionism in order to explain the reincarnation process for a modern western audience; what she did was assimilate the theory of *karma* within an already-existing western framework of spiritual progress ... It is not the case that she moved from an occidental to an oriental perspective and abandoned western beliefs in favour of oriental ones. Her fundamental belief system was an occultist version of romantic evolutionism from beginning to end ... [28]

Indeed, even today, as Malcolm Hamilton has noted, very few of the respondents to a recent study of reincarnation in England 'were interested in the idea of dissolution of individual identity. Many of those who professed a belief in reincarnation linked it to a very Western and modernist notion of self and identity that is individualistic and reflexive.'[29]

The turning east of the West, however, has not been solely dependent on the efforts and interests of Westerners. For many years there have been far more authentic sources of Eastern wisdom in the West. Beginning in the nineteenth century, numerous Eastern teachers have travelled to the West to disseminate their wisdom. The first Buddhist to visit Britain, Dharmapala (a former disciple of Olcott), arrived for five months in 1893, making return visits in 1896 and 1904.[30] Also important for Buddhism in the West was D.T. Suzuki's eleven-year sojourn in America from 1897 until 1908, following which his disciple, Nyogen Senzaki, founded Zen Buddhist groups in California from the 1920s to 1950s. In 1907, the Buddhist Society of Great Britain and Ireland was formed and a year later Ananda Metteyya and three Burmese monks arrived in Britain. Although the Buddhist Society of Great Britain and Ireland only lasted until 1924, in that year Christmas Humphreys founded the Buddhist Lodge of the Theosophical Society, which eventually, in 1943, became the Buddhist Society.

Not only did the first Buddhist visit Britain in 1893, but, in that year, Narendranath Datta, better known as Vivekananda,[31] founder of the Ramakrishna Mission, attracted great attention and became enormously popular following his appearance at the World Parliament of Religions in Chicago. As well as travelling the length and breadth of India, Vivekananda toured America and Europe, teaching the divinity of humanity and service to the poor. Significantly, during the four years he spent in the West he came to appreciate Western science and technology, believing it able to make a significant contribution to human physical well-being. This is significant because he was also convinced that for Westerners to progress spiritually they needed to turn east. Hence, Vivekananda was perhaps the first to argue that the East and the West have distinct strengths to offer humanity, an argument which subsequently entered Western consciousness and became the conviction of many during the 1960s: a key feature of progress will be the combining of Western technology with Eastern spirituality. This, of course, is an essentialist myth.[32]

The Significance of the 1893 World Parliament of Religions

The East was naturally well represented at the 1893 World Parliament of Religions, and not only by Vivekananda and Dharmapala, but also by the members of a range of faith traditions from Zoroastrianism to Shinto,[33] as well as by Western groups such as the Theosophical Society. Indeed, this gathering is worth discussing here because, far from being an obscure and insignificant meeting of the *culturati* with an arcane penchant for interfaith relations, it has a particular importance, in that it is, as Richard Roberts comments, 'generally credited with having introduced Eastern world religions to the United States in ways which were to have a growing impact on the level of mass culture and society, rather than upon a small eccentric or academic elite'.[34] More significant still is its place in the history of alternative spirituality, in that we see flowing from the confluence of the Liberal Protestant, Indian and Theosophical streams dominant at the Parliament key alternative religious currents emphasizing religious essentialism,[35] immanentism, and the significance of the self[36] – all of which, of course, had already been developed in the West (particularly within Romanticism).

Interestingly, although the prime movers of the Parliament were all Christian, its lasting impact was less so. On the one hand, Charles Carroll Bonney, a Swedenborgian who was less narrowly Christian than many of his contemporaries, insisted that the object of the gathering 'was to unite all Religion against irreligion; to make the Golden Rule the basis of this union; (and) to present to the world... the substantial unity of many religions in the good deeds of the religious life'.[37] He hoped that 'when the religious faiths of the world recognized each other as brothers, children of the one Father, whom all profess to love and serve, then, and not until then, will the nations of the earth yield to the Spirit of concord and learn war no more'.[38] On the other hand, another key mover, the Revd John Henry Burrows, pastor of the First Presbyterian Church in Chicago, a self-confessed 'Liberal Christian', was, unlike Bonney, explicit in his commitment to the superiority of the Christian faith as the universal religion: 'The idea of evolving a cosmic or universal faith out of the Parliament was not present in the minds of its chief promoters. They believed that the elements of such religion are already contained in the Christian ideal and the Christian scriptures.'[39] As Marcus Braybrooke notes, Burrows 'based his argument on the evolutionary theory of religion, whereby "lower" forms of religion are absorbed into a "higher" religion. Eventually these "higher" religions will be assimilated to the religion of Christ... Christianity was the "universal religion", the Bible the "universal book", and Jesus Christ the "universal man and saviour".'[40] The perspectives of both Bonney and Burrows, which reflect the Christian Romantic/idealist themes at the beginning of the century, are evident in the following ten purposes of the Parliament:

1. To bring together in conference, for the first time in history, the leading representatives of the great historic religions of the world.
2. To show men, in the most impressive way, what and how many important truths the various religions hold and teach in common.

3. To promote and deepen the spirit of human brotherhood among men of diverse faiths, through friendly conference and mutual good understanding, while not seeking to foster the temper of indifferentism, and not striving to achieve any formal and outward unity.

4. To set forth, by those most competent to speak, what are deemed the important distinctive truths held and taught by each religion, and by the various chief branches of Christendom.

5. To indicate the impregnable foundations of Theism, and the reasons for man's faith in Immortality, and thus to unite and strengthen the forces which are adverse to a materialist philosophy of the universe.

6. To secure from leading scholars, representing the Brahman, Buddhist, Confucian, Parsee, Mohammedan, Jewish and other Faiths, and from representatives of the various Churches of Christendom, full and accurate statements of the spiritual and other effects of the Religions which they hold upon the Literature, Art, Commerce, Government, Domestic and Social life of the peoples [among] whom these faiths have prevailed.

7. To inquire, what light each religion has afforded, or may afford, to other religions of the world.

8. To set forth, for permanent record to be published to the world, an accurate and authoritative account of the present condition and outlook of Religion among the leading nations of the earth.

9. To discover, from competent men, what light Religion has to throw on the great problems of the present age, especially the important questions connected with Temperance, Labor, Education, Wealth and Poverty.

10. To bring the nations of the earth in a more friendly fellowship, in the hope of securing permanent international peace.[41]

Hence, whilst there are tensions between Bonney's pluralistic universalism and Burrows' evolutionary Christian fulfilment theology, the end product was an overall philosophy which was basically in accord with both Romanticism and the Liberal Protestant emphasis on 'the fatherhood of God and brotherhood of humanity'. However, the significance of the Parliament is that, on the one hand, central elements of Romanticism were affirmed, and on the other hand, the Christian paradigm was challenged by an Eastern paradigm. The theological presuppositions of the Western *Christian* quest for unity were particularly questioned by Vivekananda – significantly, the speaker now most often associated with the Parliament. Whilst, like Bonney and Burrows, Vivekananda also set forth a vision of unity and universalism so evident within Romanticism, at the centre of his vision was not Christianity, or indeed any form of theism, but Vedantic Hinduism.[42] Hence, whilst Vivekananda's teaching appealed to the Romanticism and Liberalism of many of the Christians present – and indeed was eagerly received by them – it was explicitly *non*-Christian. Many present would have agreed with Vivekananda – as would Hegel, Schleiermacher, and Schelling, had they been there – that we should 'not care for doctrines … for dogmas or sects or churches or temples; they count for little compared with the essence of existence in each man which is spirituality'. And the following statement is not only consonant with Bonney's thesis, but sits comfortably with those of Hegel and Schelling: 'Every religion is only an evolving of God out of material man. The same God is the inspirer of all.'[43] However, whether it was fully understood by all present or not, for Vivekananda, Hinduism, not Christianity, had fully articulated the truth about the essential nature of things. Monism, not theism, describes reality; it is not simply that human souls are infinitely valuable, as Romanticism and Liberal

Protestantism insisted,[44] but that the human self is divine, immortal, and eternal.[45] Of course, Vivekananda was not the only attendee to hold such views. Dharmapala presented a similar thesis (although, for him, the universal religion was Buddhism and some of his concerns were strikingly nationalistic, even jingoistic[46]), and the Theosophists, antipathetic to Christianity, provided an eclectic, Western occultic version of Indian thought. This is clearly evident in Blavatsky's summary of the principal religious themes of the Theosophical Society:

> (1) To form the nucleus of a Universal Brotherhood of Humanity without distinction of race, colour, or creed. (2) To promote the study of Aryan and other Scriptures, of the World's religion and sciences, and to vindicate the importance of old Asiatic literature, namely, of the Brahmanical, Buddhist, and Zoroastrian philosophies. (3) To investigate the hidden mysteries of Nature under every aspect possible, and the psychic and spiritual powers latent in man especially.[47]

In the final analysis, such detraditionalized spirituality (which is now a significant feature of the Western religious lanscape), or what Linda Woodhead terms 'the New Spirituality', began to emerge during this period 'through the simultaneous retention, radicalization, and rejection of key themes in [Liberal] Protestantism'.[48] In particular, Woodhead quite rightly draws attention to the fact that

> it radicalized and subverted liberalism's belief in evolutionary progress towards a new universal religion and culture by broadening the category of those who would be able to participate in this new religion to include women and other races, and by denying that this new universal religion would be Protestant. And it rejected what it referred to as Liberal Protestantism's 'dualism', its belief in a theistic God and a sinful creation wholly separate from this God; in its place it offered a more 'scientific' monism which exalted each individual and gave moral and metaphysical underpinning to the idea that all was truly part of the 'One'.[49]

In other words, what she describes is the Easternization of Western Liberalism. Unfortunately, however, she does not significantly account for the Romantic elements already present in Western Liberalism, elements which easily absorbed Eastern ideas – that is, absorbed them into a *Western philosophical system*. Consequently, she suggests a process of accommodation in which Eastern thought is consciously expressed in Western terms in order to be heard: 'the necessary price for a public voice and public influence at the end of the nineteenth century ... was assent to some of the fundamental values of mainline Protestant culture ... [Even] the most radical proponents of the New Spirituality echoed the belief in progress and the ideal of religious unity, as well as in the values of industry, individualism and service.'[50] My understanding is slightly different, in that what we actually see is a conceptual shift taking place in which broadly parallel Western ideas are embracing their Eastern counterparts. Indigenous ideas of progress, evolution, immanence, individualism, and religious unity, which, although promoted by Liberalism, were not limited to Christianity, were ideal receptor concepts for Eastern ideas. Sympathetic Western philosophies welcomed and absorbed their Eastern counterparts as exalted and exotic versions of themselves. We have already seen that the very Eastern doctrine of reincarnation was simply grafted onto the Western idea of progress.[51] The idea of progress itself (the gradual improvement and, particularly, the perfection of the human individual and society), which is evident in eighteenth-century Enlightenment thought – some would say even earlier[52] – and can be found throughout the nineteenth century,[53] simply appears in an Easternized form in Theosophical thought. Again, there are strong similarities between the essentialism of Western Romanticism and that of some forms of Indian philosophy. Glyn Richards, for example, is right to point out that 'from an idealistic standpoint [Vivekananda] propounds an essentialist view of religion not dissimilar to that of Schleiermacher ... The universal religion of Vivekananda is not far removed from the primordial essence of religion found in the writings of Schleiermacher.'[54] Similarly, both immanentism and progress are developed in Hegel's teleological philosophy of history. Understood as the evolution of 'Spirit', it not only describes systematic linear progress from primitive humanity to advanced Western society and culture, but, as we have noted, the Hegelian understanding of 'Spirit' or 'Mind' reflects Vedantic philosophy. Later during the nineteeth century Absolute Idealism became particularly influential, with notable thinkers such as David Friedrich Strauss, Ferdinand Christian Baur, F.H. Bradley, Josiah Royce, and Edward Caird developing immanentist philosophies which shared many of the central ideas of Eastern thought. Again, here we see traditional Christian theism rejected, divine–human dualism challenged, and monism, if not embraced, certainly approached. For example, as Alan Sell notes, 'by arguing that nature, humanity and God are all expressions of one spiritual principle, [Caird] blurred the Creator–creature distinction so vital to orthodox [Christian] theology, and left himself open to the charge of pantheising'.[55] In other words, at the time of the Parliament, an important stream of Western philosophy is already conceptually Eastern. The themes being developed do not testify to a process of direct, unilateral Easternization, but rather to the exposition of Western Idealism.

Again one of the most widely read Christian books of the period, whilst not absolute idealist, was F.D. Maurice's 1845 Boyle Lectures, *The Religions of the World in their Relations to Christianity*, which understood humanity as 'a universal and spiritual society' and all religions to have genuine revelation within them. For Maurice, historical religions must have something more to them than the priesthood, human doctrines, and 'falsehood': 'If they have lasted a single day, it must have been because they had something better, truer than themselves to sustain them.'[56] Indeed, as Kenneth Cracknell notes with reference to Maurice's comments on the relationship between Christianity and Buddhism, 'he coined two phrases: "the Buddhist side of Christianity", and "Christian Buddhism". The ideas of complementarity and mutual fulfilment lying behind such phrases are central to Maurice's theology of religion.'[57] Similarly, with reference to the Parliament, Max Müller asserted that it 'established once and for all ... that the points on which the great religions differ are far less numerous, and certainly far less important, than are the points on which they all agree'.[58] Not only would Vivekananda have agreed with this, but, more important, so too would several notable late-Victorian Christians, including missionaries.[59]

Hence, Vivekananda travelled to the West during a period in Anglo-American religious and philosophical history when there was a growing interest in the East,[60] when the Christian mind was beginning to be opened up by the modern encounter of religions, when Absolute Idealism was having perhaps its greatest impact, and when the idea of evolutionary progress was coming to the fore. The point is that the dominant indigenous ideas in the West, many of which characterized the theology of the Parliament, were particularly receptive to a certain type of Eastern thought, a type that, fortunately for Vivekananda, he taught.

A Revolution of Consciousness:
The Sacralizing Significance of the 1960s

Particularly interesting for this study is the fundamental continuity that exists between this nineteenth-century interest in the East and what emerges in the countercultural revolution of the 1960s. As good a description as any of what I understand this continuous spiritual thread to be is Woodhead's description of 'the New Spirituality'. That said, what follows should be treated with a little caution and understood more as a mapping of tendencies than a definitive description. It is all too easy to slip into reifying, essentialist definitions, which do not reflect the heterogeneous nature of living spirituality. Hence, not all the features listed below will be manifested at the same time or to the same degree.

> … in all its forms [it] is *detraditionalized* in the sense that it rejects any form of religion which locates authority in a source which transcends the individual – whether that be God, scriptures, a particular community, its rituals, sacraments or priesthood. Instead, authority is characteristically located in the heart, feelings, intuition or experience of each individual. In more metaphysical terms, the New Spirituality is therefore *radically immanent*. It views everyday or phenomenal reality as a manifestation of a deep and unifying spirit or life-force, a stance which may also be described as *this-worldly monism*, for it maintains both that 'All is One', and that it is through the phenomenal world (natural and human) that we gain access to 'the One'. It is therefore characteristic of the New Spirituality to *divinize the human and the natural*. Furthermore, the New Spirituality's continual stress on unity gives rise to a *universalist stance* in relation to other religions and cultures, all of which are viewed as potentially one by virtue of their common ability to bear witness to 'the One'. Finally, the New Spirituality tends to be strongly *optimistic*, *evolutionary* and *progressive*, maintaining that a new age of unity, peace and spiritual enlightenment is currently dawning.[61]

The point argued in this section is that any overall religio-philosophical continuity needs to be understood in terms of neo-Romanticism. Whilst we will see that much late-modern alternative spirituality is Easternized Western religious thought, this needs to be understood in the context of a prominent stream of Western Romantic Idealism which has, for over two centuries, expounded an optimistic, evolutionary, detraditionalized, mystical immanentism.

We have seen that the roots of contemporary re-enchantment reach back at least as far as the late nineteenth century, particularly the *fin de siècle*, a period during which, as Paul Heelas notes, 'many turned to the scores of esotericists or occultists who were catering for the demand. Others … developed more theologically and philosophically informed versions of… "the contemporary rebirth of mysticism" or "union of the self with God".'[62] However, interesting and important though this period is as far as Easternization is concerned, for several good reasons some academic studies of religion in Western societies have noted the particular significance of the 1960s for the turn east. (Other major studies, such as Arthur Marwick's *The Sixties*, have fundamentally ignored it, thereby leaving a rather large hole in their otherwise comprehensive analyses of the decade.[63]) Of the sociological reasons posited, one of the more obvious is the fact that immigration from the East to America and Britain increased dramatically after 1965. In America, the quotas limiting immigration were removed from the Immigration Act in 1965 and, in the same year, many East African Hindus travelled to Britain joining other Indians who were then migrating directly, especially from Gujarat. More specifically, this migration also included several Indian gurus, most notably, in 1965, Bhaktivedanta Prabhupada, who arrived in New York and, in 1966, founded the International Society for Krishna Consciousness (ISKCON). From the 1960s there has been a steady flow of Eastern teachers visiting the West, founding organizations and attracting Westerners to India. Some, because of their presence within popular culture, moved from relative obscurity in India to being almost household names in the West.

Other reasons, including the decline of Christian belief and influence, the rise of countercultural movements,[64] the proliferation of alternative spiritualities, and the widespread political and religious idealism, make the 1960s a particularly important decade.[65] Moreover, much 1960s thought and activism was suffused with spirituality. Timothy Miller, for example, in his study of counterculturalism in the 1960s, admits that having a separate chapter on religious and spiritual groups is a little artificial, since 'a great swath of 1960s counterculturalists considered their lives and works spiritual in nature'.[66] Understandably, therefore, some have identified the 1960s, rather than 1945 or earlier, as a decade of particular importance for the rise of *new* religious movements. For example, whereas, for several reasons, I apply the term 'new' rather broadly to 'a religion, sect or alternative spirituality that emerged or *rose to prominence* during the 20th century',[67] and others limit it to religions which have appeared since 1945,[68] or 'since the 1950s',[69] there are those, such as Elisabeth Arweck, who argue that 'New Religious Movements (NRMs) – or cults, as they are popularly known – emerged as a new phenomenon in the late 1960s and early 1970s. They are mainly associated with Western societies and with the counter-culture of the 1960s.'[70] Although this definition is qualified a little later to include 'religious groups and movements which have emerged since the Second World War', the emphasis is still on the rise 'to prominence in Western societies in the late 1960s and early 1970s'.[71] However, my point in this section is not to debate the relative merits and demerits of this definition of 'new', but simply to analyse the significance which some attach to the 1960s as the decade which saw the emergence of a type of religion, the teachings of which 'were on the whole of a syncretic and eclectic nature, drawing from various traditions and belief systems'.[72]

Approaching the decade from a different angle, in his recent study of religion in Britain, Callum Brown identifies 1963 as the crucial year for the decline of Christianity and the rise of the 'secular condition':[73]

> For a thousand years, Christianity penetrated deeply into the lives of the people, enduring Reformation, Enlightenment and industrial revolution by adapting to each new social and cultural context that arose. Then, really quite suddenly in 1963, something very profound ruptured the character of the nation and its people, sending organized Christianity on a downward spiral to the margins of social significance. In unprecedented numbers, the British people since the 1960s have stopped going to church, have allowed their church membership to lapse, have stopped marrying in church and have neglected to baptise their children ... The cycle of inter-generational renewal of Christian affiliation, a cycle which had for so many centuries tied the people however closely or loosely to the churches and to Christian moral benchmarks, was permanently disrupted by the 'swinging sixties'. Since then, a formerly religious people have entirely forsaken organized Christianity in a sudden plunge into a truly secular condition.[74]

Again, driven in part by popular culture, attitudes and worldviews shifted significantly away from traditional Christianity:

> In the 1960s, the institutional structures of cultural traditionalism started to crumble in Britain: the ending of the worst excesses of moral censorship (notably after the 1960 trial of *Lady Chatterley's Lover* and the ending in 1968 of the Lord Chamberlain's control over the British theatre); the legalization of abortion (1967) and homosexuality (1967), and the granting of easier divorce (1969); the emergence of the women's liberation movement, especially from 1968; the flourishing of youth culture centred on popular music (especially after the emergence of The Beatles in late 1962) and incorporating a range of cultural pursuits and identities (ranging from the widespread use of drugs to the fashion revolution); and the appearance of student rebellion (notably between 1968 and the early 1970s).[75]

While I obviously question Brown's claim that Western societies have taken 'a sudden plunge into a truly *secular* condition', his point regarding the significance of the 1960s as a decade in which, for a variety of reasons, steps were taken away from institutional Christianity and toward countercultural alternatives is important. However, his understanding of religion in the 1960s is incomplete because, in charting the decline of Christianity, he fails to analyse emergent alternative religious vitality. Campbell reflects the religious nature of the shift more accurately:

> The cultural upheaval of the 1960s and the associated growth of new religious and spiritual movements has presented the sociologist of religion with particularly acute problems of analysis and interpretation. Prior to this decade, the image of modern society that was most widely accepted was one in which secularization, variously conceived, was considered to be the prevailing feature, although it was recognized that this process did not proceed unevenly and could be interrupted by periods of religious revival such as occurred in the United States in the mid-fifties. The various phenomena, such as the rise of Eastern religion, the occult revival, the astrology craze and the new Pentecostalism, which can collectively be called the 'new religiosity', did not, on the face of it, fit into this picture. For they did not resemble the standard pattern of religious revivals, as they were all too often in stark opposition to the churches and denominations, while at the same time, it required a fairly convoluted form of argument to maintain that such movements were evidence of continuing secularization.[76]

The point for us to note is that it is not so much a case of certain beliefs emerging as 'a new phenomenon in the late 1960s and early 1970s' (Arweck), but rather that there was, as Campbell says, 'a widespread acceptance of ones which formerly had been confined to a minority'.[77] It is this shift that dates from the 1960s, when such previously exotic beliefs 'were espoused by the significant and influential minority who comprised the counter-culture'.[78] Moreover, it was a shift that was increasingly obvious to astute thinkers and social commentators such as George Steiner who, in 1974, bemoaned the drowning of the Western culture he loved in a sea of premodern irrationalism: 'ours is the psychological and social climate most infected by superstition, by irrationalism, of any since the decline of the Middle Ages and, perhaps, since the time of the crisis in the Hellenistic world.'[79] Wuthnow's study of American religion since the 1950s also identifies the 1960s as being the key decade in this respect, in that it saw the 'decline of a spirituality of dwelling and ... the rise of a spirituality of seeking'.[80] The 1960s and 1970s 'provided new opportunities', says Wuthnow, for people 'to expand their spiritual horizons. The 1960s began with Christian theologians declaring that God was dead; it ended with millions of Americans finding that God could be approached and made relevant to their lives in more ways than they had ever imagined ... New religious movements of Asian origin, such as Zen and Hare Krishna, spread in metropolitan areas, as did the humanistic spirituality of such groups as Esalen, EST [*sic*], and Scientology.'[81] Similarly, Wade Clark Roof speaks of the emergence of a 'quest culture'.[82] The key point to note is that the 1960s saw the widespread and eclectic acceptance of older beliefs which were previously considered exotic, many of which, as Campbell argues, whether literally Eastern or not, conformed to an Eastern paradigm.

In a fairly short period of time, the West witnessed the 'de-exotification' of a range of 'Eastern' beliefs and practices. Much of this was directly due to popular culture and what became known as the psychedelic revolution (which will be discussed more fully in Chapter 7). Whereas certain privileged individuals such as Aldous Huxley and Gerald Heard had previously 'confined the distribution [of psychedelics] to a hand-picked coterie of the gifted and influential',[83] this was not the case for the man Allen Ginsberg called 'a hero of American consciousness ... faced with the task of a Messiah',[84] namely Timothy Leary. Motivated to a great extent by Leary's drive and charismatic personality, the sixties psychedelic revolution quickly became a large and influential subculture.[85] The term 'psychedelic', originally coined by Humphrey Osmond (1917–2004) in a letter to Huxley, became common currency and rapidly expanded to include all forms of culture which were thought to inspire, or to be inspired by, the use of hallucinogens and, more often than not, explicitly Eastern religious thought.[86] During the 1960s and early 1970s a great deal of time and creative energy was invested in the production of particularly music and visual art which would encourage successful psychedelic experiences. Hence, largely as a result of popular culture, the 1960s saw the flowering of Eastern-influenced psychedelic spirituality. Whether one thinks of bands such as The Incredible String Band, The Grateful Dead, The Velvet Underground, early Pink Floyd, The Doors (who took their name from the sacred text of the sixties, Huxley's book *The Doors of Perception*[87]), and even Led Zeppelin,[88] or records such as The Beatles' *Sergeant Pepper's Lonely Hearts Club Band* (the cover of which, it is worth noting, includes images of Mahatma Gandhi, Sri Yukteswar, Sri Lahiri Mahasaya, Sri Paramahansa Yogananda, Aleister Crowley, and Huxley), or the work of writers such as William Burroughs, Jack Kerouac, Hunter S. Thompson, and Allen Ginsberg, or the vibrant poster art of the period, it all reflected the impact of hallucinogens and Eastern-influenced religious thought.[89]

Reflecting on the sixties, the American Buddhist master Richard Baker Roshi makes the following comment: 'We were in San Francisco right in the middle of the whole scene from '61 on. What Suzuki-Roshi and I noticed was that people who used LSD – and a large percentage of students did – got into [Zen] practice faster than other people... My feeling is that psychedelics create a taste for a certain kind of experience.'[90] This experience, of course, is one of immediacy and self-authentication. Surya Das makes a similar observation: 'I think it is interesting to note that when I get together with my fellow Western dharma teachers, and we consider how our personal paths began (in this life at least) – very few willingly disclose that they actually entered the dharma through the portal of drugs, and the writings of A. Huxley, C. Castaneda, Ram Dass, T. Leary, R.D. Laing, etc. Yet I feel quite certain that psychedelic experience has been a great gate to the dharma for many of our generation.'[91] This was certainly the experience of Ranchor Prime, now a member of ISKCON:

> I was an art student at Chelsea Art College on the King's Road, so I was quite at the hub of things, that was in 1969. I was experiencing the freedom of being out there in society, an art student, and I found I very quickly lost faith in the materialistic sort of life. I was looking for something deep, something spiritual and of course in common with all my friends of that generation we experimented with drugs, LSD and so on. Although I know that there's a negative side to that, one of the things that it did for us was it really opened our minds, it sort of expanded our awareness... I think at that time, the East held a tremendous appeal to young people, the 'Mystic East'. It provided a tremendous spiritual tradition but one which was different to the West. My first contact with Krishna was through the musical *Hair*. It had arrived in London sometime in 1970 and one of the centrepieces of the musical was the whole cast dancing on stage and singing 'Hare Krishna'. My sister bought the record and it really caught my imagination. I used to sing 'Hare Krishna' without really knowing what it was about. Around the same time the Hare Krishna devotees had arrived in London and recorded a track with The Beatles. [I suspect he is thinking of George Harrison's 'My Sweet Lord',[92] rather than a Beatles song.] Everyone started singing it.[93]

That the shift towards the East is particularly apparent in the popular music of the period is evident from the fact that it is now difficult to think of the music of the late 1960s and early 1970s without also thinking of alternative spirituality to some extent. Again, one only has to look at album covers produced during this period to see the shift to the East and to psychedelia. For example, a personal favourite of mine is The Incredible String Band's *The 5000 Spirits or the Layers of an Onion*,[94] painted by Simon Postuma and Marijke Koger, two Dutch artists known as The Fool. The cover, which, as Robert Pendleton notes, 'became an instant psychedelic classic',[95] mixes Eastern and particularly Pagan symbolism. Indeed, it gives one a very clear sense of late-1960s eclectic, spirituality-infused culture. Pendleton describes it well: 'The composition is dominated by a winged Janus-headed hermaphrodite, embodying the eternal polarities of dark and light, male and female, life and death. Around this figure surge the great cyclic forces of growth and decay; stars and planets whirl in their courses; and strung across this phantasmagoric scene like a line of psychedelic washing are the swirling letters of THE INCREDIBLE STRING BAND.'[96] Again, The Beatles at the end of the sixties are commonly associated with Maharishi Mahesh Yogi, the founder of Transcendental Meditation, there being several popular photographs of The Beatles with the Maharishi. Indeed, one that springs to mind pictures the Maharishi in India surrounded by, amongst others, Paul McCartney, John Lennon, George Harrison, Jane Asher, Mia Farrow, and Donovan.[97] Another popular photograph taken by Linda McCartney pictures the Beach Boys sitting at the feet of the Maharishi.[98] This turn east, of course, quickly found its way into lyrics. Brown, for example, has analysed the lyrics of The Beatles and records the significant move away from the typically romantic pop songs of their early period to esoteric, psychedelic, and spiritually inspired compositions:

> The lyrics of all of the 49 songs copyrighted by The Beatles during 1963–4 were about boy–girl romance. Beatles lyrics then changed radically, with romance dropping to 83 per cent of their 1965 lyrical output, 40 per cent of 1966 output, and a mere 5 per cent of 1967 output. Despite a slight rise (to 14, 11 and 20 per cent) in the final three years of their existence, romance had been displaced by complex and varied lyrical themes influenced by amongst other things the anti-war movement, drugs, nihilism, existentialism, nostalgia and eastern mysticism.[99]

While Brown marshals such evidence simply to support his thesis regarding the decline of Christianity, arguing that 'by 1970 ... secularization was ... well under way',[100] as noted above, he also seems, by sleight of hand, to broaden his claim to religion *per se*. As I have noted above, this is problematic. Although the 1960s was a particularly significant decade for the decline of institutional Christianity, not just in Britain but throughout the Western world, the claim that a shift towards thoroughgoing secularization was the end product is less convincing. There was undoubtedly drift from the churches, which continues apace. But we have noted that the 1960s also saw the emergence of a countercultural idealism in which important and vital forms of alternative spirituality flourished.

Lemmy (Ian Kilmister) – formerly a bass player in Hawkwind and the founding member of Motörhead – while clearly unimpressed by 'talk about the cosmos and shit', which he now finds 'boring',[101] nevertheless makes the following interesting comment: 'One thing I am very glad of is that I went through the sixties. People who didn't, really don't know what they missed. We pushed a certain consciousness, a way of life and it was exciting – no AIDS, people weren't dying so much of drug abuse and it was truly a time of freedom and change.'[102] This was the post-war period of utopian idealism, of free love, of religious and political optimism, of recreational, intellectualized, sacralized, experimental drug use, of talk about bright countercultural futures, of a New Age in which 'tomorrow's people' (as Jeremy Sandford and Ron Reid called them) – attractive, healthy, free, uninhibited, peaceful individuals of the Aquarian age – would live as one. Indeed, the title page of Sandford's and Reid's *Tomorrow's People*[103] (an early account of the British festival scene) is instructive, in that it shows happy teenagers and twenty-somethings running and dancing across a field, clapping hands, laughing and playing instruments. There is no industry, no suits, no institutions, no law enforcement, no hierarchies, no disease, no disability, no drug addiction, no unhappiness. It is hippie heaven; a utopian vision of 'tomorrow's people'; a vision of society as carnival. However, the point is that, although critical of traditional organized religion, for many of these people the 'tomorrow' they had in mind was not secularized. Hippie heaven was populated by spiritual people. Even Lemmy bemoans the prospect of 'our brave new world... becoming less tolerant, *spiritual*, and educated than it ever was when I was young'.[104] However it was perceived, 'spirituality' was an important part of the consciousness of 'tomorrow's people'. As one of Jonathon Green's 'voices from the English underground', Su Small, pointed out, this was a time when people 'renounced the accepted religions and went off and started new ones'.[105] Again, Nicholas Saunders provides another interesting snapshot from the period: 'Gandalf's Garden was a shop with two big windows... [where] you could... have some sort of herb tea and there would be a room downstairs where they would have meetings and all sorts of different people – not just one guru but all sorts of different people – would give mystical enlightenment talks, or meditation talks – anything in that area, very broad. And it was all free.'[106]

In short, the 1960s saw the stream of alternative religious thought, which had for many years flowed underground, begin to surface and seep into popular culture, and permeate Western popular consciousness. Many had their presuppositions challenged and even overturned by *explicitly* Eastern ideas. Fritjof Capra provides a good illustration of this shift from a set of basic Western presuppositions to an Eastern worldview in his influential book *The Tao of Physics: An Exploration of Parallels between Modern Physics and Eastern Mysticism*. He recalls that, having 'become very interested in Eastern mysticism' in the 1960s, he was helped on his way by 'power plants' (i.e. psychoactive plants), which showed him 'how the mind can flow freely' and 'how spiritual insights come on their own, without any effort, emerging from the depth of consciousness'.[107] He then goes on to relate how he sought 'to overcome the gap between rational, analytical thinking and the meditative experience of mystical truth'. In particular, he relates a hallucinogen-induced, Easternized experience which, in 1969, led him to write *The Tao of Physics*:

> I was sitting by the ocean one late summer afternoon, watching the waves rolling in and feeling the rhythm of my breathing, when I suddenly became aware of my whole environment and being engaged in a gigantic cosmic dance. Being a physicist, I knew that the sand, rocks, water and air around me were made of vibrating molecules and atoms, and that these consisted of particles which interacted with one another by creating and destroying other particles. I knew also that the Earth's atmosphere was continually bombarded by showers of 'cosmic rays', particles of high energy undergoing multiple collisions as they penetrated the air. All this was familiar to me from my research in

high-energy physics, but until that moment I had only experienced it through graphs, diagrams and mathematical theories. As I sat on that beach my former experiences came to life; I 'saw' cascades coming down from outer space, in which particles of energy were created and destroyed in rhythmic pulses; I 'saw' the atoms of the elements and those of my body participating in this cosmic dance of energy; I felt its rhythm and I 'heard' its sound, and at that moment I *knew* that this was the Dance of Shiva, the Lord of the Dancers worshipped by the Hindus.[108]

The thesis that *The Tao of Physics* goes on to argue eloquently is that 'Eastern mysticism provides a consistent and beautiful philosophical framework which can accommodate our most advanced theories of the physical world'.[109] In particular, Capra is keen to demonstrate that contemporary physics is in accord with 'the central aim of Eastern mysticism', namely 'to experience all phenomena in the world as manifestations of the same ultimate reality'. He continues, 'This reality is seen as the essence of the universe, underlying and unifying the multitude of things and events we observe… This ultimate essence… cannot be separated from its multiple manifestations. It is central to its very nature to manifest itself in myriad forms which come into being and disintegrate, transforming themselves into one another without end. In its phenomenal aspect, the cosmic One is thus intrinsically dynamic, and apprehension of its dynamic nature is basic to all schools of Eastern mysticism.'[110] Capra's insistence on the ontological priority of the One over the many provides a good illustration of the religio-cultural shift described by the Easternization thesis. The mind of a Berkeley physicist, trained at the University of Vienna, is 'Easternized' and the Western knowledge gained is reconceptualized and viewed from a mystical perspective. Indeed, the bibliography in *The Tao of Physics* illustrates the shift well. Along with a selection of books of a scientific nature, there are far more books which are explicitly spiritual/mystical, including D.T. Suzuki's and Alan Watts' volumes on Buddhism, all of Carlos Castaneda's books on Yaqui Indian shamanism (or at least all those published when Capra completed *The Tao of Physics*), Maharishi Mahesh Yogi's translation of the *Bhagavad Gita*, Vivekananda's *Jnana Yoga*, Fung Yu-Lan's *A Short History of Chinese Philosophy*, Lama Anagarika Govinda's *Foundations of Tibetan Buddhism*, William Blake's *Complete Writings*, the *Tao Te Ching* and the *I Ching*. That said, although Capra's thought is a clear manifestation of the impact of the East, it should also be noted that his writings (including those since *The Tao of Physics*) show him to be a Westerner less interested in devotion to a particular Eastern tradition than a spiritual seeker interested in developing an eclectic style of alternative spirituality that can just as easily work with Zen or the *Bhagavad Gita* as it can with Blake or Castaneda. Indeed, in more recent works, Capra is more neo-Romantic, focusing on 'a new rise of spirituality, particularly a new kind of earth-centred spirituality'.[111]

Nevertheless, although this eclectic mix of Eastern and Western traditions should be borne in mind, and although the 1960s was a maelstrom of conflicting political, psychedelic, cultural and spiritual influences, the East scented it all. This East-oriented eclecticism, often driven by popular culture, is brought out beautifully in the account of the origins of Auroville by Savitra:

A snow-balling collage of events thunders through the tableau of the sixties ... Drugs suddenly appear – the luminous and the deadly – pouring into the converging streams, bringing another dimension to the process, pushing the revolution off the streets and into the chemistry of human consciousness. The kaleidoscope jars and the khaki-clad image of Che Guevara transposes into the figures of Leary and Huxley and Alan Watts, the credo turns from Marxist dialectics to the wanderings of Castaneda. A decade looking everywhere, opening all the doors, trying everything, all the keys, the shiny ones and the rusty, all the experiments and all the exaggerations of the experiment in that first, initial surge, swinging madly to the extremes in order to resist the formidable undertow – the counterpull of the past that would level everything, drag everything under – the gravity of the Trance. Hair lengthens, overflows or goes ascetic and bare; clothing eccentrifies, cross-breeds or dissolves; and mass music becomes an instrument of change, a ballad of the birth and struggle, a *mantra* of the moment, provocative and energizing, vital and violent, breaking the old records of His Master's Voice, the same monotonous melody dipped in syrup or mud, sticky and stuck.

And slipping in somehow amidst the turbulence of the inrushing Western tide, a faint essence of the East. The infiltration of incense, perhaps at first not so much for atmosphere as to cover the smell of grass; the sounds of the sitar through hybrid compositions of Bud Shank and Paul Horn, The Beatles and Yehudi Menuhin; and the gradual influx of a new jargon trickling into our linear language, a terse vocabulary snatched from the Sanskrit and Tibetan and Japanese that seemed more at home, more fluent, more familiar with the states and transitions through which we were passing; experiences for which our cultural dialect, derived from a unilateral rationalism, had no equivalent terms, no corresponding nomenclature.

Incense, ragas and a handful of migrant, mystic syllables. The innocuous symbols of a Revolution far more radical and dangerous, far more potent than all its surface renderings, than all the revolvings of the Earth and the stars and the flickering insurrections of men. A Revolution fundamentally subversive which finally none can resist: a takeover from Within. A Revolution of Consciousness.[112]

From the late 1960s on it would be difficult to find a Westerner who is unaware of karma, reincarnation, meditation,[113] *yin* and *yang*, or who is not familiar with symbols such as ☯ or ॐ. At the Parliament of World Religions we see a confluence of the streams of Eastern thought and Western Liberalism, and in the 1960s we see these streams widening and deepening. Dualism is challenged, immanentism is championed, reality is One, the self is deified, and reincarnation is a real possibility. Detraditionalized religion goes mainstream. The philosophies, techniques, and icons of religious traditions contribute to a process of spiritual *bricolage* in which a range of beliefs and practices are reinterpreted in terms of the experience and well-being of the seeking self:

Rising interest in Eastern faiths like Buddhism, Taoism, Hinduism, and Sufism is part of the broader move toward experiential spirituality. Eastern spirituality is grounded in what could be called 'heart knowledge', rather than 'head knowledge', of the sacred. The practice of Eastern forms of mysticism, such as meditation, does not require the same kind of loyalty to an exclusive belief system as Christianity and Islam often does. In the new millennium, many practitioners of Eastern meditation techniques will continue to see themselves as Christian, Jews, or 'none of the above'.[114]

By the late-1970s, Indian-influenced clothes, artwork, and trinkets had become very common, certainly amongst the people I knew. I have fond memories of the time spent travelling in Israel and North Africa in the early 1980s, during which I met numerous Westerners going east in search of spirituality – some of whom had been travelling since the 1960s (or so they claimed). Again, in Britain, some friends attended the local *satsangs* of the Divine Light Mission (now Elan Vital) and hung photographs of Maharaji (Prem Pal Singh Rawat) on their walls.[115] Although fundamentally Western, in their search for spirituality they had turned east.

Western Teachers in Eastern Traditions

One of the most conspicuous manifestations of Easternization has been the increasing number of Western teachers in Eastern traditions. That is to say, not only are increasing numbers of Westerners turning to Eastern spiritual teachers such as Maharaji and texts such as the Upanishads or the *I Ching* for guidance, but significant numbers are themselves becoming teachers of Eastern religion. Initially, of course, as Andrew Rawlinson points out in his seminal study of the phenomenon, Eastern thought was 'propounded by Easterners: Buddhists, Hindus, and Sufis'. But, he notes, 'gradually Westerners began to teach the Buddhist, Hindu, and Sufi versions of it. Of course, Eastern teachers are still important; but now Westerners are doing the jobs and fulfilling *all* the roles. They are the gurus and masters now.'[116] He continues: 'A century ago there were no Western masters – no Westerners who were Hindu *swamis*, Zen *roshis*, or Sufi *sheikhs*. Now there are hundreds. From a standing start, the West has produced its own spiritual teachers and traditions that were originally quite foreign. And in the last 25 years, a number of independent teachers have appeared, who belong to no tradition but teach from themselves.'[117] Moreover, says Rawlinson, '*Western* teachers need to be taken seriously' because 'they are the leaven in Western culture – and they are changing it.'[118] As to how they are changing Western culture, they are doing so, he claims, 'by making available a view of the human condition which is new in the West'.[119] In other words, Rawlinson identifies a 'spiritual psychology', which, in one form or another, is central to the thought of such Western gurus. It is, he says, based on four principles:

- Human beings are best understood in terms of *consciousness* and its modifications.
- Consciousness can be transformed by *spiritual practice.*
- There are *gurus/masters/teachers* who have done this …
- They can help others to do the same by some form of *transmission.*

There are a great number of variants of all of these.

- *Consciousness* can be seen as divine, as intrinsically pure, or as 'empty'.
- *Spiritual practice* ranges from solitary observation of the movement of the mind to temple worship and social activism.
- *Masters* can be quiet or ecstatic, trying to change the world or quite indifferent to it.
- *Transmission* ranges from formal initiation to a glance from the eye of the beloved.

We are dealing with more than a set of ideas here. These four principles, taken together, make up a way of life. I call it 'spiritual psychology' because it is concerned with the spiritual life but is based on the fundamental notion of consciousness.[120]

Rawlinson's analysis is insightful and provides another way into understanding the Easternization of Western culture. However, as I have argued above, it is also important to understand that Eastern spirituality is not parachuted unchanged into Western culture. Even Vivekananda's thought did not remain purely Eastern when taught in a Western context. It is inhistorized, inculturated, contextualized. It should, therefore, come as no surprise to learn that the spirituality taught by Western gurus and masters is distinct from that taught by their Eastern counterparts: 'a genuinely Western form of this teaching is emerging because it is only in the West that the different Eastern forms have come together so that they can be compared'.[121] Indeed, it is significant, not only that 'the West presently contains a greater variety of spiritual teachers than has ever existed in any previous time or place', or that 'hundreds of thousands of Westerners' now accept some form of this spiritual psychology, but also that 'there is more exploration going on in Los Angeles and London than there is in Tokyo or Benares'.[122] Western teachers of Eastern beliefs and practices 'are doing all the things that Eastern teachers do [and] quite a lot more besides; they are both in the tradition and also extending it'.[123] This, I would argue, is not simply because of the religiously plural context (which is also very evident in the East), but more particularly because Eastern thought is being processed in Western minds, shaped as they are by a late modern context, an eclectic, *bricolage* approach to religion, and neo-Romanticism.

Easternization? Problems and Proposals

While much of the above no doubt comes to mind when one thinks of 'Easternization', it is worth reminding ourselves that Campbell's understanding of the concept is much broader, in that he invests the term 'Eastern' with a great deal more than simply traditional conceptions of the oriental. Indeed, he invests it with a great deal that is, strictly speaking, *not* Eastern. 'I do not,' says Campbell, 'simply mean the introduction and spread within the West of recognizable Eastern "imports", whether these are products, such as spices, yoghurt and silk, practices such as yoga and acupuncture, or complete religious systems such as Hinduism and Buddhism.'[124] Whilst these are, he argues, contributing factors to the Easternization of the West, in the final analysis there needs to be something more broad-based and substantial than this in order to bring about a cultural shift on the scale we are currently witnessing:

> the introduction of 'foreign' elements such as these into an indigenous socio-cultural system may do little or nothing to change the fundamental nature of that system. They may simply be absorbed or assimilated without effecting any significant change. Indeed, these cultural imports may themselves become radically transformed as a consequence of their introduction into a new society; or, indeed, their transformation may be required before they can be successfully accommodated.[125]

As we have already noted, the thesis Campbell advances is that 'the traditional Western cultural paradigm no longer dominates in so-called "Western" societies, but… it has been replaced by an "Eastern" one. This fundamental change may have been assisted by the introduction of obviously Eastern ideas and influences into the West, *but equally important have been internal indigenous developments within that system, developments which have precipitated this "paradigm shift".*[126] His understanding of this shift is principally informed by, on the one hand, Troeltsch's discussion of mystical religion and, on the other hand, Weber's distinction between Eastern and Western worldviews.

Because there are a number of fundamental dichotomies between Eastern and Western thought, the turning east of the West requires a massive shift, which includes, at its most basic level, 'the abandonment of the traditional Western conception of the divine as transcendent and personal and its replacement by a view of the divine as immanent and essentially impersonal'.[127] Moreover,

> [the] Eastern model favours the Troeltschian religion of mysticism … with its belief in the polymorphous nature of truth, its syncretism and individualism. In addition, the Eastern concept of spiritual perfection or self-deification replaces the Western idea of salvation, the notion of a Church is replaced by a band of seekers attached to a spiritual leader or guru, while the distinction between believer and unbeliever is replaced by the idea that all beings exist on a scale of spirituality, a scale which can extend beyond this life.[128]

A very similar understanding of Eastern and Western worldviews was outlined by the psychologists Albert Gilgen and Jae Hyung Cho when, in 1979, they produced a questionnaire to measure Eastern and Western thought in order to determine the extent to which contemporary American beliefs are compatible with Eastern perspectives.[129] The Eastern perspective, operating with a non-dualistic worldview, was defined in the following way:

> (a) man and nature are one; (b) the spiritual and the physical are one; (c) mind and body are one; (d) man should recognize his basic oneness with nature, the spiritual, and the mental rather than attempt to analyze, label, categorize, manipulate, control, or consume the things of the world; (e) because of his oneness with all existence, man should feel 'at home' in any place and with any person; (f) science and technology, at best, create an illusion of progress; (g) enlightenment involves achieving a sense of oneness with the universal; it is a state where all dichotomies vanish; and (h) meditation, a special state of quiet contemplation, is essential for achieving enlightenment.[130]

The Western perspective, on the other hand, operates with a fundamentally dualistic worldview and produces the following specific beliefs:

> (a) man has characteristics which set him apart from nature and the spiritual; (b) man is divided into a body, a spirit, and a mind; (c) there is a personal God who is over man; (d) man must control and manipulate nature to ensure his survival; (e) rational thought and an analytic approach to problem solving should be emphasized; (f) science and technology have given us a good life and provide our main hope for an even better future; and (g) action and the competitive spirit should be rewarded.[131]

As Campbell notes, a modified version of the above, which lists the following 'styles of thought', was produced by David Krus and Harold Blackman (see Table 2):[132]

Table 2. *Krus and Blackman's table of categories pertaining to East–West styles of thought*

East	West
synthesis	analysis
totality	generalization
integration	differentiation
deduction	induction
subjective	objective
dogmatic	intellectual
intuition	reason
anti-science	science
personal	impersonal
moralistic	legalistic
non-discursive	assertive
affiliative	power
ecstasies	order
irrational	rational
imaginative	critical

Such stark categorization, whilst helpful in some respects, does highlight several weaknesses with the Easternization thesis. Indeed, Malcolm Hamilton has recently argued that Campbell's work is fundamentally flawed in several respects. The principal problems he identifies are as follows: 'Firstly, it is founded upon a misleading stereotypical characterisation of Eastern religions. Secondly, it is insensitive to the many and marked differences between Eastern religions. Thirdly, it too readily accepts these developments as unequivocally *religious*. Fourthly, it tends to ignore or to be unable to deal with the very inner-worldly character of trends within Western thinking.'[133] Finally, he also makes the point that it 'overlooks the way in which Eastern traditions or elements of them are modified in the process of importing them into the West'.[134]

To take the first couple of Hamilton's criticisms, whilst Campbell does not pretend to offer a phenomenological analysis of religion in the East, but rather seeks to identify dominant trends,[135] his thesis is nevertheless founded upon a misleading stereotypical characterisation of Eastern thought. Campbell does operate with a caricatured, essentialist notion of Eastern religion, which fails to account for its enormous diversity. Likewise, the lists drawn up by Gilgen and Cho and Krus and Blackman, which Campbell makes use of, fail to account for the heterogeneous plurality of Eastern and Western theologies and spiritualities. For example, on the one hand, not all *Eastern* spiritualities can be characterized as immanentist, monist, subjective, and intuitive, and, on the other hand, we have seen that important traditions of *Western* religious thought can. Again, without even considering Eastern faiths such as Zoroastrianism, which is rigorously dualist, there are theistic developments within Hinduism itself that resist monism. For example, Ramanuja vigorously refutes the monism of Shankara, the most famous Advaita philosopher.[136] On the other hand, as Aldous Huxley was keen to point out,[137] whilst clearly distinct, there are significant areas of overlap between the mysticisms of the Western Christian thinker Meister Eckhart and Shankara.[138]

Hence, the Easternization thesis tends to adopt the popular, but nevertheless erroneous, position that all Eastern philosophy, whether Indian or not, is essentially monistic and pantheistic, emphasizing the reality of the One over the many. Indeed, relying far too heavily on Max Weber's outdated categorisation of the East–West divide, he makes the following flawed statement: 'the Eastern religious world-view rejects dualism altogether, with the world viewed as a completely connected and self-contained cosmos. Thus, that contrast between the sinful natural and spiritual supernatural, so much a feature of Western religion, is rejected; for all the natural world is permeated with spirituality. This then is the fundamental East–West divide.'[139]

That said, the thesis is not irreparably damaged by this flaw. The problem is more terminological than terminal, in that, on the one hand, a paradigm shift similar to that identified by Campbell *is certainly taking place*. On the other hand, 'Easternization' may not be the best term for it. In other words, Campbell has identified an empirically verifiable shift,[140] but, operating with a faulty and outdated notion of Eastern religion, has misleadingly labelled it 'Easternization'. 'Mysticization' might perhaps be a better term, in that it indicates roughly the same shift, but does not rest on a misleading dichotomy between the East and the West. As I have already pointed out, the intellectual currents identified at the beginning of this chapter and in previous chapters suggest that much of this mysticization should be understood as part of broader process of neo-Romanticism.

Having said that, the term 'Easternization' is a useful one, though it needs to be used in a more discriminating way than Campbell does. Western seekers are treading religious paths and constructing their spiritualities from ideas that are explicitly Eastern. Whether one considers the influence of the Theosophical Society, or the increasing numbers of Westerners who accept some form of Eastern belief – such as karma, reincarnation, and *chakras* – or who practise specifically Eastern therapies – such as acupuncture or *feng shui* – or the ubiquity of Eastern symbolism and iconography in popular culture – such as pictures and statues of the Buddha, the Shiva Nataraja (the dancing Shiva), and symbols such as ☯, ✹, ॐ – or the growing popularity of daily exercises such as yoga or *t'ai chi*, it is difficult to ignore the Easternization of Western culture, if not the Easternization of consciousness. Hence, whilst it is phenomenologically true to insist that there are 'many and marked differences' within Eastern religions, and whilst simplistic discussions of the East–West divide should be challenged by scholars of religion and culture, even the most cursory analysis of the West could not fail to identify Easternization at some level. Indeed, it would be extremely odd if this were not the case. As Hamilton notes, 'religious and spiritual ideas might travel in all directions; Western ideas to the East and Eastern ideas to the West. Easternization is, in this respect, simply the other side of the coin of Westernisation.'[141] Such an exchange of influences between cultures has always been the case in human history, and increasingly so as a result of globalization.[142]

This brings us back to the qualification Campbell introduces into the thesis: 'by Easternization, I do not simply mean the introduction and spread within the

West of recognizably Eastern "imports", whether these are products, such as spices, yoghurt and silk, practices such as yoga and acupuncture, or complete religious systems such as Hinduism or Buddhism'.[143] Although he understands such 'imports' to be significant factors in the process of Easternization, as they obviously must be, we have seen that he insists that 'equally important must have been internal indigenous developments... developments which have precipitated this "paradigm shift" '.[144] Again, there are two ways of looking at this. On the one hand, my initial discussion in this chapter suggests that Campbell is right to locate sympathetic indigenous developments within the receptor culture, developments that have precipitated 'Easternization'. On the other hand, if there are Western components of the process which are at least as important as Eastern components, why label the whole process 'Easternization'? Again, if the burden of the shift is the broad category Troeltsch identified as the religion of mysticism, 'with its belief in the polymorphous nature of truth, its syncretism and individualism, [and its] concept of... self-deification',[145] why not simply use a more accommodating term for the broader process, such as 'mysticization'?

Examples of Campbell's inappropriate extension of the Easternization thesis beyond that which is explicitly Eastern can be found in his consideration of 'the recent history of the two major intellectual systems which comprise Western culture; that is Christianity, and secular progressivism, especially as manifest in Socialism and Marxism. Both of these two great theoretical systems of the West have shown clear signs of a shift towards an Eastern paradigm.' If it were not already obvious to the reader, he concedes that 'the major influence in both cases [is] not Eastern thought as such, but German Idealistic philosophy'.[146] He continues to point out that in the former case we see it developed in modern Protestant theology, and in the latter case we see it developed in the work of social and political philosophers such as Marcuse and the Frankfurt School. The first led to the New Theology and the Death of God movement, the second to the New Left. But, again, can such movements and trends be described as manifestations of *Easternization*? Take modern theology, for example. Whilst Campbell was right to declare in his 1978 article that 'the *Honest to God* controversy and the associated "New Theology" in Britain and the "Death of God Movement" in America both served to popularize ideas and attitudes consonant with a mystical and spiritual philosophy of religion',[147] this is very different from claiming they are the result of Easternizing forces. Much of the thought he identifies can be traced back to German Romanticism and Idealism. Tillich, for example, was particularly influenced by Schelling, on whose thought he wrote two doctoral dissertations. The following representative quotation from Tillich's work clearly betrays this Idealist influence: 'Where we use symbolic terms like "ground of being" we mean that we experience something that is an object of our ultimate concern, which underlies everything that is, is its creative ground or its formative unity, and cannot be defined beyond these negative terms.'[148] Hence, it is hardly a convincing argument to claim that because Tillich's theology suggests a move towards panentheistic and holistic understandings of divine–human relations it is, therefore, Easternized. Whilst it is certainly true that there are those within the theological community who are critical of dualism and seek to move towards more holistic models and methodologies, and whilst it is true that Tillich was one who did attempt to synthesize an essentially mystical and panentheistic (note, *not* pantheistic) conception of God as the 'ground of being' with a Christian theistic conception of God as personal and transcendent, in the final analysis, his theology is less indebted to Eastern spirituality than to Western philosophy and theology – particularly Jakob Boehme, Schelling, Friedrich Schleiermacher, and Troeltsch. Indeed, Tillich himself claimed that his spiritual father was Schleier-macher, his intellectual father was Schelling, and his grandfather on both sides was Boehme.[149] Hence, although there are similarities between Tillich's thought and some forms of Eastern mysticism,[150] in that, for example, there is an emphasis on immanence and, related to this, no hard and fast line of demarcation between the sacred and the secular,[151] there was actually no need for Tillich to turn east in order to develop a sophisticated immanentist theology, or indeed, should he have wished to do so, a pantheist philosophy in which divine personality is sub-ordinated, if not absent. He would have seen all he needed facing west. From Spinoza to Goethe, from Schelling to Schleiermacher, from Coleridge to Emerson, from Hegel to Teilhard de Chardin, from Henri Bergson's *élan vital* to Jan Smuts' holism, from Blake to Whitehead – there are numerous Western theological and philosophical resources.[152]

It is instructive that even those explicitly seeking to develop New Age spiritualities do not feel that they necessarily need to turn East – though, of course, most do at some point. For example, in a survey of alternative religionists conducted by the influential New Age theorist Marilyn Ferguson, 'When respondents were asked to name individuals who had influenced them, either through personal contact or through their writings', the most frequently mentioned name was the French Jesuit theologian and palaeontologist Pierre Teilhard de Chardin.[153] Indeed, of all the people most frequently mentioned, only Krishnamurti is explicitly Eastern – and even his thought is arguably Westernized.[154] Western philosophy and theology are no strangers to mystical immanentism.[155] As noted at the outset, whilst some Western thinkers, such as Hegel, Schelling, Schopen-hauer, and, in America, Emerson, Thoreau and Whitman, may have identified parallels between their own philosophizing and Eastern thought, and, in some cases, even drawn upon it,[156] their own ideas are nevertheless fundamentally Western, rather than Eastern.

The point is that, not only must Campbell's essentialist approach to Eastern thought be challenged, but so also must the methodology that searches out anything vaguely resembling 'Eastern' thought in order to include it within a process of Easternization. That a belief appears Eastern does not mean that it is Easternized or Easternizing. To claim that it is diverts attention away from other significant sources for Western spirituality. To reiterate the point, although Campbell's central thesis is that a fundamental shift has taken place (and, indeed, is still under way), and although in many cases there has been an explicit East-ernizing of Western thought and culture, and although significant streams of alternative religiosity do have an 'Eastern feel' to them, much contemporary spirituality needs to be understood in terms of neo-Romanticism, rather than explicit Easternization.[157]

This, it seems to me, is not merely another tedious academic quibble over terminology, but concerns an accurate understanding of the roots of Western sacralization. For example, Campbell's account of spiritual environmentalism and nature religion in terms of Easternization, rather than Western Paganism and Romanticism, seems forced, even Procrustean and skewed. Although we have seen that Easternization – understood narrowly as explicitly Eastern concepts and styles travelling west and the sympathetic West turning east – has fundamentally affected large areas of Western religion and culture, and is therefore crucial to any account of Western re-enchantment, it is only part of a larger process which includes, amongst other things, the neo-Romantic turn to the natural, the indigenous, and broadly speaking, the occult. Hence, in short, Easternization is part of a larger shift towards mystical immanentism in the West, which is, in turn, part of a general process of neo-Romanticization. Whilst Easternization is a useful concept, it needs to be used in such a way that it avoids caricature and essentialism, and is limited to that which is *explicitly Eastern*.

Quasi-Religion, Instrumental Activism, and Syncretism

We are now in a position to address briefly Hamilton's final three points: first, Campbell too readily accepts that which he has identified as part of the Easternizing process 'as unequivocally *religious*'; secondly, the thesis 'tends to ignore or to be unable to deal with the very inner-worldly [i.e. this-worldly] character of trends within Western thinking'; finally, the thesis 'overlooks the way in which Eastern traditions or elements of them are modified in the process of importing them into the West'.[158] To begin with the final point, the central thrust of the argument of this chapter has been that, not only does the process of importing Eastern ideas lead to modification, but the context in which the modification takes place is the occultic milieu, a central stream of which is neo-Romanticism. We have seen that Eastern beliefs, practices, and styles are not parachuted into Western culture unchanged, but are rather absorbed into sympathetic, indigenous belief systems and subcultures. As they are absorbed they change shape. Just as the religio-cultural milieu they enter is Easternized, the Easternizing elements are themselves Westernized. The process is one of syncretism. They are inhistorized, inculturated, contextualized, detraditionalized.

Hamilton's second point, of course, follows from that just made. His argument is as follows:

> While some Eastern currents of thought have adopted an inner-worldly orientation, they have been for the most part other-worldly in ethos and when they have not, their inner-worldliness … has been … markedly apathetic and non-activist in total contrast to the ethos of most Western adaptions and borrowings from such traditions … What seems to be entirely absent from this allegedly Easternized ethos is any sense of the value of renunciation which is so much a part of many Eastern traditions and, most notably, of the more philosophical and virtuoso dimensions of those traditions which, rather than folk and popular forms, have had some appeal among the spiritual intelligentsia of the

West. Renunciation is not even an ideal in the West, not even admired in the few who are successful in practising by those who are not, as is often the case in the Eastern traditions.[159]

It is not so much that certain Eastern streams of occulture are this-worldly, but more that the sea change in Western culture that Campbell is suggesting is not evident at the level of renunciation. But is it true that the West is simply not into renunciation? Are there not streams flowing through Western culture and occulture that do have renunciation as an ideal? On the one hand, the general shift towards the seeking of 'well-being' and health strongly emphasizes renunciation in some form, in that, for example, a range of practices from macrobiotic eating to fasting are not unknown. On the other hand, disciplined 'spiritual' practices from yoga to *t'ai chi*, although clearly located within Western culture, do mark a significant level of renunciation. Overall, the increasing emphasis on the significance of the self and on that which can nurture the health of the self, physically, psychologically, and spiritually, is bringing with it a belief in the value of renunciation. This is evident in Kimberly Lau's excellent study of New Age consumerism:

> The pursuit of health and wellness runs deep in the texts and textures of contemporary daily life in the United States ... Suggestions for healthy living are regular features on television and radio programs and in magazines and newspapers. As a popular and fundamental part of everyday life, the pursuit of health and wellness is dispersed from the specialized realm of medical doctors and Western biomedicine to the broader domain of alternative strategies for holistic living.[160]

She continues,

> exercise regimes are made of Eastern philosophies through the conversion of holistic practices like yoga and *t'ai chi*. Belief systems become healthy, low-impact exercises as well as training advantages for professional football and basketball players ... Superfoods derived from vaguely identified traditions of herbal medicine and special diets based on ancient and/or remote non-Western cultures suggest themselves as cures for everything from the common cold to cancer ... If you don't practice yoga or t'ai chi, you probably know someone who does. If you haven't had an aromatherapy massage, a friend has probably told you where – and especially why – to get one. Perhaps you follow a strict macrobiotic diet or maybe you have tried one of the macrobiotic options at the Ritz Carlton while on vacation ... Implicit in popular discourses surrounding aromatherapy, macrobiotic eating, and yoga and t'ai chi is the belief in personal transformation through alternative, non-Western paradigms of health and wellness.[161]

With reference to Robert Cantwell's thesis in *Ethnomimesis: Folklore and the Representation of Culture*, she points out that 'through physical and sensory "ethnomimesis" – that is, the imitation of another culture's traditions and practices – the rhetoric of holistic living is both operationalized and internalized'.[162] The point here is that this operationalizing usually requires some level of discipline and renunciation. Indeed, the individual's spirituality may evolve into that which involves relatively high levels of renunciation.

Hamilton is, of course, quite right to note of the health and fitness movement that 'it is as if spiritual goals are attainable through the material; the spiritual is redefined in terms of material regimes and disciplines; salvation through the body rather than through the soul'. That said, it is perhaps going too far to insist that 'while there may be some affinities here with Taoist thought it is, nevertheless, profoundly Western' in that, again, it is important to remember that health and spirituality in the West is very often a *bricolage* project. It is not simply Western, let alone *profoundly* Western, but also Eastern. Whilst admittedly spiritualities of life and well-being rarely lead to the austerity of Tibetan monastic life, a distinction between the East and the West cannot be made as easily as Hamilton and Campbell suggest.

Although there is obviously no blanket shift in Western culture towards an 'Eastern' form of other-worldliness (not that there is a single Eastern form of anything), when we turn from spiritualities of well-being to particular organized religions and spiritualities within occulture there is clear evidence of renunciation and discipline. Numerous small groups practise some form of renunciation, even if it is only abstinence from certain foods. Think, for example, of the Breatharians. Led by Jasmuheen, the group controversially claimed that it was possible to live on 'pranic nourishment' (i.e. light) without having to eat food. Indeed, Jasmuheen claimed to have done so for several years and, as Lynne Hume comments, 'gained some notoriety in the 1990s when media reports highlighted this claim after three people had died attempting to simulate Jasmuheen's practice'.[163] Hence, it would seem that some not only idealize renunciation, but are willing to practise extreme and austere forms of it. This may not be renunciation as it is in the Eastern tradition, and one would not expect it to be. Apart from reports that Jasmuheen never actually practised it to the extent she claimed, many who did follow her did so as part of an otherwise Western, consumerist, and spiritually eclectic lifestyle. Nevertheless, it is still renunciation with an Eastern flavour.

A more typical example of a disciplined lifestyle of renunciation can be found in the Heaven's Gate UFO group. In an attempt to withdraw from the world, several levels of renunciation, including, for example, celibacy, were strongly encouraged. Indeed, it was taught that sexual desire *per se* was the result of demonic coercion. In the words of one member, 'The "lower forces" have succeeded in totally addicting humans to mammalian behaviour. Everything from ads for toothpaste to clothing elevates human sexuality. Being from a genderless world, this behaviour is extremely hideous to us.'[164] The idea of being genderless and, particularly, celibate is understood in terms of purity. Hence, whilst Heaven's Gate thinking is typically eclectic, this aspect of their thought has more in common with certain streams of the Western Christian tradition than with Eastern religion. That is to say, celibacy in the East is not understood in quite these terms. For example, in Buddhism, the monastic code of discipline requires celibacy because 'sexual activity expresses quite strong attachment, and uses energy which could otherwise be used more fruitfully'.[165] However, the point is that a group which siphoned from the occultural reservoir a range of Eastern and Western beliefs – most of which were made up of Theosophical and Christian elements – did encourage renunciation. The following Heaven's Gate prayer (to the founders of the group) illustrates this attitude of renunciation well:

I ask for your inner strength so that I may completely withdraw this vehicle from all the inner addictions of its animal flesh, and for your keenness so that I can block all thoughts or mental pictures of mammalian behaviour, and for your consistency in maintaining non-mammalian behaviour of the Evolutionary Level Above Human – around the clock – in order that my soul (mind) will be compatible with and able to occupy a genderless vehicle from the Next Kingdom Level.[166]

Again, Eastern groups, many of the members of which are Western, such as ISKCON, the Brahma Kumaris, the New Kadampa Tradition, the Self-Revelation Church of Absolute Monism, and Ananda Marga, do have renunciation as an ideal and admire those who are able to practise it. Indeed, living in a community such as ISKCON can be particularly austere, as can many of the short retreats that Westerners from across the religious spectrum increasingly go on. The point is that, whether we think of the spiritualities of well-being or the emphasis on the health of the self, it is simply not true to say that 'renunciation is not even an ideal in the West'. It may need to be understood differently, but renunciation is certainly evident in contemporary Western religion and culture.

That said, it is also true that many Westerners adopt Eastern philosophies and techniques without also adopting the accompanying emphasis on, if not require-ment for, renunciation. And it is also true that, for the most part, Western culture *per se* is still fundamentally this-worldly. Hence, one would expect a Western worldview, even if thoroughly Easternized, to be, to some extent, this-worldly. Even when Westerners do eventually become renunciates within their chosen spiritualities, they often set out on their spiritual journey as seekers with a con-sumerist attitude to beliefs and practices from the world's religious traditions, and with little interest in world-denying austerity. At the outset, the Western seeker wants a sense of well-being, wants a healthy self, wants stress relief, wants an enhanced life – not pain and an austere lifestyle. However, that is not the same as *not* recognizing the value of renunciation, or *not* seeing renunciation as an ideal, or *not* accepting the essential truth of a world-denying philosophy.

Another perceived problem with the Easternization thesis is 'the problem of instrumental activism':

A true shift away from a Western paradigm would require a turning towards a more resigned, if not fatalistic, attitude towards the world on the part of individuals. That is to say, a rejection of that instrumental activism which has long been so characteristic of life in the West would have to occur. But is there any sign of this? Is not Western cul-ture still primarily world-affirming rather than world-denying in character? That the culture of the West is characterized by the pre-eminence accorded to instrumental activism has long been a taken-for-granted assumption in sociology.[167]

Of course, again, not all those in the East are resigned, fatalistic and unwilling to get involved in the affairs of the world in order to change it, develop it, and make the most of it, and not all those in the West are the opposite. That said, there is some truth to the following observation: 'in contradistinction to the value-profiles of other, more traditional cultures, where typically fatalist orientations prevail, modern American society is characterized by a "doing" activity orientation, one in which "getting things done" and "let's *do* something about it" are stock phrases.'[168] Does it look as if this orientation is shifting in the West? Generally speaking, the answer has to be negative. We have seen that, even when the doctrine of reincarnation is adopted in the West, it is often allied to a general doctrine of progress and a belief that one should better the self. Resignation and fatalism are very rarely found in Western alternative worldviews. They are far more often imbued with the spirit of instrumental activism: we should protect nature; we should develop the self; we should increase the health of mind–body–spirit; we should contribute to, rather than hinder, the cosmic process of spiritual evolution; we should do something about the state of the world. Even strong doctrines of predestination in hyper-Calvinism, whilst sometimes undermining Christian mission, do not entirely erode instrumental activism.[169] Hence, again, it would be surprising if Eastern beliefs did not change when residing in the Western mind. Indeed, it has to be said that Western instrumental activism seems particularly durable. For example, as John Brockington comments, whilst traumatic, the impact of British rule on India led, in due course, 'to the appearance of a series of religious and social reform movements, of which a feature …was its political aspect; social reform became less connected with religious attitudes and tended to generate political pressure groups, while religious reform took on a nationalist tone which in turn led to political involvement'.[170] The most notable such reformer was, of course, Rammohan Roy, founder of the Brahmo Samaj (in 1828) and often described as the father of modern India because of his role in its modernization and in the reformation of Hindu society and religion. As R.C. Zaehner writes of the Brahmo Samaj, 'its inspiration was Western. As in other parts of the world, Western civilization brought with it two distinct elements, the "philosophy" of progress based on the scientific revolution which looked for its philosophical justification to the eighteenth-century Enlightenment, and the Christian religion.'[171] Based on Western Christian reform movements and with a syncretistic religious worldview, the Brahmo Samaj, in its promotion of religious and social ethics, clearly demonstrates instrumental activism. Hence, the point is that, Easternization whatever else it means, will never mean the complete replacement of the Western mind with an Eastern mind. Because it is simply naïve to expect the wholesale replacement of one culture and worldview with another, religio-cultural colonialism will always be syncretistic. I suspect that instrumental activism, along with much else, will always be a feature of the West – Easternized or not.

A related area of perceived difficulty with the Easternization thesis which Hamilton notes concerns 'its assumption that the developments to which it refers are *religious* ones as opposed to certain tendencies in Western thought more broadly understood'.[172] As far as Hamilton is concerned, 'Some, at least, of these developments are better understood as representing a movement of thought away from religion *per se* and towards non-religious meaning systems, or for want of a better term, quasi-religion, rather than as change within the Western religious outlook.'[173] Similarly, Cox makes the following point:

> No deity, however terrible, no devotion, however deep, no ritual, however splendid, is exempt from the voracious process of trivialization. The smiling Buddha himself and the worldly wise Krishna can be transformed by the new gluttony into collectors'

trinkets. It was bad enough for King Midas that everything he touched turned to gold. The acquisition–accumulation pattern of the new gluttony does even more. Reversing the alchemist's course, it transforms rubies and emeralds into plastic, the sacred into the silly, the holy into the hokey.

The gods of the orient mean one thing there, and something quite different here. This is not to be blamed either on the gods themselves, or on their original devotees, or on the new seekers. It happens because when the god's migrate, or are exported to a civilization where everything is to some extent a commodity, they become commodities too.[174]

Again, on the one hand, little needs to be said about this simply because it is what one would expect in the West. Postmodern cultural pressures, argues Zygmunt Bauman, 'while at the same time as intensifying the search for peak experiences, have uncoupled the search from religion-prone interests and concerns, privatised it, and cast non-religious institutions in the role of purveyors of relevant services'.[175] On the other hand, the scholar ought to guard against patronizing and dismissive attitudes. As I have already discussed, just because something does not look like 'religion', or doesn't perform in the way the observer expects 'spirituality' to perform, or is acquired in a way not previously associated with 'serious religion', this does not mean that it can simply be labelled 'quasi-religion' or 'pseudo-spirituality'. (Indeed, the scholar might be guilty of quasi-understanding or pseudo-analysis.) It may be a case of spiritual *bricolage*, absorbing a range of ideas from occulture, and it may be practised in the service of the consuming self and in the pursuit of well-being, rather than, more self-sacrificially, in the service of others and of God, but there is a level of commitment and spirituality that cannot simply be passed off as a secular, *quasi*-religious alternative to presumably 'authentic', 'real', 'actual' religion. The dichotomy is false and betrays a failure to understand the complexity and significance of occultural spirituality. So, yes, some of it may indeed be quasi-religious, but a great deal may not. And, in the final analysis, it is difficult to determine either way from the *etic* perspective of the observer.

Concluding Comments

Hamilton, in his critique of the Easternization thesis, after noting that, as well as Eastern beliefs there are Pagan, esoteric and a range of other spiritual influences in the West, concludes by making the following point: 'What is striking, then, about the contemporary Western spiritual ethos is its extraordinary eclecticism... There does seem to be not only a plurality of influences, a supermarket of spiritual choices on offer but a clear proclivity not to choose any *one* of them. That is to say, not to make choices between them but to choose all or at least many of them.'[176] Whilst this is perhaps a rather obvious point, it does highlight the importance of stressing some of my own equally obvious points made earlier in the chapter. First, Easternization needs to be understood as part of a broader neo-Romantic, mysticizing religio-cultural stream in the West, which feeds into and drinks from the occultural pool. Secondly, Easternization should not be understood as the replacing of the Western mind with an Eastern mind, but rather as a syncretistic process whereby Eastern elements are absorbed into sympathetic

Western worldviews. Finally, Easternization should be understood to refer to the influence, absorption, import, or adoption of explicitly *Eastern* beliefs, ideas, and practices, not simply to that which looks vaguely Eastern, yet is more likely to have roots in explicitly Western traditions.

Chapter 6

POPULAR OCCULTURE: LITERATURE AND FILM

It would seem clear, without being overly speculative, that popular culture is a key sacralizing factor which has a far more influential role in the shaping and dissemination of contemporary occultural thought than is often acknowledged. As Michael Barkun has shown in relation to rejected knowledge – or, more broadly, what he prefers to term 'stigmatized knowledge'[1] – its 'volume and influence... have increased dramatically through the mediation of popular culture. Motifs, theories and truth claims that once existed in hermetically sealed subcultures have begun to be recycled, often with great rapidity, through popular culture.'[2] Of course, this should come as no surprise. On the one hand, such diffusion is, to a certain extent, not a new phenomenon.[3] On the other hand, the breathtaking spread of the electronic media, whether television, film, video games, music, or the Internet, has been central to modern cultural history. It is widely acknowledged that TV in particular, as part of the 'public sphere' (Jürgen Habermas), forms opinions and shapes attitudes. As David Lyon notes, 'TV helps to frame modes of interpretation and response to the social world by organizing experience in particular ways. Thus it has the effect of contributing to a sense of what the real world is all about.'[4] And with reference to Jean Baudrillard's work, he makes the further point that 'in fact the mass media also blur the boundaries of reality by creating a continuum from the self-confessedly fictional to the supposedly documentary'.[5] This, we will see, is clearly apparent in the reception history of science fiction and horror.

The following short analysis of popular culture is spread over two chapters. Beginning with an introduction to relevant aspects of the academic study of popular culture, this chapter focuses on literary and visual artefacts. Chapter 7 continues the discussion by focusing on the culture of popular music.

The overall treatment assumes a positive conception of popular culture, which firmly rejects the elitism of, for example, Theodor Adorno and Max Horkheimer. In particular, I do not make what I believe to be an artificial distinction between 'high' and 'low' culture, and nor do I suggest that 'mass culture' is necessarily superficial.[6] Indeed, the following discussion lends support to Jim McGuigan's cultural populist claim that 'the symbolic experiences and practices of ordinary people are more important analytically and politically [and, I would argue, spiritually] than culture with a capital C'.[7]

Popular Culture as Religious Text?

I want to begin my discussion of popular culture by commenting on a couple of issues raised by Gordon Lynch in *After Religion: Generation X and the Search for Meaning*.[8] In this short volume he takes issue with the American theologian Tom Beaudoin, who has likewise commented thoughtfully on Generation X and popular culture.[9] To summarize, Beaudoin argues that Generation X and popular culture are fundamentally related: 'GenX cannot be understood apart from popular culture, and much of popular culture cannot be interpreted without attention to Generation X.'[10] His point is that Generation X is the TV generation; the generation of children who had two busy, stressed, working parents (many of whom got divorced); the generation weaned on popular culture; the generation which, consequently, established an important relationship with electronic media. Moreover, this generational investment in popular culture happened at a time when it was undergoing a massive technological shift into the age of video recorders, digital media, and the Internet. The point is that, as Lynch notes, 'popular culture therefore developed new and exciting ways at precisely the point where a generation of children and teenagers were becoming more dependent on mass-produced popular culture as a focus for their energies and as a way of learning about the world'.[11] Popular culture became the air that this generation breathed, the principal pool of references and ideas from which they drank deeply. Similar points are made by other commentators, such as Donald Miller and Arpi Miller, who define Generation X as 'the 80 million Americans [or, less parochially, Westerners] who were born between 1961 and 1981. This is the "buster" generation, the children of the so-called baby boomers. While they are a diverse lot, they also share many common cultural experiences related to advances in technology, the failed marriages of their parents, changes in the structure of the economy, and the liberation politics that transpired during their childhood and youth.'[12]

Beaudoin, of course, goes beyond simply stating that popular culture provides an important frame of reference, and argues that it has spiritual significance, in that through it people explore values and meaning in life. While this assessment is generally sound and helpful, as Lynch goes on to note, Beaudoin does not stop there. Building on his argument about the religious significance of popular culture, he posits the thesis that the artefacts of popular culture function as texts. Any form of popular culture – book, film, song, dance, art work, fashion etc. – can function as a text. Although this is, of course, well-trodden ground in cultural studies, it is nevertheless a worthwhile point to make. The problem with Beaudoin's analysis is that his understanding of popular culture as text is too fixed and unilateral. That is to say, for Beaudoin, popular culture is not a site where meanings and values can be explored (as I want to argue); rather, he claims that it conveys 'clear and stable' meanings. Indeed, this understanding reminds me of some conservative Christian assessments of popular culture. For example, I was told by one Christian that the film *Star Wars* lured its viewers away from a Christian worldview and introduced them to a 'New Age' system of belief.[13] Although I argued that it could be read in a variety of ways, there was no question, for this person, of *Star Wars* being anything other than a corrupting artefact; it could *not* be read any other way; it was an anti-Christian text. Although Beaudoin's approach is more sophisticated, in that there is a recognition of the reader's interpretative role in the process, the same understanding of the text as conveying core meanings is nevertheless evident. As Lynch puts it, 'although Beaudoin seems to allow for the fact that people will interpret films, music, and fashion in different ways, he also seems to maintain the belief that these popular cultural "texts" do have core meanings that convey a clear theological message'.[14] This, of course, is simply not the case. When readers seek to understand the significance of cultural texts in people's everyday lives, often what they bring to the text is more important than the meaning intended by the author. Drawing on Michel de Certeau's famous work, *The Practice of Everyday Life*, Lynch makes just this point: 'individuals have a wide variety of ways of subverting the intended meanings of popular cultural "texts" and using them to serve their own interests and commitments'.[15] This is essentially the process described by cultural theorists as *bricolage*, a particular kind of 're-ordering and re-contextualization of objects to communicate fresh meanings'.[16] Related to the notion of detraditionalization, ideas and themes are detached from their original contexts and invested with new meanings in order to serve the personal interests of the individual self.

I have drawn attention to this discussion because, on the one hand, it seems to be a quick and easy way of dealing with an important issue and, on the other hand, I want readers to be clear at the outset what understanding of popular culture I am working with. I do not understand the significance of popular culture as Beaudoin does, and nor am I particularly interested in the popular cultural 'text' itself.[17] Like Lynch, I am more interested in the significance of popular culture in people's 'ordinary, lived experience … its uses and meaning for people'.[18] More specifically, I contend that, whatever meanings are intended by the producers of popular culture, there is little doubt that people are, from their own particular perspectives, developing religious and metaphysical ideas by reflecting on themes explored in literature, film, and music. However, I will also argue that we need to take account of more than this, for, at a basic level, popular culture both reflects and informs ideas, values and meanings within society as well as providing a site for the exploration of ideas, values and meanings. Hence, the relationship is a rather complex one, and, moreover, one that is implicated in the occultural milieu.

The Dilution Thesis

The occultural significance of popular culture was hinted at over a decade ago by Colin Campbell and Shirley McIver in their examination of cultural sources of support for contemporary occultism.[19] In suggesting an integration of occultic worldviews within contemporary Western culture, their study went some way to explaining why 'ordinary' individuals in the West can develop a commitment to apparently obscure occult practices and beliefs. Indeed, almost two decades earlier Marcello Truzzi had drawn attention to the significance of this relationship in his important essay, 'The Occult Revival as Popular Culture: Some Observations on the Old and Nouveau Witch'.[20] However, Truzzi did not see the occult revival as particularly significant in itself. By linking it to popular culture he wanted to indicate its superficial faddishness. He begins his discussion with a quote from Edward Sapir's 1937 essay on fashion: 'There is nothing to prevent a thought, a type of morality or an art form from being the psychological equivalent of costuming the ego. Certainly one may allow oneself to be converted to Catholicism or Christian Science in exactly the same spirit in which one invests in pewter or follows the latest Parisian models in dress.'[21] Similarly, Truzzi's essay goes on to argue that, because the occult revival is so closely allied to mass culture, the latter has the effect of trivializing occult beliefs. For example, it would be irrational both to literally believe a premodern demonology and to draw pentagrams on the floor and summon up demonic powers from beyond. That is to say, actual belief in demons as many of our medieval forebears believed in them would deter even the most adventurous occultist from summoning them. Truzzi's point is that contemporary occult interest in such supernatural beings is evidence of the demise of such beliefs: 'As long as these *mass* phenomena represent a playful and non-serious confrontation with the supernatural elements,' says Truzzi, 'they then represent a possible cleansing or purging of the old fears and myths still present in our society. The more we eliminate these old fears and myths, the more we develop a naturalistic rationalism, a scientific view of the universe.'[22] And certainly we will see that, in some cases, this is true – not least in the case of the founder of modern Satanism, the late Anton LaVey, a skilled manipulator of the media. He explicitly denied the existence of Satan, referring to his belief system as 'fun',[23] and thus, arguably, diluted the old fears and myths about Satanism.

We might call this general theory of religion and culture the *dilution thesis*. Mass culture and modern restatements of spirituality *dilute* traditional religious worldviews; they erode 'serious' occult beliefs by diluting them – thereby producing ineffective, utilitarian forms of belief; the occultural dressing-up box is raided for symbols of style and attitude; 'the occult' may even become, as is sometimes (not always) the case with astrology or Ouija boards, simply fun with a supernatural edge.[24]

While the dilution thesis is hard to refute, in that trivialization is certainly an inevitable part of the sacralization process, it should be clear by now that it is not the whole story. The progress of Western alternative spirituality is far more complex. Indeed, as I have already argued, trivialized or superficial spirituality can, over time, become serious religion. As we will see, whilst influential figures such as Anton LaVey may dilute what is perceived to be a 'traditional' expression of a religious worldview, many of their followers do not. Likewise, whilst many who read astrology columns may treat it as a bit of fun, increasingly many do not. The fact that one can now study for a postgraduate degree in astrology indicates the significance of this component of contemporary occulture.[25] Moreover, just because people do not believe in demons in the same way as their fore-bears did, does not mean that their belief is lacking in sincerity and commitment. Just because their demons are less malevolent, does not mean they are less real. That the occult is being resurrected and re-packaged in the West is not in doubt. To claim that it is therefore being diluted is a *non sequitur*; there is much to suggest that a great deal of occultural spirituality is a significant restatement of traditional religious myth rather than a dilution of it. We will see in subsequent chapters that idealized, neo-Romantic, detraditionalized concepts of spiritual powers and entities are being constructed. Whilst Westerners may not uncritically accept premodern cosmologies, this is very different from saying that the super-natural is not believed in or taken seriously anymore. Westerners are certainly not overthrowing supernaturalism for 'a naturalistic rationalism'. As Wade Clark Roof's study of American religion found,

> Talk about spirituality was often rambling and far-ranging, although several themes stood out that underscored its reflexive style. One was the rhetoric of a self-authored search, of looking inward, of wanting to grow, of 'journey' ... People seemed amazingly open to spiritual exploration: more than a few were attracted to the paranormal and to divine intervention, as evident in conversations about space-age narratives, near-death experiences, shamans, angels, and past-life regressions. Striking among these more self-reflexive types was the degree to which such spiritual phenomena mixed rather freely with Judeo-Christian symbols and themes ... Fully a fourth of our respondents said they believed in reincarnation, many of whom were committed Christians.[26]

Moreover, he demonstrates that what these beliefs and practices share is 'they persist largely as a result of loosely bound networks of practitioners, the publish-ing industry, and the media'.[27] Occulture, which is, to a large extent, being sup-ported by popular culture, is becoming ever more pervasive and influential. The emergence of popular occulture, with its consequent de-exotification of Eastern and occult themes, has led to a certain de-stigmatization. As Barkun notes of conspiracy culture: 'Surely the appearance of conspiracy themes in popular culture at least partially destigmatizes those ideas, by associating them with admired stars and propagating them through the most important forms of mass entertainment.'[28]

Again, the aim of this and the following chapter is simply to explore the ways in which this is happening through an examination of selected manifestations. (Volume II will provide further examples and develop the themes identified more fully.)

The Significance of Popular Culture

Popular culture has a relationship with contemporary alternative religious thought that is both expressive and formative.[29] That is to say, in a sense similar to Clifford Geertz's notion of religious symbols being models for and of culture,[30] so, more broadly, popular culture is both an expression of the cultural milieu from which it emerges and formative of that culture, in that it contributes to the formation of worldviews and, in so doing, influences what people accept as plau-sible. Although not discussing religion, Elizabeth Traube makes the important point that it matters little whether or not media professionals are concerned with the construction of subjectivities or with the simple telling of pleasurable stories, because the stories themselves 'are vehicles for constructing subjectivities, and hence what stories are circulated is socially consequential'.[31] This is similarly true from a religious perspective, in that whatever is intended by the producers of popular culture, there is little doubt that people are developing religious and meta-physical ideas by reflecting on themes explored in literature, film, and music (and perhaps even video games[32]) – which, in turn, reflect popular re-enchantment and thus might be understood as part of a process of modern religious 'deprivatiza-tion' (José Casanova).[33] In Casanova's words,

> Religions throughout the world are entering into the public sphere and the arena of political contestation not only to defend their traditional turf, but also to participate in the very struggles to define and set the modern boundaries between the private and the public spheres, between system and life-world, between legality and morality, between individual and society, between family, civil society, and state, between nations, states, civilizations, and the world system.[34]

I am simply suggesting that alternative spiritualities, communicated and inter-preted through popular culture, are beginning to work in this way, shaping public opinion and raising consciousness about key political issues (e.g. environmental-ism, the Chinese occupation of Tibet, globalization etc.). In other words, Casa-nova's thesis that 'religions are likely to continue playing important public roles in the ongoing construction of the modern world'[35] should not be limited to the major world religions, but also extended to occultically dependent spiritualities.

It is not insignificant that producers of popular culture are interested in alterna-tive religious and occult themes. As Campbell and McIver comment, 'commer-cial interests dictate that the interests of the majority are catered for and hence the extensive treatment of occult themes is yet further testimony to a degree of popular occult commitment'.[36] Whilst I am not claiming that this relationship with popular culture is a new development (for it clearly is not), the evidence seems to suggest that popular culture, as well as helping people to think through theological and metaphysical issues, is also providing resources for the construc-tion of religious and paranormal worldviews. As Lyon argues, 'People construct religious meanings from the raw materials provided by the media, repositioning and patterning the elements according to logics both local and global, both inno-vative and traditional.'[37]

Without disagreeing with Lyon, it is worth clarifying at this point that cultural texts are often not 'raw', in the sense that they are, to use Stuart Hall's concept, 'encoded'.[38] That is to say, rather than the media providing raw materials (Hall is principally concerned with television), they are, wittingly or unwittingly, pro-viding a package of meanings. Cultural artifacts come with interpretation or 'pre-ferred meaning' attached. The selection of, for example, images, words, their ordering, and their narrative structure all suggest particular meanings and ways of interpretation. Moreover, in order for the cultural text to make sense within a particular context (and within a particular mind) the message needs to be 'decoded'. Some people will receive what is communicated uncritically, others will reject the message, and yet others will enter into a relationship of negotiation. Some viewers of a news report, for example, or even a television series such as *The X-Files*, may uncritically accept everything communicated. Others will accept part of what is presented as an accurate representation of reality and reject other elements as distortion or simply fiction. Yet others will reject everything presented. Such decoding, of course, is influenced to a large extent by prior beliefs, commitments, and plausibility structures. Hence, for example, some conspiracy theorists I have interviewed find it very difficult to accept as trustworthy much that is presented on news programmes. Similarly, few Muslims in the Middle East uncritically accept Western media reports. Hence, production of meaning does not ensure its consumption. This is partly because of the polysemic nature of cultural artifacts and also because of the various contexts into which they are received. In other words, while texts have dominant, encoded meanings (which do guide readers, viewers and listeners towards a preferred meaning), they carry multiple possible meanings and can be interpreted in a variety of ways. Hence, if the consumers share the same cultural values as the producers, it is likely that encoded meanings will be decoded faithfully. However, if the contexts and beliefs change (e.g. social class, religion, geographical area, gender, age, race), the process of decoding is unlikely to be faithful to the encoded meaning. Hence, while popular culture is encoded, and is helping people to think through theological and metaphysical issues, it is not a one-way process. While popular culture provides resources for the construction of religious and paranormal worldviews, people are 'active audiences', occultural decoders, who are, to quote Lyon again, 'repositioning and pattering the elements according to logics both local and global, both innovative and traditional'.

To return to the principal point, and bearing the encoding–decoding model in mind, popular occulture has a shaping effect on beliefs and interests. Belief in astrology or UFOs are good examples of this popular decoding of such non-conventional, paranormal themes.[39] For example, there is evidence of a close relationship between the fact that, as John Saliba has noted, Western popular culture encourages 'the idea that space people and/or invaders exist',[40] and the fact that there are not only many people happy to entertain the existence of UFOs, but also many who are committed to notions of visitation, abduction, and related ideas. Increasingly, it would seem, encoders and decoders are sharing occultural codes. 'Belief in UFOs,' says folklorist Thomas Bullard, 'was once an oddity, a badge of craziness in the routines of popular humour. But little by little this belief has become the norm, and nearly half of the population [of the USA] now affirms that UFOs are real.'[41] Again, Paul Heelas writes, 'Prior to the later 1940s, very few would have answered affirmatively to the question "Do you believe in UFOs?" In a recent study, with which I have been involved, a quarter of those active with "alternative" spiritualities answered the same question positively. Nothing surprising about this, one might think. But what is surprising – and surely shows the extent to which ufology has entered the culture – is that around 10 per cent of regular church attendees expressed belief.'[42] In her intriguing book *Aliens in America: Conspiracy Cultures from Outerspace to Cyberspace*, Jodi Dean argues for the existence of a close two-way relationship between popular culture and seriously held conspiracy theories regarding alien abduction. This rise of interest in UFO mythology and alien abductions is not only reflected in programmes such as *The X-Files*,[43] but also stimulated and shaped by such programmes: '*The X-Files* capitalizes on and contributes to pop-cultural preoccupation with aliens';[44] 'Apparently, significant numbers of Americans are convinced. In June 1997, 17 percent of the respondents to a *Time*/CNN poll claimed to believe in abduction.'[45] Similarly, Peter Knight's discussion of conspiracy culture notes that 'more than a few *X-Files* viewers have come to take the show's conspiracy and fringe-science revelations as fact'.[46] In other words, the decoding includes what Michael Barkun has called 'fact–fiction reversals'.[47] An artifact intended as fiction has, within a particular occultural milieu, been decoded as fact.

The points for us to note are simply that it seems clear (1) that occultural worldviews have been an important source of inspiration for popular culture, (2) that popular culture has in turn been an important source of inspiration for the formation of occultural worldviews, and, consequently, (3) that popular culture is beginning to have a shaping effect on Western plausibility structures. Again, as will be discussed in more detail in Volume II, evidence for this hermeneutic circle operating between popular culture and occulture has been clearly shown in recent studies of specific new religions and alternative spiritualities.

Supernatural Horror: Vampire Fiction

It is interesting to compare contemporary supernatural horror films and the older films of the same genre made between the 1930s and the 1970s.[48] Although there are still few films which wholeheartedly endorse the occult,[49] there is a notable shift away from the unsympathetic treatments of Paganism as sinister, satanic and dangerously deviant, to more positive portrayals of it as intriguing, sexually exciting, and darkly cool. Having said that, it should also be noted that the portrayal of the occult as intriguing, mysterious and not without an element of erotic appeal is not entirely new, in that these themes can be found in Gothic literature from Horace Walpole's *The Castle of Otranto* (1765)[50] through to Bram Stoker's description of the iconic *Dracula* (1897) – the handsome, aristocratic vampire, whose appeal seems perennial.[51] However, earlier treatments of the occult either tended to conclude with rational explanations for apparently supernatural events,[52] thereby reinforcing a rationalist worldview, or were essentially moral tales warning against dabbling with the occult and demonstrating the power of the crucifix as a symbol for vanquishing evil (most obviously evident in the vampire stories), thereby reinforcing the Christian worldview. Nowadays, things have changed: the supernatural world is portrayed as fact; sceptical rationalists are made to eat their doubting words; occult powers can be used for good as well as evil; Paganism is seen as an environmentally friendly alternative to oppressive institutional religion (as, for example, in the cult classic, *The Wicker Man*); and the symbols of Christianity (particularly the crucifix) are shown to be impotent.

In the case of the vampire, traditionally, the symbols of Christianity were all that victims required in order to fend off their assailants. Throughout Bram

Stoker's *Dracula*, for example, the cross is, as Larry Kreitzer comments, 'surrounded by a sense of reverence; it is held in respect and it is recognized as possessing great protective power. Indeed, it is perhaps the primary means of defense against the evil Count Dracula, with garlic flowers and communion wafers and hawthorn bushes serving as supplementary weapons in the vampire killer's armoury.'[53] However, as Kreitzer shows, over the years the cross has gradually lost its power. Beginning with a study of the cross 'revered as a symbol of faith', he notes that in Werner Herzog's *Nosferatu: The Vampyre* (1979), a remake of F.W. Murnau's classic *Nosferatu: Eine Symphonie des Grauens* (1922),[54] 'the cross is consistently presented as a positive symbol of faith. Dracula is repelled by it, and those who wear the cross are thus protected by it.'[55] Similarly, he shows how Tobe Hooper's *Salem's Lot* (1979) – the adaptation of the 1975 novel by Stephen King – and John Badham's *Dracula* (1979) both incorporate crucifixion imagery in a similarly reverential manner (the former drawing heavily on Stoker's *Dracula*). That said, in the latter film, there is an indication that a shift is beginning to take place and that the cross is beginning to slip as a weapon of absolute power. Although throughout the film crucifixes are powerful weapons against the forces of darkness, there is an exception: 'In the dark and dank bowels of his coffin-room [Van Helsing and Jonathon Harker] confront Dracula, and Harker raises a cross in a gesture of defiance against the evil he represents. Dracula grabs the cross derisorily and it bursts into flame (apparently on his home turf and under cover of darkness the cross is not the threat it is in the daylight!). He casts the cross aside and then proclaims: "You fools! Do you think with your crosses and your wafers you can destroy me?"'[56] However, whilst there are such exceptions, generally speaking, these, along with many earlier films, portray the cross primarily as a powerful object of reverence. Dracula fears the crucifix as a symbol which has power over him. As Kreitzer notes, 'his revulsion at being confronted by a crucifix is the mirror image of the reverence in which it is held by others'.[57] Of course, this only makes sense in a predominantly Christian society, a society in which the cross is a powerful sacred symbol. Indeed, Kreitzer even seeks (a little unconvincingly) to invest the stake in Stoker's work with Christian theological significance. In particular, he draws attention to the passage in which Arthur Holmwood has to drive what is described as 'a mercy-bearing stake' through the heart of his beloved Lucy, who, as a vampire, lies in her coffin:

> Arthur placed the point over the heart, and as I looked I could see its dint in the white flesh. Then he struck with all his might.
>
> The thing in the coffin writhed; and a hideous, blood-curdling screech came from the opened red lips … But Arthur never faltered. He looked like a figure of Thor as his untrembling arm rose and fell, driving deeper and deeper *the mercy-bearing stake*, whilst the blood from the pierced heart welled and spurted up around it.[58]

This he understands to be evidence that the novel has 'an interesting theology of atonement'.[59] Although that stretches the theory a little too far, it does highlight the point I am seeking to make, namely, to understand what Stoker was doing, one needs also to understand the significance he accorded to the Bible and to the

Christian theology of atonement. Biblical imagery is frequently used, the symbol of the cross appears regularly, and key Christian rites, particularly baptism and the Eucharist, also carry significant theological weight. All of this would have made a great deal of sense in late-Victorian London, where it was written. It reflected the dominant symbols of religious authority and sacred power. However, the Western world of the late 1970s is a very different place – 'a different country'. Religious and cultural pluralism, secularization and Easternization have all begun to erode the perceived power of such symbols.

This shift in cultural context is clearly reflected in Francis Ford Coppola's *Bram Stoker's Dracula* (1992), which, despite its title, makes significant changes to Stoker's original story. One of the most significant changes to Stoker's plot is 'the way in which the relationship between Dracula and Mina Harker is transformed into a tale of lost love'.[60] More significant still, and clearly mimetic of the new Easternized religious pluralism in the West, is the fact that Coppola transforms Mina into the reincarnation of Dracula's wife Elizabeta who, two centuries previously, had committed suicide – hence the words at the centre of the promotional poster (and DVD cover) proclaiming 'love never dies'. Whereas, of course, such a theme would have been unusual and considered theosophically exotic in Stoker's *Dracula*, this is certainly not the case nowadays. As we saw in the previous chapter and as several significant studies have shown,[61] reincarnation is a widely held belief in Western culture. In Stoker's novel, Dracula's reappearance generation after generation is not the result of the transmigration of his soul, but rather because he is able to cheat death by drinking blood. Of course, this haematic appetite is also based on Judaeo-Christian teaching, being taken from Leviticus 17.11 (a passage central to Jewish and Christian theologies of sacrifice and atonement): 'For the life of the flesh is in the blood'. Indeed, Stoker has Dracula quoting this very passage – as does Coppola at the beginning of his film – indicating that the vampire is not simply a carnivorous predator seeking sustenance, but a demonic figure seeking the 'life-force' contained in the blood. In short, Stoker's Dracula is not a reincarnate entity, but an undead one living on the life-force of his victims and understood within a Judaeo-Christian theological framework. Yet, it is precisely at this point that Coppola's narrative drifts. Although he still makes use of the symbol of the cross and, indeed, keeps Dracula's opposition to Christ as a central theme, his incorporation of reincarnation into the story represents a subtle but significant shift away from Stoker's fundamentally Judaeo-Christian narrative.

As I have suggested, this shift reflects the shift taking place in the West whereby the centre of spiritual gravity is moving away from Judaeo-Christian theology to the eclecticism of occulture. Indeed, Coppola's *Dracula* is just one of an increasing number of films and books that are, in accordance with contemporary Western culture, explicitly departing from the Christian elements in the narrative and even rejecting them as irrelevant. As Kreitzer says, 'the cross is either ridiculed as a worthless trinket of a by-gone era, or replaced by another symbol, or simply rejected altogether as redundant to the concerns of the modern world'.[62] Rejection is explicit in the film *Buffy the Vampire Slayer* (1992) – the film which inspired the acclaimed and much-discussed series of the same name. The crucifix appears only twice: first, at the beginning, when Merrick (Donald Sutherland) hands Buffy (Kirsty Swanson) a crucifix along with a stake; secondly, at the end of the film, when she produces the same crucifix to fend off the evil Lothos (Rutger Hauer). The first time the crucifix is simply ignored, in that, after we see it handed over by Merrick, it does not appear again until the end of the film, the ensuing battle with a couple of vampires being won by means of stakes. Although it is explicitly used at the end of the film in the traditional way (i.e. held out between the vampire and prey), it is quickly dismissed by Lothos with the words, 'This is your defence? Puh-leaze! Your puny faith.'[63] Hence, Buffy has to discard the cross quickly and return to the far more reliable method of dispatching the modern vampire: a pointed stick and a balletic kick.

This shift away from the authority of Christian myth and symbolism is continued in the *Buffy* series.[64] For example, in an insightful essay, Gregory Erickson describes the following scene from the episode 'Who Are You?':

> The parishioners fearfully sit awaiting what seems to be certain death, or worse, as the vampires stride among the wooden pews inside the small, traditional, stone church. With the cross prominently in the background, one of the vampires looks around, admires the stained glass, approaches the altar, and shouts arrogantly, 'I've been avoiding this place for so many years, and it's nothing ... Where is the thing I was so afraid of? You know, the Lord?'[65]

As Erickson says, 'In *Buffy*, we see no heaven, no God, no Christ. There are no functioning churches, and there is no serious prayer. In isolated episodes, Cordelia prays and Riley goes to church, but both incidents are presented in humorous ways that are more about characterization than religion ... The Christian symbolism of holy water and crosses is left unstated.'[66] Indeed, the presence and effectiveness of Christian symbolism have decreased throughout the run of the series, and by the third year, in an episode entitled 'Doppelgängland', 'a vampire looks at a cross and a vial of holy water, sneers "whatever", and walks away'.[67] Concerning the specific symbol of the crucifix and what it might signify in *Buffy*, Erickson makes the following observation:

> It appears to be neither Christian nor non-Christian. It is constantly present – in the opening credits, around Buffy's neck, and in her bag of weapons along with holy water, a crossbow, and a collection of wooden stakes, knives, and axes – but it has no privileged status. The cross is no more a weapon than a crossbow, a broken pool cue, or a well-placed karate kick. The ambiguity of the cross is emphasized by Buffy's first great nemesis, the Master, who defiantly calls it 'two pieces of wood', even as he sizzles from touching it ... Buffy's cross ... is a simulacrum – a copy with no original – a sacred and powerful sign, signifying nothing.[68]

Less ambiguous is the interpretation of the cross in Neil Jordan's *Interview with the Vampire* (1994), based on Anne Rice's novel of the same name. When questioned about the significance of crucifixes, Louis, a vampire, responds incredulously: 'Crucifixes?' Probed further about whether he can look at them, he replies dismissively, 'Actually, I am quite fond of looking at crucifixes.' The point of the dialogue is explicitly to empty Christian symbolism of potency and relevance.

Noting this shift in vampire films and literature, Gordon Melton quite reasonably relates it implicitly to the general process of secularization: 'The challenge to the effectiveness of the crucifix in vampire novels symbolizes a larger challenge to the role of the supernatural in modern life. It includes a protest against the authority of any particular religion and its claims of truth in a religiously pluralistic world.'[69] There is, of course, some accuracy in these comments. However, they ignore a parallel shift towards new symbols of purity. That is to say, whilst contemporary vampire fiction seems keen to make the point that 'crosses don't do squat'[70] when it comes to repelling the forces of evil, particularly vampires, they turn instead to the products of the natural world such as silver, sunlight and garlic. These have a dramatic effect, their *natural* purity and goodness being swift in the destruction of all that is identified as 'evil'. Hence, I suggest, what we are witnessing is a shift in the locus of sacred authority towards the natural world and, in some cases, nature religion. Contrary to Melton's analysis, I would argue that the rules of sacred authority, purity and pollution are still operating, but the nature of authority, purity and pollution has been redefined. Hence, in Rice's *Interview with the Vampire*,[71] in which, as Melton points out, vampires are immune to holy objects, having 'no problem with religious symbols' and knowing 'nothing of God or a sacred space',[72] we do read, for example, of vampires being burned up in the morning sun – although, along with crosses and stakes, Louis does include garlic in his list of traditions and superstitions that are 'bullshit'.[73] Again, in both *From Dusk Til Dawn* (1996)[74] and *Blade* (1998), although 'crosses don't do squat', sunlight, silver, garlic and stakes certainly do. Indeed, in the film *Practical Magic* (1998) it is interesting that a police investigator's pentacle-shaped badge is used against the evil, undead Jimmy (Goran Visnjic) in exactly the same way as the crucifix was used in earlier vampire films, and with the same devastating effect. Similarly, whilst much Christian symbolism is employed in *Buffy*, this clear hermeneutical shift towards Paganism is also eclectically present. That said, as one would expect there to be in a North American series, there are still key identifiable Christian themes throughout, including the basic demonology, the concept of a soul which can be obsessed, possessed, lost, and even exchanged with another body (as Faith and Buffy do in the episode 'Who Are You?'), constant symbols of death, resurrection and redemption, and Buffy as the 'woman-Christ'.[75] Nevertheless, to reiterate the point, *Buffy* is also very much a manifestation of Western religious eclecticism, this being evident particularly in the dismissal of traditional Christian sacred authority in favour of magical potency.

This emphasis on the potency of the Pagan and the magical is clearly articulated in the fourth season of the series, in which Buffy's friend Willow Rosenberg develops her supernatural powers as a witch. These powers are quickly shown to be indispensable when attempts are made to destroy a being like Frankenstein's monster created by Professor Maggie Walsh from human, demon and mechanical parts and named, with obvious reference to the Genesis narrative, Adam. Unable to destroy Adam using traditional methods, Buffy finds herself in need of a more potent force. Whereas Stoker's Abraham Van Helsing would have found more than sufficient power in the crucifix, holy water, eucharistic wafers, prayer, and striking the stake 'in God's name, that all may be well with the dead that we love',[76] Buffy, in the episode 'Primeval', finds it in a conjoining spell performed by Giles, Xander and Willow – Willow's Pagan supernatural abilities being fundamental to the potency of the forces unleashed. The point is that, whereas there are Christian symbols in *Buffy*, these lack any real or distinct potency compared to occultural knowledge and forces.

Furthermore, Zoe-Jane Playden's analysis of correspondences between the religious themes in *Buffy* and both Gnosticism and goddess theologies draws the following conclusions: 'the sensibilities of *Buffy* resonate far more convincingly with those earlier spiritual traditions than they do with orthodox Christianity... Equally, the spiritual vision of *Buffy* is an immanent one, one which exists on earth, not a transcendent one in an unattainable heaven... Transformation is achieved at an individual level, by the use of personal agency and, by the extension of that agency to others, through compassion.'[77] In other words, *Buffy* reflects the eclecticism and self-centrism we have identified in Western occulture.

Cool Occulture

As noted in Chapter 3, a recent article in a British teenagers' magazine not only made the claim that Wicca is the fastest-growing religion in America, but also linked its rise, on the one hand, to popular culture and, on the other hand, to the consequent assessment of 'cool' that it had been accorded:

> Witchcraft, or Wicca, is the fastest growing 'religion' in the USA today. It is estimated that around a million and a half teenage Americans, often as young as thirteen, are practising Wiccans. Television programmes such as *Sabrina the Teenage Witch* and films like *The Craft* have sparked continent-wide interest in Witchcraft and awarded it the official Hollywood stamp of 'cool'.[78]

That it is 'cool' is worth noting, in that this coolness is fundamentally linked to its high, positive profile in popular culture.

First, however, something needs to be said about the concept of 'cool'. In their discussions of club cultures, both Sarah Thornton and Ben Malbon have explored the significance of 'hipness' or 'coolness'.[79] Drawing on Pierre Bourdieu's analysis of taste and cultural capital, Thornton develops a notion of 'hipness' as subcultural capital:

> Subcultural capital confers status on its owner in the eyes of the relevant beholder... Subcultural capital can be *objectified* or *embodied*... in the form of fashionable haircuts and well-assembled record collections... Just as cultural capital is personified in 'good' manners and urbane conversation, so subcultural capital is embodied in the form of 'being in the know', using (but not over-using) current slang and looking as if you were born to perform the latest dance styles.[80]

She shows how hierarchies of hipness/coolness are established and how that which is 'hip' is distinguished from that which is mainstream. Hence, it would seem that a series such as *Buffy* becomes subculturally 'cool' when the themes explored in the series are taken seriously. Simply to follow the series as one's parents might follow their favourite soap opera is hardly cool, in that it is main-stream behaviour. Indeed, even to be obsessively devoted to the series, collecting all the merchandise that has been produced in association with it, yet failing to progress beyond simple devotion to popular culture, while slightly cooler than watching soap operas, fails to accrue much subcultural capital. In other words, it is low on the hierarchy of coolness because it is amateurish, geekish, too close to the mainstream, and thus too uninvolved in relevant subcultural beliefs and behaviours. It is not the popular artefact which is invested with subcultural capital, but the occultural themes informing the series which are 'cool'. If *Buffy* is cool, it is because of the series' close relationship to actual occulture. Hence, *to be cool*, to accrue subcultural capital, one needs to take these underlying ideas seriously, to enter into the occultural world of rejected knowledge, and thus to place oneself outside the mainstream. Again, coolness is that which is explicitly *not* 'mainstream' and one of the principal reasons occulture is 'cool' is because it is *not* mainstream. Indeed, as we will see when we explore heavy metal music (in Volume II), that the occult is perceived as subversive, even offensive to the mainstream makes it all the more 'cool'.

'Sensations of belonging,' says Malbon, 'are partly constituted through processes, practices and experience of being cool (or not)'.[81] Cool people immediately identify and feel a sense of belonging with like-minded cool people. And, as noted above, within these communities of coolness informal hierarchies of coolness form, based on the amount of 'sub-occultural' capital individuals accrue. As Malbon argues, 'coolness is not just a quality that is ascribed and seen to be possessed, but also a hierarchically based and contextual sensation that is produced through mental-physical processes of striving, desire, fantasy and imagination'.[82] Within occultural communities, although dress, style, musical taste etc. are important, generally speaking 'being in the know' is more important. In other words, hierarchies of occultural *gnosis* form. For example, in a conversation I had with one young Wiccan who had first been inspired by films and series such as *Buffy*, it was clear that she felt she had progressed from her earlier rather 'uncool' days, in that she was no longer as ignorant and naïve as she had once been. More particularly, she was now in a position to analyse portrayals of Wicca in popular culture, distinguishing between those which were fictional and those which were genuine. Hence, as is the case in hierarchies of coolness, there was a certain amount of condescension concerning her contemporaries who could not likewise discriminate between factual and fictional occulture. Again, there was also some discrimination between good and bad popular artefacts – some films etc. seemed to be informed by genuine knowledge of the occult, whereas others simply supported mainstream stereotypes or were manifestations of the mainstream trivialization and commercialization of occulture. *Buffy*, *The Craft* (1996) and *Practical Magic* seemed to be relatively 'cool' in this respect.

Returning to popular occulture *per se*, we have seen that well before the advent of *Buffy*, coolness was being ascribed to films and television series. For example, a popular daytime soap opera in the 1960s, *Dark Shadows* (1966–71), focused on the Collins family, who were, as Ellwood notes, 'involved in everything that made the sixties counterculture. They did astrology, the Tarot cards, witchcraft, the *I Ching*.'[83] Not only did that series increasingly reflect the contours of the growing eclecticism of the late 1960s, it also established many key occultural themes as 'cool'.[84] However, few artefacts have been as significant in this respect as *Buffy*. As J. Lawton Winslade notes – and, indeed, as is recognized by the creator of *Buffy*, Joss Whedon – it has *unintentionally* (Whedon describes himself as 'a very hard-line, angry atheist'[85]) become part of 'popular occultism and marketable new age spirituality'.[86] As one Pagan excitedly observed, 'It is amazing how many people come into the Craft via shows such as *Sabrina the Teenage Witch* and *Buffy the Vampire Slayer*.'[87] For example, we have seen that a development paralleling the decrease in the presence and effectiveness of Christian symbolism in *Buffy* has been the increased prominence of Willow as a potent force in the spiritual universe of Sunnydale, her increase in potency being linked, not to anything in her Jewish background (her mother being an intellectual psychologist dismissive of the paranormal), but to her inherent supernatural powers as a witch – which are treated by the protagonists as serious powers for the mature. Indeed, there is what amounts to encouragement to take the paranormal seriously. For example, whilst superficial, faddish teen Wiccans appear in *Buffy*, they are dismissed as 'wanna-be' witches with little grasp of the true powers on offer. As Winslade notes, in the episode entitled 'Hush',

> Sunnydale's young Wiccans toss around all the buzz words associated with the contemporary feminist spirituality movement: empowerment, energy, blessing. Yet when Willow proposes they do actual magical work, like conjuring or casting spells, she is mocked and accused of both perpetuating negative stereotypes and 'sucking energy' from the group. Afterwards, Willow relates her experiences to Buffy. The following dialogue ensues:
>
> > *Buffy*: So, not stellar, huh?
> > *Willow*: Talk. All talk. Blah blah Gaia. Blah blah Moon … menstrual life force power thingy. You know, after a couple of sessions I was hoping we could get into something real, but …
> > *Buffy*: No actual witches in your group?
> > *Willow*: No. Bunch of wanna-blessed-bes. You know, nowadays, every girl with a henna tattoo and a spice rack thinks she's a sister of the Dark Ones.[88]

Willow, on the other hand, has power. No doubt reflecting the lives of many teens and young adults, Willow is a complex, talented figure, riddled with numerous adolescent insecurities. However, while struggling with such feelings, she is gradually transformed from Buffy's geeky friend to a significant occult figure in her own right: 'Willow's spells of protection and detection, discovery and subjugation, allow Team Buff [*sic*] to operate effectively on the Forces of Darkness.'[89] The awkward Willow becomes occulturally cool – and thus becomes enormously attractive as a role model.

As both Winslade and Rhonda Wilcox have noted, the very language of *Buffy* reinforces 'the theme of adult ignorance', as well as both embodying an element of 'the heroism of the teen characters' and functioning as a 'magical tool for the powerful teen who wields it'.[90] These statements are certainly borne out in discussions I have had with several teenage *Buffy* fans. Indeed, one such fan, stimulated by the series, actually pursued her fascination with Wicca and joined a local coven. This intelligent teenager, with no religious background, whilst fully aware of the fictional nature of *Buffy* and other similar artefacts, such as *The Craft* and *Practical Magic*, claimed that they had helped her to get beyond a negative interpretation of the occult and enabled her to appreciate that there might be a supernatural level of reality which could be of use to her. Positive images of witchcraft portrayed in popular series, such as *Buffy*, *Sabrina*, and *Charmed*, have transformed the popularity of occult figures to the extent that they are seen as symbols of 'girl power'. They seem to offer the hope of a degree of control to teenagers seeking to negotiate the complex emotional world of relationships and identity formation. Again, the portrayal of Willow as an insecure young adult who 'deep down feels that she is a nerd, a geekily dressed social outcast',[91] is central to the narrative of the outsider who develops special empowering gifts which can be found in much contemporary 'witch fiction'. Although *The Craft*, for example, is altogether darker, it is nevertheless a similar tale of disenfranchised teenage girls who become empowered and turn on the community that once oppressed them. This sense of empowerment, the ability to manipulate events and control relationships, is evident in much teen Wicca. For example, Jane Brum records the following interview with Rhiannon, a teenage Wiccan living in the Bronx: 'Her biggest worries are getting a boyfriend and getting rid of the braces on her teeth. "I cast a love spell a while back. I had to scatter roses on the street leading up to my apartment and then I asked the goddess to bring me the person I liked, along the path of love I had created. Well", she giggles, biting her nails, "he came, but he was only after one thing. I'm staying away from spells for now." '[92] (Such advice and spells can be found in numerous popular books with bold titles such as *How to Turn Your Ex-Boyfriend into a Toad and Other Spells*.[93])

The point is that it is difficult to avoid the evidence that such forms of alternative spirituality are perceived as 'cool' and thereby become increasingly popular, not just as interesting themes for fiction, but also as viable spiritual paths. 'Since 1996,' says Hannah Sanders, who has carried out research into 'Teen Wicca', 'it is impossible to escape the fact that Britain has seen a rise, an upsurge of interest from teenagers into magical traditions and particularly Witchcraft. This interest has been fuelled by the plethora of films and TV shows, the majority of which have been generated in the United States and all of which portray young women, or teenage girls as witches.'[94] Again, as Phyllis Curott, a New York lawyer and author of the highly successful *Book of Shadows*, put it:

> I've been a Wiccan priestess for almost twenty years, and when I began we were absolutely hidden in the back of the broom closet. Now, Wicca is out of the broom closet, in fact it's everywhere. The movie *Practical Magic* opened as number one at the box office, and every week, somewhere in the US some article is appearing in the mainstream media talking about Witchcraft and explaining, with increasing accuracy, what it's really all about. The climate of acceptance in the US is improving and increasing numbers of Wiccans and Pagans are now public and moving beyond a fringe group to becoming a real social movement rooted in the spirituality and values of the Old Religion. Universities all over the country have classes pertinent to Goddess spirituality, Paganism and Wicca and there are also many Pagan/Wiccan student groups.[95]

Furthermore, in support of this increased interest in Wicca – which, as Curott and Sanders recognize, has been stimulated by and is reflected in popular culture – Winslade notes the rapidly changing trends in publishing: 'A *Publisher's Weekly* article cited Carol Publishing as a house that prints first runs of 25,000 for its Wicca titles, about 10,000 more than for its non-Wicca offerings.'[96] Again, with reference to the phenomenal success of Curott's *Book of Shadows* – her auto-biography, subtitled *A Modern Woman's Journey into the Wisdom of Witchcraft and the Magic of the Goddess*, which sold over 25,000 copies in its first eight months[97] – Winslade notes that what this volume has done for women, 'Silver RavenWolf's *Teen Witch: Wicca for a New Generation* [which has been reprinted four times and has sold in excess of 50,000 copies] has done for teenagers, as has the *Harry Potter* series for children.'[98] Indeed, concerning J.K. Rowling's crea-tion, the Wiccan author Patricia Monaghan has argued that 'children and Wicca, once a taboo combination, is a hot buy for publishers thanks to *Harry Potter*'.[99] Similarly, Kevin Carlyon, a British Wiccan High Priest, also notes that the Harry Potter series has contributed to the growth of Paganism.[100] Again, it is difficult to avoid the commercial conclusion that 'magic is hot property these days'.[101] According to the director of trade sales for the leading publisher of occult literature Llewellyn Publishing, a significant trend began 'when the company started repackaging "classic" pagan titles with more youthful covers, and sales often jumped tenfold as a result'.[102]

The above discussion highlights an important component of the process of sacralization and occulture, namely the increasing involvement of younger people. It may be true that many organized new religions and 'New Age' net-works have an older membership, but it does seem to be the case that, certainly in Paganism, younger people are becoming involved. For example, my own impres-sionistic understanding of the average age of attendees at British Pagan Federa-tion conferences is that they are at the younger end of the spectrum (18–40).[103] This would appear to be borne out by a survey conducted by Joanne Pearson in the UK in 1996: 'the age of Wiccans ranges from 18 upwards, with most falling between the ages of 25 and 45'.[104] She continues, 'In the USA most witches are in their teens, twenties and thirties.'[105] And Lynne Hume notes of Australian Wiccan groups that 'the largest number appear to be aged between twenty-five and fifty-five, tending towards the younger end of the spectrum. In one Perth Wiccan coven, the age group is eighteen to thirty, but the organizer of the group is in his mid-sixties.'[106] Indeed, because of the increasing interest in Paganism shown by teenagers, in 1998 a network specifically catering for the needs of this age group was formed – Minor Arcana.[107]

As to why younger people are becoming involved in Paganism, it is not, I suggest, simply that many Pagan activities are relatively inexpensive (compared to, say, 'New Age' activities),[108] and therefore affordable for young people, but because the Pagan community is less 1960s-oriented, more in tune with current issues (particularly environmentalism and feminism) and, whilst it can slip into folk music, sandals and woolly jumpers, generally has a strong relationship with contemporary popular culture and mythology.

That popular culture has shaped the thinking of certain sections of Western society to the extent that some forms of new supernaturalism are perceived to be 'cool' is being cautiously welcomed by some Pagans. Christians, of course, would be delighted with such increasingly sympathetic portrayals of their own beliefs and mythologies in the visual and literary arts. However, no matter how much it is manipulated, Christian culture regularly fails to receive the stamp of 'cool'. It is difficult to imagine a book entitled *Teen Christian* becoming popular with disenfranchised Western youth. Again, this is, I suggest, because, unlike much Christianity, both popular culture and numerous new and alternative spiritualities are working with the ideas and themes drawn from occulture. Because occulture tends to be antagonistic to traditional Christian beliefs in particular, which are understood to be exclusivist, authoritarian, hierarchical and patriarchal, it not only promotes certain types of spirituality, but also implicitly excludes others. (Of course, there may be other reasons too. 'It's interesting,' says George McKay, that Christian 'music, folk, rock, rave, or otherwise, is invariably crap… [The] Devil still has the stranglehold on this aspect of culture, thank God.'[109] Regardless of the accuracy of that comment, it is interesting in itself.)

Popular Sacred Narratives

Because the connections between the occult and arts-based culture, particularly literature, film and video games, are, to quote Campbell and McIver, 'obvious and indisputable',[110] it is not surprising that some works of art should be treated as sacred narratives. For example, at the trivial end of the spectrum, I was interested to read that in 2002 the magazine *The Door* had recently named Buffy its 'theologian of the year': 'Hidden among the stupid sitcoms, copycat dramas and reality shows of broadcast TV, *Buffy the Vampire Slayer* has been acting out a modern-day morality play for seven seasons, delivering what a growing number of critics say is the edgiest show on television, dealing with topics like evil, redemption, resurrection, sex, guilt, existential angst, selflessness and sacrifice, religion and the occult, often all before the commercial break.'[111] From a more serious perspective (though, of course, I may be wrong in assuming that the nomination of Buffy was not entirely serious), in conspiracy culture – and many dominant narratives within occulture are at least conspiracist-related – as Barkun argues, 'the commonsense distinction between fact and fiction melts away'.[112] More than that, 'the two exchange places, so that in striking ways conspiracists often claim first that what the world at large regards as fact is actually fiction, and second that what seems to be fiction is really fact'.[113] Hence, when it comes to popular occulture, conspiracy theorists often interpret films and novels as accurate representations of reality. Whether understood in terms of encoded messages, originally intended for 'the inner circle of conspirators, that somehow became public',[114] or as truth purposely cloaked in fictional form, popular culture is understood to convey rejected but fundamentally accurate knowledge. This occultural epistemology has surfaced several times in my own research (and will be discussed more fully in Volume II). For example, in a recent conversation with one of the moderators of an occult website, the occultural significance of certain films was explained to me. *The Matrix* (1999), for example, was (and, no doubt, still is) understood by some occultists to be an 'initiatic' film, in that it is believed to have been created (wittingly or unwittingly) with certain 'trigger' symbols for 'those who understand'.[115] As such, it is one of a group of recent films which can initiate a person into a more enlightened, occultural understanding of reality. Indeed, following the release of the first two *Matrix* movies, the Australian magazine *New Dawn* featured an article entitled 'The "Matrix" is a Reality', which discussed a range of occultural theories and artefacts from the Masonic emblem to crop circles and a particular interpretation of quantum theory in order to demonstrate that the basic idea explored in the film is sound. On the one hand, the author, David Wilcock, argues that public opinion is being cynically manipulated and, on the other hand, he claims to reveal 'the true nature and structure of our universe'.[116] Although he doesn't discuss the content of the film, he clearly does believe it to be occulturally important. David Icke, however, is far more explicit in his endorsement of *The Matrix*, arguing that it is an important exposé.[117] He also urges those new to his ideas to study Kenneth Johnson's TV series *V* (1984–85), which, he claims, will educate people about 'what is REALLY going on.'[118] Indeed, the overlap between the basic structure of Icke's conspiracy theories and the storyline of *V* is so striking that it is hard to avoid the conclusion that the latter has been a significant factor in the construction of the former – particularly bearing in mind that it was written before Icke produced his current thesis. Icke is also keen that people study John Carpenter's *They Live* (1988), which tells the story of a drifter who accidentally uncovers an alien plot to take over America, and David Schmoeller's *The Arrival* (1990), in which an alien parasite turns a human into a vampire. 'I urge you,' says Icke, 'to think about watching these movies to get up to speed if you are new to all of this.'[119] The point is that the understandings of reality and the plausibility structures of conspiracy theorists and alternative religionists such as Icke (many of whom may only meet with other believers *virtually* on the Internet – which is becoming increasingly important as an occultural resource[120]) are directly informed and/or supported by popular culture.[121]

Turning to literature, whilst it would be wrong to make too much of children's fantasy stories, such as Rowling's tales of Harry Potter, the significance of such artefacts on contemporary worldviews is worth mentioning. In seeking to understand such popular occulture, Campbell and McIver's comments are helpful:

> no discussion of the sources of support for occultism would be complete without noting that there is at least one place where it has a secure and highly approved position within the culture of contemporary society, a place where it is not condemned but where it is heavily endorsed. This, of course, is in the context of the culture of childhood, which would be largely unrecognizable without the faeries, ghosts, alien beings and magical environments which are its stock-in-trade. Virtually all the themes of adult occultism are to be found in the books, plays and films aimed at children, although not, of course, in a fully elaborated form. Here the 'rejected' knowledge of adults is presented as the 'accepted' material for children, even if there is an attempt to do so within the framework of 'a willing suspension of disbelief' ... [This] necessarily means that almost all

members of modern society are introduced to occult material at a tender age. Occultism
is thus a central part of the world-view which they inherit and one which they must
subsequently learn to reject. It would hardly be surprising if some fail to do so.[122]

Increasing numbers of Westerners are not only failing to do so, but also are finding such narratives important spiritual resources: 'Fantasy does not necessarily
misdirect people away from consciousness raising, it need not be an opiate, but
can be the much needed catalyst for change.'[123] This is evident from numerous
accounts of individuals' paths to Paganism. As Harvey comments, 'the formation
and development of Pagan identities almost always features significant literary
resources. Even those Pagans who honestly claim to be uninfluenced by books
have generally been inspired by another Pagan who has assimilated someone
else's writings.'[124] For example, Avril Fox recalls her early 'consciousness
raising' reading: 'My childhood set the scene... I found my world in books. The
ones I read again and again were all the "coloured" fairy tales published by
Andrew Lang: *The Green Fairy Book*, *The Red Fairy Book*, etc. My mother's
copy of A.R. Hope Moncrieff's *Classic Myth and Legend* then became equally
important.'[125] Following this early introduction to fantasy and myth, later in life
she recalls turning to Wicca as a result of reading the work of Robert Graves.
Hence, even if what might be called 'popular occulture' does not inspire a relatively immediate religious response, it would seem that when it comes to thinking seriously about cosmologies and the construction of worldviews later in life,
Westerners have a store of terminological and conceptual basics on which to
draw. For example, Alan Garner's trilogy *The Wierdstone of Brisingamen*,
Elidor, and *The Moon of Gomrath* (my own childhood favourites) are, as Graham
Harvey notes, 'among the books most frequently mentioned as inspirations (and
pleasures) by Pagans – who certainly contribute to their regular reprinting. Similarly, childhood pleasure in the adventures of Asterix the Gaul and his compan-
ions has prepared some contemporary Gallic Druids for their ritual "roaring at
the sky".'[126]

A particularly interesting example of the direct influence of science fiction
literature upon contemporary alternative spirituality is Robert Heinlein's 1961
novel *Stranger in a Strange Land*, which, as Stephen May notes, 'has a gospel of
free love and anti-establishment rhetoric that has won disciples from hippies to
Charles Manson'.[127] However, more important than that is its significance as the
inspiration for the first Pagan group to obtain full state and federal recognition in
America, the Church of All Worlds.[128] The founding members of the group, Otter
Zell and Morning Glory Zell, explain:

> The Church of All Worlds took much of its initial inspiration from the 1961 science
> fiction classic, *Stranger in a Strange Land* by Robert Heinlein. In the novel, the
> 'stranger', Valentine Michael Smith, was an Earthman born on Mars and raised by
> Martians. Among his other adventures upon being brought to Earth was the formation of
> the 'Church of All Worlds'. The church was built around 'nests', a combination of a
> congregation and an expanded family. A basic concept was grokking, i.e., the ability to
> be fully empathic. It also emphasized the experience of non-possessive love and joyous
> expression of sexuality as divine union. The common greeting was 'Thou art God'; a
> recognition of immanent divinity in each person.[129]

As they go on to discuss, these basic themes, particularly the significance of sexuality and a theology of immanentism/pantheism, are developed by their own church. Indeed, not limiting their reading to Heinlein, they are keen to stress that 'science fiction [is] "the new mythology of our age" and an appropriate *religious* literature.'[130] This influence is also identified by Timothy Miller in his work on 1960s communes: 'Science fiction introduced the young to ecological issues, cultural relativity, and the ambiguities of progress.' He even notes in passing that 'one science fiction novel alone, Robert Heinlein's *Stranger in a Strange Land*, so entranced many sixties communards with its jabs at predominant social mores – especially monogamy and monotheism – that it became virtual scripture in several communes, such as Sunrise Hill in Massachusetts'.[131] Similarly, Aidan Kelly has insisted that 'The only authors who are coping with the complexity of modern reality are those who are *changing the way people perceive reality*, and these are authors who are tied in with science fiction.'[132] Indeed, while Kelly perhaps overstates the significance of science fiction *per se*, nevertheless his general point is sound, namely, popular culture is *changing the way people perceive reality*. Numerous countercultural thinkers make reference to ideas developed by science fiction writers[133] – a genre which has seen significant growth and influence since the early 1980s.[134] Popular culture is socially, psychologically, and spiritually consequential.

Perhaps the most widely discussed work of science fiction which has been understood by many to develop conspicuously occultural ideas is *Star Wars*. As Adam Possamaï comments, 'One of the most common cultural consumptions – as reflected in the Australian and UK censuses – is that of the *Star Wars* mythos.'[135] Indeed, just as the fictional Valentine Michael Smith's Church of All Worlds left the pages of *Stranger in a Strange Land* and became established on the plane of history as an influential Pagan organization, so the Jedi Knights of *Star Wars* are no longer constrained by celluloid. Through a process of spiritual *bricolage*, they have established themselves in human society as the Jedi Knight Movement and articulate a philosophy they refer to simply as 'Jediknightism'. As their website explains, 'The way of Jedi transcends the science fiction series of *Star Wars*. It encompasses many of the same truths and realizations of the major world religions, including Zen Buddhism, Taoism, Hinduism, Catholicism, and Shinto and is both a healing art and a meditative journey that the aspirant can take to improve every aspect of their life.'[136] Again, in the words of Becky, a *Star Wars* devotee interviewed by Will Brooker,

> I got into the Jedi. I think because of my Catholic Education, the Force made more sense than this patriarchal deity in heaven. It didn't coalesce into a specific being; it was all around us, as opposed to God, a single entity. I was pig sick of religion and having it rammed down my throat. So it made more sense than conventional religion, because it didn't make rulings like the Catholic Church, against contraception and abortion and things, it was just good and evil, and you could interpret that in which ever way felt right to you ... It was more of a guide than a set of rules; it just seemed more right.[137]

Another example, perhaps the supreme example, of canonized fantasy is J.R.R. Tolkien's magnum opus, *The Lord of the Rings*,[138] which itself draws on the cosmology of Norse Paganism. It would be difficult to underestimate the significance of this work. Robert Ellwood, for example, notes that, following the appearance of the American paperback edition in 1965, 'Tolkien immediately became a campus cult figure, as sales zoomed to unprecedented heights for mythopoeic fiction of this kind.'[139] As Warren Hinckle wrote in 1967, it was 'absolutely the favorite book of every hippie'.[140] Along with much other fantasy literature, Will Straw also notes that its influence can be found through the 1970s: '*Lord of the Rings* was widely read and provided motifs for a wide range of poster art, songs, album covers, and so on.'[141] Again, testifying to its enduring appeal to alternative religionists and counterculturalists, Harvey writes of its influence on contemporary Paganism: 'It is arguable that J.R.R. Tolkien's *Lord of the Rings* provided metaphorical binoculars through which the realm of Faerie became visible again ... Tolkien gave back the words for those other-than-human persons glimpsed at twilight in the Greenwood, declared Faerie to be vital and necessary – and a whole generation grew up in an enchanted, richly inhabited world.'[142] Certainly, I know several people for whom this is true, one of which is an intelligent, articulate graduate who has absolutely no doubt that he has, at least twice, witnessed an actual faerie or faerie-like being. Again, as Andy Letcher notes, 'many Eco-Pagans maintain a belief in faeries as spirits of, or spirits dwelling within, pristine nature. Occasional encounters with otherworldly beings (sometimes, but not always, triggered by the use of hallucinogens) fuel the belief that practitioners have earned access to nature's secret realms, a reward for their self-sacrifice and spiritual and ecological example. Others maintain a symbolic identification with faeries.'[143]

Elsewhere Harvey observes that, whilst academic literature has been important in the construction of contemporary Paganism,

> Tolkien's *Lord of the Rings* and other fantasy writings are more frequently mentioned by Pagans. Fantasy re-enchants the world for many people, allowing them to talk of elves, goblins, dragons, talking trees, and magic. It also encourages contemplation of different ways of relating to the world ... It counters the rationality of modernity which denigrates the wisdoms of the body and subjectivity. Alongside future fiction, the genre explores new and archaic understandings of the world, and of ritual and myth, and attempts to find alternative ways of relating technology to the needs of today.[144]

Although, like C.S. Lewis, Tolkien was writing from a Christian perspective,[145] and although many of his themes are, strictly speaking, antithetical to the Pagan worldview, *The Lord of the Rings* has encouraged a host of Tolkienesque fantasy written from an explicitly Pagan perspective. It will be interesting to see, over the next few years, the wider impact of Peter Jackson's three films based on the book. Bearing in mind Lynne Hume's claim that Paganism's reliance on literature has almost certainly contributed to the general sluggishness of its growth,[146] we should expect the wider dissemination of key fantasy works through film to lead to a significant rise in Pagan spirituality.

Finally, concerning the significance of literary resources for the formation and development of Pagan identities, while we should acknowledge the particular influence of Tolkien, who '*enabled* Pagans and others to speak of the Faerie realms without raising the spectre of Victorian whimsy',[147] and while we should acknowledge the importance of other works such as Brian Bates' *The Way of the Wyrd* or William Gibson's *Neuromancer*, particular attention should be drawn to Terry Pratchett's acclaimed Discworld series. 'It not only observes and describes a world recognizable to Pagans', says Harvey, 'but also … it *enables* a more participatory, perhaps transformative, knowledge and experience.'[148] Popular culture directly enables religious participation, transformation, understanding and experience. 'Pratchett contributes to Pagan thinking and living in this world as his narrative unfolds the Pagan world'.[149] No wonder, therefore, that Pagans refer to Pratchett's work as 'inspiring or foundational in their discovery and development of this growing Nature Religion … It is with Terry Pratchett's Discworld that a Pagan place founded in Pagan cosmology and experienced in Pagan imagination and playfulness is encountered.'[150] Indeed, it is interesting that even terms coined by Pratchett have become part of Pagan theological vocabulary. 'Octarine', for example, which describes the 'colour of magic', has been adopted by Chaos magician Peter Carroll in his book *Liber Kaos*. Hence, if Harvey is correct – and there is no reason to doubt that he is – his following point is significant: 'If academics and other observers of Paganism require texts to build their understanding on or to educate others with, they should turn primarily to [fantasy and science fiction] literature, rather than to books offering to reveal "What Witches Do".'[151]

Concluding Comments

The point is, again, that particular concepts and cosmologies explored in popular culture are not merely expressions of contemporary religious interests and concerns, but they lead, first, to familiarization and fascination, and secondly, to the development of spiritualities. In other words, although there is a complex network of reasons for the rising interest in occultural cosmologies, it seems clear that popular artefacts are, in some significant sense, contributing to the construction of new sacralized plausibility structures and worldviews. As Hume has discovered in Australian Paganism,

> Science fiction aficionados find that ritual is but an extension of the fantasy world of the future to the fantasy world of the imagination and the subconscious mind. A particular book or some character may strike a responsive chord and the image is realized through ritual. An author's approach may be taken up, a worldview espoused, from a germ of an idea put forward. Once the seed is planted, the individual then searches for others with whom to discuss, assimilate and disseminate ideas.[152]

This sacralizing significance of certain texts was recently drawn to my attention when discussing reading matter with several former 'hippies' of the 1960s and 1970s. Although the individuals I spoke to did not know each other at the time, they were reading the same texts. Similarly, Jay Stevens' research uncovered almost exactly the same reading in mid-1960s America. Indeed, he himself seems surprised at 'how esoteric the reading was'. He writes: 'Among the fiction, Hermann Hesse was the obvious bestseller – sales of *The Journey to the East,*

Steppenwolf and *Siddartha* would make Hesse[153] the largest-selling German author in America by the end of the Sixties – closely followed by the science fiction novels ... *Stranger in a Strange Land, Childhood's End,* etc.'[154] He continues: 'Balancing the fiction was a section of technical works on the psychedelic experience, Leary, Huxley, Watts, plus a variety of Eastern and occult texts, ranging from the *Tibetan Book of the Dead* to the *Zohar*.'[155] Other books that are often referred to as significant in an individual's spiritual development are those by Carlos Castaneda,[156] whose influence is, for example, made explicit in Gabrielle Roth's popular and influential book, *Maps to Ecstasy: Teachings of an Urban Shaman*.[157] (We will be exploring the relationship between psychedelics and spirituality more fully in the following chapter and Volume II.)

Chapter 7

Popular Occulture: Music

We begin our evaluation of the occultural significance of popular music by returning again to the work of the German cultural theorist Theodor Adorno. While
disagreeing somewhat with Adorno's assessment of popular music, I do, as noted
in the Introduction, agree with his understanding of it as socially and culturally
consequential. Of course, this chapter cannot possibly cover every area of popular music and will, therefore, disappoint those wanting discussions of musicians
and groups who have been particularly significant for them.[1] Generally speaking,
the focus of the chapter is determined by the genres of music that have been
influential within certain recent, occulturally significant, youth subcultures from
the 1960s to the present day. Even so, I have had to limit the discussion.

I should also note that, as with previous discussions, the following is concerned with music's socio-cultural role in the re-enchantment of the West, rather
than with any theological speculation. That is to say, unlike scholars such as
Robin Sylvan, I am not arguing for any 'numinous' or 'transcendent' content
within popular culture. While I agree with some of his conclusions about ritual
and community within music subcultures, particularly dance subcultures, I stop
short of claiming that music actually provides 'an encounter with the numinous
that is at the core of all religions'.[2] That some adherents do *claim* to have had
such an encounter is significant. Whether they *have actually had* an encounter
with the numinous is beyond the scope of this study – and, some would argue,
beyond the scope of any empirical study.

Adorno and Popular Music

In his influential essay 'On Popular Music',[3] Adorno provided some characteristically thought-provoking insights. However, I am not alone in having serious
reservations about the division he makes between 'serious' and 'popular' music.
Indeed, I simply reject his argument that, unlike classical music, the pleasure
derived from popular music is necessarily superficial[4] (just as I reject arguments
which suggest that, unlike traditional religion, contemporary alternative spirituality is generally superficial) – one only has to think, for example, of the complex
and demanding work by electronica artists such as Autechre, the avant-garde jazz
of Evan Parker, the multi-layered dub of The Rootsman or Adrian Sherwood,
or the experimental post-drum 'n' bass music of a band like Spring Heel Jack.
Although I have some sympathy with his claim that the listener becomes 'rhyth-
mically obedient' in popular music, it also has to be recognized that not all popu-

lar music creates 'slaves to the rhythm', being pre-programmed and calculated to elicit a specific, uniform response – some popular music, of course, is explicitly anti-rhythmical.[5] Again, although he is, of course, right to draw attention to the emotion-evoking qualities of popular music, it is simply naïve to go on to claim that, over against classical music, the emotions evoked by popular music are necessarily superficial because of the lesser demands made upon the listener.

Having thus judged popular music, Adorno goes further. Such music, he argues, is essentially opium for the masses, in that it contributes to the maintenance of the social relations of capitalist production. Andy Bennett helpfully summarizes his argument:

> First, it acts as a form of distraction, in unison with other forms of mass-produced leisure, ensuring that working-class consumers remain oblivious to the mechanisms of oppression that underpin the capitalist mode of production. Second, the 'patterned and pre-digested' nature of the music offers relief 'from both boredom and effort simultaneously' with the result that periods of leisure can be tailored to provide maximum relaxation and refreshment for the workforce.[6]

Part of the problem with Adorno's analysis is that it is, as Brian Longhurst has argued, 'too constrained by his own historical and social location, of being a highly educated, musically literate German intellectual of the mid-twentieth century. Owing to his lack of reflection on the effects this may have, his approach has many difficulties in coping with social and historical change in music making, as he continued to value a particular and very specific form of music.'[7] That said, to be fair to Adorno, he did not have a great deal of variety to observe in the mid-twentieth-century Western world. Since the Tin Pan Alley music of the 1930s (with which he had some familiarity), popular music has moved on considerably, developing numerous and diverse sub-genres and innovations. Hence, whereas there may have been some evidence for his argument that people receive pop music in much the same way at this early period, today it would be difficult to argue that the music of Kylie Minogue, the Sex Pistols and Nusrat Fateh Ali Khan is received and responded to in the same way: Kylie certainly is rhythmic, party-pop; the Sex Pistols' classic album *Never Mind the Bollocks* (1977), on the other hand, was countercultural, ideologically driven and, in its own way, revolutionary;[8] different again is the music of Nusrat Fateh Ali Khan, one of the best-known singers of *qawwali* (Sufi music).[9] This does not, of course, mean that individuals might not receive the Sex Pistols, or indeed Mozart, in the same way that they receive Kylie, or that Nusrat Fateh Ali Khan may not inspire that which is countercultural and ideological. It is simply to say that 'some forms of music may be valued because they are exceptionally good to dance to, others may invite contemplation, and so on.'[10] Hence, Longhurst makes the point that 'these pleasures are not all as superficial as Adorno seems to think.'[11] This overall point is surely correct, for we will see that, in some cases, the pleasures are not at all superficial and sometimes, as in the case of the Sex Pistols, have far-reaching effects. Again, the argument of this section, and indeed this chapter, concurs to some extent with McGuigan's general thesis that 'mass-popular culture is the primary terrain of cultural struggle'. Without denying that much, possibly most, popular culture is standardized and cliché-ridden, he argues that some mass-popular genres are able to 'articulate progressive possibility and disturb a prevailing sense of "reality"'.[12] Having said that, it is important to note that, for Adorno, while popular music may be superficial, its overall impact is not at all superficial. For Adorno, popular culture is, as Chris Barker notes, 'a matter not just of overt meanings, but of the structuring of the human psyche into conformist ways'.[13] According to Adorno 'the total effect of the culture industry is one of anti-enlightenment, in which... enlightenment, progressive technical domination, becomes mass deception and is turned into a means of fettering consciousness.' Consequently, 'it impedes the development of autonomous, independent individuals who judge and decide consciously for themselves... while obstructing the emancipation for which human beings are as ripe as the productive forces of the epoch permit'.[14] Such consequences are hardly superficial.

To continue the critique of Adorno's analysis of popular music in terms of mass production, whilst not wanting to deny some obvious elements of mass production and some degree of standardization, it is difficult, nowadays, to argue that *all* popular music is fundamentally controlled by the principles of mass production designed to produce a set of standardized, routinized responses, which 'reinforces the domination of society by those who control the industrial apparatus' and that 'the vast majority of the population are passive and falsely happy owing to their manipulation by the culture industry, which feeds them products they think they want'.[15] This is simply to ignore, not only the creators of music, some of which are seeking to articulate and inspire specifically anti-capitalist, anti-'culture industry' ideologies, but also the role and the power of the audience in the reception of the music. That is to say, more attention needs to be given to why people produce music and the way it is used and incorporated into personal histories. There needs to be some 'thick' description of popular music. It is not enough simply to describe what people do, we need to understand what they think they are doing when they do what they do. Once this is done, it will be seen that, in general terms, to quote some words of Nicholas Abercrombie (with reference to the theory of hegemony developed by Antonio Gramsci), 'popular culture cannot be seen as a simple imposition of dominant ideology on the subordinate classes... One cannot speak of domination here but rather for the struggle for hegemony – that is, moral, cultural and political leadership. For Gramsci, the bourgeoisie can achieve hegemony only to the extent that it can accommodate subordinate class values. The establishment of hegemony is thus a case of negotiation between dominant and subordinate values.'[16] Hence, the point is that there is *at least* a two-way, supply-and-demand relationship between listeners and the products of the culture industry. Indeed, as I will argue below, there are many instances of the relationship being essentially one-way (in the opposite direction to Adorno's thesis), in that the record companies have little to do with the process, apart from producing 'functional artefacts'. Hence, to quote John Fiske, 'I do not believe that "the people" are "cultural dopes"; they are not a passive helpless mass incapable of discrimination and thus at the economic, cultural, and political mercy of the barons of industry.'[17] In short, the Adornian passivity thesis is fundamentally flawed.

The above also, of course, has implications for the argument that popular music is a form of cultural imperialism. Some have argued, for example, that the United States imposes a certain form of music on the world and then reaps the economic benefits. This ignores the complexities of the migration and the influence of music. There is, for example, a plurality of forms of 'world music' which are now, themselves, influencing Western music and, to some extent, have themselves been influenced by Western musical styles (e.g. reggae, bhangra, and gospel).[18] As Mike Featherstone argues, 'a paradoxical consequence of the process of globalization, the awareness of the finitude of the boundedness of the planet and humanity, is not to produce homogeneity but to familiarize us with greater diversity, the extensive range of local cultures'.[19]

Finally, on Adorno, it is worth noting Bernard Gendron's argument that his thesis suffers from a confusion of 'functional' and 'textual' artefacts: 'A text (whether written or oral) is a universal, whereas a functional artefact is a particular. However, to be marketed and possessed, every universal text must be embodied in some functional artefact (paper, vinyl discs).'[20] The point is that whilst CDs are obviously mass-produced and often marketed by large corporations, we should not therefore simply assume that the text carried on the CD is, in the same sense, part of the process of mass production. In other words, as Longhurst says, 'the universal artefacts which are the product of the music industry may be produced under industrialized conditions whereas the actual recording may not be'.[21] Again, one only has to think of the various world-music artists recorded in rural communities around the world, or of the dub reggae produced in backyard sheds in Jamaica, or the ideological anarchy of a band like Crass,[22] or the left-wing politics of the late Joe Strummer (formerly of The Clash). Whilst such 'folk' music (i.e. music of the people) is sometimes mass-produced and marketed by large corporations, localized and often subversive texts should not be confused with the process. Although it should be noted that Adorno did recognize the homespun nature of some popular music, his overall thesis does not satisfactorily account for it. Regardless of mass production, standardization, rationalization and so on, new, idiosyncratic, even revolutionary music and ideologies, which have little to do with 'big business', can be disseminated widely through the functional artefacts in which they are embodied.

Hence, against the arguments of Adorno that mass culture signals the retreat of individual autonomy in favour of 'scientific-technological rationality', and against the consequent view that individuals are denied the possibility of creative participation in popular culture, simply becoming cultural puppets, this chapter explores how (in relation to spirituality) mass culture is not simply imposed from above, and how its reception is not simply a matter of pre-programming. Quoting Reebee Garofalo, Bennett makes the important point that, whilst mass culture is an arena in which 'the forces arrayed in support of the existing hegemony are formidable, there are also numerous instances where mass culture – and in particular popular music – issues serious challenges to hegemonic power'.[23] Indeed, record companies not only necessarily exercise loose control over many artists, but often they do not understand the cultural texts that they market. Hence, for example, Mary Harron has observed that in the wake of the 1960s hippie move-ment 'record companies...were confused and even alarmed by the strange groups whose music was so profitable [and had to] bring in young outsiders to tell them what would make a hit'.[24] Whether one considers rock 'n' roll, psyche-delia, punk rock, 1990s acid house, the socio-political ideologies of anti-Vietnam war songs, Rock Against Racism in 1970s Britain, or the Nation of Islam ideology of some rap music, there are numerous challenges to the Adornian passivity argument.

That said, to reiterate my earlier comments, this does not mean that Adorno's analysis can be dismissed. My point is simply that, while disagreeing with Adorno's particular negative analysis of popular music as fundamentally authori-tarian and repressive, his general argument that it is transformative and socially consequential is important. However, the process is bilateral, not unilateral.

The Occultural Significance of Popular Music

The point of the above brief discussion of Adorno and some of the issues raised by contemporary popular music theorists is not to investigate the politics of pop *per se*, but rather to provide some insights which will help us to understand ways in which it might function as a vehicle of occulture. We have seen, in particular, that the production and distribution processes of popular music are less important than the value of pop as a cultural resource. This brings me back to a point made by Campbell and McIver: 'commercial interests dictate that the interests of the majority are catered for and hence the extensive treatment of occult themes is yet further testimony to a degree of popular occult commitment'.[25] If there is some truth both to the argument concerning the significance of popular music and also to the argument concerning the emergence and significance of occulture in the West, then one would expect popular music, at certain points, to reflect occultural commitment and to be implicated in the process of sacralization. Even if we limit our analysis to the Easternization of popular music, as discussed in Chapter 5, it is not difficult to show that this is indeed the case. In short, this section explores the sacralization of popular music, arguing that it is a significant vehicle for occul-ture, in that key occultural streams use religious symbolism and even develop explicitly spiritual themes, which both reflect the countercultural interests of the producers and also contribute to the worldviews of the consumers – many of whom, of course, are already occulturally aware.[26]

Again, it is important to understand that there is a two-way, supply-and-demand relationship between listeners and the culture industry. More speci-fically, music is subculturally and homologically significant.[27] As Gary Baddeley puts it, 'Music helps to define your cultural tribe.'[28] Record companies *may* have little to do with the process, apart from producing 'functional artefacts' which disseminate and develop occultural ideas that reflect the interests and concerns of a particular subculture. On the one hand, artists not only reflect public interest in aspects of occulture, but also stimulate this interest by their association with it. Occulture is invested with subcultural capital by being associated with certain artists – i.e. it becomes 'cool'. On the other hand, to be invested with 'coolness', popular culture needs to reflect themes within the dominant milieu or within a particular subculture. Arguably, Cliff Richard lacks *subcultural* capital, not because of his musical output, but rather because the community and the beliefs with which he is identified lack subcultural capital. Again, whereas Marilyn Manson (known particularly for his Antichrist Superstar persona[29]) would, I suspect, retain much of his coolness even if he started dressing more conventionally but still remained ostensibly related to the occultural milieu, I doubt this would be the case if he continued to dress as he does now, but became a Christian and disseminated Christian cultural ideas. Of course, there are Christian artists who are appreciated because of their musical talent. However, it is enormously difficult for such artists to accrue subcultural capital because they do not reflect the prevailing cultural milieu. It may be pointed out that an artist such as Moby (Richard Melville Hall) is both Christian and, to some extent, 'cool'. However, Moby is cool *despite* his Christianity, *not* because of it. On the one hand, he is *not* conspicuously Christian, and on the other hand, he is able to accrue enough subcultural capital from beliefs he holds that resonate with occulture. That is to say, the views he is known to be passionate about are *less* identifiably those of traditional Christian culture than they are of alternative subcultures: e.g. he is a vegan and a defender of animal rights.[30] Similarly, whilst most of the band U2 are Christian, not only do they explicitly identify with a range of subcultural concerns, but there is sufficient ambiguity in their lyrics for their music to have a wide appeal. Again, although Van Morrison has travelled from Scientology to a broadly Christian faith, and even released a successful single with Cliff Richard,[31] his nature mysticism and Celtic spirituality reflect occultural concerns. Indeed, Collis argues that he is 'a pantheist at heart'[32] – though perhaps 'panentheist' would be more accurate.

Significant examples of occultural sacrilization would be, in the context of late-1960s Easternization, the Hindu mantras chanted on George Harrison's 'My Sweet Lord',[33] or the lyrics to The Beatles' 'Within You Without You'.[34] As Wilfred Mellers notes concerning the latter, it 'brings in the religious implications of the search for identity. "The space between us all" – which was the burden of most of the songs on Side 1 – will be abolished when we submit to love, and "life flows on", within us and without us. The Indian drone of eternity returns'.[35] Again, although far more influenced by Easternized psychedelia, the song 'Tomorrow Never Knows', from the album *Revolver* (1966),[36] even has John Lennon chanting words from the psychedelic classic by Timothy Leary, Richard Alpert and Ralph Metzner, *The Psychedelic Experience: A Manual Based on the Tibetan Book of the Dead*.[37] As Ian MacDonald writes in his excellent study of Beatles records, *A Revolution in the Head*, 'While Harrison was devoting himself to Indian music and McCartney to classical, Lennon had become interested in exploring his mental "inner space" with LSD. Since there was no "acid" sub-culture in Britain in 1966, he lacked any guidance to this dangerous drug and so turned to a product of the American scene: *The Psychedelic Experience*'.[38] Apparently, in January 1966, Lennon took LSD for the third time with the specific intention of embarking on a journey of self-discovery – his roadmap being *The Psychedelic Experience*. However, because it is difficult to read while 'tripping', he decided to record himself reading the book prior to taking LSD, so that he could replay the tape as the drug began to take effect. The result, as MacDonald puts it, 'was spectacular and he hastened to capture it in song, taking many of its lines directly from Leary and Alpert's text – above all its rapturous invocation of the supposed reality behind appearances: The Void.'[39] Hence, 'Tomorrow Never Knows' began life as 'The Void'. Indeed, this was the first song recorded for *Revolver*.[40] Under its eventual title the song, which exhorted the listener to 'Turn off your mind, relax and float downstream', introduced, as MacDonald says, 'LSD and Leary's psychedelic revolution to the young of the Western world, becoming one of *the most socially influential records* The Beatles ever made.'[41] Again, at Leary's request, Lennon wrote the countercultural song 'Come Together' for his campaign against Ronald Reagan for the governorship of California in 1969. Indeed, the phrase was coined by Leary as his campaign slogan.[42] 'Enthusiastically received in campus and underground circles', the song, says MacDonald (perhaps a little sensationally), 'is *the* key song of the turn of the decade, embodying a pivotal moment when the free world's coming generation rejected established wisdom, knowledge, ethics, and behaviour for a drug-inspired relativism which has since undermined the intellectual foundations of Western culture.'[43] Little wonder then that Leary hailed The Beatles as 'Divine Messiahs, the wisest, holiest, most effective avatars the human race has yet pro-duced, prototypes of a new race of laughing freemen'.[44]

As we have seen, The Beatles are, of course, not alone in this respect. The explicit influence of Sri Chimnoy can be found in the music of Carlos Santana and, particularly, John McLaughlin's Mahavishnu Orchestra.[45] From a more eclectic and Pagan perspective, thus reflecting the dominant occultural themes of the 1980s and 1990s, one might think of bands such as Ozric Tentacles (formed at the 1983 Stonehenge free festival), or the explicit Paganism of such as Inkubus Sukkubus, Catt Von Trapp, Marillion[46] and Julian Cope[47] – whose *Rite* (1992) and *Jehovahkill* (1992)[48] are particularly interesting in this respect. Concerning music within Paganism, Melvyn Willin comments, 'it is very important to twenty-first century Pagans and where it has been composed there would appear to be a move away from the stereotypical hag with broomstick etc. towards a deeper emotional interpretation that is closer in portraying contemporary Pagans and witches'.[49] Again, recent occultural trends can be found in the nature spirituality of Tori Amos,[50] the extreme right-wing Norse paganism of a band like Burzum,[51] and the Satanism of fellow Norwegian black metal group Mayhem.[52]

Interestingly, while there are discernible phases in popular music, there being, for example, a much greater emphasis on world music and indigenous cultures nowadays, there has been, since the sixties, an eclecticism which has some rela-tion to the general topography of occulture. Hence, we will see that, as well as the peace, the love and the turning east of the late 1960s and early 1970s, which reflected a certain stream of popular occultural interest, this period also saw the emergence of both Pagan and darker occultural themes, the latter being particularly evident in the music of, for example, Black Sabbath, Coven, Magick (whose founder, Graham Bond, claimed to be the illegitimate son of Crowley[53]), and particularly Black Widow's 1970 album *Sacrifice* (which entered the 'Top 40' in the UK music charts).[54] These themes are, of course, evident today in both progressive dance music (e.g. *Scorpio Rising* by Death in Vegas[55]) and particularly in heavy metal culture and the music of bands such as Mayhem and, more popularly, Marilyn Manson. Although some of these musicians and groups, such as Black Sabbath, have no personal dark occultural spiritual commitment, others do. For example, Manson is a member of the Church of Satan, having received an honorary priesthood from the Church's founder, Anton LaVey, for services to music. Indeed, he has even written the foreword to LaVey's collection of essays, *Satan Speaks*.[56]

A more significant artist within popular culture, who both shares Marilyn Manson's interest in Charles Manson and openly fraternized with LaVey, was Genesis P-Orridge – who, we saw in Chapter 4, was probably responsible for the term 'occulture'. P-Orridge is a particularly interesting case, because not only did he articulate explicit occultural ideas through music, he actually founded a new religion, Thee Temple ov Psychick Youth (TOPY).[57] TOPY, which is described as a 'worldwide network to help encourage and support the development of multi-dimensional individuals',[58] is considered by some to have been 'the most influential new occult order of the 1980s'.[59] Describing himself as an 'esoterrorist' and significantly influenced by William Burroughs, whom he knew personally, Genesis P-Orridge, first through his band Throbbing Gristle (which was disbanded in 1981) and then through Psychic TV (formed in 1982) – which functioned as the popular mouthpiece of TOPY – articulated numerous themes from occulture, both in his songs and in his live stage shows. Indeed, to help promote his anarchic occultural worldview, the respected avant-garde director Derek Jarman even made a film for him entitled *Stations of the Cross* (which was later used to falsely accuse TOPY and especially P-Orridge of satanic ritual abuse). Although he claimed in an early interview that he did not personally 'inherit and subscribe to there being Gods, demons, outside forces or anything else',[60] nonetheless he writes openly of, amongst other subjects, Enochian magick, scrying, alchemy and Freemasonry.[61] Indeed, believing the whole of history to be saturated with the occult, he is annoyed that it is not introduced into the school curriculum. He wonders why, for example, he was taught about Elizabeth I, but not about her astrologer, the much-discussed occultist John Dee.[62] Critical of Christianity,[63] and, like Crowley, emphasizing sex and sexual magick,[64] TOPY seeks to rectify this. 'There is,' he says, 'an occult side to it... For me, privately, The Temple means everything that's important to do, think and feel.'[65] As Gavin Baddeley notes of Psychic TV, 'the use of musical beats to alter consciousness and the concert experience as ritual were primary concerns... Similarly, spiritual extremes of pleasure and pain were prominent features of TOPY ritual.'[66] Indeed, Baddeley goes so far as to claim that P-Orridge, Psychic TV and TOPY played a prominent part in both the emergence of the European acid house scene and the fashion for body mortification and piercing – the latter being central to their live shows in the early 1980s.

Also significant is Thee Family ov Psychick Individuals (FOPI), which, describing itself as a 'cybertribal community', was formed by Rob Landon in 1998 as a sort of spiritual Psychic TV (PTV) fan club. In Landon's words:

> FOPI, Family ov Psychick Individuals, began as my idea to get other PTV fans involved in robbing the bank of information, and collaborating to form an archive of this information for the World Wide Web. Most of the PTV fans that I have met are archivists of various information, and my idea was to bring these archivists together to uncover the vast information that was put out by PTV and its various members. This Site has grown quite a bit from its first conception, and still there is so much more to do. Beyond just archiving the information, I also wanted to bring together the various fans of PTV. I wanted to link together their personal pages, through the 'Family' page, and through the 'Links' page.[67]

Hence, FOPI is a spiritual community fundamentally related to and engendered by popular culture. That said, whilst beginning as a group of individuals drawn together because of a common interest in 'the musick, art, magick, and philosophies related to the band Psychic TV', Landon explains that people who wish to join FOPI need not be fans of PTV: 'it is open to all open-minded individuals that wish to engage in discussion and interaction'.[68]

Even if many bands who explicitly make use of the dark occultural worldview are not personally committed to it in the way that P-Orridge and Marilyn Manson are, it is of some significance that they are, nevertheless, keen to pretend. Hence, whilst the Canadian death metal band Cryptopsy states quite categorically, 'No one really believes in religion in the band, we are not Satanists either',[69] nonetheless they are keen *bricoleurs* of dark occulture. This raises a question as to why non-religious musicians enthusiastically plunder occulture for inspiration, yet few, if any, would even consider positively adopting Christian themes and iconography. The answer is, again, that occulture is cool. (The fascination of heavy metal musicians and fans with the dark occulture will be discussed more fully in Volume II).

The Easternization of Popular Music

To return specifically to the Easternization of popular music, Ian MacDonald's insightful discussion of The Beatles illustrates well the main argument of this section:

> So in tune were they with the spirit of the times that they sometimes seemed almost god-like, especially to young listeners. In fact, The Beatles, while very observant and in some ways prescient, weren't so much causing the great social and psychological changes of the era as mirroring them. The key was that they picked up on certain special ideas before most of their immediate competitors, when these ideas were still at an elite stage of development. Moreover, by selling millions of records, the group magnified what it reflected, exporting elite trends and concepts to the intelligent and enquiring side of the mainstream.
>
> The most striking example of this is probably The Beatles' interest in oriental religion, which turned an interest shared by only a few in the West in 1965 into a subject of discussion right across Western society within two years. The group didn't invent the Western interest in Eastern thought, which had begun as an elite pursuit in the late-18th

century; however, the popular (and generally sincere) fascination with oriental wisdom
which ensued in the late-'60s and thereafter owes almost everything to The Beatles in
their role as cultural antennae of the mainstream.[70]

Essentially, The Beatles tapped into the occultural stream, which was, as Mac-
Donald recognizes, still flowing underground in 1965 and, focusing on Eastern
spirituality, they brought it bubbling excitedly to the surface. Hence, whilst he
overestimates the significance of the impact of The Beatles on the spirituality of
the 1960s (he ignores, for example, the importance of American counterculture
and, I would argue, literary figures such as Aldous Huxley, Alan Watts, Jack
Kerouac and Allen Ginsberg[71]), he is not entirely wide of the mark when he
claims that 'it was their absorption in Indian religion which started the spiritual
revival of the late-'60s … Bruce Springsteen has said that Elvis liberated people's
bodies while Dylan liberated their minds. The Beatles, though, did far more mind
liberating than Dylan, by virtue of their greater sales and because they worked in
simpler, less essentially sceptical ways.'[72] As he says, 'when The Beatles visually
namechecked their cultural icons on the cover of *Sgt. Pepper*, they meant to
encourage popular curiosity'.[73] The list of figures appearing on the famous cover
by Peter Blake – a list which was provided by The Beatles themselves[74] – include
Sri Yukteswar, Sri Lahiri Mahasaya, Sri Paramahansa Yogananda, Aleister
Crowley and Huxley. Hence, in 'being open to existing elite ideas, by themselves
being changed by these trends and concepts, and by almost immediately allowing
these changes to affect their work',[75] The Beatles were popularizing occulture,
and thereby inspiring a new generation of spiritual seekers. Hence, while some
perhaps overestimate their significance, their role in occultural sacralization
should also not be underestimated.

As noted above, there were of course many other significant figures during
this period involved in the process of occulturation. (I will argue for Huxley's
significance in Volume II.) William Burroughs and Allen Ginsberg are particularly noteworthy. For example, in the early 1960s, partly influenced by his friend
Jack Kerouac, who had been reading Buddhist texts since 1950, Ginsberg began
articulating a philosophy influenced by Eastern spirituality. In 1962 he travelled
to Europe and then on to India in search of a teacher: 'By then I was quite well
known as a poet, and I figured that the proper move, being now famous, would
be to disappear into India for a couple of years and look for some wisdom, and
also experience a different culture than the Western culture, which I thought
… was perhaps exhausted of inspiration and it was time for a second relig-
iousness, so I went to look for a teacher.'[76] He continues: 'Beginning with my
time in India in 1963, I began doing a lot of mantra chanting, and for many years
I prefaced my poetry readings with either Buddhist or Hindu chants. I used to
travel with Ram Dass and read poetry and do some chanting with him, and I
developed a voice that way, through music.'[77] Again, Michael Horrowitz recalls
arranging a reading for Ginsberg in May 1965, which turned out to be enormously successful: 'He'd just been in India and was playing his bells and
chanting, and I joined in the chanting. This Tibetan chanting I remember being
the background sound to that summer. We decided to have a bigger reading, and

Ginsberg said, "Yes, let's bring together you English assholes."... We did a lot of work, put Ginsberg on television, sprayed all the press, and quickly got masses of helpers. It was a glorious summer.'[78] Hence, in the summer of 1965, when The Beatles themselves were only just becoming occulturally aware, Ginsberg's interest in Eastern spirituality and countercultural ideals was being widely disseminated amongst 'English assholes'.

The general occultural impact stimulated by numerous icons of popular culture was such that sacralizing ripples spread throughout Western culture – and can still be felt today. Of course, many, like George Harrison (who became a lifelong devotee of the International Society for Krishna Consciousness) and Allen Ginsberg (who became a Buddhist), moved on from occultural eclecticism to formalized religious commitment. Indeed, although again, he goes too far and fails to recognize the complexity of the process of Easternization and the importance of American counterculture, there is some truth to MacDonald's claim that it was Harrison who 'inspired the West's mainstream acquaintance with Hindu religion and created the late '60s so-called spiritual revival'. He continues, 'This single-handed responsibility for such a fundamental cultural sea-change is an abiding testimony to Harrison's importance as a countercultural figure, albeit that he would have felt uncomfortable being described as such.'[79] Furthermore, even if MacDonald is not technically correct in every detail about the occultural significance of Harrison and The Beatles, this is perhaps less important than the fact that, as a music journalist, he reads cultural history in this way. In other words, it is significant in itself that he (and he is by no means alone) understands the West to have undergone such 'a fundamental sea-change' as a result of popular music.

Certainly, by the 1970s, the very sound of Eastern music was almost synonymous with 'spirituality'. For example, Susan Fast's excellent analysis of Led Zeppelin's music and, in particular, of how it has been received by fans makes this association explicit: 'Many of the fans' comments suggest that "Kashmir" [one of the band's more famous tracks] or the use of Eastern elements in their music gives it a "mystical" or "mysterious" quality, and some take this further, suggesting that there is something "ethereal," "otherworldly," and "timeless" about these elements as used by Zeppelin'.[80] Speaking specifically of 'Kashmir', the fans she spoke to confirmed this. Typically, it was identified as 'a beautiful and innovative exotic song that takes me on an ethereal journey to a far away land... It makes the music mystical'; 'Eastern elements are very welcome as I practice meditation and love the vibe. Brings their music to a new level... I love the Eastern sound.'[81] It is not surprising, therefore, as we will see later in this section, that more recently, musicians who have been involved in the composition of trance and ambient music often make use of Eastern (including Arabic) musics. Of course, as was the case with Led Zeppelin, this is usually part of a broader occultural eclecticism.

For explicitly 'New Age' musicians, of course, the rationale for the music is religious. For example, having been inspired by Stanislav Grof's *The Holotropic Mind*, Steve Roach's *The Magnificent Void* [82] was specifically composed for the nurturing of occultural spirituality. Again, Steve Hillage, who has travelled from playing with the hippie band Gong, through an enormously popular solo career in the 1970s, to become an influential techno-artist in the 1990s (with Miquette Giraudy as System 7) has not only consistently made his interest in eclectic, alternative spirituality explicit, but composed his evocative *Rainbow Dome Musick*[83] especially for the 1979 New Age Mind–Body–Spirit Festival. (There are also many artists whose work is 'implicitly New Age' – in that they are musicians to which the term 'New Age' is sometimes ascribed, their music being conducive to meditative states – but who often do not understand their own work in such terms. Such artists would include Steve Reich, Brian Eno, and Holgar Czukay.[84])

Another good example of the explicit, occultural Easternization of popular music can be found in the work of Japan's former lead singer, David Sylvian. Along with his wife, the singer and dancer Ingrid Chavez, he became a devotee of Sri Sri Mata Amritanandamayi (Shree Ma), to whom he has since dedicated his compilation album *Camphor*[85] and his tour 'Slow Fire'. Indeed, the album *Dead Bees on a Cake*[86] offers, as Christoph Cox says, 'glimpses into the Hindu mysticism to which [he had] become devoted'.[87] After completing *Dead Bees on a Cake*, Sylvian, Chavez and their three children moved to Napa Valley to live with their guru for a short while, after which they moved to New Hampshire, where Sylvian set up his own record label, Samadhi Sound. Sylvian is one of many musicians to understand music to have spiritual properties. This is conspicuous in his comments about a recording of Tuvan shamanic singing (he entitled his 1988 tour 'In Praise of Shamans'): 'I'm very interested in the power of music to work on this level. My guru, Amma, she also sings. And Shree Ma is a beautiful singer. They choose to work through music to elevate the spirit. With them, music is pure light.'[88] (He has recorded Shree Ma singing on his composition 'Praise'.[89]) Although Sylvian does not understand his music in this 'pure light' spiritual sense, it is nevertheless couched in spirituality. More significantly, this is the way many of his fans understand his recent work. In the words of one music journalist, 'He's become a guru, a god… People actually rush to the stage to shake his hands, kiss them, rest their foreheads on his palms.'[90] Again, tongue firmly in cheek, Ryan Gilby comments: 'I swear I saw him turn somebody's mineral water into Chablis.'[91] Although I feel sure that Sylvian is not looking explicitly for this sort of adulation, the hype surrounding him certainly has a sacralizing effect. He wears traditional Indian garb and his merchandizing often includes soft-focus photographs of him in iconic poses. Indeed, his biographer Martin Power is very critical of what he calls 'the rampant mythologising' of Sylvian's image. The posters for the Slow Fire tour 'featured blurred shots of David, arms outstretched, as if welcoming his followers'. Such 'iconographic aspects of the merchandising' created a certain 'messianic aura'.[92] He continues, 'if one added the poetic, almost mystical aspect of his lyrics to the overall package, a… religious undertone behind the marketing of Slow Fire began to emerge.'[93]

To return to where this section began, the psychedelic period of the 1960s and 1970s was (as we have seen in Chapter 5) enormously significant for the popular dissemination of a range of broadly Eastern occultural ideas,[94] which continued into the 1980s and 1990s, and is still with us today. Increasingly, items such as tablas,[95] *qawwali* singers, and sitars are becoming ubiquitous spiritual signifiers in contemporary music. That said, likewise following occultural trends in the 1960s, we have seen that we cannot speak simply in terms of Easternization. As the inclusion of individuals such as Crowley on The Beatles' *Sgt. Pepper* cover and the title of The Rolling Stones' *Their Satanic Majesties Request* (1967) suggest, even during the 1960s the truly eclectic nature of occulture was becoming apparent. This has continued. Because it was (and is) not drawing directly on, for example, Indian culture, but rather on Western occulture, it was (and is) very rarely entirely Eastern. Jay Stevens notes that

> Aldous Huxley would have been overjoyed at this intermingling of East and West, but he might have been a trifle disturbed at the amount of occult chaff that was getting mixed in with the grains of perennial philosophy. Although Huxley had predicted that LSD would waken the Baby Boom's slumbering appetite for spiritual meaning, he hadn't anticipated what would happen once this hunger began searching for something to feed upon ... [The] perennial philosophy came heavily spiced with astrology, numerology, alchemy, black magic, voodoo; a crazy quilt of arcane practice and contemporary jargon that affronted the Western intellect's need to formalize, to abstract out a workable map from anarchic reality.[96]

As we have seen, a good example of such occultural eclecticism is The Incredible String Band's *The 5000 Spirits or the Layers of an Onion* (1967), the cover of which depicts a Janus-faced, half-male, half-female, winged being holding a serpent in one hand and an ankh in the other,[97] and the music of which betrays a mix of Indian and Celtic influences. 'If the album possesses a single theme,' says Robert Pendleton, 'it is that of the transcendent imagination, the mind's ability to generate and perceive alternate realities. Before we even place the record on the turntable, the cover gives us some strong pointers towards this. Both front and rear covers express an unfolding cosmic vision of the wonder and variety of natural forms perceived by the single, unified eye of mystical perception'.[98] As Rowan Williams, the Archbishop of Canterbury, writes of their music *per se*, 'the literacy you might have needed to pick up all the allusions was and is intimidating – Sufism, Celtic myth, Biblical and Gnostic symbols... For those of us who fell in love with the ISB, there was a feeling of breathing the air of a very expansive imagination indeed. It was alright to be enchanted... by colossal antique symbols.'[99] Again, George McKay indicates the occultural eclecticism of this period in his comments about Nicholas Saunders' classic directory of the underground, *Alternative London*:

> The first edition of *Alternative London*, from December 1970, contains a short section on alternative religions, mainly Eastern ones such as Hinduism, Buddhism, Sufism. By the third edition, for the summer solstice of 1972, Saunders is including a section on English mysticism, which explains that 'There is a current reawakening of English mysticism – quite apart from the Druids. Over the last few years some quite separate legends and phenomena have begun to be understood as part of the same pattern...' Other Londoners too were looking for their own spiritual answers...[100]

Finally, it is perhaps worth noting that, although versions of hippie culture continued for many years, by 1970 the countercultural idealism and utopianism of 'flower power' was severely eroded. The reasons for this are many, but central to the sense of disillusionment were the horrific murders by Charles Manson's followers in August 1969, quickly followed in December by the tragedy at The Rolling Stones' Altamont festival. Concerning the latter, following the famous Woodstock festival, which suggested to many that peace, love and utopian community were a real possibility,[101] The Rolling Stones decided to hold their own festival in Golden Gate Park, San Francisco – which was effectively the geographic centre of the hippie movement. However, their plans were thwarted and they had to move it to the nearby speedway track at Altamont. At the suggestion of their support band, The Grateful Dead, they hired Hell's Angels to take care of the security. Needless to say, crowd control was carried out with ruthless enthusiasm. Tragically, the violence eventually erupted into a riot, during which 100 people were injured and three people murdered. Not only did this lead Jagger to turn his back on the occultism with which he had been flirting,[102] but it also stands as a significant milestone in the demise of the love generation – the 1960s had come to an end and it was clear to many that The Beatles mantra 'all you need is love' was nice, but naïve.

Nevertheless, the point of this section has been to argue that Easternized, neo-Romantic occulture, which surfaced in the 1960s, has continued and, particularly during the last couple of decades, has surfaced and is beginning to shape mainstream popular culture. Westerners are becoming increasingly fluent in their use of new spiritual signifieds and signifiers.

Festival Culture

Concerning these Easternized, and particularly Pagan and neo-Romantic, elements of occulture, they emerge explicitly in the music festivals of the period, particularly the free festivals that took place with increasing frequency throughout the 1970s and into the 1980s. Kevin Hetherington, for example, persuasively argues that a continuity exists between 1960s hippie culture and the more eclectic free festivals.[103] Promoting an idealistic, romanticized notion of love, community, spirituality, and relationship to the land, 'the most lively [young people] escape geographically and physically to the "Never Never Land" of a free festival where they become citizens, indeed rulers, in a new reality'.[104] In 1972 the first Windsor Free Festival was held, and a couple of years later the first Stonehenge festival (1974), the latter becoming the longest-lasting annual 'free' countercultural event. Its location is, of course, significant, in that it was not chosen because of its archaeological interest as a historic monument. Festival-goers were not members of the National Trust interested in pottering around ancient monuments; they were countercultural Pagans interested in both music and sacred space – Stonehenge being understood to have links with pre-Christian, Druidic spirituality (as is very clear from the posters advertising the events, many of which include illustrations of Druids). Here, music, countercultural politics, and contemporary Pagan spirituality meet. While music has always been central to free festivals, they were often much more than simply music events, music being, as Clarke notes, 'only one of a variety of activities which, apart from participation in running the site, and preparing and distributing food, may include arts and crafts of various sorts, music and forms of theatre, folk dancing, fireworks and various manifestations of commitment to ecological awareness and to the occult'.[105] I remember, for example, attending one at the Horseshoe Pass in Wales in the late 1970s at which there was very little music, the main attractions simply being the gathering of like-minded people, vegetarian food, magic mushrooms, and a general acceptance of some amorphous, romantic nature spirituality.

Music festivals since the late 1960s are worth dwelling on, therefore, not only because of their overall importance as countercultural events, but also because they provide a window through which to view the occultural significance of popular music. Stonehenge, which was held between 1974 and 1984, is generally acknowledged to be the most important of the free festivals. The child of occultural spirituality, it was initiated by Philip Russell, who was 'a kind of charismatic hippy mystic'.[106] (That said, Tim Abbot notes that, although 'a psychedelic anarchist, he had a strong traditional streak'.[107]) Known to his friends as Wally Hope, he and a group of his followers, the 'Wallies', squatted the site in 1974 and held a small summer solstice festival, declaring that 'Our generation is the best mass movement in history – experimenting with anything in our search for love and peace. Our temple is sound, we fight our battles with music, drums like thunder, cymbals like lightning, banks of electronic equipment like nuclear missiles of sound.'[108] So began a significant occultural and countercultural annual event, which has, over the years, realized Russell's dream of reclaiming Stonehenge as a focus for 'spiritual activism'.[109] While very clearly *not* a Christian event, I was interested to read the letter sent by Wally Hope 'to the farmer of the land around Stonehenge' in spring 1974, in that it actually reflects a deeply Christian spirituality (spelling and grammar left unchanged):

Dear Sir,

With all well meaning respect, Our Lord God and his son Jesus Christ, have ordained a spiritual Pilgrimage to Stonehenge on 20th June 21st etc., to fulfill the

TWO COMMAND MEANTS

LOVE GOD

Love your neighbour.

You are and will be our neighbour we beg you for help, friendship and trust, if the gathering is overflowing big, we will give you any help you need, but you must respect we are to GOD'S law, and trying to balance the violence, cormption [competition], insuing 3rd world war, oily energy crisis, to manual communal farming love peace and freedom.

Your Best mate WALLY

For the Kids x
HELP[110]

Stonehenge, of course, was not the first music festival, or indeed the first 'free festival'. As Michael Clarke has shown, not only can festivals, as cultural gatherings, be traced back many centuries, but twentieth-century popular music festivals, held as commercial ventures, began many years before the free festivals of the 1970s, with folk and jazz events in America.[111] More significant for the emergence of the festival as a countercultural 'happening' were several large-scale events in the 1960s, most notably Woodstock in the US[112] and the Isle of Wight in the UK. Emerging partly as a protest against the commercialism and capitalism of the large-scale festivals, a *free* festival was initially a festival at which no profit was made by the organizers. However, Hetherington is quite right to argue that they quickly became much more than this: 'Free festivals developed not only as a critique of larger commercial festivals but also as a utopian model of an alternative society, aiming to offer an ethos of freedom from constraints and an economy based on reciprocity and gift around principles of mutual aid rather than money.'[113] This was certainly the way my friends and I viewed them in the mid- to late 1970s. Indeed, veteran free-festival space rockers Hawkwind, who have been strongly critical of the commercialism of later festivals, began their own small 'Hawkfests' in the UK (the first of which was in Devon in 2002 and the second of which is, as I type this, kicking off in Lancashire – 9 August 2003): 'We wanted to recreate the atmosphere of festivals of old, as an alternative to the now heavily commercialized events such as Glastonbury etc. A place that was safe, and where everyone who attended shared the same vision.'[114] In keeping with contemporary occulture and in response, they say, to popular demand, the 2003 Hawkfest introduced 'mind, body and spirit areas'.

One of the contemporary by-products of the free festivals in the 1970s was the phenomenon of the significantly named 'New Age traveller'. As the free festival scene developed and as increasing numbers were taking place,[115] so groups of people organized their summers around them, travelling from one to the next: 'By the end of the 1970s a regular summer circuit had been established. From May Hill at the beginning of May via the Horseshoe Pass, Stonehenge, Ashton Court, Ingleston Common, Cantlin Stone, Deeply Vale, Meigan Fair, and various sites in East Anglia, to the Psilocybin Fair in mid-Wales in September, it was possible to find a free festival or a cheap community festival almost every weekend.'[116] Travelling this circuit, setting up festivals and, often, selling psychedelics along the way was a countercultural band of hippies known to me, at the time, simply as 'the convoy'. It was essentially this free festival convoy that evolved into the 'New Age travellers', a countercultural community which established, as Simon Reynolds puts it, 'a neo-medieval economy based around crafts, alternative medicine and entertainment: jugglers, acrobats, healers, food vendors, candle makers, clothes sellers, tattooists, piercers, jewellers, and drug peddlers'.[117] Indeed, he notes that despite the concerted efforts of the authorities to bring an end to the nomadic lifestyle of these 'medieval brigands' (as Douglas Hurd, then Home Secretary, termed them), by the end of the 1980s some calculated that the number of travellers had reached 40,000.

As to their inspiration, although Donovan Wylie's disturbing collection of photographs charting the progress of a group of travellers during the 1990s shows their decline into heroin and alcohol addiction,[118] in the 1970s and 1980s (and still for some today) they promoted an idealism permeated with occultural meaning. Hence, the label they came to bear is particularly significant because, like the free festivals in which they had their genesis, they drew on many of the ideas and practices commonly associated with 'New Age' spirituality. Indeed, while, on the one hand, Hetherington is perhaps correct to note that it would be wrong to overemphasize the religious element, he is, on the other hand, guilty of underestimating its significance. Although he concedes that there was 'some resonance between the Travellers' outlook and that of the wider New Age movement',[119] initially, at least, there was more than *some* resonance. Indeed, Hetherington himself even acknowledges that 'Many of the forms of religiosity and therapy associated with the New Age [he mentions involvement and interest in astrology, Paganism, earth mysteries, and ancient healing techniques] are of interest to many Travellers.'[120] Moreover, his further point that 'many of these beliefs and practices are construed in modern societies as forms of rejected knowledge'[121] is also an important one, in that part of the ideology of free festival counterculture is the recovery of such *rejected* knowledge – a return to the land and to indigenous mysteries associated with the land: ley lines, faery culture, spirits of place, the power of ancient sacred sites, and so on. For example, speaking of the Stonehenge festival, Nik Turner (of Hawkwind) recalls: 'I remember I designed this fertility ritual for the 1984 solstice at the stones, the last Stonehenge Free as it happens (so far anyway). It was an all-night thing, the death of the sun-king in the evening and the rebirth of the new with the solstice sunrise.'[122] Similarly, handfastings (Pagan weddings) and other rites were frequently performed at 'the stones'. Hence, again, whilst Hetherington's study is excellent in many respects, it is a shame that too little attention is given to this aspect of free festival counterculture. Although there was little religion in the traditional 'organized' sense, the experience was, for many, both deeply meaningful and understood to be spiritual. As Andy Letcher has noted, much of the Eco-Paganism of the road protest movement has its roots in this free festival culture: 'Because many protestors were originally travellers, Eco-Paganism exhibits what has been termed a "new tribalism"...'[123]

Occultural significance, of course, is not limited to free festivals. As many who attended festivals at the time will testify, and as is evident from the posters and the magazines of the period – indeed, as is still evident at many commercial festivals – underlying and informing the counterculture of the festival are numerous occultural ideas. For example, at the WOMAD festival[124] (held on the banks of the Thames at Reading each year) in 2003 – from which, as I write this, I have just returned – hippie idealism was still very much evident. As well as the usual psychedelic aspects and the emphasis on vegetarianism, the whole experience was very similar to earlier festivals – though the toilets are, thankfully, more adequate than they used to be (when there were any!). For example, as campers walk from their tents, of which there are thousands in all shapes and sizes – including the odd tipi and painted bus – to the main, brightly decorated site to listen to one of the bands, they walk through an informal area perfumed with incense and strongly reminiscent of earlier festivals. Numerous stalls sell all manner of occultural artefacts, people meditate, spiritual symbols are ubiquitous, signs on tents offer massage, tarot readers set out their cards, colourfully painted people dance, exotic food is prepared – sometimes with a little extra ingredient to help the consumer 'chill'. Reynolds' neo-medieval economy is alive and well. The jugglers, acrobats, healers, food vendors, candle-makers, clothes sellers, tattooists, piercers, jewellers, and drug peddlers are all still plying their respective trades. The point is that the festival experience today, although far more commercial and organized than earlier festivals, and although attracting a much wider section of society, still preserves that which is countercultural and occultural.

The most important music festival in the UK is Glastonbury. First held in 1970, Glastonbury Fayre, as it was called in its early days, has become the best-known music festival in the world. However, Hetherington is incorrect to claim that it has 'continued to the present day'.[125] Because of complaints by local residents about the 10,000 or so festival-goers in 1971, formal gatherings ceased at Worthy Farm, Pilton (just outside Glastonbury) until another small free festival was held in 1978.[126] Glastonbury was then officially revived in 1979. Since then, apart from the odd fallow year, it has continued to be, in the words of Michael Eavis, the Methodist organizer and owner of the farm on which it takes place, 'a kind of utopia, really, something outside of the normal world we all live in'.[127] However, although the countercultural element has been eroded in recent years, most simply going to see a few of their favourite artists (some of whom are likewise hardly icons of counterculture – e.g. Rod Stewart, Tom Jones, Tony Bennett and Rolf Harris – difficult to believe, but sadly true), for others it is also an occultural event – something which has always been a protected feature of Glastonbury. Tim Beckerley's report of the 2002 festival includes the following description of activities in one of the areas of the festival site known as 'the Green Fields':

> A 12 feet high wickerwoman, a field full of tipis, a rest garden, healing workshops, innovative arts and crafts, alternative energy, yoga classes, the Greenpeace tent, veggie stalls, you get the picture. At the end of the site there is a small, undulating field with a stone circle for those who wish to marvel at the midnight firework displays, watch the sun rise at four in the morning or to get away from the crowds and just chill. The Green Fields are composed of a self-confident community of kindred spirits... There is a tangible sense of peace and calm amid the myriad of sounds and music emanating from the festival. It would be easy to poke fun at this mix 'n' match of vibrant spontaneity and miscellaneous spirituality, but many of the Green Fielders wish to live a self-sustainable and natural existence away from the materialistic, money-driven trappings of western society – and they offer a tangible glimpse of alternative possibilities.[128]

Glastonbury 1971 (20–4 June), which included sets by David Bowie and the main free festival band of the period, Hawkwind (who had gained countercultural credibility as a result of playing for free outside the fences of the Isle of Wight festival in 1970), featured the now-famous pyramid stage. This itself is an interesting manifestation of contemporary occulture, in that it is fundamentally linked to the ideas discussed in John Michell's hippie occult classic, *The View Over Atlantis*.[129] As the *New Musical Express* (*NME*) reports (a little simplistically and sensationally), 'A year before the first festival at Worthy Farm, a book called *View Over Atlantis* was published. [It] immediately became the catalyst for a cult of New Age practitioners who rejected all beliefs based on modern science and put their faith, instead, in the Olde Ways.' Basically, Michell argues that there is a 'sacred relationship' between the dimensions of Stonehenge, Glastonbury and the Great Pyramid at Giza, Egypt. 'And so it was, for that sole reason, that ... the stage was built pyramid-shaped.'[130] Based on a scaled-down version of the Great Pyramid, it was constructed in 1971 from polythene and scaffolding. Furthermore, it was situated over a 'blind spring' on the St Michael ley line (located by dowsing) in order to tap hidden, ancient powers. Indeed, McKay notes that the organizers of the Glastonbury 1971 festival, Bill Harkin and Andrew Kerr, 'rang Michell from Worthy Farm, and were advised by him to base the proportions of the pyramid on the dimensions of Stonehenge'.[131] According to Michell, the Great Pyramid 'was constructed for a magical and sacred purpose, as a vehicle for transcending the material state, for travel in space, through time and into a further dimension'.[132] Similarly inspired, Hawkwind, who have, over the years, made much of such occultural mythology – and who later in the 1970s went on to make creative use of the science fiction of Michael Moorcock (who, indeed, replaced lead singer Robert Calvert for a short while in 1975) – transported a much smaller pyramid stage around the free festivals. Although Hawkwind's work has always been more tongue-in-cheek, and although they were more concerned with psychedelic experience and the creation of their own mythologies, nevertheless, their early albums – in particular I suggest their live album, *Space Ritual* – provide an insight into the fantasy-based occulture of the period. More recently, Banco de Gaia (a.k.a. Toby Marks), who produces principally ambient dance music, travelled to Egypt to record his album *Igizeh*. As he tells us on the cover, 'Parts of this album were recorded inside the Great Pyramid of Giza, the Temple of Seti 1 at Thebes, and other locations in Egypt.' That it was recorded in these locations significantly increases the appeal of the CD, it becoming, for some, a spiritual as well as a popular cultural artefact. Similarly, attracted by the occultural significance of the sacred sites of Egypt, The Grateful Dead, played in front of the pyramids at Giza in September 1978, during which there was an eclipse of the moon. As McKay writes, with reference to Glastonbury, 'Hundreds of West Coast Americans fly in for the ancient and cosmic vibe. (British hippies have a stage in the shape of a pyramid; Californian ones fly to the real thing.)'[133]

There are numerous tales of the paranormal and the spiritual emanating from these festivals – particularly those associated with 'sacred sites'. Of course, according to the classic doctrine of the festival, as interpreted by Roger Caillois, this should be expected, for at a festival the group has 'recourse to the sacred'.[134] For example, at the first Glastonbury, 'Mad Mick', the festival MC, responding to a 'rainbow-like apparition' above the stage, was inspired to make the following request: 'Whatever you are, please talk to us!'[135] According to the report in *Melody Maker*, the following Glastonbury festival in 1971 seems to have elicited equally spiritual feelings: 'The freaking was wholesome. You could stand back and laugh or kneel and pray in the shadow of Glastonbury Tor'.[136] Again, as one of the organizers put it: 'It is the very heart of this body of England ... What drew these people to Glastonbury was a feeling that from this ancient, sacred place a new spirit is to spread among men. They were here to bear witness to the birth of a new era, the Age of Aquarius.'[137] More formally, at the 1971 festival, Guru Maharaji of the Divine Light Mission (now Elan Vital) stood on the pyramid stage and addressed the crowd.

As we have seen, part of the appeal of Glastonbury, just as it was the appeal of Stonehenge, is the sense of sacred place. This connection between popular music and ancient sacred sites is still significant and, indeed, has recently been explored on the trance compilation CD *Sacred Sites*. As Chris Deckker says in the booklet accompanying the CD:

> To create this compilation, some leading international producers of the psychedelic dance scene were asked to choose a sacred site that inspired them. Their task was to visit the site, feel the energy and then create a track expressing through music the power of the site. This album represents a global journey. It is an attempt to reconnect with the ancient spirits of the earth, reminding us of the power we once felt as we danced the sacred path. The power we again feel today. We dedicate this album to our beautiful planet 'Gaia' and all her devas.[138]

This spiritual sense of connectedness to the Earth/Gaia, primarily felt at 'sacred sites', is an important element of free festival culture – as well as, of course, to the related Pagan and eco-protest cultures.[139] Unlike Hetherington, McKay is far more aware of this, recognizing that 'the mystical side of the place' has helped Glastonbury to become the phenomenon that it is today:[140]

> Calling the large 1971 free festival 'Glastonbury Fayre' – despite the greater proximity of the village of Pilton and the well-known festival town of Shepton Mallet alike – was an informed marketing stroke of genius, which tapped into the emerging zeitgeist of the Aquarian and later New Age ideals, and lay some of the strongest foundations for the festival's longer term claims to having an alternative ethos and atmosphere ... If we buy a ticket for the festival, we buy into a little bit of Glastonbury, its mystical magic, its palimpsestic fictions, its topography.[141]

Hence, as Patrick Benham says, Glastonians 'have had to put up with all manner of strange and wild specimens of humanity drawn to the place by strange and wild rumours of lines of power and forthcoming revelations'.[142] Again, Benham, an ex-hippie who is clearly not happy with the large commercial phenomenon that the Glastonbury festival has become, makes the following point: 'What was interesting about the earlier festivals at Pilton was the underlying New Age mythos which provided a sense of metaphysical approbation for the event. The site was said to be on the ley line between Glastonbury and Stonehenge.'[143] Whilst many in Glastonbury, including Benham,[144] would like to see an end to the festival, the 'alternative' Glastonbury community of spiritual seekers are, according to one commentator, 'genuinely pleased to see the travellers here, doing their bit towards the rebirth of Glastonbury as a place of planetary service and spiritual renewal ... Glastonbury is an internationally famous place of tourism and pilgrimage.'[145]

An equally culturally significant festival in the US, the Burning Man Festival, held for a week each year on the prehistoric lakebed of the Black Rock Desert, is likewise infused with occultural significance. Having its genesis in 1986 as a small gathering of friends on a San Francisco beach, it has since had to move to the desert and now hosts over 29,000 people.[146] It is described as 'A feast for the senses… [merging] the enchantment and playfulness of children's worlds with adult content'.[147] It is this mix of elements, says Sarah Pike, that 'draws participants of all ages from across the country, from New York, to nearby Reno.'[148] Organized around visual art rather than music[149] – though music, of which 'there [is] an immense variety', is clearly important[150] – Burning Man explicitly incorporates, more than many commercial British festivals, key occultural and countercultural elements. Pike refers to it as a Neo-Pagan religious site that offers 'an experiential intensity that participants find lacking in other religious institutions.'[151] This is evident from the following description of one of the zones at the 2003 festival, the theme of which was 'Beyond Belief':

> Beginning with the dawn of human consciousness, mystics have sought out this realm of super-charged experience. They have retreated into caves, removed themselves to mountaintops, and disappeared into the solitude of desert space. They have relentlessly emptied themselves of our world; they have fasted, prayed, and kept vigils – all in pursuit of that which cannot be compared to any other thing. What these pilgrims have encountered on their outward journeys into nothingness is a matter for conjecture. The only proper answer of the faithful to the sceptic is that one must be there if one hopes to understand. In the year 2003, we'll populate this world beyond our world with artworks that evoke such visions. Other theme-related artworks will line the processional ways that converge on the Great Temple.[152]

As this description clearly indicates, Burning Man is explicitly viewed by festival-goers as sacred space, to be distinguished from the wider 'outside' (profane?) world. Just as the major dance hit by Faithless, 'God is a DJ', speaks of the dance environment as 'my Church', the place 'where I heal my hurts',[153] so, for many Burning Man participants, the festival is understood in ecclesiological terms. Indeed, the following statement by one festival-goer makes precisely this connection: 'this is our church, this is our respite from suffering through 358 days of Christian-inspired, bore-me-to-death society with all its mind-numbing institutions, corporations, and television. This is where we pray, this is our sacred place.'[154] And, in the words of another attendee, 'When life returns to the desert, Humanity is rejuvenated; with dew on our lips and paint on our bodies we enter the kingdom of god.'[155] Michael Eavis's comments about the significance of Glastonbury (quoted above) express this same sense of moving from the outside world to a meaningful space: the festival becomes 'a kind of utopia, really, something outside of the normal world we all live in'.

However, more than that the organizers note that, like the growth of religious communities, 'the impact of the Burning Man experience has been so profound that a culture has formed around it'. Consequently, they have felt the need to create a virtual community on the Internet, 'Black Rock City Year-Round'. We might call this an *e.kklesia* (i.e. an electronic/virtual community).[156] Indeed, more significant still, the *e.kklesia* is gradually being transformed into an *ekklesia* – physical gatherings of the faithful. (Indeed, to press the terminology a little further, we could even speak of some gatherings in terms of an *E-kklesia* – communities shaped by shared drug-induced experiences within a common, usually musical, environment.)[157] However, the overall point is that Burning

Man is understood to be enormously significant at the core of a new spiritual movement within an evolving Western society:

> What we do here is rather like consumerism. What does consumerism tell us every day of our lives? It says, as we sit in front of our TV, 'Be all that you can be. Be real. Be authentic. You can be yourself.' It's a simulacrum of being. It's the unhallowed trafficking in sacred things, in which things have been substituted for states of being. Here, we offer the same thing, but it happens to be authentic, it originates in their soul. It doesn't blind them to their inner resources; it doesn't make them empty and lonely and hungry ... We are creating a national organization, a network. I think that a great discourse is beginning, and a value system has emerged. But the reality of it naturally generates out of this spontaneous interaction between people. So, instead of an ideology, what we're creating is an internalized ethos. Now that may sound idealistic, but if through spiritual rituals you renew that ethos – not only at this event but repeatedly, hundreds of times – then it becomes the basis of a new kind of spirituality that can begin to inform the lives of people. Without being bidden, our community is already forming its own regional gatherings ... The numbers of people affected by us will be far greater than the ones who ever come to [Burning Man], or even regional events. And ultimately, then, I think that will become a new kind of basis for democracy, which will be value based, community based, and can more than countervail the forces that are corrupting it.[158]

Concerning the explicitly sacralized nature of this festival, Pike recalls,

> what most intrigued me about the festival was that for many participants Burning Man was an event of *religious* significance, characterized by powerful ritual, myth, and symbol; experiences of transcendence or ritual ecstasy; experiences of personal transformation; a sense of shared community; relationship to deity/divine power; and perhaps, most important, sacred space ... This festival is an important cultural and religious site that exemplifies the migration of religious meaning-making activities out of American temples and churches into other spaces.[159]

Burning Man participants (and all attendees are expected to *participate* – 'participation is at the very core of Burning Man'[160]) take this perception very seriously, even going so far as to understand their annual journey to the site in terms of pilgrimage and expecting transformation when they get there. Whilst many in the UK, although imbibing occulture, would not understand their festival experience in such explicitly religious terms, there are those who do: 'It's about enlightenment.'[161] Indeed, interestingly, the Burning Man festival has acquired a sacralized status even in the UK, the journey to it being understood in terms akin to pilgrimage. Andy Smith's comments about the festival are explicit in this respect: 'If it is the obligation of every Muslim to visit Mecca at least once in a lifetime, then attending the "Burning Man" could be considered a pilgrimage that every confirmed "festival head" should make, at least once.'[162]

Moreover, as with British free festivals, it is clear that the spirituality encouraged at Burning Man is explicitly non-Christian. Although Burning Man is an eclectic, occultural event that makes use of symbolism and ideas from a range of sources, when it makes use of Christian symbolism it almost always does so negatively, as parody. This is both because 'Judaeo-Christian culture' is, as indicated in some of the comments quoted above, the culture over against which the festival stands, and because many of the key themes and ideas are drawn from occulture. Because, as I have already discussed, occulture tends to be antagonistic to traditional Christian beliefs, which are understood to be restrictive, exclusivist, authoritarian, hierarchical, patriarchal, and so on, it not only promotes certain types of spirituality, but it implicitly excludes others. Hence, as Pike observes, 'One of the most effective ways Burning Man establishes itself as a "church" of sorts is through antireligious [i.e. principally anti-Christian] art and the subversive appropriation of familiar symbols... Although festival-goers contrast their Burning Man experience to life in the outside world, they borrow the idioms of that world in order to criticize organized religion, consumerism, and social mores.'[163] For example, she describes the following artefact, 'a confessional in the shape of a large wooden nun painted colourfully with flames coming up from the bottom of her robe and words along her head reading "Sacred Disorder of the Enigmata!?!" and "Confess Your Conformities!": 'When I walked through the confessional's curtains I was faced by a round mirror decorated and painted with a message: "Be Your Own Messiah".'[164] As she says, this use of religious symbolism (nuns, confessionals and Messiah language) 'both reifies and critically comments on Catholic practice. It is a playful display, yet serious in its underlying critique, an attitude in dozens of other festival appropriations of religious symbolism.'[165]

Hence, as with British music festivals, Burning Man functions as, to use Foucault's term, a 'heterotopia', a 'counter-site, a kind of effectively enacted utopia in which... all other real sites... are simultaneously represented, contested, and inverted'.[166] In many ways this accords with Jean Duvignaud's analysis of festivals as sites of belief and behaviour which have an inherent 'subversive spirit' that involves 'a real awakening of consciousness'.[167] Festivals aren't merely, as he says, the 'world turned topsy-turvy', they are 'a powerful denial of the established order'.[168] As one participant put it, 'I enjoy like, when things are not qualified, and they just become completely... quantified, that's when I like it.'[169] More particularly, I would argue, the festival is an island of countercultural utopianism where *rejected* ideas and behaviours can be explored and celebrated. Therefore, the type of spirituality the festival-goer delights in is necessarily countercultural, subversive, and rejected – occultural.

Concerning this celebration of *rejected* and *hidden* (i.e. occult) spirituality, I have been interested to see the emergence of festivals explicitly devoted to the celebration of the occult – most of which, like Burning Man, incorporate popular music. Perhaps the most interesting of these in the UK is 'Occulture'.[170] As noted above, the festival, which began in Brighton in 1999, 'started out as a tiny event featuring various Wiccans, chaos magicians and Satanists'. Although it was attacked in the local press by people who were concerned that they were 'sacrificing animals', and although there was some antipathy between the different occult traditions attending (e.g. I was told that 'some prominent Wiccans had issues about appearing on the same stage as, for example, a member of the Church of Satan'), it has gone from strength to strength. Indeed, Justin Hankinson (one of the founders of the festival) is clear that 'this is exactly the reason why we created Occulture', namely to inform people about and widen people's experience of occult belief and practice. The festival is now beginning to attract a range of prominent speakers and musicians. For example, I was told that they were expecting Genesis P-Orridge in 2003, but, due to an accident, he was unable to make it. They did, however, include sessions by, amongst others, Colin Wilson, the popular writer on all things occultural, and Jaz Coleman, the front man for the once popular band Killing Joke, who gave a solo performance entitled 'Activating the Double Current: A Study of Music and the Occult'.

Psychedelic Trance Culture

As has already been indicated, and as we have seen is the case at Burning Man, there is a great deal of continuity between the psychedelic hippie culture of the sixties and certain aspects of 1980s and 1990s rave culture.[171] Indeed, not only is there a recent CD setting contemporary dance music to the words of Timothy Leary,[172] but also there are a range of contemporary groups and musicians who betray the influence of Leary and the psychedelic subcultures of the 1960s and early 1970s. For example, the following words are taken from the Porcupine Tree's *Voyage 34* album: 'the LSD trip is a pilgrimage far out beyond your normal mind into that risky and revelatory territory which has been explored for thousands of years by mystics, visionaries and philosophers'. Although, admittedly, Porcupine Tree is a contemporary psychedelic rock group, one could cite numerous 'trance' music pieces which are also explicitly occulturally psychedelic. As Sheila Whitely observes in her discussion of contemporary music and culture:

> there is a strong sense of shared identity between the sixties hippy philosophy and that of nineties alternative culture. Similarities are present in the music, the influence of the drug experience, an awareness of the destruction and ruination of the Earth and the poisoning of the seas. New Age Travellers share the hippie philosophy of alternative family groupings and the freedom to opt out of mainstream society, whilst free festivals and raves provide the space both to trip and experience a range of house and ambient bands. Publications such as the *Freak Emporium* provide guidance to a range of psychedelic music, magazines and books, whilst *Bush Telegraph* provides features on cannabis and the dream mechanism, homeopathy and growing hemp in the UK. Collective experience, music and drugs appear, once again, to provide the means whereby young people can explore the politics of consciousness, to set up an alternative lifestyle.[173]

Indeed, there is an interesting geographic connection between the hippie culture of the 1960s and recent psychedelic rave culture, namely Goa on the southwest coast of India. A Portuguese colony up until 1961, this Christian state in India, to which many hippies travelled in the 1960s and 1970s, became in the 1980s a utopian destination for the devotees of another form of Western popular occulture. Easternized psychedelic hippie culture was transformed into Easternized psychedelic trance culture. Trance, as a musical genre, was arguably begun in the 1980s by a man known simply as Goa Gil, who, having worked as a DJ in Goa throughout the 1970s playing rock and reggae, decided in the 1980s to experiment with the post-punk electronica that was coming out of Europe. Sharing ideas with the international community of DJs working in Goa and influenced by Indian classical music, he began to develop a new Easternized form of electronica. The trance DJ Ray Castle describes the Goa scene in the mid-1980s as follows:

> The freaks and the hippies used to collect the most mind-boggling psychedelic dance music they could find and bring it to India and play it at these parties, and we used to exchange this music... In the old days we used to call it 'special music'. It was very obscure and it was very hard to get your hands on. You were a real connoisseur or collector, and Goa was a kind of fraternity of the obscure, weird psychedelic music collectors getting together, getting stoned, and getting off on the music; and sharing each other's music, exchanging it, copying it, and making parties out of it.[174]

Goa Gil was at the centre of this culture developing his own particular brand of dance music. Inspired by the use of LSD in particular, which had become central to many of the Goa beach parties (there even being free 'acid punch' available in the early years), psychedelic trance emerged as the most popular and influential genre. However, it was not just the pulse of the beat and the hallucinogens that made Goa trance 'special music', there was also a sense of transcendence; a sense that the music was connecting the raver to that which was beyond the mundane and the entertaining; a sense that the dancers were gathering as a spiritual community. In the words of one Goa DJ, 'India and psychedelic trance-dance is for those who want to shed their egos and embrace something quite numinous (spirit reflecting) and potentially more psychically edifying.'[175] Goa trance was mystical music, a rave was a *satsang*, the DJ was a guru. One fan remembers Goa Gil looking like 'a Sadhu... with locks down to his bum', who, when he plays, 'puts a Shiva in front of him and incense sticks'. Indeed, it is interesting to note that this fan goes so far as to say, 'He really was a religious leader.'[176] Certainly, as we will see, the Goa DJ takes on, if not a guru-like, then a shamanic-like role, in which he (and it was a 'he' in the early years) was often understood, and understood himself, to be taking ravers on a spiritual journey during the course of an all-night party.

Also at the heart of the trance scene was the TIP record label and dance organization, one of the founders of which was another old hippie, Ron Rothfield, known simply as 'Raja Ram'. (Interestingly, Raja Ram is an Australian musician who used to be in the Indian-inspired psychedelic hippie band, Quintessence.) Again, the praise Raja Ram receives goes beyond that which would normally be given to a DJ. He is not just a great DJ, says one fan, but 'Raja Ram is the most inspiring person I ever met.'[177] I am not arguing that people actually worshipped DJs in Goa or that they responded to them as other Westerners in India were responding to gurus such as Satya Sai Baba. I am simply noting that, within the early Goa trance scene, the relationship between the raver and the DJ is a meaningful, often spiritually charged one. Jane Bussmann hints at this in her excellent, popular overview of dance culture: 'Those who stuck with [trance] went totally hippie: instead of the middle ground of the odd Nehru shirt and a pair of sandals, they went deep into the trance with a bindi on their bonce. Goa seemed an appropriate destination for the mystical raver.'[178]

Des Tramacchi's research has likewise uncovered something of the occulturally eclectic nature of doofs/raves in Australia (evidence of which I have witnessed, in some form or another, at similar events and festivals in the UK):

> A 'trance space' had been set up on a small flat area next to the creek. In the centre of this space was a large installation consisting of a billowing three-rayed fabric structure, mostly suspended from ropes, but descending into an excavated crater at the centre of the dancing ground. At the outer corners of this structure were three, brilliantly-coloured sarong-like banners. One depicted a 'school' of all-seeing eyes swimming against a multi-coloured geometric background. Another represented the Hindu deity Ganesha, while a third was decorated with flying saucers.[179]

Elsewhere Tramacchi argues that 'the various psychedelic dance-cultures contain virtually all the elements of putative new religious movements. Indeed, certain characteristics of "the sacred" are present to a remarkable degree. Elements of the iconography of Hinduism and Buddhism, such as the elephant-headed divinity Ganesha or the mantra ॐ (*om*), are frequently represented at doofs. Influences from the New Age, Human Potential Movement, Transpersonal Psychology and Neo-Paganism are also often present.'[180] Hence, while the music has changed – as popular music does – the Easternized, psychedelic, occultural eclecticism remains intact. This is conspicuously evident on most, if not all, CDs released on trance labels such as TIP, Flying Rhino, and Return to the Source, in that the covers and titles of many tracks consistently contain explicit references to spirituality and psychedelia. For example, on Return to the Source products (T-shirts, CDs, posters, flyers etc.), images of the Buddha are ubiquitous, as are those of Hindu deities, and track listings frequently include references to shamanic, Pagan and psychedelic themes.

Indeed, it is interesting to note that the followers of the Indian guru Rajneesh/Osho have strong links with some forms of contemporary dance culture, particularly the trance music scene. As Anthony D'Andrea comments,

> The Osho movement is a good case for exploring the relations between New Age and techno. Music, therapy, celebration, and meditation pervade daily life in the 'Osho Ashram' [in Poona, India]. In the huge camp-like Buddha Hall, hundreds of practitioners (about 80 per cent Westerners) do one-hour 'dynamic meditations', which begin with cathartic stages of chaotic dance and gibberish, moving towards introspective stages of silent stillness and relaxation ... Notably predominant music styles are techno, house, trance, ambient, and New Age music ...[181]

Bussmann even notes that 'since the sixties, followers of the late Guru Osho, formerly the Bhagwan Shree Rajneesh ... had had a base on Ibiza where he advocated the use of ecstasy for social understanding, personal development and dancing a lot. The followers ... were trance dancing and practising free-love culture before it made the most unexpected transition to the bleak British inner cities. Clubbers were impressed by what they saw.'[182] D'Andrea is much more explicit concerning the enormous significance of the Osho movement for Western rave culture. He notes, for example, that following the closing of Osho's ashram in Oregon,

> many *sannyasins* returned to Ibiza ... While participating in the nightclub life, they also introduced New Age techniques from the USA, including the use of MDMA for

meditation and body therapies. Although 'ecstasy' was already known in European gay and anti-psychiatric circles, it was through the interaction between the *sannyasins* and late-1980s clubbers in Ibiza that MDMA became an explosive discovery for European youth ... The phenomenon flowed from the underground to the mainstream, from Poona, to America, to Ibiza, to London, to the world. Within multiple flows of alternative subjects, objects, and imaginaries across East and West, Osho *sannyasins* were a bridge between the 1960s counterculture and the 1990s Techno movement.[183]

Bussmann also highlights this continuity of rave culture with the 1960s:

Having the doors in their minds opened wasn't enough for some people: they wanted the back wall knocked out and a psychic patio built. Just like John Lennon, Peter Sellers and London's happening scene of the sixties, people are finding themselves cross-legged on the floor all over again. Shamanism, yoga, Sanjasin [*sic*], paganism, Special Brew ... now there are all kinds of ways to get on a spiritual one ...[184]

Of course, as I have already indicated (and as we will see in Volume II), central to the spirituality of psychedelic trance culture has been the recreational use of hallucinogens – hence the adjective 'psychedelic'. As Ben Osborne notes, 'Still catering for cheap drugs, the ultimate Goan pilgrimage is to a Full Moon party [originally begun by, among others, Goa Gil]. Here you can trip to the deep throb of electronic music until the first rays of the Asian dawn lift the dew from the palm leaves ... [Goa] became a fixed stop-off point on the international party trail from Ibiza to Amsterdam, New York, and Mikanos, but differed from these scenes largely through its base in psychedelic drugs.'[185]

While much early psychedelic spirituality at Goa was, as might be expected, inspired by Indian religions, we have also indicated that, as with contemporary psychedelia generally,[186] so psychedelic trance became increasingly more eclectic. Indeed, the Goa DJ Ray Castle had already in 1987 begun to organize trance parties in Europe under the name of 'Pagan Productions'. Similarly, as trance culture travelled to Australia, initially becoming established at the northern New South Wales hippie destination of Byron Bay, it became less Indian and more Pagan. I am not suggesting that the eclectic occultural mix was not evident at Goa – even Goa Gil understood trance as 'the revival and awareness of ancient tribal practices'[187] – only that as the location changed the balance of spiritual ideas shifted. As trance travelled from the beaches of Goa to the West it became more Pagan/Shamanic and Earth-centred, often focusing on the indigenous religious traditions of the area (e.g. Aboriginal in Australia; Celtic in the UK; Native American in the US). Castle certainly makes much of the notion that trance is a revival of Pagan and tribal cultures: 'Like the Aborigine, eons ago, that contemplated the planetsphere, whilst hitting their sticks, blowing through a pipe (didgeridoo). These open-air, wilderness, tribedelic, pagan-like parties (rituals) are along this line of primordial communion.'[188] This is reflected in the music, in that Eastern sounds (e.g. Islamic and Indian singing, the tambura, the sitar, and the tabla) were supplemented (sometimes replaced) by explicitly Pagan singing (e.g. Cat Von Trapp's 'Reaper Girl'[189]), samples of the singing of indigenous tribal peoples (e.g. Ceba's 'Sky Spirit',[190] Zion Train's 'Shaking Tent',[191] and the more commercial music of Deep Forest), or the sound of indigenous instruments, especially the didgeridoo (e.g. Insectoid's 'Tribadelic Nomads'[192] and the music of in particular, Dr Didge and Tribal Drift). Moreover, those who have attended such events or been to see any of these musicians perform, as I have, will know that one is presented with a range of religio-cultural influences – comments made by the musicians, the samples used, the images screened, the dress and body art, all evocatively communicate an eclectic mix of ideas drawn from Earth mysteries, indigenous religion, and contemporary nature spiritualities. This shift of occultural emphasis was recognized and welcomed by Leary shortly before his death.[193] As Tramacchi found, 'Neo-pagan spiritualities have ... exerted an influence on *doof* ideologies, Chaos Magick and symbolism being particularly prominent.'[194] Similarly, in the UK Simon Reynolds observed that, 'instigated by anarcho-mystic outfits like Spiral Tribe and by neo-hippie travellers on the "free festival" circuit ... the techno-pagan spirit' evolved. Spiral Tribe, he points out, 'preached a creed they called Terra-Technic, arguing that ravers' non-stop ritual dancing reconnected mankind with the primordial energy of the Earth'.[195] Again, as Graham St John comments, 'The rhythmic soundscapes of electronic dance music genres are thought to inherit the sensuous ritualism, percussive techniques and chanting employed by non-Western cultures and throughout history for spiritual advancement.'[196] As we have seen was the case in Goa, the DJ becomes a shaman,[197] 'a kind of channeller of frequencies and beats to massage and activate the unconscious and the superconscious via ecstatic, meditative, trance-dance – which becomes a form of euphoric, collective catharsis'.[198] There are several CDs that make this DJ–shaman connection explicit, such as Tsuyoshi Suzuki's *Shamanic Trance: Dada Funk Mix*[199] and Mark Allen's *Shamanic Trance: Psiberfunk Mix*.[200]

This type of essentially Neo-Pagan, 'shamanic' spirituality has been particularly promoted by Terence McKenna, probably the most important contemporary psychedelic thinker to have had an impact on rave culture.[201] Certainly I have found that, for those interested in dance and psychedelics, McKenna's *Food of the Gods* is the most frequently mentioned text. Indeed, at a recent Pagan gathering, I was surprised to learn from a couple of attendees that they too had found McKenna's book helpful in the development of their own spirituality. Similarly, Tramacchi's research reached the same conclusion: 'all my informants were familiar with the work of Terence McKenna, a highly charismatic spokesperson for the psychedelic community, who encourages the exploration of the traditional shamanic tryptamine hallucinogens ... as an essential element in an "archaic revival" '.[202] (McKenna will be discussed in detail in Volume II.) Nevertheless, the point is that, whether influenced by McKenna or not (and he does seem to have a large and growing following), as in the 1960s and 1970s a certain form of McKennaesque shamanic mysticism has been propagated largely through music. This is clearly evident in groups such as the Shamen, Zuveya, and Spacetime Continuum, who have made their indebtedness to McKenna explicit and have even lent their services to his evangelistic efforts, in that they have, for example, included samples of him expounding his ideas in their music.[203]

Similarly Fraser Clark, like McKenna, sought to inject house music and dance culture in general with hippie idealism and Pagan spirituality. As Matthew Collin recalls, 'Clark clearly… believed that the house scene was a contemporary version of the ancient dance-drug rituals of tribal shamans (perhaps his greatest success is that this idea has passed into popular currency and is endlessly repeated by those attempting to discern the "meaning" of house culture)… Clark also had a romantic vision of a New Age Britain revitalized by pagan energies generated by a fission between the house generation and the green movement.'[204] Likewise, Douglas Rushkoff has noted that techno and house music 'events are Cyberia's spiritual conventions. House is more than a dance craze or cultural sensation. House is cyberian religion.'[205] (Rushkoff's notion of 'cyberia' will be discussed in Volume II.) Clark, in his own way, explains: 'A kid grows up in a Christian culture and thinks he's probably the only one questioning these ideas. When he comes to house… he suddenly realizes he's got a whole alternative history. He might get into UFOs or whatever there is – drugs, witches, it's all in there.'[206] Again, a little more forcefully, he makes the following statement: 'As the depression in the dominator system deepens into final collapse, the co-operative free festy/rave/squatter/new new age/techno tribal traveller cross-over counter-culture will grow unstoppably into the new dominant goddess-worship-ping techno-tipi dwelling eco-culture that will inherit a cleaned planet.'[207] A psy-chedelic, Pagan, utopian eschatology!

The controversial drug at the centre of rave culture in the 1980s and 1990s was, of course, 'E' or 'Ecstasy' (MDMA – methylene-dioxymethampheta-mine).[208] Although not a psychedelic in the sense that LSD, mescaline, psilocybin and other powerful hallucinogens were psychedelics, it could lead, says Mary Anna Wright, to experiences which 'involved intense insights into the depth of the human psyche that touched on a spiritual revelation or metanoia'.[209] How-ever, generally speaking, it would seem that, whilst mood-altering, Ecstasy did not have the same sort of 'spiritual' or 'transcendent' impact that LSD did in the 1960s. It tended to lead simply to egoistic hedonism, rather than a spiritual quest. (Users I have spoken to confirm this assessment.) I am not arguing that psyche-delics do not engender hedonistic or egoistic attitudes (for they clearly do), but only that they also, partly because of their particular hallucinogenic properties, tend to contribute to a more spiritually reflective disposition. This can be observed in the underlying philosophy of the Spiral Tribe, which seems to have become more spiritual as a direct result of moving from primarily using E to the use of LSD and psilocybin. That is to say, the shift in drug use led to a shift in ideology, from the simply hedonistic pursuit of happiness to the development of 'an alternative lifestyle, based around psychedelic drugs, tribal techno music, and New Age belief systems'.[210] In the words of Spiral Tribe's Mark Harrison,

MDMA has its place, but once you've taken it a couple of times, its lessons are learned very quickly and it becomes unnecessary… From what I've seen I don't think it has very much to show you, whereas I don't think you can go wrong with LSD and magic mushrooms. They are much more important… LSD and magic mushrooms have a much more creative influence, not just on raves, but on life, on one's understanding of oneself and the world around.[211]

However, the point is that the Longstock festival (where this shift in drug use took place) was the context of *both* a 'revelatory, life-changing LSD experience' *and*, more specifically, as Harrison says, 'the Tribe's spiritual awakening'. That said, as I have argued elsewhere[212] (and will discuss more fully in Volume II), the context and presuppositions, spiritual or otherwise, of an individual significantly contributes to the overall induced effect. Many of those involved in the house and club scene were not ideologically aware to anything like the degree that earlier generations of hippies and punks were. It was, for many, simply a hedonistic pursuit. People took drugs simply to 'get off their heads', not to experience the divine within. That the Spiral Tribe became ideologically and spiritually driven, we will see below, had as much to do with their involvement with the New Age traveller community as it did with psychedelics (though the influence of the latter must not be underestimated).

The Spiral Tribe were not the only ravers disillusioned with the superficiality of E culture and its lack of countercultural and spiritual content. Such ravers were particularly unhappy with what was understood to be the commercialization of rave culture. For example, reflecting on this development and commercialization, Goa DJ Steve Psyko makes the following comment: 'The parties are made for money... the music is made for money... It reflects the Western mentality. What attracted me in the beginning of electronic music was that it didn't reflect the Western mentality. I am not really interested in any music that reflects that... where consumption is the basis of the mentality.'[213] Increasingly, rave music and culture was becoming too closely associated with, if not the product of, 'big business'. Indeed, it was in danger of becoming a paradigm of Adorno's thesis. Consequently, it was shunned by those with countercultural sympathies. Indeed, because the term 'rave' itself had been frequently used in the marketing of mass-produced dance music, for many it had become corrupted, representing that which they opposed. For example, Tramacchi's research found that a distinction was beginning to be made between 'raves' and 'doofs', the latter being non-commercial 'psychedelic gatherings' or 'bush parties' organized at grass roots level for those 'in the know'.[214] Hence, in Australia, non-commercial psychedelic gatherings with a more explicitly Pagan orientation than raves were organized. Similarly, in the UK, inspired by sound systems such as, of course, the Spiral Tribe, a rekindled interest in the occultural and the countercultural began to emerge. (Interestingly, I have found that in the UK 'rave' is the term used for *unofficial*, non-commercial gatherings, not 'doof', which is generally unknown.[215]) As Harrison of the Spiral Tribe recalls about their 'awakening' at the Longstock summer solstice free festival in 1991:

> Up until that point I thought ley lines, solstices and all that mumbo-jumbo was just hot air, I had no belief in it. Suddenly that all changed. Something just clicked, we were on a groove and we knew who we were. We got an inkling of the gravity of what we were up to and what we were about. It was bigger than all of us! It wasn't just Spiral Tribe as organizers or co-ordinators, it was also the people around us. We would all be on that kind of buzz, realizing that what we had here extended beyond each and every one of us and beyond the material thing of having a sound system. This is where the whole philosophy of the Spiral Tribe has its roots. But what was a great mystery and surprise – and still is – is that it was already within us.[216]

Also at this time, the Spiral Tribe joined with the New Age travellers, imbibed much of their philosophy, and, like the free festival convoy before them, began travelling around the English countryside from festival to festival setting up their sound system. They quickly became, as Reynolds witnessed, 'prime movers on the scene, luring thousands of urban ravers to party at disused airfields and abandoned quarries'.[217] Moreover, we have already noted that as the 1990s progressed they became increasingly ideological and Eco-Pagan. Believing the countryside to be a politically charged, spiritually significant environment,[218] they developed

> a romantic, purist philosophy, based on their background, the situations they found themselves in and the people they came into contact with ... They began to believe that techno was ... the voice of the culturally dispossessed ... [and] that the Spiral Tribe were in some way connected to prehistoric tribes of nomads who had celebrated music and dance thousands of years earlier in the same surroundings; that free parties were sha-manic rites which, using new musical technologies in combination with certain chemi-cals ... preferably in settings of spiritual significance, could reconnect urban youth with the earth to which they had lost contact, thus averting imminent ecological crisis.[219]

This is supported by Reynolds' recollection of one Spiral Tribe event:

> Spiral MC, crop-headed Simone, hollers 'Let's lose it, together', then chants the chorus ... which quotes the lament of a nineteenth-century American Indian chieftain. 'I am a savage, and I can't understand | How the beauty of the Earth can be sold back to man', toasts Simone. Dancing with the stars overhead, it's not hard to succumb to the back-to-Nature romanticism. It's all part of the Spiral Tribe's eco-mystical creed, which is crystallized in the buzzword 'terra-technic': using technology to unlock the primal energy of Mother Earth.[220]

It is interesting to note that, in the wake of the Criminal Justice and Public Order Act (3 November 1994), which dealt a heavy blow to outdoor events such as Spiral Tribe's terra-technic 'raves', the culture began to go mainstream. Whilst certain elements of the scene went underground, others went overground in the form of licensed clubs. The most important of these was Club Dog, which, as Reynolds notes, created 'a milieu in which the original free-party revellers min-gled with part-time crusties, non-aligned trance fans and recent converts from rock to techno'.[221] At roughly the same time (1996), Easternized 'Goa trance' also went overground and 'exploded into media consciousness'.[222] As it did, sha-manism, Paganized romanticism and dance as meditation surfaced in mainstream popular culture. Mainstream DJs such as Danny Rampling produced trance CDs prominently displaying religious symbols, such as ॐ or ☯. Less mainstream, but nevertheless accessible clubs, labels, and artists such as Return to the Source, Dragonfly, TIP, Green Nuns of the Revolution, Psykick Warriors of Gaia, Shamanic Tribes on Acid, and Prana introduced eclectic versions of shamanism and Paganism, and consequently invested them with some subcultural capital.

It should be noted, of course, that I am not saying that just because religious symbolism is used religious significance is attached to it, or that, just because people have an uplifting experience dancing in clubs they believe they are, there-fore, having a spiritually significant encounter with a divine reality beyond them-selves. Many are not. They are simply having a good night out, and that's it.

Hence, much use of religious symbolism in club culture is, not only what Gordon Lynch has referred to as 'post-religious',[223] but also 'pseudo-religious', in the sense that it is collected and used simply as religious kitsch, fashionable cultural baggage with no discernable *spiritual* significance. Hence, although many clubbers will be familiar with ॐ, it is little more than a flavour of the East. The symbol has been detached from its original location within the Indian religious tradition. Again, in skateboarding culture, the accessory company Lord spell their name backwards and insert it inside an inverted crucifix, and the skate company Thresher use the popular inverted pentacle of the Church of Satan. I have spoken to several skaters and few were aware of its occult significance – it just looks 'cool' because, it would seem, it symbolizes that which is dark and rejected. Indeed, for some, it just looks cool – and that's it. There is, of course, some significance in the fact that such symbols have accrued subcultural capital without, it seems, a great deal being known about what is symbolized. As we will see in Volume II, even Satan, like Che Guavara in the 1970s, has become a popular icon within a counterculture who know next to nothing about Christian demonology. The symbols have become detached from their original contexts and now float free as emblems of a countercultural, occultural, anti-establishment rejection of that which is 'safe and decent'.

Finally, to come right up to date, a recent manifestation of rave-oriented spiritual *bricolage* is currently being developed by Robbie Wootton, an Irish 'restaurant entrepreneur, music industry veteran, and general entertainment capitalist'. Known to many within the music industry, a close friend of the band U2, and one of the founders of Windmill Studios in Dublin (where U2 have recorded some of their most successful albums), he began a process that he hopes will lead to the establishment of seven nightclubs around the globe, specifically located at 'the light centers of the earth'.[224] The idea had its genesis in the African bush, where he received what he describes as 'a "calling" to open up seven "Spirit" clubs around the world, whose mission it would be to "take a role in encouraging people to evolve to a new plane of consciousness" '.[225] Spirit Dublin was the first and Spirit New York, which opened in November 2003, the second. His aim is to open further clubs in Cape Town, Athens, Sydney, Shanghai, and Rio de Janeiro.

Interestingly, his clubs differ from many of the earlier clubs and festivals, in that they seek to be drug-free. The rave itself is the 'medium for transcendence': 'House, techno, trance: whatever you want to call it, music is understood by ravers as far more than just entertainment – for them, it's literally a medium for transcendence.'[226] He recognized, says Maura O'Connor, 'that the positive elements of entertainment, such as music and togetherness, were potential tools to be used in the spiritual awakening of others…But this would only work as long as the negative elements, such as the consumption of drugs, were kept out of the picture…Nontoxic raves…'[227] That the clubs are not simply entertainment venues is immediately apparent. Spirit New York, for example, has three floors – Mind, Body, and Soul – the third of which is 'open most of the week and houses several studios for holistic healers, aroma therapists, and yoga instructors'.[228] The second floor is home to a large vegetarian and raw-food restaurant and the ground floor is a 2,000-capacity dance floor, which also includes a stage on which 'spiritual' artists and dancers, such as Gabrielle Roth, perform.[229] He is particularly concerned to employ spiritually aware DJs: 'For the last ten years a lot of ravers have been saying that God is a DJ because they've been having these religious experiences on the dance floor. What we are trying to say is: Yes, God can be a DJ; God is Music; God is Sound; God is Vibration; everything in the Universe is Vibration.'[230] With a strong emphasis on the development of the *holistic* self,[231] the spiritual well-being rave has arrived – non-toxic, holistic, health-conscious, macrobiotic, vegetarian, spiritually oriented, dance events.

Chilling Out with Ambient and Dub

Having discussed dance and rave, it is time to briefly chill out. We begin with a short introduction to a genre of music which, although arguably having a long history, is related to the psychedelia of the 1960s, became popular during the 1970s as a result of the work of Brian Eno in particular;[232] evolved eclectically during the post-punk years of the 1980s, was then used as a form of post-Rave 'come down' or 'chill-out' music in the 1990s, and seems to have been particularly associated, on and off, with spirituality, namely 'ambient'.[233] Ambient music, particularly Eno's *Discreet Music, Evening Star* (with Robert Fripp), *Music for Airports, The Plateaux of Mirror* (with Harold Budd), *On Land, Thursday Afternoon, Neroli,* and *The Shutov Assembly*[234] is, generally speaking, minimalist, atmospheric music designed to create soothing soundscapes. Hence, it became enormously popular in New Age circles as music to be piped into flotation tanks and meditation suites. This, of course, led to the genre being termed (often dismissively) 'New Age music'. Indeed, such are its qualities, ambient is not only the preferred music for those seeking to create atmospheres conducive to meditation, but it has also been used in therapy and has even been used in hospitals to aid childbirth.[235] Ambient is, therefore, a typical example of what might be described as a 'technology of mood', in that it is able to stimulate emotional change.

By the 1990s ambient had evolved in several interesting directions: most notably it was often mixed with digital dub (at the core of which is the use of bass and echo) in order to provide spiritually evocative, atmospheric music. Dub is a particularly interesting genre. The term 'dub', which is now used widely and indiscriminately by producers of dance and chill-out music, was originally applied to a remixing technique pioneered in Jamaica as far back as 1967. Recording engineers produced reggae tracks on which the efforts of the producer were often more evident than those of the musicians – these heavily engineered tracks were termed 'versions'. The techniques used to produce versions quickly evolved into what we now know as 'dub'. As Steve Barrow, perhaps the foremost historian of Jamaican dub, comments, 'dub, in the now familiar sense of radically remixed versions, arrived in 1972, and was largely the contribution of one man: Osbourne Ruddock, aka King Tubby, boss of the leading sound system in Kingston and a superb engineer'.[236] Over the decades dub itself evolved, especially in the UK in the 1980s. Creative British producers, most notably Adrian Sherwood, brought groups of musicians together such as the New Age Steppers, Creation Rebel, and Dub Syndicate, in order to experiment with the dub sound. This led to the development of a form of dub music produced principally electronically, namely 'digital dub' or 'digi-dub'. Again, many of the most important producers of digi-dub are British: e.g. Jah Warrior, the Bush Chemists, the Disciples, East Meets West, Hydroponics. Experimentation has continued and there are now numerous bands and artists making eclectic use of electronica, instruments, and a range of genres in their dub explorations. Indeed, some of the most interesting such music is being produced in France by groups such as High Tone and EZ3kiel.[237]

As for the process of producing dub, I like David Toop's description:

> When you double, or dub, you replicate, reinvent, make one of many versions. There is no such thing as an original mix, since music stored on a multi-track tape, floppy or hard disc, is just a collection of bits. The composition has been decomposed, already, by the technology. Dubbing, at its very best, takes each bit and imbues it with new life, turning a rational order of musical sequences into an ocean of sensation.[238]

The aesthetic impact of this is well described in Richard Williams' account of his experience of the genre in a 1976 *Melody Maker* article (when it was very new in the UK). He describes the slight sense of reality-shift that dub can induce: 'One's overriding impression, on initial exposure to dub at the high volume for which it is intended, is that this is the nearest aural equivalent to a drug experience, in the sense that reality (the original material) is being manipulated and distorted.'[239] Not only that, but when listened to live (which, in my experience, is usually very loud), along with this intriguing manipulation of sound, one feels the bass internally, as if being massaged within. This experiential dimension is perhaps why it has become, since its humble origins in Jamaica, one of the most important contemporary musical genres. Not only has it continued to evolve as a genre, but its influence has been enormous, it being evident in, for example, most forms of dance and trance music, hip-hop, contemporary electronica, and drum 'n' bass. However, the point I want to highlight here is that ambient dub has proved particularly appealing to those wanting to create spiritual music. The echo and reverb of dub and its sonorous bass give it a mystical, ethereal quality. This almost spiritual quality of dub is identified in Toop's poetic analysis:

> Dub music is like a long echo delay, looping through time. Regenerating every few years, sometimes so quiet that only a disciple could hear, sometimes shatteringly loud, dub unpicks music in the commercial sphere. Spreading out a song or a groove over a vast landscape of peaks and deep trenches, extending hooks and beats to vanishing point, dub creates new maps of time, intangible sound sculptures, sacred sites, balm and shock for mind, body and spirit.[240]

Of course, with its roots in reggae, from its genesis dub has often been invested with Rastafarian religious significance. Reggae artists known for their interest in mystical spirituality seem to find dub a particularly appealing genre through which to express themselves. One such artist was Augustus Pablo

(Horace Swaby), whose 'deep mysticism found the right vehicle in dub music';[241] 'Pablo's music [is]... for spiritual upliftment'.[242] Often understood as mystical reggae and consciousness-raising music, eclectic spirituality is increasingly evident in much dub music. For example, I was told by 'the Drunken Master' from Lotus Sounds, a new dub band based in Liverpool, that the name of the band, the recording studio (Sunyata Studios), and the particular dub music produced were all inspired by a love of the Lotus Sutra, psychedelia, and Rasta spirituality.[243] Even a cursory glance through a list of contemporary dub artists, CDs, and track listings reveal the prevalence of this sacralized interpretation of the genre: Alpha and Omega significantly entitled one of their CDs *The Sacred Art of Dub*;[244] the Disciples' *Infinite Density of Dub* includes tracks such as 'Higher Dimensions', 'Astral Flame', and 'Ritual Drum';[245] the Hazardous Dub Company's *Dangerous Dubs Vol. 2* includes tracks such as 'Mystical Dub' and 'Spiritual Dub';[246] Jah Shaka's *Dub Symphony* includes the tracks 'Immortal Dub' and 'Mystic Dub';[247] together the Disciples and The Rootsman produced an album entitled *Rebirth*[248] – the list could be a very long one.

Again, to return to ambient *per se*, this too is pervaded with occultural and mystical references, ranging from Hillage's *Rainbow Dome Musick*, explicitly produced, as noted above, for a New Age gathering, to *Tibetan Bells* by Henry Wolff and Nancy Hennings, to the more dance-oriented neo-gothic work of Michael Cretu (working under the name Enigma), which includes amongst other spiritual references Gregorian chant, Indian melismas and samples from Spielberg's *Close Encounters of the Third Kind*.[249]

Part of the reason for the sacralization of ambient and dub in particular, as indicated above, is the nature of the music itself, in that it evokes a sense of timelessness and space. As Reynolds quite rightly argues, 'the mystical aura of echo and reverberance is a thread connecting most twentieth century musics that aspire to timelessness: psychedelica, dub reggae, ambient, and the New Age sub-genre of "resonant music" (recorded in temples, cathedrals, and giant cisterns)'.[250]

The soothing atmospheres evoked by ambient and dub led to a further development of rave culture – 'chill-out' music. Although, for years, ravers had been going home with friends and putting on some mellow ambient to help them come down from the night's high, it eventually surfaced as a prominent stream of popular culture. Clubs and festivals, such as Tribal Gathering, provided chill-out spaces with large cushions for ravers to recline on while listening to ambient; record companies started producing compilation CDs of chill-out music, such as Return to the Source's *Ambient Meditations*;[251] and dance musicians began experimenting with the genre. Gradually it became apparent that increasing numbers of people were more interested in chilling than dancing. Again, Reynolds describes the chill-out revolution well:

> In October 1993, the fifth Telepathic Fish took place at Cooltan, an art-space/gallery/dancehall set up by squatters in an abandoned unemployment office on Brixton's Coldharbour Lane, where Prime Minister John Major had once signed on... Mentally creased and physically crumpled after a night's raving, my friends and I found Telepathic Fish Number 5 the perfect place for 'getting your head together.' In stark contrast to the stress-makingly staccato (strobes, cut-up beats) assault of your average

...rave, Telepathic Fish was a womb-adelic sound-and-light bath. The DJs massaged our ears with a seamless mix of mostly beat-and-vocal free atmospherics... The lights, oil projections, and 'deep-sea décor' soothed eyes sore from the previous night's blitz.[252]

That said, as he insightfully comments, such ambient chill-outs often produced more than simply pleasurable atmospheres:

Chill-out zones and ambient parties resemble R. Murray Shafer's pipe-dream of the 'somniferous garden': acoustically designed bowers where city-dwellers can go to have their ears cleansed of 'noise pollution', where you can get your soul's pH balance restored... With its samples of bird-song and trickling water, ambient techno is a digital update of nineteenth-century programme music – the pastoral symphony that imitates Nature, as with the aqua-mysticism and forest idylls of Claude Debussy works like *La Mer, Jardins sous la pluie* and *Prelude à l'après-midi d'un faune*.[253]

More specifically, much chill-out music has an occultural, 'New Age' orientation. For example, a popular provider of music for chill-out DJs, Pete Namlock, began his career in the New Age band Romantic Warrior. Reynolds recalls the effect of Namlock's mass-produced chill-out: 'All lambent horizons of celestial synth, psalmic melodies and wordless seraphim-on-high harmonies... transformed your living room into a sacro-sanctuary of sensuously spiritual sound.'[254] While many may not like the term 'New Age music', in actual fact the New Ager in the flotation tank and the raver reclining on a cushion in the chill-out tent are using the similar music in similar ways for similar ends.

The Sacred Art of Dub

Dub is spiritual music, and today's freedom seekers, and travellers, have adopted Dub, and intuitively recognized its resonance with their own aspirations. Remember, roots music was created by the seekers of freedom, and this vibration is the essence of the music. Now the 'system' struggles to accommodate the implications of the higher consciousness. The power brokers can feel their grip on our lives slipping away. They scornfully deride and attack those who like alternative lifestyles. We must be grateful to the Rastas, the travellers, true revolutionaries, and people of real vision... Long live de Dub.

(Benjamin Zephaniah and Dr Love)[255]

As someone who has had an interest in reggae and dub since the late 1970s, I have been particularly interested in the emergence of the post-punk dub scene in the UK and, increasingly, in Europe. Since the early 1990s in particular a fascinating and evocative form of dub has emerged, much of which seeks to cultivate a specifically spiritual ambience. While some of this has been produced by Rastafarians (such as, most influentially, Jah Shaka), increasingly dub, although informed by Rasta culture (in that it makes use of the terminology: 'Jah Rastafari'; 'conscious sounds'; 'I an' I'; 'Babylon'; 'dread'; 'the chalice' etc.), is nevertheless produced by non-Rastafarians who, understandably (particularly if they are white), feel uncomfortable referring to traditional reggae themes, such as 'war inna Babylon' (i.e. oppressive white society), devotion to Ras Tafari (Haile Selassie of Ethiopia), and 'the days of slavery'. Hence, not only is much contemporary dub instrumental (apart from a few voice samples), but it has progressed, both musically and spiritually, beyond its Jamaican and Rastafarian roots, developing and mixing influences from other cultures and musical traditions. Although the umbilical cord connecting it to Jamaican dub techniques and rhythms[256] has not been entirely severed, British producers such as the Mad Professor (a.k.a. Neil Fraser) and Adrian Sherwood have been truly eclectic in their interpretation of dub. This cultural eclecticism has, arguably, led to some of the most interesting and creative work in the genre. For example, Little Axe (a.k.a. Skip McDonald) has produced three superb albums seamlessly blending blues with dub.[257] The Twinkle Brothers (who began their career in Jamaica) not only have a significant following in Eastern Europe, but they have recorded tracks in Warsaw with a traditional Polish wedding band, the Trebunia-Tutki Family. Their *Higher Heights (Twinkle Inna Polish Stylee)* includes violins, a cello and a Polish family singing folk songs over their rhythms.[258] Again, the Moroccan band Aisha Kandisha's Jarring Effects have developed a form of 'tribal dub', which is shaped by their North African Islamic faith and culture.[259]

One of the most interesting producers of dub in the UK, who has worked with and been influenced by Aisha Kandisha, is The Rootsman (a.k.a. John Bolloten). From the early 1990s, when he produced his first EP, *Koyaanisqatsi* (1994), The Rootsman has established himself as one of the more creative and innovative artists on the European dub scene. However, he is particularly interesting because, although we have seen that dub *per se* lends itself to spiritual interpretation, perhaps more explicitly than many other producers he has been keen to use his music and his label as vehicles to explore spirituality and, to some extent, politics. From explicitly spiritual works such as *Rebirth* (1997) and *Union of Souls* (1998) to his more musically difficult and politically engaged work with Muslimgauze,[260] especially the *Al Aqsa Intifada* EP,[261] the music of The Rootsman can hardly be described as either superficial or secularized. It is consciously religious music. (It is worth noting, for example, that when I discussed his work with him he indicated more than once that he was not interested in the 'slack' (i.e. sexually explicit) themes that often characterize reggae, but rather he sought to create something more meaningful and spiritual.)

The Rootsman converted to Islam in the late 1990s. However, as we chatted and listened to some of his latest work in the Third Eye studio (in the basement of his house), it was evident that this was no ordinary Muslim household. Although the name of Allah (in Arabic script) hung prominently in the studio, I was a little surprised to see that other faiths and cultures were more conspicuously represented than Islam. There were statues of the Buddha, African art, images of Guru Nanak, paintings of Rama and Krishna, Chinese artefacts, numerous images of Christ, and even the odd extraterrestrial relaxing in the sublime surroundings. Indeed, the small Third Eye studio is very nearly covered wall-to-wall with religious imagery from around the world. All this intrigued me. How was this eclecticism held together with his Islamic faith? To what extent was spirituality a significant and formative part of The Rootsman's life? And how did all this relate to his life as a musician and producer of dub reggae?[262]

Brought up within a Christian family, he attended a Church of England Sunday school as a child. However, unlike many children with a similar upbringing, he refused to be confirmed. This, he says, greatly embarrassed and disappointed his parents. 'I was a little rebellious punk and had no time for such stuffy old-fashioned ideas like religion!' Inspired by punk rock, in 1978, while living in Edinburgh, he taught himself to play guitar and, at the age of 13, formed his first band, State Oppression. Although their debut concert in 1981 was as support for the Angelic Upstarts, rather surprisingly, after only three concerts, he decided against being a punk guitarist and left the band. However, during this time other genres of popular music were beginning to attract his attention. 'After leaving State Oppression in 1981 I played in a couple of other bands but never did any more live gigs. By 1982 I was more interested in listening to American psychedelic punk, the Stooges, Jimi Hendrix, Cream, a lot of blues and blues-rock and southern soul music. I gave up any ambitions to be a musician and even though I was playing on reggae sound systems from the mid-80s, I only dabbled in the production of rhythms.' That said, it was well before the mid-1980s, during his time as a punk, that John became interested in reggae.

If it seems rather unlikely that the follower of a rebellious, often violent form of music might appreciate a genre such as reggae, it needs to be understood that one of the most interesting (even socially important) alliances of the punk era is that between punk and reggae.[263] As Stephen Colegrave and Chris Sullivan comment, 'There were similarities between the anti-establishment ethic of punks and Rastafarian culture. Both groups were generally viewed as outsiders, and both employed contentious sloganeering as a means of promotion.'[264] People such as Don Letts in particular, a DJ at London's Roxy Club, introduced reggae and dub into the punk scene in the late 1970s.[265] Other performers associated with punk, such as Patti Smith and The Clash, also incorporated reggae into their acts. Perhaps most famously, following the breakup of the Sex Pistols, Johnny Rotten, with Don Letts, accompanied Richard Branson to Jamaica to find reggae artists for what was to be Virgin's 'Frontline' reggae label. As Dennis Morris notes, 'Johnny Rotten was instrumental in bringing reggae to the forefront... John did a Radio 1 show with John Peel. He had been asked to bring along his favourite records. All the records he brought, except for one, were reggae, and they really were the best. As he was such a strong figurehead for all the punks, they thought reggae was really cool and what they had to be listening to.'[266] However, the point for us to note is that the young John Bolloten was one of those punks who quickly acquired an appreciation of reggae (as well as 1960s soul music). Indeed, interestingly, the first band he saw live was the reggae band Matumbi (who were supporting Ian Dury and the Blockheads). Again, in 1979 he saw Steel Pulse, who were one of the most significant British reggae bands of the period. Inspired, he began what is now an enormous collection of reggae records.

In 1983, he moved to Bradford, Yorkshire, and, he says, 'quickly immersed himself into the local reggae scene'. He worked for a couple of years in the 'Roots Record Shop', where he picked up the nickname 'The Rootsman', and then in 1985 became involved in local reggae sound systems and pirate radio stations. Eventually, in 1991, he founded his own successful club night, 'Dub Me Crazy', which both promoted roots reggae and dub in the north of England and provided a platform for new artists. In 1993 he was invited to be the resident DJ at Soundclash in Leeds, where he played alongside some of the most important and innovative producers of dub and electronica in the early 1990s, such as Alex Patterson (of the Orb), Andrew Weatherall (of The Sabres of Paradise) and Justin Robertson (of Lionrock). His growing popularity and entrepreneurial instincts suggested to him that a label devoted to innovative dub music might be success-ful. Hence, in 1994 he founded the Third Eye Music label, the debut album for which was *Storm Clouds* by Dayjah and the Disciples. Also, at this time, follow-ing the demise of the short-lived Soundclash club night and the increased demand for dub music, he began recording his own material, producing his debut EP in May 1994, *Koyaanisqatsi*. As he recalls of that period: 'As Dub Me Crazy became more popular, I started to work on more rhythms that I could play in the dances. One of these was the infamous "*Koyaanisqatsi*". It was the popularity of this track as a dub plate that led to it being released. After following it up with a second EP, the *Soundclash City Rockers* EP, I thought to myself that I could do something with this in the long term. That is when I began to take it more seriously' (i.e. from 1994 onwards). After a well-received five-track session for Andy Kershaw's BBC Radio 1 world music programme in 1995, he produced his first album, *In Dub We Trust* (1995). Since then, as well as producing and remix-ing numerous artists, from Black Star Liner and Dub Syndicate to heavy metal bands such as Soulfly, he has released a steady stream of his own albums, EPs, and tracks for compilations, which have included collaborations with important reggae artists such as Horace Andy, Johnny Clarke, Sugar Minott, and Michael Prophet.

As the title of his second album *International Language of Dub* (1995) indi-cates, throughout his career he has been interested in developing dub as a cross-cultural world music. This is evident on the album he produced with Celtarabia, *Union of Souls* (1998). Of the album, he writes,

> What we have tried to create here is an innovative mix of styles that has never been attempted before. We have fused medieval melodies and instrumentation with digital technology, all held together with the depth and heartbeat of dub. We pay homage to the musicians and artists who created and developed the variety of styles of music that have inspired and influenced us throughout this work. We have drawn from the great tra-ditions of countries like Turkey, Algeria, Egypt, Morocco, Spain, France, Germany and Eastern Europe, as well as Jamaica and the contemporary ideas within dance music in Britain today.[267]

However, he does not stop there. Increasingly, he has been interested in dub as a way of exploring spirituality. Writing again of the *Union of Souls* album, he explains that 'the most important thing for us overall was to try and create an uplifting collection that was in touch with the human soul and spirit'.[268]

The spirituality articulated within The Rootsman's music is shaped by Islamic faith and culture. His CD covers often include religious images from the Islamic world (e.g. dervishes, Sufis, Arabic text) as well as, sometimes, personal statements of gratitude to Allah and quotations from the Qur'an: 'I give thanks and praises to the Most High Allah for guidance and inspiration.'[269] His limited edition EP, *Al Aqsa Intifada*, is, as the title indicates, explicitly religio-political from a Palestinian perspective. On the cover and the CD itself, in Arabic and English, are the following words: 'the massacre through which innocent victims were slaughtered, will always remain in our memory until the end of time'.[270] *Al Aqsa Intifada* is intended as a contribution to that memory.

This Islamic influence, however, is tempered by an eclectic and inclusive approach to spirituality. Although indebted to Islam, it is very clear that he is offended by exclusivist and dogmatic belief systems. Indeed, he described himself to me as one who has moved 'beyond Islam'. This sense of innate, universal spirituality, informed by an Islamic faith, reminded me of the perennialism developed by thinkers such as Seyyed Hossein Nasr[271] or even the Western Sufism of a teacher such as Frithjof Schuon.[272] As he puts it, 'all humanity is one basically and it is the same God, the same feelings, the same spirituality between all people – it's just manifested in different ways'. It is this spirituality 'deep within' that, on the one hand, takes him beyond Islam and, on the other hand, he has found within his music. Indeed, it was music that first helped him to experience and articulate his spirituality: 'I always found a spirituality in reggae that spoke to me and I continue to identify strongly with that.' It is not surprising, therefore, that, as we have seen is the case for some within rave culture, John spoke very movingly of the sense of spirituality and community evoked during live club/dub events: 'When I was doing the dub thing in its best years (1990–1998), often I could feel a certain spirituality in the dances, like the music was taking people into a deeper level. So I think that scene could certainly give people some kind of "spiritual experience"'. He was very clear that there were always some people for whom the music meant a lot more than its aesthetic appeal and with whom he felt he could connect on a spiritual level when performing. That is to say, while some people on the dance floor were simply there for the music, and while others were enjoying it as a result of the drugs they had taken,[273] some were experiencing the event at a deeper, explicitly spiritual level. Consequently, The Rootsman feels a sense of connection and common purpose with such people: 'There are some who understand what I am doing and I focus on them when I'm playing.' Hence, when I asked whether performing his music engendered an *explicitly spiritual* experience, he said 'definitely'.

This inclusive, pluralist approach to spirituality is articulated musically through culturally eclectic sampling. (At this point, my temptation to drift off into artsy-fartsy analogies about the spirituality of dub and its eirenic potential is very great – but I shall resist.) As he says, 'By the time I converted to Islam, I had had a few years experience of travelling to North Africa and the Middle East and was also familiar with other musics where spirituality had a high place.' Hence, when other samples and styles from other cultures are woven into his dub, they are not done so unthinkingly – the motivation is always spiritual: 'In my music, I always try to put in a certain depth or spirituality ... by using samples and sounds from the Middle East and elsewhere'. Again, 'Faith'[274] on The Rootsman's *New Testa-*

ment album (2002) is a good example of this approach to music. Although the song is clearly devotional, it is significant that it refers to the object of devotion in a way that explicitly does not locate the divine within a particular tradition. In other words, it is intentionally non-specific – it could be sung by devotees of most faiths.

Finally, as noted above, the Third Eye studio itself reflects The Rootsman's approach to spirituality. It seems that wherever John travels around the world he returns with some icon, image or piece of religious kitsch. This last point needs to be noted, in that he is not only a person deeply interested in spirituality, but also an occasional collector of religious kitsch. Alongside images and texts that obviously mean a great deal to him, there are, for example, wind-up Buddhas and pictures that are valued more for their quirky and aesthetic qualities than for any spiritual significance. Again, when I asked him about the titles of particular tracks and albums, often there was no particular reason they had been chosen. It was simply that together they reflected his particular spirituality and approach to life.

Concluding Comments

These final two chapters, needless to say, could have discussed a great deal more than they have. Numerous films, television programmes, pop videos, festivals, musicians, songs, and genres could have been trawled through analytically in order to identify the articulation of occultural themes and concepts. For example, much might have been made of the video game genre, which, replete with occultural baggage, puts the elusive powers sought by occultists *virtually* into the hands of the player. The individual enters the occultural matrix and acquires occultural-like knowledge and skills in order to manipulate supernatural forces. Again the occultural themes within some 'subcultures', such as Goth culture, which Julia Winden Fey argues is essentially a spiritual culture,[275] could have been fruitfully explored, as could heavy metal culture (which will be discussed in Volume II).[276]

The aim of these chapters, however, has simply been to draw attention to the relationship that exists between popular culture, the cultures they generate, and occulture. Hopefully, I have surveyed enough of the landscape, and done so sufficiently well, to elucidate the close two-way relationship that exists between popular culture and occulture. We have, for example, seen evidence of this in the relationship that exists between literature and film and their religio-cultural contexts, noting the subtle shifts that have taken place, particularly in vampire fiction, away from Judaeo-Christian themes towards those more consistent with occulture. Again, in relation to popular music, we have seen that an Adornian passivity thesis is fundamentally flawed, in that much popular music is not a cultural opiate, manufactured by large corporations, but rather the product of artists, many of whom identify with, or at least speak to, countercultures, and some of whom challenge social norms, capitalist ideals, and 'mainstream' traditional religion in an exploration of 'rejected knowledge'. As such they articulate and disseminate not only countercultural concerns, but often also occultural ideas. Although when in the cultural mainstream, as a component of mass culture, occulture is regurgitated and disseminated by large corporations keen to market popular artefacts, this does not mean that the occultural content is necessarily trivialized and made impotent – although it may be. It does, however, mean that occulture/non-traditional spirituality becomes increasingly less alternative, less exotic, less deviant, and more respectable – it becomes *popular* occulture.

As I was putting the finishing touches to this volume, an interesting collection of essays entitled *Predicting Religion* was published.[1] It brings together a group of sociologists to predict the future of religion. Some predictions are gloomy, others less so, some even cautiously positive about the future of religion/spirituality in the West. Not surprisingly, those essays that are gloomier tend to focus on *Western* (predominantly *European*) Christianity and Christian sectarianism and those that are more sanguine examine *non-Western* Christianity and *Western* alternative forms of spirituality closely associated with what I have identified as 'occulture' – indeed, those most optimistic about the future of Christianity discuss 'soft' or 'alternative' expressions, which are more self-oriented. Although not all the commentators on alternative and paranormal beliefs understood them to be particularly significant, the overall impression left by the volume is that the discussion of secularization theory within the sociology of religion has focused too heavily on Christianity within Western, particularly European, societies. The problem with such analyses is that not only is Christianity flourishing in large areas of the non-Western world, but there are new vigorous forms of spirituality in the West supported in various ways by an increasingly significant occulture.

That said, as I have noted in this book, and will argue in Volume II, I am not claiming that Christian beliefs and related ideas are wholly unpopular and insignificant in the West, for they are not. We will see, for example, that Christian demonology is still dominant. However, to be palatable to Westerners, increasingly such beliefs need to be consumed as part of a dish with other ingredients. Whether we think of the rise of interest in reincarnation or the rejection of dualism, many Westerners seem uncomfortable with the traditional Christian package. Hence, although Christian terminology may be used, it is often used as part of a broader 'occultural' vocabulary.

Kate Hunt's research, reported in *Predicting Religion*, discovered that 'belief itself is important. "I definitely believe in something" is a phrase that occurs in nearly every conversation.'[2] Although she says that often the belief appeared to have 'little, if any, substance', her own evidence seems to contradict the statement. While it is no doubt true that some beliefs will have little substance, she immediately goes on to suggest that the problem is not so much one of the *substance* of belief, but rather of the *articulation* of belief. That is to say, the vocabulary that people have at their command to describe significant belief is very limited. Indeed, she acknowledges that religious experience is 'difficult to put into words, even by professional theologians'.[3] So how do our contemporaries describe their belief? While some use Christian, often 'Sunday School' imagery, she notes that 'they instinctively know that these images are inadequate – they do not reflect *their own experience of God*'.[4] Hence, in seeking to articulate their experience of the divine, some speak of 'universal consciousness', 'driving force', 'divine energy' and 'a journey into spiritual enlightenment', all terms which we have seen are popular within the emerging spiritual milieu. In the final analysis, I agree with Hunt's prediction that not only will 'spiritual awareness... continue', but 'the way that spirituality is expressed will continue to evolve. The language and symbols of Christianity will become increasingly remote to most people.'[5] However, I question her further concern regarding a lack of a 'shared language'. Increasingly, occulture/popular occulture is supplying that language. The rules of the Western, spiritual 'language game', to use Wittgenstein's famous terminology, are being set, not by Christian culture, but by occulture. Increasingly, Westerners are using the language of occulture to articulate significant religious experience and belief. Unlike our Western forebears, whose worldviews were shaped by a largely Christian culture, many of our contemporaries are not familiar with or sympathetic to the Christian notions of 'a personal God', 'incarnation', and 'atonement', and certainly not to the epistemic and soteriological exclusivism that these theological concepts often engender. However, they do seem to be sympathetic to 'reincarnation', 'chakras', '*feng shui*', 'universal consciousness', 'life force' and 'spiritual enlightenment'.

To pilfer another concept – this time from the post-liberal theologian George Lindbeck – *very broadly speaking*, occulture is leading to the establishment of a cultural-linguistic community[6] – indeed, an *occultural*-linguistic community. This, I would argue, accounts for a gradual occultural ecumenism which some have noticed. For example, Jo Pearson has noted that not only is there a gradual blurring of the boundaries between Pagan traditions, but there is increasingly less opposition to certain forms of Christianity.[7] As Gay Pilgrim's study of Quakerism indicates,[8] it seems clear that, to the extent that this is true, it is traditional, 'hard' Christian belief that is losing out here, not 'soft' occulture-friendly Christian belief. Hence, again, when seeking to understand the emergence of soft religion/spirituality, the ecumenical blurring of traditional boundaries, the significance of the self and epistemological individualism, Easternized belief, Pagan and eco-spiritualities, *occulture* is the key. Western spiritual seekers are starting to speak the same language. There may be little homogeneity in the particular way concepts and terms are used, but increasingly occulture is providing a *lingua franca*.

Moreover, as I noted in Chapter 3, the shift from what Robert Wuthnow calls 'spiritualities of dwelling' to 'spiritualities of seeking' need not be as traumatic as some secularization theorists suggest. Although, as both Steve Bruce and Peter Berger have argued, pluralism in Western societies tends to undermine taken-for-granted certainties, as Berger notes, 'it is possible to hold beliefs and live by them even if they no longer hold the status of taken-for-granted verities'.[9] Indeed, this, it would seem, is one of the strengths of these hardy new forms of spirituality. This should not come as a surprise. Why would a form of spirituality that has recently evolved in the West, and which necessarily functions quite differently from an older form of religion which evolved in a different society, be vulnerable to the same forces? New alternative spiritualities serve the needs of a different people in a different age. The reason they are flourishing is because they function in a very different way, having adapted to a new environment.[10]

I am, of course, very aware that concepts such as 'occulture' can be reinterpreted by conspiracy theorists. Indeed, rather worryingly, this book is ripe for conspiratorial interpretation. So, for those readers who have skipped (or simply forgotten) previous chapters, particularly Chapter 4, and turned to these brief concluding comments, I am not describing a global occultural network and certainly do not predict the rise of an anti-Christian evil empire. Although I have discussed overlapping ideas, themes, and concerns, as well as the possibility of a broad occultural ecumenism and *lingua franca*, there is nothing homogeneous or systematic about the new spiritual milieu in the West. Indeed, many ideas and themes *may not* overlap, agree or be tolerant of each other. Occulture does not refer to a hierarchical organization, or even a network – it is simply a broad type of 'culture'. Of course, we have seen that 'culture' itself is a notoriously slippery term which has been invested with numerous meanings. However, in this book it has been used simply of an environment/reservoir/library of beliefs, ideas, meanings and values which inform the processes of thinking, of symbolizing, and of reflecting on experience. Consequently, it influences the way people do things in their everyday lives. Without adopting his particular political analysis (helpful though that may be), another useful way of understanding how 'culture' is used here is with reference to the definition provided by the British cultural theorist Raymond Williams: culture 'is constituted by the meanings and practices of ordinary men and women. Culture is lived experience: the texts, practices and meanings of all people as they conduct their lives.'[11] Bearing in mind the definition of 'occult' developed in Chapter 4, 'occulture' signifies the spiritual/mythic/paranormal background knowledge that informs the plausibility structures of Westerners. Hence, because the centre of gravity is shifting from Christian culture to occulture, the spiritualities and worldviews resourced and encouraged do not look and behave like those of the past.

Occulture tends to be antagonistic to scientism, secularism, and views that dismiss the significance of the sacred. Consequently, I predict that some form of spirituality will continue to inform the lives of Western individuals. Again, it will not be a homogeneous spirituality. It will be a milieu of constantly changing spiritualities and religious trends. Within the occultural milieu, new religious groups will coalesce, of which some will fade and others grow. Spiritualities will emerge stimulated by occultural peaks – such as interest in UFOs, fascination with ancient societies, apocalyptic speculation, eco-spiritualities, and so on – and then fade with the general fading of media and public interest. Others will emerge around particular charismatic figures, only to die with their passing. For some, routinization may lead to the continuation of new religions and alternative spiritualities for many years. Again, religion, as Anastasia Karaflogka and others have enthusiastically argued, has and will continue to evolve in cyberspace: 'cyberreligion may reshape the structure of the religious economy and imagination... In one way or another... the future will bring remarkable transformation not only of religion, but of the study of religion.'[12]

Some are bold enough to predict that 'Britain in 2030 will be a secular society'.[13] I do not hesitate to contradict such predictions. Occulture, alternative spiritualities and 'soft religion' will increase in significance in the West. That this is so will become more evident as the twenty-first century progresses.

NOTES

Introduction

1.   It is worth noting that the term 're-enchantment' is not always used in this way. For example, Murray Bookchin's thoughtful book, *Re-Enchanting Humanity*, is sharply critical of the new spiritual milieu, which, he argues, 'disenchants' our humanity. Of course, Bookchin is principally concerned with environmentalism. Hence, his argument in that book concerns what he believes to be the misanthropy of much New Age and deep ecological spirituality. We are, he says, encouraged 'to regard ourselves as an ugly, destructive excrescence of natural evolution… The New Age mentality… demonises human beings… [as] a delinquent species in an otherwise amiable biosphere or "circle of beings"…' (3). Bookchin's interpretation of 're-enchantment', informed by his political radicalism, is thus quite distinct from my use of the term.

2.   See for example, Bruce, *God is Dead*, 63–70; 'The Demise of Christianity in Britain'. See also Peter Brierley's various volumes (which provide Bruce, the Church and many others with much of their statistical data): *A Century of British Christianity*; *Religious Trends No.1*; *Religious Trends No.2*; *The Tide is Running Out*.

3.   Martyn Percy, for example, has argued that the decline of charismatic Christianity is already under way: 'So far as Charismatic Christianity is concerned, the party is largely over. The celebrations, the abundance and the optimism of the last quarter of the 20th century have reached their peak, and while people are still crowding in through the front door, plenty have already left through the back door too. The charisma that has driven the movement has been routinized, and the cognitive dissonance will ultimately settle on the corporate Charismatic psyche, ameliorating memory but also postponing (indefinitely) the realization of promises and prophecies for the future' ('A Place at High Table?', 106).

4.   A characteristically thoughtful analysis of revival in the eighteenth century, which shows how it was very much a movement of its time, is provided by David Bebbington in his essay 'Revival and Enlightenment in Eighteenth Century England'.

5.   This claim, of course, is not accepted by all theorists. Rodney Stark, for example, has been particularly critical of the thesis that pre-industrial European societies were more religious than the contemporary West. See Stark and Iannacconne, 'A Supply-Side Reinterpretation of the "Secularization" of Europe'. The opposing case, which argues for the traditional view of the pre-industrial past as more religious, is made by Steve Bruce. See, for example, *God is Dead*, 43–59.

6.   Note that I am not here referring to the traditional sociological premises relating to European normativity, modernization and secularization. To my mind, the big issue regarding Christianity and secularization is not whether it is happening, but whether Europe is exceptional or normative. Is Europe a paradigm of the future of world Christianity? Those sociologists who answer this question positively often argue for the rather patronizing thesis which assumes that when other areas of the world catch up with the West in terms of modernization, they too will abandon religious enthusiasm and Christianity. That it now flourishes in the southern hemisphere (and even in the USA) cannot simply be explained away by using traditional sociological assumptions. On the USA, see particularly Casanova, 'Beyond European and American Exceptionalisms'. More generally and on the southern hemisphere see Martin, 'On Secularization and Its Prediction'; Berger, 'The Desecularization of the World'. See also Martin, 'The Evangelical Upsurge and its Political Implications'; Martin, *Pentecostalism*; Cox, *Fire from Heaven*; Jenkins, *The Next Christendom*; Freston, *Evangelicals and Politics in Asia, Africa and Latin America*.

7.   Both these quotations are taken from Smith's *Against the Stream*, 52.

8.   Brierley, *The Tide is Running Out*, 236.

9.   For a good collection of papers analysing the significance of Toronto, see Hilborn (ed.), *'Toronto' in Perspective*.

10.   See particularly Davie, 'Believing Without Belonging: Is This the Future of Religion in Britain?'

11.   An interesting collection of papers on Christian revival can be found in Walker and Aune (eds.), *On Revival*.

12.   Duncan, *The Christ, Psychotherapy and Magic*, 55. Duncan was not even referring to a broad occultic milieu, but only to the type of esotericism outlined above. Influenced by the prominent occultist Gareth Knight, he was an Anglican clergyman with a particular interest in kabbalistic occultism.

13.   See Adorno, 'On Popular Music'.

14.   Barker, *Cultural Studies*, 45.

15.   Adorno, *The Culture Industry*, 92.

16.   This essay can be found in Benjamin, *Illuminations*.

Chapter 1

1.   Bruce, *God is Dead*.

2.   There are, of course, other typologies of secularization, most notably Larry Shiner's 'The Concept of Secularisation'.

3.   Woodhead and Heelas (eds.), *Religion in Modern Times*, 307.

4.   Ibid., 308.

5.   See e.g. Nietzsche, *The Twilight of the Idols*, in *Thus Spoke Zarathustra*.

6.   Gerth and Mills, 'Introduction: The Man and His Work', 53.

7.   For one such history see particularly Gilbert, *The Making of Post-Christian Britain*, 2–99. For a more idiosyncratic interpretation, see Gauchet, *The Disenchantment of the World*. See also Martin, *A General Theory of Secularization*, chs 1–3.

8.   See particularly Weber, *The Protestant Ethic and the Spirit of Capitalism*.

9.   Gilbert, *The Making of Post-Christian Britain*, 17–18.

10.   Ibid., 18.

11.   Ibid., 19.

12.   Ibid. (emphasis in original).

13.   Jolly, *Popular Religion in Late Saxon England*, 170–1. See also Kieckhefer, *Magic in the Middle Ages*.

14.   Thomas, *Religion and the Decline of Magic*, 28.

15.   Berger, 'The Desecularization of the World', 2. As we will see, this essay is written in opposition to the paradigm he so clearly articulated earlier in his career. He now refers to his early thesis (and those of like-minded thinkers) as 'a big mistake'.

16.   Bruce, *God is Dead*, 2.

17.   Wilson, *The Social Dimensions of Sectarianism*, 122.

18.   This common phrase was popularized by Wilson – see *Religion in Secular Society*, 14.

19.   See De Graaf and Need, 'Losing Faith: Is Britain Alone?'; Greeley, 'Religion in Britain, Ireland and the USA'.

20.   Bruce, *God is Dead*, 37.

21.   Ibid., 37–8.

22.   Bruce, 'The Charismatic Movement and the Secularization Thesis', 227.

23.   Bruce, *God is Dead*, 39.

24.   Bruce, 'The Charismatic Movement and the Secularization Thesis', 227 (my emphases).

25.   Ibid., 227.

26.   Milbank, *Theology and Social Theory*.

27.   A worthwhile discussion of Nietzsche and atheism can be found in Buckley, *At the Origins of Modern Atheism*, 28ff.

28.   Bruce, *God is Dead*, 39.

29. See Comte, 'A Science of Society', 285–7.

30. See Freud, *The Future of an Illusion*.

31. Bruce, *Religion in the Modern World*, 38.

32. See Wilson, 'Secularization: The Inherited Model'.

33. Gerth and Mills, 'Introduction', 51.

34. Bruce, *Religion in the Modern World*, 48–9.

35. Bruce, *God is Dead*, 8.

36. Ibid., 8.

37. Dobbelaere, 'Secularization: A Multi-Dimensional Concept'.

38. Hefner, 'Secularization and Citizenship in Muslim Indonesia', 150.

39. Berger, *The Sacred Canopy*, 151.

40. Ibid., 156.

41. Ibid., 127.

42. Ibid.

43. Bruce, 'Pluralism and Religious Vitality', 170.

44. For a good discussion of new religions, equal rights and laws, see Wilson, *The Social Dimensions of Sectarianism*, ch. 4.

45. Walker, *Telling the Story*, 6.

Chapter 2

1. Weber, 'The Protestant Sects and the Spirit of Capitalism', 304–5.

2. Ibid., 305–6.

3. Weber, 'The Meaning of Discipline', 262 (my emphasis). See also his 'The Sociology of Charismatic Authority'.

4. Quoted in Niesel, *Reformed Symbolics*, 32–3.

5. From its original two volumes in 1890 *The Golden Bough* expanded to three volumes in the second edition (1900) and finally to twelve volumes for the third and final edition, which was published between 1911 and 1915. That said, it is primarily the 1922 abridged edition that most people are familiar with nowadays (if they are familiar with it at all), a cheap edition of which has recently been published by Wordsworth Editions.

6. For a good basic introduction to Scientology, see Melton, *The Church of Scientology*.

7. Tumminia, 'When the Archangel Died'.

8. Quoted in Drescher, *Ernst Troeltsch*, 122.

9. Troeltsch, *The Social Teaching of the Christian Churches*, 2 vols.

10. Drescher, *Ernst Troeltsch*, 222.

11. See particularly Troeltsch, *The Social Teaching of the Christian Churches*, vol. 1, p. 338ff.

12. Ibid., 331.

13. Ibid.

14. Ibid.

15. Ibid., 332.

16. Ibid., 377.

17. Drescher, *Ernst Troeltsch*, 233–4.

18. Troeltsch, *The Social Teaching of the Christian Churches*, vol. 1, p. 338.

19. Ibid.

20. For an interesting discussion of sect and church which demonstrates the difficulty of applying Troeltsch's typology more broadly, see van der Leeuw, *Religion in Essence and Manifestation*, 261–8.

21. For more on this see Partridge, 'Truth, Authority and Epistemological Individualism in New Age Thought'.

22. Niebuhr, *The Social Sources of Denominationalism*.

23. Ibid., 19.

24. Ibid., 19–20.

25. Ibid., 3.

26. See esp. ibid., chs 2–4.

27. Ibid., 71.

28. Ibid., 28.

29. Wilson, 'An Analysis of Sect Development', 26.

30. For an influential typology of sectarianism, see Wilson, *Religious Sects*, 36–47.

31. Wilson, *The Social Dimensions of Sectarianism*, 47.

32. See Wilson's discussion of the Exclusive Brethren, in *The Social Dimensions of Sectarianism*, ch. 5. 'When there is persistent wrong-doing or false teaching, the local assembly becomes concerned, and if the case cannot be resolved by rebuke, then an unrepentant individual is said to be "shut up", a term used to indicate that he is not admitted to the Brethren's meetings, and in particular, to the meeting for the "breaking of bread". One who fails to repent is then "withdrawn from" or "put out", and any brother who fails so to dissociate himself from the unrepentant himself becomes subject to the same form of censure. Little as such measures might be appreciated by outsiders, they are well understood by those who have committed themselves to the fellowship as something unfortunate but essential to the maintenance of its purity' (92).

33. Wallis, *The Road to Total Freedom*, ch. 1.

34. Wallis, *The Elementary Forms of the New Religious Life*.

35. See Martin, 'The Denomination'.

36. See Robertson, *The Sociological Interpretation of Religion*, ch. 5. Wallis makes particular use of Robertson's discussion of unique and pluralistic legitimacy.

37. Stark and Bainbridge discuss the problems involved in classifying Mormonism and conclude that, in the final analysis, it fits their particular definition of a 'cult' rather than a 'sect'. See *The Future of Religion*, 245ff. It should be noted that the definition of 'cult' provided by Stark and Bainbridge is distinct from that provided by Wallis (outlined in the next paragraph of the text).

38. Becker, *Systematic Sociology on the Basis of the* Bezeihungslehre *and* Gebildelehre *of Leopold von Wiese*.

39. Yinger, *Religion, Society and the Individual*. Yinger delineated a sixfold typology: (1) the universal church (e.g. the medieval Catholic Church, which transcends individual nations and societies); (2) the ecclesia (i.e. a less inclusive, less universal established national church such as the Church of England); (3) the denomination (i.e. an organization limited to particular people and thus even less universal and inclusive); (4) the established sect (i.e. a more established development of the sect which resists denominationalism, a typical example of which is the Quakers); (5) the sect (i.e. Troeltsch's sect); (6) the cult (i.e. a form of religion which is oriented around the individual, has little organizational structure, is focused on a charismatic figure, and is usually short-lived).

40. See Bruce, *God is Dead*, 76–9.

41. Wallis, 'Ideology, Authority and the Development of Cultic Movements', 304.

42. I have explored the notion of epistemological individualism in relation to the New Age in 'Truth, Authority and Epistemological Individualism in New Age Thought'.

43. Over the last half-century, the most influential Evangelical assessments of new religious movements include the following books, all of which, to some degree, adopt the broad, negative definition of cult: Hoekema, *The Four Major Cults*; Sanders, *Heresies and Cults*; Larson, *Larson's Book of Cults*. Of course, there are a variety of understandings of 'cult'. For a good discussion of types of cult, see Nelson, *Cults, New Religions and Religious Creativity*, 53–66. For a good discussion of definitions of 'cult' used by the Christian counter-cult movement, see Cowan, 'Exits and Migrations', 341–4.

44. See Melton, *The Church of Scientology*, 25–38 (esp. 30–3).

45. See Stark and Bainbridge, *The Future of Religion*, 208–33.

46. Wallis, *The Road to Total Freedom*, 94, 96.

47. Stark and Bainbridge, *The Future of Religion*, 25.

48. Ibid.

49. Ibid., 28.

50. Ibid., 26.

51. Wallis, *The Elementary Forms of the New Religious Life*, 4.

52. Ibid., 9.

53. See Hall, *Apocalypse Observed.*

54. Wallis, *The Elementary Forms of the New Religious Life*, 20–1.

55. Russell, *The TM Technique*, p. vii.

56. Ibid., 4.

57. Wallis, *The Road to Total Freedom*, 14.

58. Wallis, *The Elementary Forms of the New Religious Life*, 35.

59. The term 'modern times' is deliberately chosen by Woodhead and Heelas because, they claim, it is broader than the term 'modernity': 'The former designates simply a period of time; the latter the socio-cultural attributes of the so-called "developed" societies distinctive of the West (and now, increasingly, of other parts of the world as well)' (Woodhead and Heelas [eds.], *Religion in Modern Times*, 4). But surely the term 'modern' still carries the baggage they are seeking to offload.

60. Ibid., 3.

61. Ibid., 2–3.

62. See particularly Eliade, *The Sacred and the Profane.*

63. See Bruce, 'The New Age and Secularization', 233.

64. See Bruce, 'Religion in Britain at the Close of the 20th Century'.

65. Bruce, *God is Dead*, 70–1.

66. Bruce, *Religion in the Modern World*, 222.

67. Bruce, *God is Dead*, 79.

68. Ibid.

69. Wilson, *The Social Dimensions of Sectarianism*, 273–4.

70. Others, of course, have denied that it constitutes a religion, or, like David Bromley and Mitchell Bracey, have argued that it is 'one of the clearest examples of a quasi-religious therapy system' (Bromley and Bracey, 'The Church of Scientology: A Quasi Religion', 152).

71. Wilson, *The Social Dimensions of Sectarianism*, 288.

72. Wilson, *Social Change and New Religious Movements*, 5. Interestingly, this is a small booklet written for and published by the Church of Scientology.

73. Wilson, *The Social Dimensions of Sectarianism*, 288.

74. See Wilson's discussion of the broadening of the concept of religion in relation to new religions, ibid., ch. 4.

75. Bruce, *God is Dead*, 79 (emphasis in original).

76. Ibid.

77. Bruce, 'The New Age and Secularization', 233.

78. See Swatos, 'Enchantment and Disenchantment in Modernity'.

79. See e.g. Wilson, *Contemporary Transformations of Religion.*

80. Wilson, ' "Secularization": Religion in the Modern World', 207.

81. Bruce, *God is Dead*, 82.

82. 'Insofar as [the New Age] is popular, it is so because its individualistic epistemology, consumerist ethos and therapeutic focus resonate with the rest of our culture. The New Age is important not for the changes it will bring but for the changes it epitomises' (Bruce, 'The New Age and Secularization', 234).

83. For more on this see Partridge, 'Truth, Authority and Epistemological Individualism in New Age Thought'. See also Partridge and Elliot, 'The Spiritual Nature of Human Beings'.

84. Bruce, *God is Dead*, 83.

85. *Alternatives*, Spring/Summer 2002.

86. Ibid., 1.

87. *Inspiration* 3 (2002), 1.

88. Woodhead, 'Studying Religion and Modernity', 9.

89. Bruce, *God is Dead*, 86.

90. Berger, *The Heretical Imperative*, 28 (emphasis in original).

91. Bruce, *God is Dead*, 94.

92. Ibid., 95.
93. Ibid., 97.
94. Ibid.
95. Ibid.
96. Ibid., 98.
97. Ibid., 99.
98. Ibid. (emphasis in original).
99. Ibid., 101.
100. Ibid.
101. Ibid., 102.
102. See Heelas, Lash and Morris (eds.), *Detraditionalization*.
103. A particularly strident account of the significance of new religions and alternative spiritualities can be found in Gregory Baum's *Religion and the Rise of Scepticism*, 186–97.
104. Bruce, 'The New Age and Secularization', 234.
105. Bruce, *God is Dead*, 105.
106. Bruce, 'The New Age and Secularization', 235.
107. Bruce, 'The Demise of Christianity in Britain', 61.

Chapter 3

1. Nelson, *Cults, New Religions and Religious Creativity*, 2. See also Mayer, 'The Emergence of a New Religiosity in the Western World'.
2. See Partridge (ed.), *Fundamentalisms*.
3. See the essays in Berger (ed.), *The Desecularization of the World*.
4. Survey carried out for the BBC series *Soul of Britain* (2000).
5. Berger, 'The Desecularization of the World', 3. His thesis in this essay has baffled and been directly challenged by his disciple, Steve Bruce, in 'The Curious Case of the Unnecessary Recantation'.
6. Berger, 'The Desecularization of the World', 9–10 (emphasis in original).
7. Ibid., 10.
8. Ibid., 11. A similar point is made by Wouter Hanegraaff on Keith Thomas, who, in his important study *Religion and the Decline of Magic* (1971), declared, in the face of an emerging occult counterculture, that magical beliefs 'are now rightly disdained by intelligent persons'. As Hanegraaff comments: 'one wonders whether he had ever left his study and his archives to take a look around the real world' ('How Magic Survived the Disenchantment of the World', 357–8).
9. See, for example, Stark and Bainbridge, *The Future of Religion*; Stark, 'Modernization, Secularization, and Mormon Success'; Stark, 'Rationality'.
10. Stark and Bainbridge, *The Future of Religion*, 429–30.
11. Berger, 'The Desecularization of the World', 9–10.
12. The oppositionalist nature of the cultic milieu is explored in a collection of articles edited by Kaplan and Lööw, *The Cultic Milieu*: 'The cultic milieu is oppositional by nature' (Kaplan and Lööw, 'Introduction', 3).
13. Hanegraaff, 'How Magic Survived the Disenchantment of the World', 358 (emphasis in original).
14. Ibid., 359–60 (emphasis in original).
15. Luhrmann, *Persuasions of the Witch's Craft*.
16. See e.g. Zalewski, *Golden Dawn Enochian Magic*.
17. Luhrmann, *Persuasions of the Witch's Craft*, 164.
18. Ibid., 177–8.
19. Campbell, 'The Secret Religion of the Educated Classes', 147.
20. Ibid., 150.
21. Stark and Bainbridge define religions as 'human organizations primarily engaged in providing general compensators based on supernatural assumptions' (*The Future of Religion*, 8).
22. Ibid., 6–8 (emphasis in the original).

23. Campbell, 'The Secret Religion of the Educated Classes', 150.

24. Ibid.

25. White, 'Re-Enchanting the World', 347.

26. Adorno, 'The Stars Down to Earth', 37.

27. 'Disenchantment...has more than one cause. Reason expelled magic and God from ordinary events of nature and history. But it also ejected other methods of knowing, relegating them to marginal, specialist interests, outside the public domain. The far point of separation is now most obviously recognizable in what is called postmodernism: a world in which any number of private interpretations of reality is allowed, but none trusted to lay claim to a common public arena... In a further twist, radical postmodernism sees reason itself as privatized, distorted by personal agendas. So *everything* is fragmented and unreliable, nothing can be commonly held. Which brings us full circle. It is a recipe for new superstition and magic... No wonder we would like to re-enchant the world' (White, 'Re-enchanting the World', 349–50; emphasis in original). Another interesting theological discussion, which draws on contemporary 'ritual studies' and includes a critique of contemporary secularization theses, is Lieven Boeve's 'The Sacramental Interruption of Rituals of Life' (see esp. 406–9).

28. This view is supported by the work of writers such as Robert Wuthnow, Wade Clark Roof and Paul Heelas. See, for example, Wuthnow, *After Heaven*; Roof, *Spiritual Marketplace*; Heelas, *The New Age Movement*.

29. Marty, 'The Occult Establishment', 214.

30. Bell, 'The Return of the Sacred?'.

31. See Chan, 'The Sacred–Secular Dialectics of the Reenchanted Religious Order'.

32. Wuthnow, *After Heaven*, 2.

33. Ibid., 3.

34. Green, *Church Without Walls*, p. x.

35. Frost, *A Closer Look at New Age Spirituality*, 9, 13. The book is actually a fascinating and illuminating account of an Evangelical's open-minded and informed engagement with alternative spiritualities. Indeed, it might almost be described as an account of the re-enchantment of a deeply Evangelical mind.

36. Ibid., 13.

37. Ibid., 119.

38. Berger, 'Postscript', in Woodhead *et al.* (eds.), *Peter Berger and the Study of Religion*, 194.

39. Brierley, 'Religion'.

40. Ibid., 667.

41. Brown, *The Death of Christian Britain*, 11–12.

42. Lyon, *Jesus in Disneyland*, 21.

43. Dyson, 'Spellbound', 30 (my emphasis); quoted in Cavallaro, *Cyberpunk and Cyberculture*, p. xii.

44. York, 'Alternative Spirituality in Europe', 131.

45. Brum, 'Smells Like Teen Spirit', 146.

46. See Stuart, 'The Home Counties Witch Project', 20.

47. Jorgensen and Russell, 'American Neopaganism: The Participants' Social Identities', 330.

48. See Stuart, 'The Home Counties Witch Project', 20.

49. Burke, 'No Rest for the Wicca'.

50. In 1930 occult books constituted 7 per cent of religious books published. This gradually rose to 17 per cent in 1990, dipped to 11 per cent in 1995 and rose again to 15 per cent in 2000. See Brierley, 'Religion', 666–7.

51. Anonymous, 'The Road Well Trodden: How to Succeed in Publishing', 35.

52. 'Occult beliefs have increased dramatically in the United States during the last two decades. Far from being a "fad", preoccupation with the occult now forms a pervasive part of our culture. Garden-variety occultisms such as astrology and ESP have swelled... Ouija boards overtook Monopoly as the nation's best-selling board game in 1967... Occult beliefs are salient not only among the lay public, but also among college students, including those at some of our science

oriented campuses. The occult trend shows no signs of diminishing' (Singer and Benassi, 'Occult Beliefs', 384).

53. Heelas, 'Prosperity and the New Age Movement', 71.

54. Heelas, 'Expressive Spirituality and Humanistic Expressivism', 240 (emphasis in original).

55. For Heelas's calculations, which are based, interestingly, on the figures Bruce uses, see ibid.

56. Brooks and Morgan, 'Losing Our Religion', 13. These results were also reported in the BBC's *Soul of Britain* survey (2000).

57. Hunt, 'Understanding the Spirituality of People Who Do Not Go to Church', 160, 162 (my emphasis).

58. Rushkoff, 'Foreword', in St John (ed.), *Rave Culture and Religion*, p. xv (my emphasis).

59. Cited in Wuthnow, *After Heaven*, 2, 199.

60. Cornbleth, *Hearing America's Youth*, 115–16.

61. Ibid., 116.

62. Ibid., 118–19.

63. Ibid., 120.

64. Fey, 'Spirituality Bites: Xers and the Gothic Cult/ure', 32.

65. The Gallup Index of Leading Religious Indicators/Princeton Religion Research Index records the following: 'Belief in God or a universal spirit: This percentage has been very high in the U.S. over the last six decades – consistently in the mid-90 per cent range. However, considerably fewer (8 in 10) believe in a personal God, that is, a God who watches over humankind and answers prayers', accessed 12 Sept. 2001 (http://www.gallup.com/poll/releases/pr010329.asp). See also Brierley, 'Religion', 663.

66. Brierley (ed.), *UK Christian Handbook: Religious Trends No.1*, pt. 10, p. 4.

67. Brooks and Morgan, 'Losing Our Religion', 13.

68. Barker, 'New Religious Movements: Their Incidence and Significance', 19. There would seem to be more people who hold recognizably religious beliefs than people who want to describe themselves as either 'religious' or 'spiritual'. Andrew Greeley's discussion of belief in God in Britain highlights the importance of using the right words to ask the right question in the right way. People are clearly sensitive about how they are perceived when it comes to religious belief. See Greeley, 'Religion in Britain, Ireland and the USA', 66–8.

69. Wuthnow helpfully describes spirituality as follows: 'Spirituality consists not only of implicit assumptions about life but also of the things people talk about and the things they do: the stories they construct about their spiritual journeys, the prayers they offer, the inspirational books they read, the time they spend meditating, their participation in retreats and at worship services, the conversations they have about it with their friends, and the energy they spend thinking about it. At its core, spirituality consists of all the beliefs and activities by which individuals attempt to relate their lives to God or to a divine being or some other conception of a transcendent reality. In a society as complex as that of the United States, spirituality is expressed in many different ways. But spirituality is not just the creation of individuals; it is shaped by larger social circumstances and by the beliefs and values present in the wider culture' (Wuthnow, *After Heaven*, pp. vii–viii).

70. Paul Heelas has recently identified the shift discussed in this chapter as a shift from 'religion' to 'spirituality' ('The Spiritual Revolution').

71. Hunt, 'Understanding the Spirituality of People Who Do Not Go to Church', 161.

72. Wainwright, 'Church Fears Modern Beliefs are Undermining Traditional Values', 3. Similarly, in 1998, Archbishop Zycinski, commenting on the encyclical *Fides et Ratio*, bemoaned the reduction of grand philosophical questions to 'naïve faith in UFOs, astrology and the New Age' (quoted in Lyon, *Jesus in Disneyland*, 53).

73. Wainwright, 'Our Candid Cardinal', 19 (emphasis mine).

74. Beckford, 'The Mass Media and New Religious Movements', 103–19.

75. Campbell, 'The Easternization of the West', 36.

76. See Partridge (ed.), *UFO Religions*. In this volume I have discussed alien abduction spirituality at some length (26–37).

77. Whilst some New Agers have sought to convince me that this is not the case and that Jesus

actually taught reincarnation, and although such thoughtful Christians as Leslie Weatherhead and, more recently, Geddes MacGregor have seriously considered the doctrine, in the final analysis it is difficult to disagree with John Whale's blunt conclusion that 'there is not a shred of evidence for this doctrine of Karma or a series of Reincarnations in the New Testament' (55). See MacGregor, *Reincarnation in Christianity*, 'Is Reincarnation Compatible with Christian Faith?', 89–98; Weatherhead, *The Christian Agnostic*, ch. 14; Whale, *The Christian Answer to the Problem of Evil*, 53–5.

78. An interesting overview of Western parapsychological interest in the area is provided by John Beloff, in *Parapsychology*, 206–15.

79. Walter, 'Reincarnation, Modernity and Identity', 21.

80. See Barker, 'New Religious Movements', 19.

81. Walter, 'Reincarnation, Modernity and Identity', 21.

82. Waterhouse, 'Reincarnation Belief in Britain', 107 (emphasis in original).

83. William Bloom makes the following point: 'It is in the field of healthcare that the holistic approach has probably had its greatest impact over the last thirty years. Originally the medical and scientific establishment was deeply distrustful of all holistic and complementary approaches, regarding these alternative strategies as at best naïve and at worst fatally dangerous. This attitude is understandable, for Western medicine has its foundation in the certainties of empirical science and because medical doctors daily face life and death crises. Indeed, the success of Western medicine can be witnessed in infant survival rates, the extension of life and the general relief of pain... In the face of such a successful track record, based in a scientific approach, the complementary therapies can easily be seen as irrelevant and dangerous. But public demand for a holistic approach and the pragmatic reality of its effectiveness have forced mainstream medicine to widen its boundaries to include the complementary strategies' (*Holistic Revolution*, 149).

84. Eisenberg *et al.*, 'Unconventional Medicine in the United States', 251.

85. Survey for BBC series, *Soul of Britain*.

86. Heelas and Seel, 'An Ageing New Age?', 234–5.

87. Springhouse Corporation, *Nurse's Handbook of Alternative and Complementary Therapies*, p. ix. See also Rankin-Box, *Nurse's Handbook of Complementary Therapies*.

88. See my discussion of the significance of the pre-modern in alternative religious worldviews: 'Truth, Authority and Epistemological Individualism in New Age Thought', 87–8.

89. Springhouse Corporation, *Nurse's Handbook of Alternative and Complementary Therapies*, 3.

90. Walter, 'Reincarnation, Modernity and Identity', 22.

91. Other terms, such as 'normalization' or 'domestication', might have been used, but these carry meanings I do not intend. 'De-exotification', simply indicates a belief's or artifact's or practice's loss of exotic status.

92. Rose, 'An Examination of the New Age Movement', 10.

93. Ibid.

94. For more on self-spirituality and modernity see particularly Heelas, *The New Age Movement*.

95. Campbell, 'The Secret Religion of the Educated Classes', 152.

96. Ibid., 153.

97. Ibid., 153–4.

98. Richardson, 'Studies of Conversion', 107.

99. For an excellent, critical treatment of Celtic Christianity, ancient, modern and postmodern, see Meek, *The Quest for Celtic Christianity*.

100. Campbell, 'The Easternization of the West', 37.

101. Heelas, *The New Age Movement*, 124.

102. See Lee, *Earth First!* and Plows, 'Earth First! Defending Mother Earth, Direct-Style'.

103. Taylor, 'Earth and Nature-Based Spirituality (Part 1)'; 'Earth and Nature-Based Spirituality (Part 2)'.

104. Hay, *Companion to Environmental Thought*, 94.

105. Dalton and Rohrschneider, 'The Greening of Europe'; Witherspoon, 'The Greening of Britain'.

106. See Potts, 'Imagining Gaia'.

107. See Ruether, *Gaia and God*; Diamond and Orenstein (eds.), *Reweaving the World*; Gottlieb, *This Sacred Earth*, 383–470.

108. See Devall and Sessions, *Deep Ecology*. For key texts on 'spiritual deep ecology' see Gottlieb, *This Sacred Earth*, 471–508. A helpful essay explaining the attraction of ecological spiritualities is Charlene Spretnak's 'The Spiritual Dimension of Green Politics'. Another good article which discusses the outworking of green consciousness politically in direct action and spiritually in Paganism, and their relationship, is Letcher, ' "Gaia Told Me To Do It": Resistance and the Idea of Nature within Contemporary British Eco-Paganism'.

109. As an aspect of the process of contextualization, the concept of inculturation has been developed within contemporary Christian missiology. For an excellent overview of contemporary Christian missiological usage of contextualization and inculturation, see Bosch, *Transforming Mission*, 420–32, 447–57.

110. Wilson, ' "Secularization": Religion in the Modern World', 207.

111. Ostwalt, *Secular Steeples*, 28–9.

112. Depeche Mode, 'Personal Jesus' on *Violator*.

113. Johnny Cash, 'Personal Jesus' on *American IV*.

114. See Ostwalt's discussion of Christian rock music (*Secular Steeples*, 193ff.). Indeed, although he is clearly not a fundamentalist Christian and does not actually interpret such music as 'the Devil's music', the premise of his analysis would not be out of place in fundamentalist discourse. In one hermeneutic of suspicion the Devil is everywhere apparent, compromising and subverting true religion; in another hermeneutic of suspicion, the secular is everywhere apparent, compromising and subverting true religion.

115. Ibid., 30–1.

116. Ibid., 1.

117. See particularly his discussion of the 'megachurch' movement (ibid., 57–76).

118. On softer, more syncretic forms of Christian 'spirituality' see Yip, 'The Self as the Basis of Religious Faith: Spirituality of Gay, Lesbian and Bisexual Christians'; Pilgrim, 'The Quakers'.

119. Pearson, 'Witchcraft Will Not Soon Vanish from This Earth', 179.

120. Bruce, 'The Demise of Christianity in Britain'.

121. See Tony Walter's discussion of reincarnation in everyday conversation: 'Reincarnation, Modernity and Identity', 26–7.

122. Anderson, *Reality Isn't What It Used To Be*, 187.

123. Woodhead, 'The World's Parliament of Religions and the Rise of Alternative Spirituality', 81. See also Martin, *The Religious and the Secular*, 108, and Heelas, 'Expressive Spirituality and Humanistic Expressivism', 239.

124. As Leonard Glick urges, 'those of us who study people's responses to new religious ideas should not labour with the misconception that our world is one in which religion is disappearing. For, to the contrary, the evidence is that new religions are arising all the time, that people do not respond to new problems by abandoning religion but by developing a new religion on the ruins of the old' (quoted in Anderson, *Reality Isn't What It Used To Be*, 114).

125. See particularly Davie, 'Believing Without Belonging'; *Religion in Britain Since 1945*.

126. Davie, 'Believing Without Belonging', 462.

127. We will see in the next volume that this seems to be the case with contemporary demonologies in the West.

128. Davie, *Religion in Britain Since 1945*, 83.

129. Hay, *Exploring Inner Space*.

130. Hay, *Religious Experience Today*.

131. Spencer, 'Are the Stars Coming Out?', 214.

132. Sjödin, 'The Paranormal in Swedish Religiosity', 203.

133. The decrease in Church of Sweden membership has been relatively minimal, membership being still around 85 per cent (ibid.).

134. Ibid.

135. Lyon, *Jesus in Disneyland*, 104.

Chapter 4

1. Troeltsch, *The Social Teaching of the Christian Churches*, vol. 1, p. 377.

2. Again, this individualistic eclecticism is outlined by Troeltsch with regard to Christianity: a 'third sociological type of Christian thought, which does not depend, like the Church, upon the institution, not like the sect on the literal interpretation of the Law of God in the Bible, but which is an individualism which freely combines Christian ideas with all kinds of other elements, and which is either entirely unorganized, or else exists alongside of the Church and assumes its necessity for the mass of mankind' (ibid., vol. 1, p. 378).

3. See Partridge, 'Truth, Authority and Epistemological Individualism in New Age Thought'.

4. Troeltsch, *The Social Teaching of the Christian Churches*, vol. 1, 381 (my emphasis).

5. A good example of this sort of coalescence would seem to be the emergence of Spiritualism. See Nelson, *Spiritualism and Society*; and also Beloff, *Parapsychology*, 38–63.

6. See Rawlinson, 'The Rise and Fall of Lifewave', 11–14.

7. See Bradby, '*A Course in Miracles*'; Drane, '*The Celestine Prophecy*'.

8. See Wallis, 'Scientology: Therapeutic Cult to Religious Sect'; *The Road to Total Freedom*.

9. Campbell, 'Clarifying the Cult'.

10. To be fair, since the book is not mentioned by Campbell, it probably came out too late for him to take account of it.

11. See also Campbell, 'The Secret Religion of the Educated Classes'.

12. Becker, quoted in Campbell, 'Clarifying the Cult', 377.

13. Ibid. (emphasis in original).

14. Ibid. (emphasis in original). He is referring here to Talcott Parsons' notion of 'residual category' as discussed in *The Structure of Social Action*, 16–19.

15. Ibid., 381.

16. Ibid., 382.

17. Troeltsch, *The Social Teaching of the Christian Churches*, vol. 2, 734; quoted in ibid. Campbell, 'Clarifying the Cult', 381.

18. Troeltsch, *The Social Teaching of the Christian Churches*, vol. 2, p. 734; quoted in Campbell, 'Clarifying the Cult', 382.

19. See Hocking, *Living Religions and a World Faith*.

20. See Schuon, *Transcendent Unity of Religions*.

21. See Huxley, *The Perennial Philosophy*.

22. See, for example, Hughes, 'Mysticism: The Perennial Philosophy?'.

23. Campbell, 'The Secret Religion of the Educated Classes', 150.

24. Ibid.

25. Campbell, 'Clarifying the Cult', 383.

26. Ibid., 385.

27. Troeltsch, *The Social Teaching of the Christian Churches*, vol. 2, 745; quoted in Campbell, 'Clarifying the Cult', 383–4.

28. Campbell, 'Clarifying the Cult', 385.

29. Sutcliffe, 'A Colony of Seekers', 215. See also Sutcliffe, *Children of the New Age*, 150–73. For a good earlier study of the community, see Rigby and Turner, 'Findhorn Community, Centre of Light'.

30. Hamilton, 'An Analysis of the Festival of Mind–Body–Spirit, London', 188.

31. See Partridge (ed.), *UFO Religions*; Grünschloß, 'Ufology and UFO-Related Movements'.

32. A short biography and her views on vegetarianism and spirituality can be found in Ching Hai, *Key to Enlightenment*. See also Irons, 'Suma Ching Hai'.

33. See Dawson and Hennebry, 'New Religions and the Internet'.

34. Campbell, 'The Cult, the Cultic Milieu and Secularization', 122.

35. Kaplan and Lööw, 'Introduction', 3.

36. Campbell, 'The Cult, the Cultic Milieu and Secularization', 122. For a collection of essays discussing the contemporary relevance of Campbell's thesis, see Kaplan and Lööw (eds.), *The Cultic Milieu*.

37. This is evident from the breadth of Kaplan and Lööw (eds.), *The Cultic Milieu*. Robert Ellwood's recommendation on the cover of the book is worth quoting: 'What do deep ecologists, neo-Nazis, Goths, black nationalists, and urban shamans have in common? They are all part of a "cultic milieu," an underground culture that embraces everyone, right or left, good or bad, that thrives on standing in opposition to the social mainstream'.

38. See the essays in Partridge and Gabriel (eds.), *Mysticism East and West*.

39. Jantzen, 'Mysticism and New Religious Movements', 11 (emphasis in original).

40. Ibid., 11 (emphasis in original). See also McIntosh, *Mystical Theology*.

41. See Stark and Bainbridge, *The Future of Religion*, 322.

42. See ibid.

43. See <http: www.occulture.tv>. The aim of Occulture is to celebrate and draw together the occult subculture. 'It started out as a tiny event', Justin Hankinson told me, 'featuring Wiccans, chaos magicians and Satanists.' Indeed, recalling that it was initially 'slated in the local press by individuals claiming we were "sacrificing animals",' he commented that 'this is exactly the reason why we created Occulture'.

44. For an interesting interview with Genesis P-Orridge, see Watson, 'Beyond Evil'.

45. Kane, 'In Thrall to New Age Thrills'.

46. McKay, *Senseless Acts of Beauty*, 51–2.

47. 'The cultic milieu is oppositional by nature' (Kaplan and Lööw, 'Introduction', 3).

48. It should be noted that, although often confused, the terms 'esotericism' and 'occultism' are not synonymous. Robert Gilbert, for example, makes the following point: 'This is now the preferred term of use, among academics, for categorising and describing a constellation of practices and belief systems that are among the constituent parts of what has commonly been labelled "occultism". The term is not synonymous with occultism, for although it incorporates many of the occult arts and "sciences", it excludes others and takes in also various initiatic systems that are often considered to be simply fraternal societies, together with schools of thought more usually placed within the confines of western spirituality' ('Western Esotericism', 304).

49. Laurant, 'The Primitive Characteristics of Nineteenth-Century Esotericism', 277, 287.

50. Ibid., 287.

51. See Copenhaver (trans.), *Hermetica* for a reliable and accessible English translation of the *Corpus Hermeticum*.

52. Perhaps the most influential recent occultic interpretation of the Kabbalah is Knight, *A Practical Guide to Qabalistic Symbolism*. Also important are the following: Fortune, *The Mystical Qabalah*; Regardie, *The Tree of Life*; Mathers, *The Kabbalah Unveiled*.

53. See, for example, Zalewski, *Golden Dawn Enochian Magic*. Even a cursory glance through this volume with its many tables, diagrams and symbols, including the so-called Enochian script, reveals the complexity of some occult systems.

54. Gilbert, 'Western Esotericism', 305.

55. For an overview of such organizations and systems, see Partridge, *Encyclopedia of New Religions*, 301–56.

56. Jung, for example, is carefully used by the prominent Wiccan High Priestess, Vivianne Crowley: e.g. *Wicca: The Old Religion in the New Millennium*. On the use of Jung in the New Age, see Main, 'Religion, Science and the New Age'.

57. Duncan, *The Christ, Psychotherapy and Magic*, 55.

58. Clarke, 'The Occult and Newly Religious in Modern Society', 1.

59. See Lewis (ed.), *Magical Religion and Modern Witchcraft*.

60. Lööw, 'The Idea of Purity'; Kaplan, 'The Postwar Paths of Occult National Socialism'; Simonelli, 'Thriving in a Cultic Milieu'.

61. See e.g. Taylor, 'Diggers, Wolves, Ents, Elves and Expanding Universes'.

62. e.g. Gonzalez-Wippler, *Return of the Angels*.

63. A great deal of material in the occult milieu, from the massive *A Course in Miracles* to more traditionally Spiritualist messages from those 'who have passed over', to communications from extraterrestrials (e.g. George King's messages from Aetherius), is claimed to have been channelled.

Indeed, such is the popularity of spirit guides such as Seth (Jane Roberts), Lazaris (Jach Pursel), Ramtha (J.Z. Knight), and Mafu (Penny Torres) that they themselves could be considered to have attained celebrity status within the occult milieu. For a helpful overview of the some of the principal channellers and entities, see Melton, Clark and Kelly, *New Age Almanac*, ch. 2.

64. e.g. The International Institute of Projectiology and Concientiology (IIPC), which advertises itself as 'a non-profit research and educational organization dedicated to the study of the Evolution of Consciousness, Psychic Phenomena, and Out-of-Body Experience' (i.e. astral projection), claims to develop 'techniques for producing an OOBE' (out-of-body experience) (quotations from IIPC leaflet).

65. e.g. Bonewitz, *New Cosmic Crystals*.

66. e.g. Miller, *10,000 Dreams Interpreted*.

67. e.g. Bloom (ed.), *The New Age*, ch. 4; Chryssides, *Exploring New Religions*, ch. 8.

68. e.g. Gilbert and Cotterell, *The Mayan Prophecies* claims to 'unlock the secrets of a lost civilization'; see also Collins, *Gateway to Atlantis*.

69. There are few beliefs and practices as widespread throughout the occult milieu as astrology. A good, recent discussion of astrology can be found in Spencer, 'Are the Stars Coming Out?'.

70. e.g. Mitchell, *Naturopathy*; Angelo, *Spiritual Healing for Today*.

71. e.g. Giles, *Tarot*; Barrett, *Tarot*. Tarot has also been suggested as a possible spiritual path for Christians: Drane, Clifford and Johnson, *Beyond Prediction*.

72. e.g. Ducie, *Principles of Numerology*; *Do It Yourself Numerology*.

73. e.g. Gonzales-Wippler, *Kabbalah for the Modern World*; Crowley, *Woman's Kabbalah*; Fortune, *The Mystical Qabalah*.

74. e.g. Too, *Complete Illustrated Guide to Feng Shui*.

75. e.g. Hogue, *Nostradamus: New Revelations*; *Nostradamus: The Complete Prophecies*; *Nostradamus: The New Millennium*.

76. e.g. Coghlan, *Illustrated Encyclopaedia of Arthurian Legends*; Blake and Lloyd, *Keys to Avalon*.

77. e.g. Wallace-Murphy and Hopkins, *Rosslyn*.

78. e.g. Matthews (ed.), *Celtic Seers Source Book*; Carr-Gomm (ed.), *Druid Renaissance*.

79. e.g. Cunningham, *Wicca*; Crowley, *Principles of Wicca*.

80. e.g. Fitch, *Rites of Odin*. See also Harvey, 'Heathenism'.

81. e.g. West, *The Complete Illustrated Guide to Palmistry*.

82. e.g. Roth, *Maps to Ecstasy*; Meadows, *Where Eagles Fly*.

83. e.g. Starhawk, *The Spiral Dance*.

84. e.g. Bloom (ed.), *The New Age*, ch. 5; Fox, *Creation Spirituality*; Simpson, *The Healing Energies of the Earth*.

85. Capra, *The Tao of Physics*; Zukav, *The Dancing Wu Li Masters*; Dhamija, *Quest for the Eternal*.

86. e.g. Mack, *The Lost Gospel*; Kersten, *Jesus Lived in India*; Hogue, *The Last Pope*.

87. See Partridge (ed.), *UFO Religions*; Lewis, *The Gods Have Landed*.

88. Apart from specialized studies of esotericism and occultism, this broad understanding of 'the occult' is adopted by many academic commentators from Theodor Adorno to Peter Clarke. See Adorno, *The Stars Down to Earth*, 34ff., 128–33; Truzzi, 'The Occult Revival as Popular Culture'; Singer and Benassi, 'Occult Beliefs', 384–92; Clarke, 'The Occult and Newly Religious in Modern Society'; 'The Occult and Newly Religious in Modern Society. Part II'.

89. One of the strengths of the volume edited by Kaplan and Lööw, *The Cultic Milieu*, is that, as a collection of essays, such continuities are made explicit.

90. Bainbridge, for example, claims that 'the cultic milieu' is 'roughly the same thing' as the 'New Age movement' (*The Sociology of New Religious Movements*, 368). As the range of areas rightly discussed in Kaplan and Lööw (eds.), *The Cultic Milieu* indicate, the cultic milieu is far broader.

91. Indeed, many who were traditionally identified as 'New Agers' reject the term nowadays and, commercially (in book and music stores etc.), the term has been replaced by such as 'mind,

body, spirit'. Hence, whilst there are still some 'insiders' who are happy with it as a term of self-definition, such as William Bloom, it has become an etic term of categorization largely confined to the academic community. See Bloom, *The New Age*.

92. Spangler, 'The New Age', 80.

93. See, for example, Bloom, *The New Age*: 'The New Age movement represents several very different dynamics, but they thread together to communicate the same message: *there is an invisible and inner dimension to all life – cellular, human and cosmic. The most exciting work in the world is to explore this inner reality*' (p. xvi; emphasis in original).

94. Heelas, 'The New Age in Cultural Context', 110.

95. For an excellent treatment of Romanticism in the eighteenth and nineteenth centuries see Reardon, *Religion in the Age of Romanticism*.

96. 'The immediate feeling of absolute dependence is presupposed and actually contained in every religious and Christian self-consciousness as the only way in which, in general, our own being and the infinite Being of God can be one in self-consciousness' (Schleiermacher, *The Christian Faith*, 131).

97. The capitalized word 'Self' is used when referring to that which transcends or seems to transcend the individual 'self' (with a lower-case 's').

98. John 14.6.

99. MacLaine, *Going Within*, 82–3.

100. Ibid., 82.

101. Ibid., 108 (emphasis in original).

102. Ferguson, *The Aquarian Conspiracy*, 418.

103. Trevelyan, *Exploration into God*, 8.

104. See Campbell, 'The Easternization of the West'. The following chapter provides a discussion of this thesis.

105. Boltwood, 'Channelling', 41.

106. Ibid., 40.

107. Ibid., 40–3.

108. Besant, *Revelation, Inspiration, Observation*, 4.

109. Quoted in Heelas, 'The Sacralization of the Self and New Age Capitalism', 145; and also in Heelas, *The New Age Movement*, 58 (italics in original).

110. Quoted in Bruce, *Religion in the Modern World*, 203.

111. See Spink, *A Christian in the New Age*, chs 11–12; Fox, *Original Blessing*, ch. 6.

112. Fox, *Original Blessing*, 90.

113. Roth, *Maps to Ecstasy*, 29–30.

114. Quoted in Perry, *Gods Within*, 147.

115. Heelas, *The New Age Movement*, 21 (emphasis in original).

116. McLaughlin, 'How to Evaluate Channelling', 52.

117. Ultramarine, 'Stella', *Every Man and Woman is a Star*; listen also to the excellent alternative version, 'Stella Connects (edit)', on Ultramarine, *Companion*.

118. Quoted in Thompson and Heelas, *The Way of the Heart*, 33.

119. Ibid., 33–4 (emphasis in original).

120. Quoted ibid., 34.

121. Spink, *A Christian in the New Age*, 63.

122. Ibid., 38.

123. Heelas, *The New Age Movement*, 23.

124. See Bowman, 'The Noble Savage and the Global Village'.

125. See Starhawk, *Dreaming the Dark*, 5ff.

126. Insectoid, 'Aboriginal Sites, Australia', 50.

127. It should be noted that some New Agers invest particular significance in premodern cultures, not simply because of their wisdom and union with Gaia and possibly other cosmic powers etc., but because of their relationship with extra-terrestrial intelligence. For example, in a discussion of the 'remarkable similarities in the beliefs of isolated primitive peoples', John Keel writes: 'from Africa

to Australia there are early myths that the gods came from Pleiades, a cluster of six stars visible to the naked eye… How did this particular myth get started? And why are the Pleiades universally known as "the Seven Sisters" when only six stars are visible? Is it possible that early peoples everywhere were actually being visited by seemingly supernatural beings who claimed to be from another planet?' (*The Cosmic Question*, 29) More recently, reflecting on the Pyramids, Ann Walker provides answers to questions such as how an ancient civilization had the knowledge and technology to design and construct them. Guided by White Arrow, a Native American spirit, she tells us that, not only are the pyramids built in the shape of a spacecraft, but buried between the Pyramids and the Sphinx there has 'for millions of years' been a spaceship known as 'the Hall of Records' from which humanity started life. The argument is that this is one of a number of spaceships containing aliens who had escaped from a dying planet (Walker, *The Stone and the Plough*).

128. For example, the following is taken from three leaflets picked randomly from my pile of recent New Age literature: in his leaflet 'Mysterious Tremendum', Gongmaster Don Conreaux begins by telling us that he stands in 'the lineage of ancient tradition'; Paulinne Delcour-Min, in her leaflet 'Realize Your Potential through Past Life Therapy', declares that her brand of 'Soul therapy' is 'derived from Native American healing practices'; and the Isle of Avalon Foundation informs us that Glastonbury has 'powerful and *ancient* energies' and that it is 'a place which has long been recognised as a sacred site … [and from] the earliest days this energy has drawn people to it to find healing' (taken from the leaflet 'Glastonbury: Isle of Avalon'; emphasis in original).

129. Harvey, *Listening People, Speaking Earth*, 219–20.

130. Ibid., 219.

131. Ibid., 220.

132. In the Pagan calendar there are eight major festivals which together make up 'the Wheel of the Year': (1) Samhain is generally understood to be the beginning of the Wheel of the Year and is celebrated by many as the Celtic New Year (Hallowe'en/All Hallows Eve). (2) Midwinter (also Yule or Winter Solstice) is celebrated by all Pagans (as are Midsummer and both equinoxes). (3) Imbolc (also Oimelc or Candlemas) welcomes the return of the bright sun and celebrates the emergence of new life. (4) Spring Equinox, the point in the calendar when the hours of darkness are equal to those of light, is the time when Pagans celebrate fertility, and the power of the life force. (5) Traditionally the time for May queens and Maypoles (which are sometimes reinvested with religious significance by Pagans, the May queen symbolizing the Goddess and the Maypole symbolizing the God), Beltane celebrates the emergence out of spring and into the full bloom of summer. (6) Midsummer (also Summer Solstice) celebrates the power of the Sun and often focuses on a solar deity. Many Pagans (and some New Agers) will gather to observe the Sun rise. (7) Lammas (or Lughnasadh) is the Old English term for 'loaf mass' or 'loaf feast', the celebration of the first loaf baked from the newly harvested corn. Lammas is a firstfruits festival that is traditionally celebrated with fairs and games. This is still a popular cultural event in some British towns, such as St Andrews, Scotland. (8) At the Autumn Equinox the Wheel of the Year has turned full circle and the previous year is reflected upon.

133. Harvey, *Listening People, Speaking Earth*, 219; Adler, *Drawing Down the Moon*, 420.

134. See Lau, *New Age Capitalism*. Lau draws attention to the links between New Age ideologies, health, and politics. From a slightly different perspective, Heelas has drawn attention to the New Age 'sanctification of capitalism'. See Heelas, *The New Age Movement*, 95–6; 'The Sacralization of the Self and New Age Capitalism'; 'The Limits of Consumption on the Post-Modern "Religion" of the New Age'.

135. Ezzy, 'New Age Witchcraft?'

136. See Valiente, *ABC of Witchcraft*, 118–23; Maclean, 'Devas' – an extract from *The Findhorn Garden* reprinted in Bloom (ed.), *The New Age*, 180–2.

137. Maclean, 'Devas', 180.

138. Ibid.

139. Ibid., 180–1.

140. Ibid., 180 (italics in the original).

141. Valiente, *ABC of Witchcraft*, 123.

142. Ibid., 118.
143. Ibid., 119.
144. Harvey, *Listening People, Speaking Earth*, 220.
145. Ibid., 218.
146. See, for example, Crowley, *Principles of Paganism*: 'Pagans are not Satanists… [and] Paganism does not advocate Black Magic or animal sacrifice' (11).
147. Compare the lists of deities in, for example, LaVey, *The Satanic Bible* (58–60, 145–6) and Williams and West, *Born in Albion* (37).
148. See, for example, the following debate in the Pagan Federation journal, *Pagan Dawn*: Hannam, 'Why Deny Satan?', 29; Crone, 'Satan? Who's That?', 30; Howard, 'The Bright and the Dark', 30–1.
149. See Urban, 'The Beast with Two Backs'.
150. Hardman, 'Introduction', in Harvey and Hardman (eds.), *Paganism Today*, p. ix.
151. Some insight into the person and beliefs of LaVey can be gained from his interview with Lawrence Wright (Wright, 'Sympathy for the Devil').
152. LaVey, *The Satanic Bible*, 62 (emphasis in original).
153. LaVey, *The Devil's Notebook*, 9–10.
154. LaVey, *The Satanic Bible*, 25.
155. The term, used by McRitchie, is from Coughlin's *Out of the Shadows*. See McRitchie, 'A Critique of Evangelical Understandings of Satanism', ch. 3.
156. See ibid., 56.
157. Harvey, 'Satanism in Britain Today', 288.
158. There is a widening stream of books on everything from reading tea leaves to dowsing to seashell divination. For a popular overview see Matthews (ed.), *The World Atlas of Divination*. On seashell divination see Gonzalez-Wippler, *Introduction to Seashell Divination*.
159. For a short introduction to Heathenism, see Harvey, 'Heathenism'; *Listening People, Speaking Earth*, ch. 4.
160. Taylor, 'The Message of the Runes', 34.
161. Ibid., 42.
162. The term 'other-than-human persons' was coined by the anthropologist Irving Hallowell ('Ojibwa Ontology, Behavior and World View'). See also Morrison, 'The Cosmos as Intersubjective'.
163. Lamond, *Religion Without Beliefs*, 141 (emphasis in original).
164. See Partridge, 'Pagan Fundamentalism?'.
165. See Pagan Federation, *Information Pack*: 'The Pagan Ethic: "If it harms none, do what thou wilt." This is a positive morality expressing the belief in individual responsibility for discovering one's own true nature and developing it fully, in harmony with the outer world and community' (4).
166. Possamaï, 'Alternative Spiritualities and the Cultural Logic of Late Capitalism', 36.
167. Ritzer, *The McDonaldization of Society*, 1.
168. See particularly ibid., 21ff.
169. Possamaï, 'Alternative Spiritualities and the Cultural Logic of Late Capitalism', 42.
170. See ibid., 33. See also Possamaï, 'Not the New Age: Perennism and Spiritual Knowledges'.

Chapter 5

1. On the influence of esotericism on Western culture see Gibbons, *Spirituality and the Occult* and Beloff, *Parapsychology*, 1–15.
2. See, for example, Glock and Bellah, *New Religious Consciousness*; Green, 'Buddhism in Britain'; Heelas, *The New Age Movement*, 54ff.; Hummel, 'Contemporary New Religions in the West'; Wilson, 'The Westward Path of Buddhism'; Wuthnow, *Consciousness Reformation*; Rawlinson, *Book of Enlightened Masters*, 3–56.
3. Cox, *Turning East*, 96.
4. Ibid. (emphasis in original).
5. Ibid., 95–100.
6. Ibid., 92.

7. Ibid., 97.

8. Dunne, *The Way of All the Earth*, p. vii.

9. Bell, 'The Return of the Sacred?', 443.

10. Wuthnow, *After Heaven*, 75.

11. Walter, 'Reincarnation, Modernity and Identity', 21.

12. See Barker, 'New Religious Movements', 19. A survey carried out by Opinion Research Business for the BBC series *Soul of Britain* (2000) similarly found that around 30 per cent of British people believe in reincarnation.

13. Walter, 'Reincarnation, Modernity and Identity', 21.

14. Campbell, 'The Easternization of the West', 41.

15. A good, concise discussion of, for example, the history of the emerging Western interest in Tibetan Buddhism can be found in Bishop, *Dreams of Power*, 22–76.

16. MacNicol, *Is Christianity Unique?*, 77.

17. Hegel, *The Phenomenology of Spirit*.

18. Radhakrishnan, *Eastern Religions and Western Thought*, 248.

19. Wilhelm Halbfass, quoted in Obeyesekere, 'Buddhism', 65.

20. Quoted ibid.

21. Ibid.

22. MacNicol, *Is Christianity Unique?*, 77–8.

23. Ibid., 78.

24. Radhakrishnan, *Eastern Religions and Western Thought*, 248.

25. Quoted ibid.

26. On the significance of the Theosophical Society for the spread of Buddhism in the West, see Obeyesekere, 'Buddhism', 67–71.

27. See Tingay, 'Madame Blavatsky's Children', 37–50.

28. Hanegraaff, *New Age Religion and Western Culture*, 471–2. Indeed, as Hanegraaff argues, an evolutionary teleology is a central feature of New Age spirituality (158).

29. Hamilton, 'The Easternization Thesis', 247; Walter, 'Reincarnation, Modernity and Identity'. See also the following: Walter and Waterhouse, 'Lives-Long Learning'; Walter and Waterhouse, 'A Very Private Belief'; Waterhouse, 'Reincarnation Belief in Britain'.

30. For a concise, helpful discussion of Dharmapala, see Obeyesekere, 'Buddhism', 71ff.

31. Selections from the writings of Vivekananda can be found in Richards (ed.), *A Source-Book of Modern Hinduism*, 77–90.

32. As Stephen Neill noted many years ago, the thesis 'disregards both the glorious spiritual history of the West and the earthly materialism that is to be found in the East as much as in any other part of the world' (*Christian Faith and Other Faiths*, 77).

33. On the World Parliament of Religions see Chattopadhyaya, *World's Parliament of Religions, 1893*. The volume contains an interesting selection of facsimiles of the original press coverage of the meeting. For an authoritative treatment of the Parliament and its significance, see Braybrooke, *Pilgrimage of Hope*, 7–42, and Seager, *The World's Parliament of Religions*.

34. Roberts, *Religion, Theology and the Human Sciences*, 248.

35. The essentialist approach is expressed well by H.H. Farmer: 'I shall assume that there is underlying all genuinely religious phenomena a common defining essence of some sort, by which they are all constituted genuinely religious phenomena and distinguished from other phenomena which merely look like religion or are usually closely associated with religion' (*Revelation and Religion*, 24). See also Partridge, *H.H. Farmer's Theological Interpretation of Religion*, 52ff.; Thomas (ed.), *Attitudes toward Other Religions*, 21–2; Richards, *Studies in Religion*, 129–39.

36. See Woodhead, 'The World's Parliament of Religions'.

37. Quoted in Braybrooke, *Pilgrimage of Hope*, 13.

38. Quoted ibid., 13.

39. Quoted ibid., 15.

40. Ibid.

41. Chattopadhyaya, *World's Parliament of Religions*, 2–3; see also 323–4.

42. See Glyn Richards' study of 'Vivekananda and Essentialism' (*Studies in Religion*, 129–39).

43. Burrows (ed.), *The World's Parliament of Religions*, 977.

44. This emphasis can be found in, for example, the work of the great Liberal Protestant theologian Adolf von Harnack, for whom the essence of the Gospel is 'God the father and the infinite value of the human soul' (*What is Christianity?*, 51).

45. See Burrows (ed.), *The World's Parliament of Religions*, 971.

46. See Obeyesekere, 'Buddhism', 71.

47. Blavatsky, *The Key to Theosophy*, 39.

48. Woodhead, 'The World's Parliament of Religions', 94.

49. Ibid.

50. Ibid., 95.

51. See also Partridge, 'Truth, Authority and Epistemological Individualism in New Age Thought', 80.

52. e.g. Nisbet, *History of the Idea of Progress*.

53. Indeed, stimulated greatly by the emergence of evolutionary theory, it was fundamental to much early theorizing about religion and culture. See, for example, Sharpe, *Comparative Religion*, 47–71.

54. Richards, *Studies in Religion*, 137.

55. Sell, *The Philosophy of Religion 1875–1980*, 20. This charge was also levelled against (and subsequently rejected by) Friedrich Schleiermacher. See Schleiermacher, *On Religion*, 97, 115f. See also Partridge, *H.H. Farmer's Theological Interpretation of Religion*, 78ff.

56. Maurice, *The Religions of the World in their Relations to Christianity*, 8.

57. Cracknell, *Justice, Courtesy and Love*, 44.

58. Quoted in Sharpe, *Faith Meets Faith*, 17.

59. See ibid., 17.

60. This interest was manifested particularly in the publication of the fifty volumes of *The Sacred Books of the East*, edited by Müller.

61. Woodhead, 'The World's Parliament of Religions', 81–2 (emphasis in original).

62. Heelas, *The New Age Movement*, 42–3, quoting Le Rider, *Modernity and Crises of Identity*. See also Weber, *France Fin de Siècle*, and his *Apocalypses* (7–26).

63. Marwick, *The Sixties*. In his otherwise useful list of 'the characteristics of a unique era' spirituality is neglected (16–20).

64. As Marwick notes without reference to spiritualities, the sixties witnessed a 'formation of new subcultures and movements, generally critical of, or in opposition to, one or more aspects of established society' (ibid., 17).

65. See Heelas, *The New Age Movement*, 124.

66. Miller, *The 60s Communes*, 92.

67. Partridge, 'Introduction', in Partridge (ed.), *Encyclopedia of New Religions*, 20 (emphasis in original).

68. Clarke (ed.), *The New Evangelists*, 5.

69. Barker, *New Religious Movements*, 9.

70. Arweck, 'New Religious Movements', 264.

71. Ibid., 265.

72. Ibid.

73. Andrew Rawlinson also identifies 1963 as the year in which the 'full bloom' of Eastern religions in the West began. That said, his discussion does not make it clear why this is a significant year. Perhaps it was because Chogyam Trungpa and Akong Rinpoche arrived in Oxford (Rawlinson, *Book of Enlightened Masters*, 56, 58, 82).

74. Brown, *The Death of Christian Britain*, 1.

75. Ibid., 176.

76. Campbell, 'The Secret Religion of the Educated Classes', 146.

77. Campbell, 'The Easternization of the West', 37. See also Heelas, *The New Age Movement*, 124.

78. Campbell, 'The Easternization of the West', 37.

79. Quoted in Hanegraaff, 'How Magic Survived the Disenchantment of the World', 358.

80. Wuthnow, *After Heaven*, 54.

81. Ibid., 53.

82. See Roof, *Spiritual Marketplace*, ch. 2.

83. Cody, 'Gerald Heard: Soul Guide to the Beyond Within', 68.

84. Ginsberg, 'A Tale of the Tribe (from Preface to "Jail Notes")'.

85. See Miller, *The 60s Communes*, 26–9, 205–8.

86. On the popularization of the religious use of psychedelics see Partridge, 'Sacred Chemicals?'.

87. Although the book does not use the term 'psychedelic', it is often cited as one of the founding texts, if not *the* founding text, of psychedelia. See Huxley, *Doors of Perception and Heaven and Hell*.

88. See Susan Fast's discussion of the 'East' in the music of Led Zeppelin: *In the Houses of the Holy*, 86ff. (It is perhaps worth noting that one Led Zeppelin album is titled *The Houses of the Holy*.)

89. See particularly Stevens, *Storming Heaven*.

90. Baker *et al.*, 'The Roundtable', 103.

91. Dass, 'What Does Being a Buddhist Mean to You?', 43.

92. 'My Sweet Lord' appears on Harrison's 1970 album *All Things Must Pass*.

93. Akhtar and Humphries, *Far Out*, 33.

94. If you are not familiar with the cover, it may be found on a very helpful website devoted to Incredible String Band album covers: <http://www.knott32.fsnet.co.uk/isbp/spirits.jpg>.

95. Pendleton, 'Kindred Spirits', 81.

96. Ibid.

97. The photograph I have in mind is reproduced in Phil Sutcliffe's 'Go Forth and Rock', 72.

98. McCartney, *Linda's Pictures*, plates 34–5.

99. Brown, *Death of Christian Britain*, 178–9.

100. Ibid., 180.

101. Kilmister, *White Line Fever*, 179.

102. Ibid., 287.

103. Sandford and Reid, *Tomorrow's People*.

104. Kilmister, *White Line Fever*, 289 (my emphasis).

105. Green, *Days in the Life*, 296.

106. Quoted ibid., 296.

107. Capra, *The Tao of Physics*, 12.

108. Ibid. (emphasis in original), 11.

109. Ibid., 12–13.

110. Ibid., 209.

111. Capra, Steindl-Rast, and Matus, *Belonging to the Universe*, 70.

112. Savitra, *Auroville: Sun-Word Rising*, 17–18.

113. As Gananath Obeyesekere notes, 'it is no accident that [meditation]…has spread globally in recent times, particularly after the 1960s…' ('Buddhism', 73–5).

114. Cimino and Lattin, *Shopping for a Faith*, 21.

115. For a good recent discussion of the Divine Light Mission/Elan Vital, see Geaves, 'From Divine Light Mission to Elan Vital and Beyond'.

116. Rawlinson, *Book of Enlightened Masters*, p. xviii (emphasis in original).

117. Ibid., p. xvii.

118. Ibid., 63 (emphasis in original).

119. Ibid., p. xvii.

120. Ibid.

121. Ibid., p. xviii.

122. Ibid.

123. Ibid., 3.

124. Campbell, 'The Easternization of the West', 40–1.

125. Ibid., 41.

126. Ibid. (my emphasis).

127. Ibid., 41.

128. Ibid., 42.

129. Gilgen and Cho, 'Questionnaire to Measure Eastern and Western Thought', 835–44.

130. Ibid., 836.

131. Ibid. See also Krus and Blackman, 'East–West Dimensions of Ideology'.

132. Krus and Blackman, 'East–West Dimensions of Ideology', 951; Campbell, 'The Easternisation of the West', 43.

133. Hamilton, 'The Easternization Thesis', 246 (emphasis in original).

134. Ibid.

135. Dwelling far too much on this, Hamilton's first two criticisms betray some misunderstanding of the central thrust of Campbell's argument.

136. Of all the Indian philosophies, Advaita ('non-dual') Vedanta is perhaps the most famous. However, Advaita is not the only the only interpretation of vedantic thought. See Flood, *Introduction to Hinduism*, 238–46; Klostermaier, *Survey of Hinduism*, 412–26; Sharma, *Critical Survey of Indian Philosophy*, 239–385.

137. Huxley, *Perennial Philosophy*, 8.

138. See Rudolf Otto's famous study of the two thinkers, *Mysticism East and West*.

139. Campbell, 'The Easternization of the West', 41.

140. The work done by Gilgen and Cho, for example, was 'tested on college students, a group of Buddhists, some transpersonal psychologists and some businessmen; a test which strongly suggested its validity' (ibid., 43).

141. Hamilton, 'The Easternisation Thesis', 254.

142. See Juergensmeyer, 'Thinking Globally about Religion'. Cf. Robertson, 'Antiglobal Religion'; and Smart, 'The Global Future of Religion'.

143. Campbell, 'The Easternization of the West', 40–1.

144. Ibid., 41.

145. Ibid., 42.

146. Ibid., 43.

147. Campbell, 'The Secret Religion of the Educated Classes', 151.

148. Tillich, *Ultimate Concern*, 43.

149. See Ferré, 'Tillich and the Nature of Transcendence', 11.

150. It is perhaps worth noting that Tillich became particularly interested in Eastern religion following a visit to Japan later in life. See Tillich, *Christianity and the Encounter of the World Religions*, ch. 3; *The Future of Religions*. In the latter volume see particularly the tribute by Mircea Eliade: 'Paul Tillich and the History of Religions'.

151. For an interesting discussion which draws out what might be broadly understood as the Eastern aspects of Tillich's thought, see Richards, *Studies in Religion*, 91–102.

152. Bergson and Smuts in particular have both had an influence on alternative religious thinking. For example, both are specifically mentioned by the influential New Age theorist Marilyn Ferguson in *The Aquarian Conspiracy*, 150, 168–9, 180, 200. 'Wholeness, Smuts said, is a fundamental characteristic of the universe – the product of nature's drive to synthesize … The wholes – in effect, these unions – are dynamic, evolutionary, creative. They thrust towards ever-higher orders of complexity and integration. "Evolution", Smuts said, "has an ever deepening, inward spiritual character."' Ferguson then goes on to point out, in a way similar to Capra, that 'General Systems Theory, a related modern concept, says that each variable in any system interacts with the other variables so thoroughly that cause and effect cannot be separated. A single variable can be both cause and effect. Reality will not be still. And it cannot be taken apart! You cannot understand a cell, a rat, a brain structure, a family, or a culture if you isolate it from its context. *Relationship is everything*' (169; emphasis in original). The principal works of these two thinkers are Bergson, *Creative Evolution* and Smuts, *Holism and Evolution*.

153. For excellent discussions of Teilhard's mystical thought, see King, *Towards a New Mysticism* and *Christ in All Things*. See also Zaehner, *Evolution in Religion*; Delfgaauw, *Evolution: The Theory of Teilhard de Chardin*. For Teilhard's own works, see particularly *Le Milieu Divin*.

154. Ferguson, *The Aquarian Conspiracy*, 462–3.

155. Panentheist and immanentist thought is explicit in process theology. An older, though still excellent introduction to process theology, in which useful comparisons are made with Teilhard's thought, is Cousins (ed.), *Process Theology*. Creation spirituality and ecofeminism are also important in this respect. See Fox, *Creation Spirituality* and Ruether, *Gaia and God*. See also Gillian McCulloch's critique, *The Deconstruction of Dualism in Theology*. Again, as Donald Bloesch comments, 'Paul Tillich, Alfred North Whitehead, Charles Hartshorne, Henry Nelson Wieman, Schubert Ogden, Bernard Meland, John Cobb and Rosemary Ruether... illustrate the dawning of a new mysticism' (*God the Almighty*, 15).

156. As Nicol MacNicol commented many years ago in his 1935 Wilde Lectures, 'That Thoreau, Emerson and even Walt Whitman were attracted by certain elements in the teaching of the Oriental sages is indeed proved by their own testimony. The first two certainly read the Vedas and the Upanishads, and Thoreau tells us that "the pure Walden water is mingled with the sacred water of the Ganges." ... Emerson... is drawn to the speculations of the Indian sages because he finds there the same thirst which, if less urgently, moves him as also moved them – the thirst for an ultimate unity of things. In that quest he stretches the idea of God beyond personality to something that becomes as impalpable and unreal as Brahman itself' (*Is Christianity Unique?*, 89–90). Later, of course, other thinkers, in particular Carl Jung, were inspired by Eastern thought. See Coward, *Jung and Eastern Thought*.

157. Interestingly, although Krus and Blackman have entitled their paper 'East–West Dimensions of Ideology', they speak of the West in terms of Romanticism. Indeed, their work focuses less on Eastern and Western perspectives than it does on rationalist and Romantic perspectives: 'Theoretical analysis contrasting both historical and contemporary romantic–rational attitudes suggests a strong connection between romanticism and antiscience with resulting emotional reactions against the technological society. The prevalence of either pole of the rational–romantic dichotomy also seems to determine the future creativity and productivity of society, values placed on the individual's liberty and freedom and the individual's decision-making power with respect to economic and political issues' (954).

158. Hamilton, 'The Easternization Thesis', 246.

159. Ibid., 251.

160. Lau, *New Age Capitalism*, 2–3.

161. Ibid., 3.

162. Ibid.

163. Hume, 'Jasmuheen and the Breatharians', 354.

164. Glnody, 'Why We Must Leave at This Time'.

165. Harvey, *Introduction to Buddhism*, 225.

166. Brnody, 'Up the Chain'.

167. Campbell, 'The Easternization of the West', 45–6.

168. Ibid., 46.

169. See Cracknell, *Justice, Courtesy and Love*, 20–7.

170. Brockington, *The Sacred Thread*, 173.

171. Zaehner, *Hinduism*, 150.

172. Hamilton, 'The Easternization Thesis', 250 (emphasis in original).

173. Ibid.

174. Cox, 'Eastern Cults and Western Culture', 42.

175. Bauman, 'Postmodern Religion?', 70; quoted in Hamilton, 'The Easternization Thesis', 250–1.

176. Hamilton, 'The Easternization Thesis', 255 (emphasis in original).

Chapter 6

1. He defines 'stigmatized knowledge' as follows: 'claims to truth that the claimants regard as verified despite the marginalization of those claims by the institutions that conventionally distinguish between knowledge and error – universities, communities of scientific researchers, and the like'. He further divides 'stigmatized knowledge' into five categories: (1) forgotten knowledge; (2) superseded knowledge; (3) ignored knowledge; (4) rejected knowledge; (5) suppressed knowledge. See Barkun, *A Culture of Conspiracy*, 26ff.

2. Ibid., 33.

3. As Paul Heelas comments, 'New Age themes, of course, have long been spreading through culture. The Romantics were – and continue to be – quite widely read; journals edited by Orage or *Bibby's Annual* (published out of Liverpool) served to spread the message at the beginning of [the twentieth century]' (*The New Age Movement*, 128).

4. Lyon, *Jesus in Disneyland*, 62.

5. Ibid.

6. See Adorno, *The Culture Industry*.

7. Quoted in Barker, *Cultural Studies*, 47.

8. Lynch, *After Religion*.

9. Beaudoin, *Virtual Faith*.

10. Beaudoin, *Virtual Faith*, 22; quoted in Lynch, *After Religion*, 54.

11. Lynch, *After Religion*, 54.

12. Miller and Miller, 'Understanding Generation X', 3.

13. Of course, other Christians have used it missiologically, drawing comparisons between, as Will Brooker notes, 'its mythical aspects and the teachings of the Bible'. The good–evil dualism in the films is, it is argued, a diluted version of spiritual reality. See Brooker, *Using the Force*, 6–11.

14. Lynch, *After Religion*, 59.

15. Ibid., 64.

16. John Clarke, quoted in Barker, *Cultural Studies*, 325.

17. Some interesting discussions which do take this approach can be found in Forbes and Mahan (eds.), *Religion and Popular Culture in America*.

18. Lynch, *After Religion*, 68.

19. Campbell and McIver, 'Cultural Sources of Support for Contemporary Occultism'.

20. Truzzi, 'The Occult Revival as Popular Culture'.

21. Ibid., 16.

22. Ibid., 36 (emphasis in original).

23. LaVey, *The Devil's Notebook*, 9–10.

24. Wayne Spencer, for example, found that although astrology is widely used, and although it 'seems likely to serve as at least part of the private spiritual explorations of "relatively small numbers of serious adherents", it 'is mostly produced and consumed as mass entertainment' (Spencer, 'Are the Stars Coming Out?', 224–5).

25. For example, Bath Spa University College, England, have recently validated a MA in sacred astronomy.

26. Roof, *Spiritual Marketplace*, 82–3. See also Wuthnow, *After Heaven*, 142ff.

27. Roof, *Spiritual Marketplace*, 38.

28. Barkun, *A Culture of Conspiracy*, 35.

29. Ohmann (ed.), *Making and Selling Culture* is an interesting volume discussing the extent to which film directors, television and radio producers, advertising executives, and marketing companies merely reflect cultural trends, beliefs and desires, and to what extent they consciously shape culture.

30. Geertz, *Interpretation of Cultures*, 90–1.

31. Traube, 'Introduction', in Ohmann (ed.), *Making and Selling Culture*, p. xvi.

32. It is significant that interactive video games in which fantasy worlds are explored, occult symbols deciphered, new ethical frameworks constructed, and supernatural powers utilized, are not only easily outstripping the sales of films and books, but they are also being discussed as important forms of art.

33. Casanova, *Public Religion in the Modern World*.

34. Ibid., 6.

35. Ibid.

36. Campbell and McIver, 'Cultural Sources of Support for Contemporary Occultism', 46.

37. Lyon, *Jesus in Disneyland*, 57.

38. See Hall, *Culture, Media, Languages*, and also the edited extract from this work: Hall, 'Encoding, Decoding'.

39. See Partridge (ed.), *UFO Religions*; Lewis (ed.), *UFOs and Popular Culture*.

40. Saliba, 'Religious Dimensions of UFO Phenomena', 20.

41. Bullard, 'Foreword: UFOs – Folklore of the Space Age', p. ix.

42. Bullard, 'Foreword', in Partridge (ed.), *UFO Religions*, p. xiv.

43. On the cultural significance of The X-Files, see Lavery, Hague and Cartwright (eds.), *Deny All Knowledge*, and also Barkun, *A Culture of Conspiracy*, 34ff.

44. Dean, *Aliens in America*, 25.

45. Ibid., 30.

46. Knight, *Conspiracy Culture*, 47.

47. Barkun, *A Culture of Conspiracy*, 29–33.

48. An early example would be the film the founder of the Church of Satan, Anton LaVey, described as 'the best paid commercial for Satanism since the Inquisition', namely *Rosemary's Baby*. LaVey himself served as a consultant on the film as well as playing the role of Satan who impregnated Rosemary (Mia Farrow). For an interesting interview with LaVey about the film, see Baddeley, *Lucifer Rising*, 88: 'It was the best ad for Satanism ever screened… For the first time, *Rosemary's Baby* presented Satanists as sophisticated, reasonable people, instead of stoned freakouts.' See also Wright, 'Sympathy for the Devil'.

49. Perhaps the most notable examples of such films are notorious underground films of Kenneth Anger which explore the Satanic subculture: *Scorpio Rising* (1964); *Invocation of My Demon Brother* (1969); *Lucifer Rising* (1973). Attracting a cult following, *Scorpio Rising* has even recently been referred to by the rock-dance band Death in Vegas with their album of the same name.

50. Walpole, *The Castle of Otranto*. For a good discussion of the supernatural in the works of Horace Walpole and Ann Radcliffe, see Cavaliero, *The Supernatural and English Fiction*, 23ff.

51. For an excellent analysis of the significance and popularity of 'vampire fiction', see Gelder, *Reading the Vampire*.

52. Whilst there are of course exceptions, it does seem to be the case that whilst the Enlightenment mind was fascinated with the occult, it was also dismissive of it. For example, Ann Radcliffe closed her novels with rational explanations for apparently supernatural events, and, as Gamer comments, whilst Walter Scott produced many works with occultic and supernatural themes, 'he nevertheless moves from producing texts that celebrate black magic and the supernatural to debunking these same subjects in his critical writing – doing so with cool rationality in *Letters on Demonology and Witchcraft* (1830)' (Gamer, *Romanticism and the Gothic*, 33).

53. Kreitzer, 'The Scandal of the Cross', 185.

54. The significance of this film is explored by Gelder, in *Reading the Vampire*, 94ff.

55. Kreitzer, 'The Scandal of the Cross', 198.

56. Ibid., 201.

57. Ibid.

58. Stoker, *Dracula*; quoted in Kreitzer, 'The Scandal of the Cross', 193 (emphasis added by Kreitzer).

59. Kreitzer, 'The Scandal of the Cross', 194.

60. Ibid., 202.

61. See Walter, 'Reincarnation, Modernity and Identity'; Walter and Waterhouse, 'Lives-Long Learning'; Walter and Waterhouse, 'A Very Private Belief'; Waterhouse, 'Reincarnation Belief in Britain'.

62. Kreitzer, 'The Scandal of the Cross', 209.

63. The reference to Buffy's 'puny faith' might be taken as referring to her own puny faith. If this is so, then the implication is that should a believer of greater faith wield the crucifix, the vampire would be constrained to submit to its authority. However, there is no indication in the film that Christianity has any of its traditional authority. Buffy is simply turning to the traditional symbols she assumes will have power over vampires. But the symbols have no power. It is clear that Lothos' response, 'Your puny faith', is directed toward the faith to which the symbols refer (i.e. the Christian faith), rather than to any personal faith that Buffy may or may not possess.

64. This, of course, is not surprising, since Joss Whedon, the creator of *Buffy*, wrote and directed many of the episodes of the series, as well as writing the screenplay for the film.

65. Erickson, ' "Sometimes You Need a Story": American Christianity, Vampires, and *Buffy*', 109.

66. Ibid., 114.

67. Ibid.

68. Ibid., 114–15.

69. Melton, *The Vampire Book*, 155.

70. These are the words of Abraham Whistler (Kris Kristofferson), the vampire hunter in the film *Blade* (1998).

71. Rice, *Interview with a Vampire*.

72. Melton, *The Vampire Book*, 155, 369.

73. Rice, *Interview with a Vampire*, 22.

74. *From Dusk Til Dawn* was directed by Robert Rodriguez and written by Quentin Tarantino.

75. The notion of Buffy as 'woman-Christ' is suggested by Playden, in 'What You Are, What's To Come', 129–32.

76. Stoker, *Dracula*, 230.

77. Playden: 'What You Are, What's To Come', 135.

78. Brum, 'Smells Like Teen Spirit', 146.

79. See Thornton, *Club Cultures*; Malbon, *Clubbing*.

80. Thornton, *Club Cultures*, 11 (emphasis in original).

81. Malbon, *Clubbing*, 51.

82. Ibid., 56.

83. Ellwood, *The Sixties Spiritual Awakening*, 202.

84. For more on the series, which still has a large 'cult following', see Scott (ed.), *Dark Shadows Companion*.

85. Quoted in Lavery, ' "A Religion in Narrative": Joss Whedon and Television Creativity'.

86. Winslade, 'Teen Witches, Wiccans, and "Wanna-Blessed-Be's" '.

87. Wrigley, 'TV and Wicca', 57.

88. Winslade, 'Teen Witches, Wiccans, and "Wanna-Blessed-Be's" '.

89. Overby and Preston-Matto, 'Staking in Tongues', 79.

90. Winslade, 'Teen Witches, Wiccans, and "Wanna-Blessed-Be's" '. See also Wilcox, ' "There Will Never Be a 'Very Special' *Buffy*" '.

91. Winslade, 'Teen Witches, Wiccans, and "Wanna-Blessed-Be's" '.

92. Brum, 'Smells Like Teen Spirit', 152.

93. Starwoman and Gray, *How to Turn Your Ex-Boyfriend into a Toad and Other Spells*. Ezzy provides an interesting discussion of this and two other popular spell books in 'New Age Witchcraft?'.

94. Sanders, 'Why are the Young Attracted to the Goddess?'

95. Angela and Martin, 'A Review of *The Book of Shadows* and Interview with the Author, Phyllis Curott, Wiccan High Priestess', 34–5.

96. Winslade, 'Teen Witches, Wiccans, and "Wanna-Blessed-Be's" '.

97. Curott, *Book of Shadows*.

98. Winslade, 'Teen Witches, Wiccans, and "Wanna-Blessed-Be's" '. See RavenWolf, *Teen Witch*.

99. Reported ibid.

100. Quoted in Harrison, 'Harry, Sabrina and Buffy Help Paganism Grow'.

101. Winslade, 'Teen Witches, Wiccans, and "Wanna-Blessed-Be's" '.

102. Ibid.

103. See for example, York, *The Emerging Network*, 180.

104. Pearson, 'Witches and Wicca', 142.

105. Ibid.

106. Hume, *Witchcraft and Paganism in Australia*, 103.

107. See, Pearson, 'Witches and Wicca', 142.

108. As noted above (p. 79), according to Margot Adler, 'There is a funny saying in the Pagan movement: "The difference between Pagan and 'new age' is one decimal point." In other words, a two-day workshop in meditation by a 'new age' practitioner might cost $300, while the same course given by a Pagan might cost $30' (*Drawing Down the Moon*, 420).

109. McKay, *Glastonbury*, 74.

110. Campbell and McIver, 'Cultural Sources of Support for Contemporary Occultism', 54.

111. Skippy, '*The Door* Theologian of the Year'. Thanks to Ross Wiley, one of my students, for drawing this to my attention.

112. Barkun, *A Culture of Conspiracy*, 29.

113. Ibid.

114. Ibid., 29–30.

115. See also Gordon Lynch's short discussion of a range of mainly Christian interpretations of *The Matrix* in *After Religion* (58–65). Indeed, it is perhaps worth noting that other commentators see nothing beyond banal eclecticism in *The Matrix*. As I type this footnote (3 Nov. 2003) I am listening to the BBC Radio 4 arts programme *Front Row*, and have just heard Mark Lawson (the presenter) and another reviewer discuss the final film of the trilogy. Their conclusion? Laughable 'New Age tosh'.

116. Wilcock, 'The "Matrix" is a Reality', 55.

117. Icke, *Children of the Matrix*, p. xvii.

118. Icke, 'The Reptilian Connection' (emphasis in original).

119. Ibid.

120. This will be discussed more fully in Volume II.

121. Again, as will be discussed in Volume II, some Satanic and vampire religions are informed to some extent by popular culture. See Jenkins, 'Satanism and Ritual Abuse', 231–2. See also Partridge, 'The Temple of the Vampire', 353–4.

122. Campbell and McIver, 'Cultural Sources of Support for Contemporary Occultism', 58.

123. Harvey, 'Fantasy in the Study of Religions'.

124. Ibid.

125. Fox, 'Solitary Pagans', 43.

126. Ibid.

127. May, *Stardust and Ashes*, 99.

128. The novel's influence is not limited to the Church of All Worlds. For example, certain words used by spiritually inspired environmental activists such as 'grok' (meaning 'understand') are taken directly from *Stranger in a Strange Land*. See Taylor, 'Earth and Nature-Based Spirituality (Part 1)', 232, 242.

129. Zell and Zell, 'Where on Earth is the Church of All Worlds?', 47.

130. Quoted in Adler, *Drawing Down the Moon*, 286 (my emphasis). The works of H.P. Lovecraft have also had a direct influence on certain groups, not least Satanist groups. The influence is explicit in the writings of Anton LaVey.

131. Miller, *The 60s Communes*, 5.

132. Quoted in Adler, *Drawing Down the Moon*, 285 (my emphasis).

133. For example, Terence McKenna was clearly impressed by the work of science fiction writers such as Philip K. Dick and William Gibson: *Food of the Gods*, 218; *The Archaic Revival*, 41, 235.

134. 'As far back as January 1984 the top four money-making films in history were science fiction films… What was regarded twenty years ago as an amiable eccentricity has become the norm of modern culture' (May, *Stardust and Ashes*, 1). Things have not changed appreciably since then. For an excellent analysis of the philosophical significance of science fiction, see Clark, *How to Live Forever*.

135. Possamaï, 'Alternative Spiritualities and the Cultural Logic of Late Capitalism', 34. On the intense fandom surrounding *Star Wars* see Will Brooker's analysis, *Using the Force*.

136. <http://groups.yahoo.com/groups/Jedi_Knight_Movement/>; quoted in Possamaï, 'Alternative Spiritualities and the Cultural Logic of Late Capitalism', 34.

137. Brooker, *Using the Force*, 212–13.

138. Tolkien, *The Lord of the Rings*.

139. Ellwood, *The Sixties Spiritual Awakening*, 134.

140. Hinckle, quoted ibid., 201.

141. Straw, 'Characterizing Rock Music Culture: The Case of Heavy Metal', 379.

142. Harvey, 'Fantasy in the Study of Religions'.

143. Letcher, 'Eco-Paganism: Protest Movement Spiritualities', 302.

144. Harvey, *Listening People, Speaking Earth*, 181–2.

145. See Duriez, 'The Theology of Fantasy in Lewis and Tolkien'; 'Mysticism and Fantasy in Lewis, Tolkien and Barfield'.

146. Pearson, 'Witches and Wicca', 136.

147. Harvey, 'Fantasy in the Study of Religions' (my emphasis).

148. Ibid. (emphasis mine).

149. Ibid.

150. Ibid.

151. Ibid.

152. Hume, *Witchcraft and Paganism in Australia*, 80.

153. As Timothy Leary comments, 'For millions of post-World War II youths Herman Hesse's heroes served as models for personal transformation/evolution and for the triumph of the individual' (*Flashbacks*, 208).

154. Stevens, *Storming Heaven*, 408.

155. Ibid.

156. Although Castaneda wrote more volumes towards the end of his life, perhaps his most influential works, some of which have been reprinted several times are *The Teachings of Don Juan*; *A Separate Reality*; *Journey to Ixtlan*; *Tales of Power*; *The Second Ring of Power*.

157. Roth, *Maps to Ecstasy*.

Chapter 7

1. I am often reminded just how culturally significant popular music is when people are either literally shocked that a particular song or artist has not been discussed, or immediately light up when one is mentioned. For example, more than a few times individuals (usually academics) have commented on the significance of Tthe Incredible String Band for them – some even quoting lyrics. Indeed, the Archbishop of Canterbury, Rowan Williams, did himself no harm at all by revealing his knowledge of the group and their lyrics, and how much they meant to him. He was even invited to write the Foreword to a recent compendium of articles about them. See Rowan Williams, 'Foreword', in Whittaker (ed.), *beGLAD*, 5–6.

2. Sylvan, *Traces of the Spirit*, 4.

3. Adorno, 'On Popular Music'.

4. See Bennett, *Popular Music and Youth Culture*; Middleton, *Studying Popular Music*.

5. For example, 'Flutter' on Autechre's *Anti EP* (1994) was, the label tells the listener, 'programmed in such a way that no bars contain identical beats and can therefore be played at both forty five and thirty three revolutions under the proposed new law [i.e. the Criminal Justice and Public Order Act]. However,' they continue (tongue firmly in cheek), 'we advise DJs to have a lawyer and a musicologist present at all times to confirm the non-repetitive nature of the music in the event of police harassment.' Much of Spring Heel Jack's avant-garde *The Sound of Music EP* (1999) is similarly demanding.

6. Bennett, *Popular Music and Youth Culture*, 37.

7. Longhurst, *Popular Music and Society*, 13.

8. As Roger Sabin notes, 'one of the key defining elements of punk was an emphasis on class

politics' (Sabin, 'Introduction', in Sabin [ed.], *Punk Rock*, 3). See also Garnett, 'Too Low to be Low: Art Pop and the Sex Pistols', 17–30.

9.   See, for example, the interview with Khan in Dimitri Ehrlich, in *Inside the Music*, 117–24. For an interesting discussion of *qawwali* in an Islamic community in Britain, see Baily, '*Qawwali* in Bradford'.

10.   Longhurst, *Popular Music and Society*, 13.

11.   Ibid.

12.   McGuigan, *Modernity and Postmodern Culture*, 68.

13.   Barker, *Cultural Studies*, 45.

14.   Adorno, *The Culture Industry*, 92.

15.   Longhurst, *Popular Music and Society*, 8, 10.

16.   Quoted ibid., 20.

17.   Quoted ibid., 21.

18.   An example of this process can be found in Veit Erlmann's discussion of South African music ('Africa Civilized, Africa Uncivilized'). See also Banerji and Baumann, 'Bhangra 1984–8'.

19.   Featherstone, 'Global and Local Cultures', 169.

20.   Quoted in Longhurst, *Popular Music and Society*, 11.

21.   Ibid.

22.   George McKay describes Crass well: 'Crass were a radical anarcho-pacifist, anarcha-feminist, vegetarian collective', espousing 'a lifestyle and worldview they developed through a combination of hippie idealism and resistance, punk energy and cheek, and some of the cultural strategies of the Situationists' (*Senseless Acts of Beauty*, 75). Indicating their continuing influence, along with numerous contemporary artists, Crass's anti-war song 'Nagasaki Nightmare' was recently used on the fundraising CD for the global peace movement, *Peace Not War*.

23.   Quoted in Bennett, *Popular Music and Youth Culture*, 40.

24.   Quoted ibid., 41.

25.   Campbell and McIver, 'Cultural Sources of Support for Contemporary Occultism', 46.

26.   An interesting collection of interviews with popular musicians about spirituality can be found in Ehrlich, *Inside the Music*. For examples of recent 'music press' discussions of religious trends in popular music see Sutcliffe, 'Go Forth and Rock'; Wilding, 'Lucifer Rising'.

27.   The concept of 'homology' was introduced by Paul Willis to describe the 'fit' between a person's/group's social position, social values, and the cultural symbols and styles which are used to express themselves: '[Homology] is concerned with how far, in their structure and content, particular items parallel and reflect the structure, style, typical concerns, attitudes and feelings of the social group. Where homologies are found they are actually best understood in terms of structure. It is the continuous play between the group and a particular item which produces specific styles, meanings, contents and forms of consciousness' (Willis, *Profane Culture*, 191). Dick Hebdige developed the thesis with particular reference to British punk culture in his seminal *Subculture: The Meaning of Style*.

28.   Baddeley, *Lucifer Rising*, 89.

29.   Note his recording *Antichrist Superstar*.

30.   e.g. Moby, *Animal Rights*.

31.   'Whenever God Shines His Light', on Van Morrison, *Avalon Sunset*.

32.   Collis, *Van Morrison*, 118. Interestingly, on his 1991 album *Hymns to the Silence*, there seems to be a conscious mixing of Christian theology and nature mysticism. Along with tracks such as 'By His Grace' and the hymn 'Be Thou My Vision', there is the evocative 'Pagan Streams'.

33.   On Harrison, *All Things Must Pass*.

34.   On The Beatles, *Sgt. Pepper's Lonely Hearts Club Band*.

35.   Mellers, *Twilight of the Gods: The Beatles in Retrospect*, 94, 96.

36.   Robert Ellwood is wrong to locate the beginnings of The Beatles' experimentation with Eastern thought and sounds in 1967 (*The Sixties Spiritual Awakening*, 201).

37.   Leary, Metzner and Alpert, *The Psychedelic Experience*.

38.   MacDonald, *A Revolution in the Head*, 164.

39. Ibid., 166.
40. On the writing of 'The Void', see Irvin, 'Into Tomorrow', 45.
41. MacDonald, *A Revolution in the Head*, 166 (my emphasis).
42. Concerning the figure described by Lennon in the song, MacDonald writes: 'The archetype of countercultural anti-politics as presented in "Come Together" was the head-gaming hippie sage: a bewildering guru/shaman modelled on Timothy Leary, Ken Kesey, Carlos Castaneda's fictional Don Juan, and "trickster" figures like Mullah Nasruddin and Zen masters from the Orient. The amalgam of these (with perhaps a dash of cartoonist Robert Crumb's lampoon Mr Natural), the character presented in Lennon's lyric has "juju eyeball(s)" which suggest the cover of Dr John the Night Tripper's pseudo-voodoo album *Gris-Gris*, released in 1968 and a big hit in Britain's student/underground circles' (ibid., 287–8).
43. Ibid., 288 (emphasis in original).
44. Quoted ibid., 153.
45. Listen particularly to the Mahavishnu Orchestra's *The Inner Mounting Flame*.
46. See Krys Boswell's interview with Marillion: 'Marillion: Latter Day Druidic Bards'.
47. See Cope, 'From Punk to Pre-History', 25.
48. See also Cope, *The Modern Antiquarian*.
49. Willin, 'Music and Paganism', 43.
50. See, for example, Tom Doyle's interview with her ('Ready, Steady, Kook!'). Referring to her marriage in woodland in West Wycombe, which had an Arthurian theme, she says: 'Yeah, I really believe in that force, I believe in the elementals. I believe that when you call on certain forces and if you respect them, sometimes, they are there for you. I figured if I had [the wedding] where there were trees and water then maybe the fairies would show up' (88).
51. Such 'Viking' themes are particularly clear on their album *Hlidhskjalf* (1999).
52. Listen particularly to Mayhem, *De Mysteriis Dom Sathanas* (1994). See also <www.thetruemayhem.com>.
53. Graham Bond is an interesting figure, in as much as he played with some of the most influential musicians of the 1960s and is often claimed to be 'the Godfather of British R&B'. See Strong, *The Great Rock Discography*, 114.
54. For a discussion of the emergence of these themes in music see Baddeley, *Lucifer Rising*, 89–99.
55. Death in Vegas, *Scorpio Rising*.
56. M. Manson, 'Foreword', in LaVey, *Satan Speaks*, pp. xiii–xix.
57. See <http://www.uncarved.org>.
58. Neal, *Tape Delay*, 19. See also TOPY, 'TOPY London Interviewed by AntiClockwise Magazine 1991'.
59. Baddeley, *Lucifer Rising*, 156.
60. Quoted in Neal, *Tape Delay*, 26.
61. See ibid., 24.
62. Ibid.
63. Ibid., 23.
64. Ibid., 24. On Crowley and sex magic, see Urban, 'The Beast with Two Backs'.
65. Neal, *Tape Delay*, 21.
66. Baddeley, *Lucifer Rising*, 156.
67. Landon, 'What is FOPI?'.
68. Ibid.
69. <http://home.nestor.minsk.by/emn/interview/cryptops.html> (accessed 2 Feb. 2004).
70. MacDonald, 'The Psychedelic Experience', 31.
71. See Stevens, *Storming Heaven*, 394–415.
72. MacDonald, 'The Psychedelic Experience', 31. Dylan was far less Eastern-oriented and *spiritually* countercultural than The Beatles. For example, a recent study traces the influence of the Bible on his poetry and lyrics (Gilmour, *Tangled Up in the Bible*).
73. MacDonald, 'The Psychedelic Experience', 31.

74. Blake's brief discussion of the project is printed in the booklet provided with the *Sgt. Pepper's Lonely Hearts Club Band* CD (EMI, 1987), 4.

75. MacDonald, 'The Psychedelic Experience', 32.

76. Quoted in Ehrlich, *Inside the Music*, 133.

77. Quoted ibid., 126, 128.

78. Quoted in Green, *Days in the Life*, 67.

79. MacDonald, 'The Psychedelic Experience', 36.

80. Fast, *In the Houses of the Holy*, 90–1.

81. Ibid., 91.

82. Roach, *The Magnificent Void*.

83. Hillage, *Rainbow Dome Musick*. Note the spelling of 'musick' (like 'magick').

84. See Hoek, *Steve Reich*, 1–25; Tamm, *Brian Eno*.

85. Sylvian, *Camphor*.

86. Sylvian, *Dead Bees on a Cake*.

87. Cox, 'Invisible Jukebox', 21.

88. Ibid., 22.

89. Sylvian, 'Praise', on *Camphor*.

90. Sylvie Simmons from *Mojo*, quoted in Power, *David Sylvian*, 183.

91. Quoted in Power, *David Sylvian*, 183.

92. Ibid.

93. Ibid., 183–4.

94. For example, reflecting on drug use and spirituality during the 1960s, Richard Baker Roshi, the leader of a Zen Buddhist community in Colorado, makes the following interesting comment: 'We were in San Francisco right in the middle of the whole scene from '61 on. What Suzuki-Roshi and I noticed was that people who used LSD – and a large percentage of students did – got into [Zen] practice faster than other people ... My feeling is that psychedelics create a taste for a certain kind of experience' (Baker *et al.*, 'The Roundtable', 103).

95. The popularity of the inspirational, dance-oriented tabla music of Talvin Singh is a good example of this. Not only has he produced his own well-received CDs (e.g. *Ha*), but he has been sampled and has appeared on the CDs of numerous other musicians.

96. Stevens, *Storming Heaven*, 408–9.

97. Readers who are not familiar with this cover can, as noted above, view it on < http://www.knott32.fsnet.co.uk/isbp/spirits.jpg>.

98. Pendleton, 'Kindred Spirits', 69. This article is an excellent analysis of the whole album.

99. Rowan Williams, 'Foreword', in Whittaker (ed.), *beGLAD*, 6.

100. McKay, *Glastonbury*, 67.

101. See the excellent documentary (DVD) by Michael Wadleigh, *Woodstock*.

102. According to Marianne Faithful, following Altamont, 'Mick took all our magic books and made a great pyre of them in the fireplace' (quoted in Baddeley, *Lucifer Rising*, 51).

103. Hetherington, *New Age Travellers*, 41–2.

104. McKay, *Senseless Acts of Beauty*, 15.

105. Clarke, *The Politics of Pop Festivals*, 85.

106. Hetherington, *New Age Travellers*, 47.

107. Abbott, 'Wally Hope', 42.

108. Quoted in Collin, *Altered States*, 185.

109. Ibid., 186.

110. Reproduced in Abbott, 'Wally Hope', 42.

111. Clarke, *The Politics of Pop Festivals*.

112. See Wadleigh's *Woodstock*.

113. Hetherington, *New Age Travellers*, 48.

114. <http://hawkwind.com> (accessed 9 Aug. 2003).

115. McKay has provided a helpful 'Time-Line of Festival Culture', in his *Glastonbury*, 87–114.

116. Aitken, '20 Years of Free Festivals in Britain', 19.

117. Reynolds, *Energy Flash*, 136.
118. See Wylie, *Losing Ground*.
119. Hetherington, *New Age Travellers*, 12.
120. Ibid.
121. Ibid.
122. From an interview with McKay, in his *Glastonbury*, 148.
123. Letcher, 'Eco-Paganism: Protest Movement Spiritualities', 301.
124. WOMAD – World of Music, Arts and Dance. WOMAD was founded by Peter Gabriel in Britain in 1980 and organized its first festival in 1982 – which actually lost a great deal of money.
125. Hetherington, *New Age Travellers*, 47.
126. Linda Edwards makes the following incorrect statement: 'Today [Glastonbury] is a New Age center attracting thousands of spiritual travellers each year, especially to its music festival, which was revived in its present form in 1971 (*A Brief Guide to Beliefs*, 477). As we have seen, this is misleading on three counts: (1) the festival was not *revived* in 1971; (2) its form then was not its *present* form – it has evolved significantly; (3) it is inaccurate to say that the current Glastonbury Festival particularly attracts New Age seekers. Although the occultural element is still part of the Glastonbury experience, nowadays it is primarily a music event, the tickets for which sell out within the first few hours. This year (2004), because a friend was a couple of hours late going online to purchase his ticket, he missed out.
127. Quoted in McKay, *Glastonbury*, 29.
128. Beckerley, 'Glastonbury Entertains', 10.
129. A selection from the revised, 1983 edition of the book, entitled *The New View Over Atlantis*, can be found in Bloom (ed.), *Holistic Revolution*, 138–42.
130. Both quotations from *NME*, 'The Pyramid', 10.
131. McKay, *Glastonbury*, 69.
132. Quoted ibid.
133. Ibid., 101.
134. Quoted in Duvignaud, 'Festivals: A Sociological Approach', 15.
135. Quoted in *NME*, 'Time Line: A History of the Glastonbury Festival', 12.
136. Quoted ibid.
137. Quoted in Clarke, *The Politics of Pop Festivals*, 90.
138. Deckker, 'Introduction' to the booklet of the CD *Sacred Sites*, 5.
139. See Letcher, ' "Gaia Told Me to Do It" '.
140. McKay, *Glastonbury*, 48.
141. Ibid., 59.
142. Ibid., 49.
143. Benham, *The Avalonians*, 235.
144. ' … its organizers are incapable of seeing that it has made its statement and that it is about time that the beleaguered inhabitants of the village of Pilton and the countryside itself were given a permanent break from the city-size intrusion of more than 80,000 souls into a few fields around Worthy Farm at midsummer' (ibid.).
145. Ann Morgan, quoted in McKay, *Glastonbury*, 51.
146. See Kozinets and Sherry, 'Dancing on Common Ground', 287.
147. Pike, 'Desert Goddesses and Apocalyptic Art', 155.
148. Ibid.
149. See Van Rhey, 'The Art of Burning Man'.
150. Although there is a great variety of music, Kozinets and Sherry note that 'techno' provides the principal soundtrack to the festival ('Dancing on Common Ground', 289). This is supported by Steenson's comments: 'As a hardcore raver, I was in absolute heaven at the fact that there were dozens of places to party at any time of the day or night. Even during the worst of the dust storms there were people blasting Techno music in complete defiance of the potential peril they were in. My booty was exceptionally well shaken after this event … It felt like every sound system west of the Mississippi was there playing something a little different' ('What is Burning Man?').
151. Pike, *Earthly Bodies, Magical Selves*, p. xxiii.

152. Quoted in Smith, 'Burning Man', 23.

153. The track can be found on Faithless, *Sunday 8pm*.

154. Quoted in Pike, 'Desert Goddesses and Apocalyptic Art', 160.

155. Quoted ibid., 156.

156. See <http://www.burningman.com>. Originally the term *ekklesia* ('assembly') was not identified exclusively with the Christian community. It was, for example, also used of Jewish communities. After the admission of Gentiles, however, the distinction between Christian and Jewish assemblies became acute, and gradually the term became attached primarily to the former.

157. I will develop these ideas of *ekklesia*, *e.kklesia*, and *E-kklesia* (the last being a community shaped by induced experiences – not just the drug E/Ecstasy/MDMA) in Volume II.

158. Quoted in Robertson, 'Naked on Stilts', 26.

159. Pike, 'Desert Goddesses and Apocalyptic Art', 157 (emphasis in original). This point is also made forcefully by Kozinets and Sherry, 'Dancing on Common Ground', 287–303.

160. See the statement on obligatory participation on the website: <http://www.burningman.com/participate>.

161. Robertson, 'Naked on Stilts', 27.

162. Smith, 'Burning Man', 23.

163. Pike, 'Desert Goddesses and Apocalyptic Art', 161.

164. Ibid., 161–2.

165. Ibid., 162.

166. Quoted ibid., 160. A recent, interesting use of Foucault's 'heterotopia' is provided by Gay Pilgrim in 'The Quakers: Towards an Alternate Ordering' (see particularly 147–8). Pilgrim makes particular use of Kevin Hetherington's interpretation in *The Badlands of Modernity*.

167. Duvignaud, 'Festivals', 18.

168. Ibid., 19.

169. Quoted in Robertson, 'Naked on Stilts', 27.

170. For details of the festival, visit <http://www.occulture.tv>.

171. See Whiteley, 'Altered Sounds', 121–42; Reynolds, 'Back to Eden', 143–65.

172. Leary, *Beyond Life with Timothy Leary* (1997). If I am not mistaken, the following hip-hop track also puts the words of Leary to music: 'The Time Has Come' by U.N.K.L.E. vs the Major Force Orchestra. This can be found on *Headz: A Soundtrack of Experimental Hip-Hop Jams*.

173. Whiteley, 'Altered Sounds', 139.

174. Quoted in Cole and Hannan, 'Goa Trance'.

175. Ray Castle in dialogue with Eugene ENRG: ENRG, 'Psychic Sonics', 165.

176. Quoted in Bussmann, *Once in a Lifetime*, 134.

177. Quoted ibid.

178. Ibid., 108.

179. Tramacchi, 'Field Tripping', 205.

180. Tramacchi, 'Chaos Engines', 172. See also Sylvan, *Traces of the Spirit*.

181. D'Andrea, 'Global Nomads', 243.

182. Bussmann, *Once in a Lifetime*, 3.

183. D'Andrea, 'Global Nomads', 244.

184. Bussmann, *Once in a Lifetime*, 147.

185. Osborne, *A–Z of Club Culture*, 113–14.

186. See, for example, DeKorne, *Psychedelic Shamanism*.

187. Cole and Hannan, 'Goa Trance'.

188. Quoted in ENRG, 'Psychic Sonics', 159.

189. 'Reaper Girl' can be found on the compilation CD *Sacred Sites*.

190. 'Sky Spirit' can be found on the same CD.

191. 'Shaking Tent' can be found on the compilation CD *Tribal Futures: The Way Ahead*.

192. 'Tribabdelic Nomads' can be found on *Sacred Sites*.

193. Leary, *Your Brain is God*, 17.

194. Tramacchi, 'Field Tripping', 203.

195. Reynolds, 'Back to Eden', 159. See also his discussion in *Energy Flash*, 134–54.

196. St John, 'Introduction', 4. See also Sylvan, *Traces of the Spirit*, ch. 4.

197. Bill Brewster and Frank Broughton, in their history of the disc jockey, comment that 'the DJ is part shaman, part technician, part collector, part selector and part musical evangelist' (*Last Night a DJ Saved My Life*, 17).

198. Ray Castle, quoted in Cole and Hannan, 'Goa Trance'.

199. Suzuki, *Shamanic Trance*.

200. Allen, *Shamanic Trance*.

201. The Shamen, for example, are clearly sympathetic to the views of McKenna, who appears on their album *Boss Drum*.

202. Tramacchi, 'Field Tripping', 202–3.

203. e.g. 'Re-Evolution', on *Boss Drum*; and 'Re-Evolution (Shamen Mix)', on *The Shamen Collection*.

204. Collin, *Altered States*, 191.

205. Rushkoff, *Cyberia*, 91.

206. Quoted ibid., 96.

207. Quoted in Collin, *Altered States*, 191.

208. For a concise discussion of 'dance-drugs' and their use within 'rave' culture, see Rietveld, *This is Our House*, 175–88.

209. Wright, 'The Great British Ecstasy Revolution', 228.

210. Osborne, *Club Culture*, 273. On the Spiral Tribe, see particularly Reynolds, *Energy Flash*, 134–54.

211. Quoted in Collin, *Altered States*, 205.

212. Partridge, 'Sacred Chemicals?', 114ff.

213. Quoted in F. Cole and M. Hannan, 'Goa Trance'.

214. See Tramacchi, 'Field Tripping', 201–13.

215. Although I have used the term 'rave' fairly indiscriminately, it does feel a little passé nowadays. As with the term 'New Age', while a useful catch-all term, not only has it become a little too broad, amorphous and hence imprecise, it has actually become an *etic* term which is not used very much by 'insiders'. As one raver told me, 'it is just not used of music anymore. Rave music is house, early Prodigy, that sort of mid-nineties music, *definitely not* the type of drum 'n' bass that is often played at unofficial events nowadays.' That said, he did indicate that, as noted above, the term is still used within his particular subculture for such *unofficial* gatherings (which often get interrupted by the police). Hence, strictly speaking, it would seem that, in the UK, a distinction needs to be made between the music (which may include a range of genres, but usually not 'rave') and the event, which may be *unofficial*, or *official*, and thus a dance/club event. (No doubt, by the time this is published, these definitions will have shifted again.) However, I suppose the point is that, as ever, we academics find it hard to keep up with the speed of contemporary popular culture and alternative spirituality. Consequently, in seeking to develop a vocabulary, we reify social and cultural terminology, styles and movements. To some extent this cannot be helped, but I simply raise this point here as something that needs to be borne in mind by those of us interested in understanding subcultures, countercultures and alternative spiritualities.

216. Quoted in Collin, *Altered States*, 200.

217. Reynolds, *Energy Flash*, 136.

218. For a good discussion of Eco-Pagan beliefs (which will be discussed more fully in Volume II), see Letcher, 'Eco-Paganism: Protest Movement Spiritualities', 300–2; ' "Gaia Told Me To Do It" ', 61–84.

219. Collin, *Altered States*, 203–4.

220. Reynolds, *Energy Flash*, 138.

221. Ibid., 149.

222. Ibid., 151.

223. Lynch, *After Religion*, 88–9.

224. O'Connor, 'God is a DJ', 20.

225. Ibid.

226. Quoted ibid.

227. Ibid., 21.

228. Ibid., 22.

229. Gabrielle Roth, who describes herself as an urban shaman, is a choreographer and author of the influential *Maps to Ecstasy*.

230. Quoted in O'Connor, 'God is a DJ', 21.

231. For more on this emphasis in New Age thought generally, see Hedges and Beckford, 'Holism, Healing, and the New Age', 169–87.

232. Eno is a seminal figure in the history of contemporary ambient. The best appreciation of his work is Eric Tamm's *Brian Eno: His Music and the Vertical Color of Sound*. A good concise discussion of him can be found in Prendergast, *The Ambient Century*, 115–32 – to which Eno has written the Foreword (pp. xi–xii).

233. The definitive history of ambient, or perhaps the definitive history of twentieth-century music interpreted from the perspective of ambient, is provided by Prendergast, ibid.

234. Eno, *Discreet Music*; *Music For Airports*; *On Land*; *Thursday Afternoon*; *Neroli*; and *The Shutov Assembly*; Eno and Fripp, *Evening Star*; Eno and Budd, *The Plateaux of Mirror*.

235. This point is made with reference to Eno's *Neroli* by the discographer Martin Strong in his massive *The Great Rock Discography*, 347.

236. Barrow and Dalton, *Reggae*, 199.

237. See particularly High Tone, *Opus Incertum*; EZ3kiel, *Handle with Care*. Sadly, this interesting and creative music is still little known in the Anglophone world. Indeed, when I recently contacted one small French company producing dub I was told that I was the first English-speaking person to contact them.

238. Toop, *Ocean of Sound*, 115–16.

239. Williams, 'The Sound Surprise', 146.

240. Toop, *Ocean of Sound*, 115.

241. From the sleeve notes to Pablo and Perry, *Augustus Pablo Meets Lee Perry at the Black Ark*.

242. From the sleeve notes to Pablo, *Pablo meets Mr. Bassie*.

243. For more on Lotus Sounds, go to <hhtp://www.lotussounds.com>.

244. Alpha and Omega, *The Sacred Art of Dub*.

245. The Disciples, *Infinite Density of Dub*.

246. The Hazardous Dub Company, *Dangerous Dubs Vol. 2*.

247. Jah Shaka, *Dub Symphony*.

248. The Disciples Meet the Rootsman, *Rebirth*.

249. Enigma, *MCMXC A.D.*

250. Reynolds, *Energy Flash*, 171.

251. *Ambient Meditations*.

252. Reynolds, *Energy Flash*, 174.

253. Ibid., 175–6.

254. Ibid., 177.

255. From the sleeve notes to Zephaniah and The Hazardous Dub Company, *Back to Roots*.

256. What is now referred to as dub is largely the genre, particularly the work developed by the Jamaican recording engineer Osbourne Ruddock, popularly known as King Tubby. Others have since followed and developed the genre, such as Prince Jammy, Scientist, Errol Thompson, Herman Chin Loy, Augustus Pablo, and Lee Perry.

257. Little Axe, *The Wolf That House Built*; *Slow Fuse*; *Hard Grind*.

258. Twinkle Brothers, *Higher Heights (Twinkle Inna Polish Stylee)*. The dub versions can be found on Twinkle Brothers, *Dub with Strings*.

259. Listen particularly to the album produced by Bill Laswell, *Shabeesation*.

260. Muslimgauze, a.k.a. Bryn Jones (1961–1999), was one of the most creative and innovative producers of dub and electronica. In many ways he was the Damien Hirst of contemporary dub, much of his work being politically engaged and musically provocative. For a good introduction to

and overview of the music of Muslimgauze, listen to the compilation CD *The Inspirational Sounds of Muslimgauze*.

261. The Rootsman Meets Muslimgauze, *Al Aqsa Intifada*. Benjamin Zephaniah has also addressed the Palestinian issue 'in dub': 'Palestine', on *Back to Roots*. Indeed, so has Steve Reich (see Hoek, *Steve Reich*, 19).

262. Although much of what follows is the result of email correspondence (which took place betwen Sept. and Dec. 2003) and an interview at his house (29 Sept. 2003), a brief autobiographical overview can be found on the Third Eye Music website: <http://www.thirdeyemusic.co.uk>.

263. This alliance has been challenged recently by Roger Sabin, who makes use of fanzines etc. to show that some punks were not interested in reggae or, indeed, in left-wing, anti-racist politics ('"I Won't Let That Dago By"'). Obviously there were such punks and thus there is evidence to support this thesis. I myself attended concerts where such sentiments were expressed. I also attended an event in the late 1970s at which John Peel was the DJ, during which he was verbally abused by hippies for playing punk and by punks for playing reggae (not that this necessarily means the protestors were racist). Again, a friend attended a concert at which Joe Strummer invited the reggae musician Mikey Dread to perform with The Clash. This led to jeers from the crowd, followed by a short speech from Joe Strummer who, in no uncertain terms, denounced racism and told them to be quiet or The Clash would leave as well. The rest of the concert was an enjoyable mix of punk and reggae. So, yes, some punks did not like reggae. So what? Punk rock was not a homogeneous movement. Many punks (and hippies) did enjoy reggae, did get involved in Rock Against Racism, and did buy such seminal albums as The Clash's *Sandinista!* (1980) or UB40's *Signing Off* (1980) – which use reggae very effectively. Moreover, there is no doubt that dub had an ideological impact on punk and hippie countercultures and that this was the time when reggae made significant inroads into British popular culture. To deny this simply flies in the face of the facts. Furthermore, that punk *bricolage* included the liberal appropriation of symbols that would be offensive, including swastikas and so on, did not necessarily indicate right-wing politics, just as the Sex Pistols' use of Union Jacks or singing 'God Save the Queen' did not indicate that they were royalists. The Rootsman is by no means alone in moving from punk to reggae. Indeed, in the book edited by Sabin, one contributor, the former punk Frank Cartledge, notes that he made this shift after hearing the Specials ('Distress to Impress?', 152).

264. Colegrave and Sullivan, *Punk*, 186.

265. An excellent collection of tracks from this period compiled by Don Letts can be found on volume II of the Social Classics series: *Dread Meets the Rockers Uptown* (2001). The booklet accompanying the CD contains an interesting autobiographical essay by Letts.

266. Quoted in Colegrave and Sullivan, *Punk*, 203.

267. Sleeve notes to the Rootsman meets Celtarabia, *Union of Souls* (1998).

268. Ibid.

269. Ibid. Listen also too the Rootsman, *New Testament*.

270. The Rootsman meets Muslimgauze, *Al Aqsa Intifada*.

271. On Nasr's perennialism see Aslan, *Religious Pluralism in Christian and Islamic Perspective*.

272. For a good introductory overview of Schuon's thought, see Rawlinson, *Book of Enlightened Masters*, 517–24.

273. It is worth noting that, although the Rootsman has taken his share of drugs and alcohol, unlike many of those he works with, he does not smoke marijuana and only rarely drinks alcohol.

274. 'Faith' is the opening track on *New Testament*.

275. See Fey, 'Spirituality Bites'.

276. A general overview of contemporary Goth culture has been provided by Massimo Introvigne ('The Gothic Milieu'). Unfortunately, his discussion provides no theory of the milieu and, in my opinion, spreads the net rather too widely, covering everything from Joy Division (who were existentially dark, but hardly Gothic) and New Order (who were certainly not Gothic, being upbeat electronica) to Scandinavian Black Metal, contemporary Satanism, and *Buffy the Vampire Slayer*. That said, it is true that much heavy metal and Gothic-inspired bands (whether spoof, such as the Damned, or serious, such as Venom and Deicide), as well as films and TV series about vampires,

draw from the same dark occultural pool of symbols and ideas. 'Dark occulture' will be discussed more fully in Volume II.

Concluding Comments

1. Davie *et al.* (eds.), *Predicting Religion*.
2. Hunt, 'Understanding the Spirituality of People Who Do Not Go to Church', 163.
3. Ibid.
4. Ibid. (my emphasis).
5. Ibid., 168.
6. Lindbeck's 'cultural-linguistic' approach, which owes a great deal to Wittgenstein, can be found in his *Nature of Doctrine*.
7. Pearson, 'Witchcraft Will Not Soon Vanish from this Earth'.
8. Pilgrim, 'The Quakers'.
9. Berger, 'Postscript', 194.
10. Jean-François Mayer makes the point that, although the future is uncertain, 'we can be sure of one thing and that is that the challenge to the Christian churches will not come from this or that new religious movement but rather from new worldviews which will have an impact on an ever-growing number of people in the Western world who are not necessarily members of a NRM'. He also quotes the following interesting prediction by Mircea Eliade in one of the last interviews he gave prior to his death: 'It is quite possible that some day we will see absurd, strange things appearing which may well be new expressions of the experience of the sacred...I believe...we will experience difficulties in recognizing immediately the new expressions of the experience of the sacred' ('The Emergence of a New Religiosity in the Western World', 67, 68).
11. Barker, *Cultural Studies*, 40–1.
12. Karaflogka, 'Religion On', 200. Cyber-spirituality will be discussed more fully in Volume II.
13. Bruce, 'The Demise of Christianity in Britain', 62.

BIBLIOGRAPHY

Abbott, T., 'Wally Hope', *Festival Eye*, 1990, 42.

Abercrombie, N., and A. Warde (eds.), *Social Change in Contemporary Britain* (London: Polity, 1992).

Adler, M., *Drawing Down the Moon: Witches, Druids, Goddess Worshippers, and Other Pagans in America Today* (New York: Penguin/Arkana, 1986).

Adorno, T., 'On Popular Music', in Frith and Goodwin (eds.), *On Record*, 301–14.

—*The Culture Industry: Selected Essays on Mass Culture*, ed. J. Bernstein (London: Routledge, 1991).

—*The Stars Down to Earth and Other Essays on the Irrational in Culture*, ed. S. Crook (London: Routledge, 1994).

Aichele, G., and T. Pippin (eds.), *The Monstrous and the Unspeakable: The Bible as Fantastic Literature* (Sheffield: Sheffield Academic Press, 1997).

Aitken, D., '20 Years of Free Festivals in Britain', *Festival Eye*, 1990, 18–21.

Akhtar, M., and S. Humphries, *Far Out: The Dawning of New Age Britain* (Bristol: Sansom and Co./Channel 4, 1999).

Anderson, W.T., *Reality Isn't What It Used To Be: Theatrical Politics, Ready-to-Wear Religion, Global Myths, Primitive Chic, and Other Wonders of the Postmodern World* (San Francisco: Harper and Row, 1990).

Angela and Martin, 'A Review of *The Book of Shadows* and Interview with the Author, Phyllis Curott, Wiccan High Priestess', *Pagan Dawn* 132 (Lughnasadh 1999), 34–5.

Angelo, J., *Spiritual Healing for Today: Energy Medicine for Today* (Shaftesbury: Element, 1999).

Anonymous, 'The Road Well Trodden: How to Succeed in Publishing', *The Economist*, 19 May 2001, 35.

Arweck, E., 'New Religious Movements', in Woodhead *et al.* (eds.), *Religions in the Modern World*, 264–88.

Aslan, A., *Religious Pluralism in Christian and Islamic Perspective: The Thought of John Hick and Seyyed Hossein Nasr* (London: Curzon, 1998).

Baddeley, G., *Lucifer Rising* (London: Plexus, 1999).

Badham, P. (ed.), *Religion, State, and Society in Modern Britain* (Lampeter: Edwin Mellen, 1989).

Baily, J., '*Qawwali* in Bradford: Traditional Music in Muslim Communities', in Oliver (ed.), *Black Music in Britain*, 153–65.

Bainbridge, W.S., *The Sociology of New Religious Movements* (New York: Routledge, 1997).

Baker, R., R. Dass, J. Halifax, and R. Aitken, 'The Roundtable', *Tricycle: The Buddhist Review* 6:1 (Fall 1996), 101–9.

Banerji, S., and G. Baumann, 'Bhangra 1984–8: Fusion and Professionalization in a Genre of South Asian Dance Music', in Oliver (ed.), *Black Music in Britain*, 137–52.

Barber, K., *Readings in African Popular Culture* (Oxford: James Currey, 1997).

Barker, C., *Cultural Studies: Theory and Practice* (London: Sage, 2000).

Barker, E., *New Religious Movements: A Practical Introduction* (London: HMSO, 1989).

—'New Religious Movements: Their Incidence and Significance', in Wilson and Cresswell (eds.), *New Religious Movements*, 15–32.

Barkun, M., *A Culture of Conspiracy: Apocalyptic Visions in Contemporary America* (Berkeley: University of California Press, 2003).

Barrett, D.V., *Tarot* (London: Dorling Kindersley, 1995).

Barrow, S., and P. Dalton, *Reggae: The Rough Guide* (London: Rough Guides, 1997).

Bates, B., *The Way of the Wyrd* (London: Century, 1983).

Baum, G., *Religion and the Rise of Scepticism* (New York: Harcourt, Brace and World, 1970).

Bauman, Z., 'Postmodern Religion?', in Heelas *et al.* (eds.), *Religion, Modernity and Postmodernity*, 55–78.

Beaudoin, T., *Virtual Faith* (San Francisco: Jossey-Bass, 1998).

Bebbington, D., 'Revival and Enlightenment in Eighteenth Century England', in Walker and Aune (eds.), *On Revival*, 71–86.

Becker, H., *Systematic Sociology on the Basis of the Bezeihungslehre and Gebildelehre of Leopold von Wiese* (New York: Wiley, 1932).

Beckerley, T., 'Glastonbury Entertains', *Festival Eye*, 2003, 10.

Beckford, J., 'The Mass Media and New Religious Movements', in Wilson and Cresswell (eds.), *New Religious Movements*, 103–20.

Bell, Daniel, 'The Return of the Sacred? The Argument on the Future of Religion', *British Journal of Sociology* 28 (1977), 419–9.

Bell, David, *An Introduction to Cybercultures* (London: Routledge, 2001).

Bell, David, and B.M. Kennedy (eds.), *The Cybercultures Reader* (London: Routledge, 2000).

Beloff, J., *Parapsychology: A Concise History* (London: Athlone Press, 1993).

Benham, P., *The Avalonians* (Glastonbury: Gothic Image, 1993).

Benjamin, W., *Illuminations* (London: Fontana, 1973).

Bennett, A., *Popular Music and Youth Culture* (London: Routledge, 2000).

Bennett, J., 'The Enchanted World of Modernity: Paracelsus, Kant, and Deleuze', *Cultural Values* 1 (1997), 1–28.

Berger, A., and J. Berger (eds.), *Reincarnation: Fact or Fable?* (Wellingborough: Aquarian Press, 1991).

Berger, H., *A Community of Witches: Contemporary Neo-Paganism and Witchcraft in the United States* (Columbia, SC: University of South Carolina Press, 1999).

Berger, P., 'The Desecularization of the World: A Global Overview', in Berger (ed.), *The Desecularization of the World*, 1–18.

—*The Heretical Imperative: Contemporary Possibilities of Religious Affirmation* (London: Collins, 1980).

—*The Sacred Canopy: Elements of a Sociological Theory of Religion* (New York: Anchor Books, 1967).

—'Postscript', in Woodhead *et al.* (eds.), *Peter Berger and the Study of Religion*, 189–98.

Berger, P. (ed.), *The Desecularization of the World: Resurgent Religion and World Politics* (Grand Rapids: Eerdmans, 2000).

Bergson, H., *Creative Evolution*, trans. A. Mitchell (New York: Henry Holt, 1911).

Besant, A., *H.P. Blavatsky and the Masters of Wisdom* (London: Theosophical Publishing House, 1907).

—*Revelation, Inspiration, Observation: An Approach to them for Theosophical Students* (Madras: Theosophical Publishing House, 1909).

Bird, M., B. Curtis, T. Putnam, G. Robertson, and L. Tickner (eds.), *Mapping the Futures: Local Cultures, Global Change* (London: Routledge, 1993).

Bishop, P., *Dreams of Power: Tibetan Buddhism and the Western Imagination* (London: Athlone Press, 1993).

Blake, S., and S. Lloyd, *The Keys to Avalon: The True Location of Arthur's Kingdom Revealed* (Shaftesbury: Element, 2000).

Blavatsky, H.P., *The Key to Theosophy* (London: Theosophical Publishing House, 1889).

—*The Secret Doctrine: The Synthesis of Science, Religion and Philosophy*, 2 vols; Adyar, India: Theosophical Publishing House, 1978).

Bloesch, D.G., *God the Almighty: Power, Wisdom, Holiness, Love* (Carlisle: Paternoster Press, 1995).

Bloom, W. (ed.), *Holistic Revolution: The Essential Reader* (London: Allen Lane, 2000).

—*The New Age: An Anthology of Essential Writings* (London: Rider, 1991).

Boeve, L., 'The Sacramental Interruption of Rituals of Life', *Heythrop Journal* 44 (2003), 401–17.

Boltwood, G., 'Channelling', in Deckker (ed.), *Sacred Sites*, 40–3.

Bonewitz, R.A., *New Cosmic Crystals: The Ultimate Course in Crystal Consciousness* (San Francisco: HarperCollins, 2000).

Bookchin, M., *Re-Enchanting Humanity: A Defense of the Human Spirit against AntiHumanism, Misanthropy, Mysticism and Primitivism* (London: Cassell, 1995).

Bosch, D., *Transforming Mission: Paradigm Shifts in Theology of Mission* (Maryknoll, NY: Orbis, 1991).

Boswell, K., 'Marillion: Latter Day Druidic Bards', *Pagan Dawn* 140 (Lammas 2001), 20–2.

Bowman, M., 'The Noble Savage and the Global Village: Cultural Evolution in New Age and Neo-Pagan Thought', *Journal of Contemporary Religion* 10 (1995), 139–49.

Bradby, R., '*A Course in Miracles*', in Partridge (ed.), *Encyclopedia of New Religions*, 348–9.

Braun, W., and R.T. McCutcheon (eds.), *Guide to the Study of Religion* (London: Cassell, 2000).

Braybrooke, M., *Pilgrimage of Hope: One Hundred Years of Global Interfaith Dialogue* (London: SCM, 1992).

Brewster, B., and F. Broughton, *Last Night a DJ Saved My Life: The History of the Disc Jockey* (London: Headline, 1999).

Brierley, P., 'Religion', in Halsey and Webb (eds.), *Twentieth-Century British Social Trends*, 650–74.

Brierley, P. (ed.), *A Century of British Christianity: Historical Statistics 1900–1985 with Projections to the Year 2000* (London: MARC Europe, 1989).

—*Religious Trends No.1: 1999/2000* (London: Christian Research Association, 1999).

—*Religious Trends No.2: 2000/01* (London: Christian Research Association, 2000).

—*The Tide is Running Out* (London: Christian Research Association, 2000).

—*UK Christian Handbook*, 1998–9 edn (London: Christian Research; Carlisle: Paternoster Press, 1997).

Brnody, 'Up the Chain', <http://www.heavensgatetoo.com/exitchk.htm> (accessed 26 Aug. 1999).

Brockington, J., *The Sacred Thread: Hinduism in its Continuity and Diversity* (Edinburgh: Edinburgh University Press, 1981).

Brockway, A.R., and J.P. Rajashekar (eds.), *New Religious Movements and the Churches* (Geneva: WCC Publications, 1987).

Brooker, W., *Using the Force: Creativity, Community, and* Star Wars *Fans* (New York: Continuum, 2002).

Brooks, R., and C. Morgan, 'Losing Our Religion', *Sunday Times*, 15 May 2001, 13.

Bromley, D.G., and M. Bracey, 'The Church of Scientology: A Quasi Religion', in Zellner and Petrowsky (eds.), *Sects, Cults, and Spiritual Communities*, 141–56.

Brown, C., *The Death of Christian Britain: Understanding Secularisation 1800–2000* (London: Routledge, 2001).

Bruce, S., 'The Charismatic Movement and the Secularization Thesis', *Religion* 28 (1998), 223–32.

—'The Curious Case of the Unnecessary Recantation: Berger and Secularization', in Woodhead (ed.), Peter Berger and the Study of Religion, 87–100.

—'The Demise of Christianity in Britain', in Davie *et al.* (eds.), *Predicting Religion*, 53–63.

—*God Is Dead: Secularization in the West* (Oxford: Blackwell, 2002).

—'The New Age and Secularization', in Sutcliffe and Bowman (eds.), *Beyond New Age*, 220–36.

—'Pluralism and Religious Vitality', in Bruce (ed.), *Religion and Modernization*, 170–94.

—'Religion in Britain at the Close of the 20th Century: A Challenge to the Silver Lining Perspective', *Journal of Contemporary Religion* 11 (1996), 261–74.

—*Religion in the Modern World: From Cathedrals to Cults* (Oxford: Oxford University Press, 1996).

Bruce, S. (ed.), *Religion and Modernization: Historians Debate the Secularization Thesis* (Oxford: Oxford University Press, 1992).

Brum, J., 'Smells Like Teen Spirit', *Marie-Claire*, Nov. 2000, 146–52.

Buckley, M.J., *At the Origins of Modern Atheism* (New Haven: Yale University Press, 1987).

Bullard, T., 'Foreword: UFOs – Folklore of the Space Age', in Lewis (ed.), *UFOs and Popular Culture*, pp. ix–xxv.

Burke, K., 'No Rest for the Wicca', *Sydney Morning Herald*, 30 June 2003 (accessed via WorldWide Religious News, <http://wwrn.org/parse.php?idd=9001andc=14>, 12 Nov. 2003).

Burrows, J.H. (ed.), *The World's Parliament of Religions* (Chicago: Parliament Publishing Company, 1893).

Bussmann, J., *Once in a Lifetime: The Crazy Days of Acid House and Afterwards* (London: Virgin Books, 1998).

Campbell, C., 'Clarifying the Cult', *British Journal of Sociology* 28 (1977), 375–88.

—'The Cult, the Cultic Milieu and Secularization', in Hill (ed.), *Sociological Yearbook of Religion in Britain 5*, 119–36; also pub. in Kaplan and Lööw (eds.), *The Cultic Milieu*, 12–25.

—'The Easternisation of the West', in Wilson and Cresswell, *New Religious Movements*, 35–48.

—'The Secret Religion of the Educated Classes', *Sociological Analysis* 39 (1978), 146–56.

Campbell, C., and S. McIver, 'Cultural Sources of Support for Contemporary Occultism', *Social Compass* 34 (1987), 41–60.

Cantwell, R., *Ethnomimesis and the Representation of Culture* (Chapel Hill: University of North Carolina Press, 1993).

Capra, F., *The Tao of Physics: An Exploration of Parallels between Modern Physics and Eastern Mysticism* (London: Fontana, 1976).

Capra, F., D. Steindl-Rast, and T. Matus, *Belonging to the Universe: New Thinking about God and Nature* (Harmondsworth: Penguin, 1992).

Carr-Gomm, P. (ed.), *The Druid Renaissance: The Voice of Druidry Today* (London: Thorsons, 1996).

Carroll, P., *Liber Kaos* (York Beach, Me.: Weiser, 1993).

Cartledge, F., 'Distress to Impress? Local Punk Fashion and Commodity Exchange', in Sabin (ed.), *Punk Rock*, 143–53.

Casanova, J., 'Beyond European and American Exceptionalisms: Towards a Global Perspective', in Davie *et al.* (eds.), *Predicting Religion*, 17–29.

—*Public Religion in the Modern World* (Chicago: University of Chicago Press, 1994).

Castaneda, C., *Journey to Ixtlan* (London: Penguin, 1975).

—*The Second Ring of Power* (London: Arkana, 1990).

Castaneda, C., *A Separate Reality* (London: Penguin, 1973).
—*Tales of Power* (London: Arkana, 1990).
—*The Teachings of Don Juan* (London: Penguin, 1970).
Cavaliero, G., *The Supernatural and English Fiction* (Oxford: Oxford University Press, 1995).
Cavallaro, D., *Cyberpunk and Cyberculture: Science Fiction and the Work of William Gibson* (London: Athlone Press, 2000).
Certeau, M. de, *The Practice of Everyday Life* (Berkeley: University of California Press, 1984).
Champion, S., 'Goa', in *Deep Trance and Ritual Beats,* a booklet accompanying the CD *Deep Trance and Ritual Beats*, 36–51.
Chan, C., 'The Sacred–Secular Dialectics of the Reenchanted Religious Order – the Lungsu Exo-Esoterics in Hong Kong', *Journal of Contemporary Religion* 15 (2000), 45–63.
Chattopadhyaya, R., *World's Parliament of Religions, 1893* (Calcutta: Minerva Associates Publications, 1995).
Ching Hai, Suma, *The Key to Enlightenment* (Formosa, China: Suma Ching Hai International Association Publishing, 1996).
Chryssides, G.D., *Exploring New Religions* (London: Cassell, 1999).
Cimino, R., and D. Lattin, *Shopping for a Faith: American Religion in the New Millennium* (San Francisco: Jossey-Bass, 1998).
Clark, S.R.L., *How to Live Forever: Science Fiction and Philosophy* (London: Routledge, 1995).
Clarke, M., *The Politics of Pop Festivals* (London: Junction Books, 1982).
Clarke, P.B., 'The Occult and Newly Religious in Modern Society', *Religion Today* 7:2 (Spring 1992), 1–5.
—'The Occult and Newly Religious in Modern Society. Part II: In the Mirror of History', *Religion Today* 7:3 (Summer 1992), 1–3.
Clarke, P.B. (ed.), *The New Evangelists: Recruitment Methods and Aims of New Religious Movements* (London: Ethnographica, 1987).
Cody, J.V., 'Gerald Heard: Soul Guide to the Beyond Within', *Gnosis* 26 (1993), 64–70.
Coghlan, R., *The Illustrated Encyclopaedia of Arthurian Legends* (Shaftesbury: Element, 1994).
Cole, F., and M. Hannan, 'Goa Trance: A Psykotropic Trip through Tribedelic Transcapes', <http://www.princeton.edu/~cspock/Goa_Trance.htm> (accessed 20 Aug. 2003).
Colegrave, S., and C. Sullivan, *Punk: A Life Apart* (London: Cassell, 2001).
Collin, M., *Altered States: The Story of Ecstasy Culture and Acid House*, 2nd edn (London: Serpent's Tail, 1998).
Collins, A., *Gateway to Atlantis: The Search for the Source of a Lost Civilization* (London: Headline, 2000).
Collis, J., *Van Morrison: Inarticulate Speech of the Heart* (London: Warner Books, 1996).
Comte, A., 'A Science of Society', in Tierney and Scott (eds.), *Western Societies*, 285–7.
Cope, J., 'From Punk to Pre-History', *Kindred Spirit* 45 (1998–9), 25–8.
—*The Modern Antiquarian: A Pre-Millennial Odyssey through Megalithic Britain* (London: Thorsons, 1998).
Cornbleth, C., *Hearing America's Youth: Social Identities in Uncertain Times* (New York: Peter Lang, 2003).
Coughlin, J.J., *Out of the Shadows: An Exploration of Dark Paganism and Magick* (Bloomington, Ind.: 1st Books Library, 2001).
Cousins, E.H. (ed.), *Process Theology: Basic Writings* (New York: Newman Press, 1971).
Cowan, D.E., 'Exits and Migrations: Foregrounding the Christian Countercult', *Journal of Contemporary Religion* 17 (2002), 339–54.
Coward, H.G., *Jung and Eastern Thought* (Albany, NY: State University of New York Press, 1984).
Cox, C., 'Invisible Jukebox: David Sylvian', *The Wire* 232 (June 2003), 20–4.

Cox, H., 'Eastern Cults and Western Culture: Why Young Americans Are Buying Oriental Religions', *Psychology Today*, July 1977, 36–42

—*Fire From Heaven: Pentecostalism, Spirituality and the Reshaping of Religion in the Twenty-First Century* (London: Cassell, 1996).

—*Turning East* (New York: Simon and Schuster, 1977).

Cracknell, K., *Justice, Courtesy and Love: Theologians and Missionaries Encountering World Religions, 1846–1914* (London: Epworth Press, 1995).

Crone, 'Satan? Who's That?', *Pagan Dawn* 133 (Samhain 1999), 30.

Crowley, V., *Principles of Paganism* (London: Thorsons, 1996).

—*Principles of Wicca* (London: Thorsons, 1997).

—*Wicca: The Old Religion in the New Millennium* (London: Thorsons, 1996).

—*A Woman's Kabbalah: Kabbalah for the 21st Century* (London: Thorsons, 2000).

Cunningham, S., *Wicca: A Guide for the Solitary Practitioner* (St Paul: Llewellyn, 1988).

Curott, P., *Book of Shadows: A Modern Woman's Journey into the Wisdom of Witchcraft and the Magic of the Goddess* (New York: Broadway Books, 1998).

Dalton, R., and R. Rohrschneider, 'The Greening of Europe', in Jowell *et al.* (eds.), *British (and European) Social Attitudes: How Britain Differs: The 15th Report*, 101–23.

D'Andrea, A., 'Global Nomads: Techno and New Age as Transnational Countercultures in Ibiza and Goa', in St John (ed.), *Rave Culture and Religion*, 236–55.

Dass, S., 'What Does Being a Buddhist Mean to You?', *Tricycle: The Buddhist Review* 6:1 (Fall 1996), 43.

Davie, G., 'Believing Without Belonging: Is This the Future of Religion in Britain?', *Social Compass* 37 (1990), 455–69.

—*Religion in Britain Since 1945: Believing Without Belonging* (Oxford: Blackwell, 1994).

Davie, G., P. Heelas, and L. Woodhead (eds.), *Predicting Religion: Christian, Secular and Alternative Futures* (Aldershot: Ashgate, 2003).

Dawson, L.L., and J. Hennebry, 'New Religions and the Internet: Recruiting in a New Public Space', *Journal of Contemporary Religion* 14 (1999), 17–39.

Dean, J., *Aliens in America: Conspiracy Cultures from Outerspace to Cyberspace* (Ithaca, NY: Cornell University Press, 1998).

Deckker, C., 'Introduction', in Deckker (ed.), *Sacred Sites*, 4–5.

Deckker, C. (ed.), *Sacred Sites*, booklet accompanying *Sacred Sites* CD (Return to the Source, 1997).

De Graaf, N.D., and A. Need, 'Losing Faith: Is Britain Alone?', in Jowell *et al.* (eds.), *British Social Attitudes: The 17th Report*, 119–36.

DeKorne, J., *Psychedelic Shamanism: The Cultivation, Preparation and Shamanic Use of Psychotropic Plants* (Port Townsend, Wash.: Loompanics Unlimited, 1994).

Delfgaauw, B., *Evolution: The Theory of Teilhard de Chardin*, trans. H. Hoskins (London: Fontana, 1969).

Devall, B., and G. Sessions, *Deep Ecology: Living as if Nature Mattered* (Salt Lake City: Peregrine Smith Books, 1985).

Dhamija, J.N., *A Quest for the Eternal: Poetry, Physics and Philosophy* (Shaftesbury: Element, 1999).

Diamond, I., and G.F. Orenstein (eds.), *Reweaving the World: The Emergence of Ecofeminism* (San Francisco: Sierra Club Books, 1990).

Dobbelaere, K., 'Secularization: A Multi-Dimensional Concept', *Current Sociology* 29 (1981), 1–216.

Doyle, T., 'Ready, Steady, Kook!', *Q* 140 (May 1998), 80–8.

Drane, J., 'Celebrity-Centric Religion', in Partridge (ed.), *Dictionary of Contemporary Religion in the Western World*, 185–8.

—'*The Celestine Prophecy*', in Partridge (ed.), *Encyclopedia of New Religions*, 355.

Drane, J., R. Clifford, and P. Johnson, *Beyond Prediction: The Tarot and Your Spirituality* (Oxford: Lion, 2001).

Drescher, H.-G., *Ernst Troeltsch: His Life and Work*, trans. J. Bowden (London: SCM, 1992).

Ducie, S., *Do It Yourself Numerology: How to Unlock the Secrets of Your Personality with Numbers* (Shaftesbury: Element, 1999).

—*Principles of Numerology* (London: Thorsons, 1998).

Duncan, A.D., *The Christ, Psychotherapy and Magic: A Christian Appreciation of Occultism* (London: George Allen and Unwin, 1969).

Dunne, J.S., *The Way of All the Earth: An Encounter with Eastern Religions* (London: Sheldon Press, 1973).

Duriez, C., 'Mysticism and Fantasy in Lewis, Tolkien and Barfield', in Partridge and Gabriel (eds.), *Mysticism East and West*, 230–54.

—'The Theology of Fantasy in Lewis and Tolkien', *Themelios* 23 (1998), 35–51.

During, S. (ed.), *The Cultural Studies Reader* (London: Routledge, 1993).

Duvignaud, J., 'Festivals: A Sociological Approach', *Cultures* 3 (1976), 13–25.

Dyson, J., 'Spellbound', *Vogue*, British edn, May 1999, 30–3.

Edwards, L., *A Brief Guide to Beliefs, Ideas, Theologies, Mysteries, and Movements* (Louisville: Westminster John Knox Press, 2001).

Ehrlich, D., *Inside the Music: Conversations with Contemporary Musicians about Spirituality, Creativity, and Consciousness* (Boston: Shambhala, 1997).

Eisenberg, D., R.C. Kessler, C. Foster, F.E. Norlock, D.R. Calkins, and T.L. Delbanco, 'Unconventional Medicine in the United States: Prevalence, Costs, and Patterns of Use', *New England Journal of Medicine* 328 (1993), 246–52.

Eliade, M., 'Paul Tillich and the History of Religions', in Tillich, *The Future of Religions*, 31–6.

—*The Sacred and the Profane: The Nature of Religion*, trans. W.R. Trask (New York: Harcourt Brace Jovanovich, 1959).

—*Shamanism: Archaic Techniques of Ecstasy* (New York: Pantheon Books, 1964).

Elliot, M. (ed.), *The Dynamics of Human Life* (Carlisle: Paternoster Press, 2001).

Ellwood, R.S., *The Sixties Spiritual Awakening: American Religion Moving from the Modern to the Postmodern* (New Brunswick, NY: Rutgers University Press, 1994).

Eno, B., 'Foreword', in Prendergast, *The Ambient Century*, pp. xi–xii.

ENRG, E., 'Psychic Sonics: Tribadelic Dance Trance-Formation', in St John, *FreeNRG*, 157–69.

Erickson, G., '"Sometimes You Need a Story": American Christianity, Vampires, and *Buffy*', in Wilcox and Lavery (eds.), *Fighting the Forces*, 108–19.

Erlmann, V., 'Africa Civilized, Africa Uncivilized: Local Culture, World System, and South African Music', in Barber (ed.), *Readings in African Popular Music*, 170–7.

Ezzy, D., 'New Age Witchcraft? Popular Spell Books and the Re-Enchantment of Everyday Life', *Culture and Religion* 4 (2003), 49–65.

Faivre, A., and J. Needleman (eds.), *Modern Esoteric Spirituality* (London: SCM, 1993).

Farmer, H.H., *Revelation and Religion: Studies in the Theological Interpretation of Religious Types* (London: Nisbet, 1954).

Fast, S., *In the Houses of the Holy: Led Zeppelin and the Power of Rock Music* (Oxford: Oxford University Press, 2001).

Featherstone, M., 'Global and Local Cultures', in Bird *et al.* (eds.), *Mapping the Futures*, 169–87.

Ferguson, D.S. (ed.), *New Age Spirituality: An Assessment* (Louisville: Westminster/John Knox Press, 1993).

Ferguson, M., *The Aquarian Conspiracy: Personal and Social Transformation in Our Times* (London: Paladin, 1982).

Ferré, N.F.S., *Paul Tillich: Retrospect and Future* (Nashville: Abingdon, 1966).

Fey, J.W., 'Spirituality Bites: Xers and the Gothic Cult/ure', in Flory and Miller (eds.), *Gen X Religion*, 31–53.

Fitch, E., *The Rites of Odin* (St Paul: Llewellyn, 1997).

Flood, G., *An Introduction to Hinduism* (Cambridge: Cambridge University Press, 1996).

Flory, R.W., and D.E. Miller (eds.), *Gen X Religion* (New York: Routledge, 2000).

Forbes, B.D., and J.H. Mahan (eds.), *Religion and Popular Culture in America* (Berkeley: University of California Press, 2000).

Fortune, D., *The Mystical Qabalah* (London: Ernest Benn, 1935).

Foucault, M., *Religion and Culture*, ed. J. Carrette (London: Routledge, 1999).

Fox, A., 'Solitary Pagans', *Pagan Dawn* 145 (Samhain 2002), 43–4.

Fox, M., *Creation Spirituality: Liberating Gifts for the People of the Earth* (San Francisco: HarperCollins, 1991).

—*Original Blessing* (Santa Fe: Bear and Co., 1983).

Frayling, C., *Nightmare: The Birth of Horror* (London: BBC Books, 1996).

Frazer, J.G., *The Golden Bough* (London: Wordsworth Editions, 1993).

Freston, P., *Evangelicals and Politics in Asia, Africa and Latin America* (Cambridge: Cambridge University Press, 2001).

Freud, S., *The Future of an Illusion*, trans. J. Strachey (New York: Norton, 1961).

Frith, S., *Performing Rites: Evaluating Popular Music* (Oxford: Oxford University Press, 1996).

Frith, S., and A. Goodwin (eds.), *On Record: Rock, Pop and the Written Word* (London: Routledge, 1990).

Frost, R., *A Closer Look at New Age Spirituality* (Eastbourne: Kingsway Publications, 2001).

Gamer, M., *Romanticism and the Gothic: Genre, Reception, and Canon Formation* (Cambridge: Cambridge University Press, 2000).

Garnett, R., 'Too Low to be Low: Art Pop and the Sex Pistols', in Sabin (ed.), *Punk Rock*, 17–30.

Gauchet, M., *The Disenchantment of the World: A Political History of Religion*, trans. O. Burge (Princeton: Princeton University Press, 1997).

Geaves, R., 'From Divine Light Mission to Elan Vital and Beyond: An Exploration of Change and Adaption', *Nova Religio: The Journal of Alternative and Emergent Religions* 7 (2004), 45–62.

Geertz, C., *The Interpretation of Cultures* (New York: Basic Books, 1973).

Gelder, K., *Reading the Vampire* (London: Routledge, 1994).

Gerth, H.H., and C. Wright Mills, 'Introduction: The Man and His Work', in Gerth and Mills (trans. and eds.), *From Max Weber*, 1–74.

Gerth, H.H., and C. Wright Mills (trans. and eds.), *From Max Weber: Essays in Sociology* (London: Routledge, 1948, repr. 1991).

Gibbons, B., *Spirituality and the Occult: From the Renaissance to the Twentieth Century* (London: Routledge, 2000).

Gibson, W., *Neuromancer* (London: HarperCollins, 1995).

Giddens, A., *Modernity and Self-Identity: Self and Society in a Late Modern Age* (Oxford: Polity Press, 1991).

Gilbert, A., and M. Cotterell, *The Mayan Prophecies* (Shaftesbury: Element, 2000).

Gilbert, A.D., *The Making of Post-Christian Britain: A History of the Secularization of Modern Society* (London: Longman, 1980).

Gilbert, R.A., 'Western Esotericism', in Partridge (ed.), *Encyclopedia of New Religions*, 304–8.

Giles, C., *Tarot: The Complete Guide* (London: Robert Hale, 1992).

Gilgen, A.R., and J.H. Cho, 'Questionnaire to Measure Eastern and Western Thought', *Psychological Reports* 44 (1979), 835–44.

Gilmour, M.J., *Tangled Up in the Bible: Bob Dylan and Scripture* (New York: Continuum, 2004).

Ginsberg, A., 'A Tale of the Tribe (from Preface to "Jail Notes")', from the sleeve notes to the CD, *Beyond Life with Timothy Leary* (Mercury Records, 1997).

Gittins, I., 'Return to the Source', in *Deep Trance and Ritual Beats*, a booklet in the CD *Deep Trance and Ritual Beats* (Return to the Source, n.d.), 4–17.

Glnody, 'Why We Must Leave at this Time' <http://www.heavensgatetoo.com/exitchk.htm> (accessed Aug. 26, 1999).

Glock, C., and R. Bellah, *The New Religious Consciousness* (Berkeley: University of California Press, 1976).

Gonzalez-Wippler, M., *Introduction to Seashell Divination* (New York: Original Publication, 1992).

—*Return of the Angels* (St. Paul: Llewellyn, 2000).

Gottlieb, R.S., *This Sacred Earth: Religion, Nature, Environment*, 2nd edn (New York: Routledge, 2004).

Greeley, A., 'Religion in Britain, Ireland and the USA', in Jowell *et al.* (eds.), *British Social Attitudes: The 9th Report*, 51–70.

Green, D., 'Buddhism in Britain: Skilful Means or Selling Out?', in Badham (ed.), *Religion, State, and Society in Modern Britain*, 277–91.

Green, J., *Days in the Life: Voices from the English Underground, 1961–1971* (London: Pimlico, 1998).

Green, M. (ed.), *Church Without Walls: A Global Examination of Cell Churches* (Carlisle: Paternoster Press, 2002).

Grünschloß, A., 'Ufology and UFO-Related Movements', in Partridge (ed.), *Encyclopedia of New Religions*, 372–6.

Haining, P. (ed.), *The Walls of Illusion: A Psychedelic Retro* (London: Souvenir Press, 1998).

Hall, J.R., *Apocalypse Observed: Religious Movements and Violence in North America, Europe and Japan* (London: Routledge, 2000).

Hall, S., *Culture, Media, Language* (London: Unwin Hyman, 1990).

—'Encoding, Decoding', in During (ed.), *The Cultural Studies Reader*, 90–103.

Hallowell, I., 'Ojibwa Ontology, Behaviour and World View', in Harvey (ed.), *Readings in Indigenous Religions*, 18–49.

Halsey, A.H., and J. Webb (eds.), *Twentieth-Century British Social Trends* (Basingstoke: Macmillan, 2000).

Hamilton, M., 'An Analysis of the Festival of Mind–Body–Spirit, London', in Sutcliffe and Bowman (eds.), *Beyond New Age*, 188–200.

—'The Easternisation Thesis: Critical Reflections', *Religion* 32 (2002), 243–58.

Hammer, O., *Claiming Knowledge: Strategies of Epistemology from Theosophy to the New Age* (Leiden: Brill, 2001).

Hammond, F., and I.M. Hammond, *Pigs in the Parlor* (Kirkwood, Mo.: Impact, 1973).

Hammond, P.E. (ed.), *The Sacred in a Secular Age: Toward Revision in the Scientific Study of Religion* (Berkeley: University of California Press, 1985).

Hanegraaff, W., 'How Magic Survived the Disenchantment of the World', *Religion* 33 (2003), 357–80.

—*New Age Religion and Western Culture: Esotericism in the Mirror of Secular Thought* (Leiden: Brill, 1996).

Hannam, M., 'Why Deny Satan?', *Pagan Dawn* 133 (Samhain 1999), 29.

Hardman, C., 'Introduction', in Harvey and Hardman (eds.), *Paganism Today*, pp. ix–xix.

Harnack, A. von, *What is Christianity?*, trans. T.B. Saunders (Philadelphia: Fortress, 1986).

Harner, M., 'The Sound of Rushing Water', in Lehmann and Myers (eds.), *Magic, Witchcraft and Religion*, 122–7.

Harris, K., '"Roots"?: The Relationship between the Global and the Local within the Extreme Metal Scene', *Popular Music* 19 (2000), 13–30.

Harrison, P., 'Harry, Sabrina and Buffy Help Paganism Grow', Reuters, 19 June 2003 (accessed via WorldWide Religious News <http://www.wwrn.org, 24 June 2003).

Harvey, G., 'Fantasy in the Study of Religions: Paganism as Observed and Enhanced by Terry Pratchett', *Discus* 6 (2000), <http://www.uni-marburg.de/religionswissenschaft/journal/diskus>

—'Heathenism: A North European Tradition', in Harvey and Hardman (eds.), *Paganism Today*, 49–64.

—*Listening People, Speaking Earth: Contemporary Paganism* (London: Hurst, 1997).

—'Satanism in Britain Today', *Journal of Contemporary Religion* 10 (1995), 283–96.

Harvey, G. (ed.), *Indigenous Religions: A Companion* (London: Cassell/Continuum, 2000).

—*Readings in Indigenous Religions* (London: Continuum, 2002).

Harvey, G., and C. Hardman (eds.), *Paganism Today: Wiccans, Druids, the Goddess and Ancient Earth Traditions for the Twenty-First Century* (London: Thorsons, 1995).

Harvey, P., *An Introduction to Buddhism: Teachings, History and Practices* (Cambridge: Cambridge University Press, 1990).

Hay, D., *Exploring Inner Space: Scientists and Religious Experience* (Harmondsworth: Penguin, 1982).

—*Religious Experience Today: Studying the Facts* (London: Mowbray, 1990).

Hay, P., *A Companion to Environmental Thought* (Edinburgh: Edinburgh University Press, 2002).

Hebdige, D., *Subculture: The Meaning of Style* (London: Routledge, 1979).

Hedges, E., and J.A. Beckford, 'Holism, Healing, and the New Age', in Sutcliffe and Bowman (eds.), *Beyond New Age*, 169–87.

Heelas, P., 'Expressive Spirituality and Humanistic Expressivism', in Sutcliffe and Bowman (eds.), *Beyond New Age*, 237–54.

—'Foreword', in Partridge (ed.), *UFO Religions*, pp. xiv–xv.

—'The Limits of Consumption on the Post-Modern "Religion" of the New Age', in Keat, Whiteley and Abercrombie (eds.), *The Authority of the Consumer*, 102–15.

—'The New Age in Cultural Context: The Premodern, the Modern, and the Postmodern', *Religion* 23 (1993), 103–16.

—*The New Age Movement: The Celebration of the Self and the Sacralization of Modernity* (Oxford: Blackwell, 1996).

—'Prosperity and the New Age Movement: The Efficacy of Spiritual Economics', in Wilson and Cresswell (eds.), *New Religious Movements*, 51–78.

—'The Sacralization of the Self and New Age Capitalism', in Abercrombie and Warde (eds.), *Social Change in Contemporary Britain*, 139–66.

—'The Spiritual Revolution: From "Religion" to "Spirituality"', in Woodhead *et al.* (eds.), *Religions in the Modern World*, 357–78.

Heelas, P. (ed.), *Religion, Modernity and Postmodernity* (Oxford: Blackwell, 1998).

Heelas, P., S. Lash, and P. Morris (eds.), *Detraditionalization: Critical Reflections on Authority and Identity* (Oxford: Blackwell, 1996).

Heelas, P., and B. Seel, 'An Ageing New Age?', in Davie *et al.* (eds.), *Predicting Religion*, 229–47.

Hefner, R.W., 'Secularization and Citizenship in Muslim Indonesia', in Heelas (ed.), *Religion, Modernity, and Postmodernity*, 147–68.

Hegel, G.W.F., *The Phenomenology of Spirit*, trans. A.V. Miller (Oxford: Oxford University Press, 1977).

Hermetica, trans. B. Copenhaver (Cambridge: Cambridge University Press, 1992).

Hetherington, K., *The Badlands of Modernity: Heterotopia and Social Ordering* (London: Routledge, 1996).

—*New Age Travellers: Vanloads of Uproarious Humanity* (London: Cassell, 2000).

—'Stonehenge and its Festival: Spaces of Consumption', in Shields (ed.), *Lifestyle Shopping*, 83–98.

Hilborn, D. (ed.), *'Toronto' in Perspective: Papers on the New Charismatic Wave of the Mid-1990s* (Carlisle: Paternoster Press, 2001).

Hill, M. (ed.), *Sociological Yearbook of Religion in Britain 5* (London: SCM, 1972).

Hocking, W.E., *Living Religions and a World Faith* (London: George Allen and Unwin, 1940).

Hoek, D.J., *Steve Reich: A Bio-Bibliography* (Westport, Conn.: Greenwood Press, 2002).

Hoekema, A.A., *The Four Major Cults: Christian Science, Jehovah's Witnesses, Mormonism, Seventh-Day Adventism* (Exeter: Paternoster Press, 1963).

Hogue, J., *Nostradamus: The Complete Prophecies* (Shaftesbury: Element, 1999).

—*Nostradamus: The New Millennium* (Shaftesbury: Element, 2002).

—*Nostradamus: New Revelations* (Shaftesbury: Element, 1994).

Howard, M., 'The Bright and the Dark', *Pagan Dawn* 133 (Samhain 1999), 30–1.

Hughes, D., 'Mysticism: The Perennial Philosophy?', in Partridge and Gabriel (eds.), *Mysticism East and West*, 306–24.

Hume, L., 'Doofs and Raves in Australia', in Partridge (ed.), *Encyclopedia of New Religions*, 416–18.

—'Jasmuheen and the Breatharians', in Partridge (ed.), *Encyclopedia of New Religions*, 354–5.

—*Witchcraft and Paganism in Australia* (Victoria: Melbourne University Press, 1997).

Hummel, R., 'Contemporary New Religions in the West', in Brockway and Rajashekar (eds.), *New Religious Movements and the Churches*, 16–29.

Hunt, K., 'Understanding the Spirituality of People Who Do Not Go to Church', in Davie *et al.* (eds.), *Predicting Religion*, 159–69.

Hunt, S., *Alternative Religions: A Sociological Introduction* (Aldershot: Ashgate, 2003).

Hutson, S., 'Technoshamanism: Spiritual Healing in the Rave Subculture', *Popular Music and Society* 23 (1999), 53–77.

Hutton, R., *The Triumph of the Moon: A History of Modern Pagan Witchcraft* (Oxford: Oxford University Press, 1999).

Huxley, A., *The Doors of Perception and Heaven and Hell* (London: Flamingo, 1994).

—*The Perennial Philosophy* (London: Chatto and Windus, 1946).

—'A Visionary Prediction', in Haining (ed.), *The Walls of Illusion*, 210–21.

Icke, D., *The Biggest Secret* (Scottsdale, Ariz.: Bridge of Love, 1999).

—*Children of the Matrix* (Scottsdale, Ariz.: Bridge of Love, 2001).

—'The Reptilian Connection', <http://www.davidicke.com/icke/temp/reptconn.html> (accessed: 6 Jan. 2003).

Insectoid, 'Aboriginal Sites, Australia', in Deckker (ed.), *Sacred Sites*, 48–50.

Introvigne, M., 'The Gothic Milieu: Black Metal, Satanism, and Vampires', in Kaplan and Lööw (eds.), *The Cultic Milieu*, 138–51.

Irons, E., 'Suma Ching Hai', in Partridge (ed.), *Encyclopedia of New Religions*, 263–5.

Irvin, J., 'Into Tomorrow', *Mojo: Special Limited Edition – 1000 Days that Shook the World* (2002), 45.

Jantzen, G., 'Mysticism and New Religious Movements', *Religion Today* 5:3 (1988), 10–12.

Jenkins, P., *The Next Christendom: The Coming of Global Christianity* (New York: Oxford University Press, 2002).

—'Satanism and Ritual Abuse', in Lewis (ed.), *The Oxford Handbook of New Religious Movements*, 221–42.

Jolly, K.L., *Popular Religion in Late Saxon England: Elf Charms in Context* (Chapel Hill: University of North Carolina Press, 1996).

Jorgensen, D.L., and S.E. Russell, 'American Neopaganism: The Participants' Social Identities', *Journal for the Scientific Study of Religion* 38 (1999), 325–38.

Jowell, R., *et al.* (eds.), *British Social Attitudes: The 9th Report* (Aldershot: Dartmouth Publishing, 1992).

—*British Social Attitudes: The 11th Report* (Aldershot: Dartmouth, 1994).

—*British (and European) Social Attitudes. How Britain Differs: The 15th Report* (Aldershot: Ashgate, 1998).

—*British Social Attitudes: The 17th Report* (London: Sage, 2000).

Juergensmeyer, M., 'Thinking Globally about Religion', in Juergensmeyer (ed.), *Global Religions*, 3–13.

Juergensmeyer, M. (ed.), *Global Religions: An Introduction* (Oxford: Oxford University Press, 2003).

Kane, P., 'In Thrall to New Age Thrills', *Guardian*, 4 Jan. 1995, sect. 2, p. 13.

Kaplan, J., 'The Postwar Paths of Occult National Socialism: From Rockwell and Madole to Manson', in Kaplan and Lööw (eds.), *The Cultic Milieu*, 225–64.

Kaplan, J., and H. Lööw, 'Introduction', in Kaplan and Lööw (eds.), *The Cultic Milieu*, 1–11.

Kaplan, J., and H. Lööw (eds.), *The Cultic Milieu: Oppositional Subcultures in an Age of Globalization* (Oxford: AltaMira Press, 2002).

Karaflogka, A., 'Religion On – Religion in Cyberspace', in Davie *et al.* (eds.), *Predicting Religion*, 191–202.

Kaufmann, W. (ed.), *The Portable Nietzsche* (New York: Viking Press, 1954).

Kaveney, R. (ed.), *Reading the Vampire Slayer: An Unofficial Critical Companion to Buffy and Angel* (London: Tauris Parke, 2001).

Keat, R., N. Whiteley and N. Abercrombie (eds.), *The Authority of the Consumer* (London: Routledge, 1994).

Keel, J., *The Cosmic Question* (Frogmore: Granada, 1978).

Kersten, H., *Jesus Lived in India* (Shaftesbury: Element, 1994).

Kieckhefer, R., *Magic in the Middle Ages* (Cambridge: Cambridge University Press, 1989).

Kieckhefer, R., and G.D. Bond (eds.), *Sainthood: Its Manifestations in the World Religions* (Berkeley: University of California Press, 1988).

Kilmister, L., *White Line Fever: The Autobiography* (London: Simon and Schuster, 2002).

King, U., *Christ in All Things: Exploring Spirituality with Teilhard de Chardin* (London: SCM, 1997).

—*Towards a New Mysticism: Teilhard de Chardin and Eastern Religions* (London: Collins, 1980).

Klostermair, K., *A Survey of Hinduism*, 2nd edn (Albany, NY: State University of New York Press, 1994).

Knight, G., *A Practical Guide to Qabalistic Symbolism*, 2 vols. (Cheltenham: Helios, 1965).

Knight, P., *Conspiracy Culture: From Kennedy to The X-Files* (London: Routledge, 2000).

Kozinets, R.V., and J.F. Sherry, 'Dancing on Common Ground: Exploring the Sacred at Burning Man', in St John (ed.), *Rave Culture and Religion*, 287–303.

Kreitzer, L.J., 'The Scandal of the Cross: Crucifixion Imagery and Bram Stoker's *Dracula*', in Aichele and Pippin (eds.), *The Monstrous and the Unspeakable*, 181–219.

Krus, D.J., and H.S. Blackman, 'East–West Dimensions of Ideology Measured by Transtemporal Cognitive Matching', *Psychological Reports* 47 (1980), 947–55.

Lamond, F., *Religion Without Beliefs: Essays in Pantheist Theology, Comparative Religion and Ethics* (London: Janus Publishing, 1997).

Landon, R., 'What is FOPI?', <http://www.fopi.net> (accessed 3 Aug. 2003).

Larson, B., *Larson's Book of Cults* (Wheaton, Ill.: Tyndale House, 1989).

Lau, K., *New Age Capitalism: Making Money East of Eden* (Philadelphia: University of Pennsylvania Press, 2000).

Laurant, J.-P., 'The Primitive Characteristics of Nineteenth-Century Esotericism', in Faivre and Needleman (eds.), *Modern Esoteric Spirituality*, 277–87.

Lavery, D., ' "Emotional Resonance and Rocket Launchers": Joss Whedon's Commentaries on the *Buffy the Vampire Slayer* DVDs', *Slayage: The Online International Journal of Buffy Studies* 6 (Sept. 2002): <http://www.slayage.tv/essays/slayage6/lavery.htm>.

—' "A Religion in Narrative": Joss Whedon and Television Creativity', *Slayage: The Online International Journal of Buffy Studies* 7 (Dec. 2002): <http://www.slayage.tv/essays/slayage7/lavery.htm>.

Lavery, D., A. Hague and M. Cartwright, 'Introduction: Generation X – *The X-Files* and the Cultural Moment', in Lavery *et al.* (eds.), *Deny All Knowledge*, 1–21.

Lavery, D., A. Hague and M. Cartwright (eds.), *Deny All Knowledge: Reading* The X-Files (London: Faber & Faber, 1996).

Lavery, D., and R. Wilcox (eds.), *Encyclopedia of Buffy Studies*, <http://www.slayage.tv/EBS>.

LaVey, A.S., *The Devil's Notebook* (Portland: Feral House, 1992).

—*The Satanic Bible* (New York: Avon Books, 1969).

—*The Satanic Rituals* (New York: Avon Books, 1972).

—*Satan Speaks* (Portland: Feral House, 1998).

Leary, T., *Flashbacks: An Autobiography* (New York: Tarcher/Putnam, 1990).

—*Your Brain is God* (Berkeley: Ronin Publishing, 2001).

Leary, T., R. Metzner and R. Alpert, *The Psychedelic Experience: A Manual Based on the Tibetan Book of the Dead* (New Hyde Park, NY: University Books, 1964).

Lee, M.F., *Earth First! Environmental Apocalypse* (Syracuse: Syracuse University Press, 1995).

Leeuw, G. van der, *Religion in Essence and Manifestation*, trans. J.E. Turner (Princeton: Princeton University Press, 1986).

Lehmann, A.C., and J.E. Myers (eds.), *Magic, Witchcraft and Religion: An Anthropological Study of the Supernatural* (Mountain View, Calif.: Mayfield Publishing Co., 1997).

Le Rider, J., *Modernity and Crises of Identity: Culture and Society in Fin de Siècle Vienna* (Cambridge: Polity Press, 1993).

Letcher, A., 'Eco-Paganism: Protest Movement Spiritualities', in Partridge (ed.), *Encyclopedia of New Religions*, 300–2.

—' "Gaia Told Me To Do It": Resistance and the Idea of Nature within Contemporary British Eco-Paganism', *Ecotheology: The Journal of Religion, Nature and the Environment* 8 (2003), 61–84.

Lewis, J.R., *The Gods Have Landed: New Religions from Other Worlds* (Albany: State University of New York Press, 1995).

—*Legitimating New Religions* (New Brunswick, NY: Rutgers University Press, 2003).

—'Legitimating Suicide: Heaven's Gate and New Age Ideology', in Partridge (ed.), *UFO Religions*, 103–28.

Lewis, J.R. (ed.), *Magical Religion and Modern Witchcraft* (Albany: State University of New York Press, 1996).

—*The Oxford Handbook of New Religious Movements* (New York: Oxford University Press, 2004).

Lindbeck, G., *Nature of Doctrine: Religion and Theology in a Postliberal Age* (London: SPCK, 1984).

Longhurst, B., *Popular Music and Society* (Oxford: Polity, 1995).

Lööw, H., 'The Idea of Purity: The Swedish Racist Counterculture, Animal Rights and Environmental Protection', in Kaplan and Lööw (eds.), *The Cultic Milieu*, 193–210.

Luhrmann, T., *Persuasions of the Witch's Craft: Ritual Magic in Contemporary England* (Cambridge, Mass.: Harvard University Press, 1991).

Lynch, G., *After Religion: 'Generation X' and the Search for Meaning* (London: Darton, Longman and Todd, 2002).

Lyon, D., *Jesus in Disneyland: Religion in Postmodern Times* (Cambridge: Polity Press, 2000).

MacDonald, I., 'The Psychedelic Experience', *Mojo: Special Limited Edition – 1000 Days that Shook the World* (2002), 30–6.

—*A Revolution in the Head: The Beatles Records and the Sixties*, 2nd edn (London: Pimlico, 1998).

MacGregor, G., 'Is Reincarnation Compatible with Christian Faith?', in Berger and Berger (eds.), *Reincarnation*, 89–98.

—*Reincarnation in Christianity* (Wheaton, Ill.: Theosophical Publishing House, 1978).

MacLaine, S., *Going Within* (London: Bantam Books, 1990).

Maclean, D., 'Devas', in Bloom (ed.), *The New Age*, 180–2.

Mack, B.L., *The Lost Gospel* (Shaftesbury: Element, 1994).

Mack, J.E., *Abduction: Human Encounters with Aliens* (London: Simon & Schuster, 1994).

MacNicol, N., *Is Christianity Unique? A Comparative Study of the Religions* (London: SCM, 1936).

Main, R., 'Religion, Science and the New Age', in Pearson (ed.), *Belief Beyond Boundaries*, 192–214.

Malbon, B., *Clubbing: Dancing, Ecstasy, and Vitality* (London: Routledge, 1999).

Martin, D., 'The Denomination', *British Journal of Sociology* 12 (1962), 1–13.

—'The Evangelical Upsurge and its Political Implications', in Berger (ed.), *The Desecularization of the World*, 37–49.

—*A General Theory of Secularization* (Aldershot: Gregg Revivals, 1978).

—'On Secularization and its Prediction: A Self-Examination', in Davie *et al.* (eds.), *Predicting Religion*, 30–9.

—*Pentecostalism: The World Their Parish* (Oxford: Blackwell, 2002).

—*The Religious and the Secular: Studies in Secularization* (London: Routledge and Kegan Paul, 1969).

Marty, M., 'The Occult Establishment', *Social Research* 37 (1970), 212–23.

Marwick, A., *The Sixties: Cultural Revolution in Britain, France, Italy, and the United States c.1958–c.1974* (Oxford: Oxford University Press, 1998).

Mathers, S.L.M., *The Kabbalah Unveiled* (New York: Weiser, 1968).

Matthews, J. (ed.), *The Celtic Seers Source Book: Vision and Magic in the Druid Tradition* (London: Blandford, 1999).

—*The World Atlas of Divination: The Systems, Where They Originate, How they Work* (Twickenham: Tiger Books International, 1998).

Maurice, F.D., *The Religions of the World in Their Relations to Christianity* (London: Macmillan, 1886).

May, S., *Stardust and Ashes: Science Fiction in Christian Perspective* (London: SPCK, 1998).

Mayer, J.-F., 'The Emergence of a New Religiosity in the Western World', in Brockway and Rajasheker (eds.), *New Religious Movements and the Churches*, 60–8.

Mazur, E.M., and K. McCarthy (eds.), *God in the Details: American Religion in Popular Culture* (New York: Routledge, 2001).

McCartney, L., *Linda's Pictures: A Collection of Photographs* (New York: Ballantine Books, 1977).

McCulloch, G., *The Deconstruction of Dualism in Theology: With Special Reference to Ecofeminist Theology and New Age Spirituality* (Carlisle: Paternoster Press, 2002).

McGuigan, J., *Modernity and Postmodern Culture* (Buckingham: Open University Press, 1999).

McIntosh, M., *Mystical Theology* (Oxford: Blackwell, 1998).

McLaughlin, C., 'How to Evaluate Channelling', in Bloom (ed.), *The New Age*, 51–5.

McKay, G., *Glastonbury: A Very English Affair* (London: Victor Gollancz, 2000).

—*Senseless Acts of Beauty: Cultures of Resistance since the Sixties* (London: Verso, 1996).

McKay, G. (ed.), *DIY Culture: Party and Protest in Nineties Britain* (London: Verso, 1998).

McKenna, T., *The Archaic Revival: Speculations on Psychedelic Mushrooms, the Amazon, Virtual Reality, UFOs, Evolution, Shamanism, the Rebirth of the Goddess, and the End of History* (San Francisco: Harper, 1991).

—*Food of the Gods* (London: Rider, 1999).

McRitchie, J.K., 'A Critique of Evangelical Understandings of Satanism', unpub. M.Th. diss., Chester College, 2001.

Meadows, K., *Where Eagles Fly: A Shamanic Way to Inner Wisdom* (Shaftesbury: Element, 1995).

Meek, D.E., *The Quest for Celtic Christianity* (Edinburgh: Handsel Press, 2000).

Melechi, A. (ed.), *Psychedelia Britannica: Hallucinogenic Drugs in Britain* (London: Turnaround, 1997).

Mellers, W., *Twilight of the Gods: The Beatles in Retrospect* (London: Faber and Faber, 1976).

Melton, J.G., *The Church of Scientology* (Turin: Signature Books, 2000).

—'The Contactees: A Survey', in Lewis (ed.), *The Gods Have Landed*, 1–14.

—*The Vampire Book: The Encyclopedia of the Undead* (Detroit: Visible Ink Press, 1999).

Melton, J.G., J. Clark and A.A. Kelly, *New Age Almanac* (New York: Visible Ink, 1991).

Michell, J., 'The New View Over Atlantis', in Bloom (ed.), *Holistic Revolution*, 138–42.

—*The View Over Atlantis* (London: Abacus, 1973).

Middleton, R., *Studying Popular Music* (Milton Keynes: Open University Press, 1990).

Milbank, J., *Theology and Social Theory* (Oxford: Blackwell, 1990).

Miller, D.E., and A.M. Miller, 'Understanding Generation X: Values, Politics, and Religious Commitments', in Flory and Miller (eds.), *Gen X Religion*, 1–12.

Miller, G.H., *10,000 Dreams Interpreted: An Illustrated Guide to Unlocking the Secrets of Your Dreamlife* (Shaftesbury: Element, 1999).

Miller, T., *The 60s Communes: Hippies and Beyond* (Syracuse: Syracuse University Press, 1999).

Miller, T. (ed.), *America's Alternative Religions* (Albany: State University of New York Press, 1995).

Mitchell, S., *Naturopathy: Understanding the Healing Power of Nature* (Shaftesbury: Element, 1999).

Morrison, K.M., 'The Cosmos as Intersubjective: Native American Other-Than-Human Persons', in Harvey (ed.), *Indigenous Religions*, 23–36.

Neal, C., *Tape Delay* (Wembley: SAF Publications, 1987).

Neill, S., *Christian Faith and Other Faiths: the Christian Dialogue with Other Religions*, 2nd edn (Oxford: Oxford University Press, 1970).

Nelson, G.K., *Cults, New Religions and Religious Creativity* (London: Routledge and Kegan Paul, 1987).

Niebuhr, H.R., *The Social Sources of Denominationalism* (New York: Meridian Books, 1957).

Niesel, W., *Reformed Symbolics: A Comparison of Catholicism, Orthodoxy, and Protestantism*, trans. D. Lewis (Edinburgh: Oliver and Boyd, 1962).

Nietzsche, F.W., *Thus Spoke Zarathustra*, trans. R.J. Hollingdale (Harmondworth: Penguin, 1961).

Nisbet, R., *History of the Idea of Progress* (London: Heinemann, 1980).

NME, 'The Pyramid', in *Glastonbury: A Celebration of the World's Greatest Festival – NME Special* (2003), 10.

NME, 'Time Line: A History of the Glastonbury Festival', in *Glastonbury: A Celebration of the World's Greatest Festival – NME Special* (2003), 12–15.

Obeyesekere, G., 'Buddhism', in Juergensmeyer (ed.), *Global Religions*, 63–77.

O'Connor, M.R., 'God is a DJ: Robbie Wootton has a Vision for Spiritual Nightlife from NYC to Shanghai', *What is Enlightenment?* 24 (Feb.–Apr. 2004), 20–2.

Ohmann, R. (ed.), *Selling Culture: Magazines, Markets and Class at the Turn of the Century* (Hanover, NH: Wesleyan University Press, 1996).

Oliver, P. (ed.), *Black Music in Britain: Essays on the Afro-Asian Contribution to Popular Music* (Milton Keynes: Open University Press, 1990).

Osborne, B., *The A–Z of Club Culture* (London: Sceptre, 1999).

Ostwalt, C., *Secular Steeples: Popular Culture and the Religious Imagination* (Harrisburg, Pa.: Trinity Press International, 2003).

Otto, R., *Mysticism East and West: A Comparative Analysis of the Nature of Mysticism*, trans. B.L. Bracey and R.C. Payne (New York: Living Age Books, 1957).

Pagan Federation, *Information Pack*, 4th edn (London: Pagan Federation, 1996).

Partridge, C., 'Alternative Spiritualities, New Religions and the Re-Enchantment of the West', in Lewis (ed.), *The Oxford Handbook of New Religious Movements*, 39–67.

—*H.H. Farmer's Theological Interpretation of Religion: Towards a Personalist Theology of Religions* (Lewiston, NY: Edwin Mellen, 1998).

—'Pagan Fundamentalism?', in Partridge (ed.), *Fundamentalisms*, 155–80.

—'Sacred Chemicals? Psychedelic Drugs and Mystical Experience', in Partridge and Gabriel (eds.), *Mysticisms East and West*, 96–131.

—'The Temple of the Vampire', in Partridge (ed.), *Encyclopedia of New Religions*, 353–4.

—'Truth, Authority and Epistemological Individualism in New Age Thought', *Journal of Contemporary Religion* 14 (1999), 77–95.

—'Understanding UFO Religions and Abduction Spiritualities', in Partridge (ed.), *UFO Religions*, 3–42.

Partridge, C. (ed.), *Dictionary of Contemporary Religion in the Western World* (Leicester: IVP, 2002).

—*Encyclopedia of New Religions: New Religious Movements, Sects and Alternative Spiritualities* (Oxford: Lion Publishing, 2004); pub. in US as *New Religions: A Guide* (New York: Oxford University Press, 2004).

—*Fundamentalisms* (Carlisle: Paternoster Press, 2001).

—*UFO Religions* (London: Routledge, 2003).

Partridge, C., and M. Elliot, 'The Spiritual Nature of Human Beings', in Elliot (ed.), *The Dynamics of Human Life*, 117–73.

Partridge, C., and T. Gabriel (eds.), *Mysticisms East and West: Studies in Mystical Experience* (Carlisle: Paternoster Press, 2003).

Pearson, J., 'Witchcraft Will Not Soon Vanish from this Earth: Wicca in the 21st Century', in Davie *et al.* (eds.), *Predicting Religion*, 170–82.

—'Witches and Wicca', in Pearson (ed.), *Belief Beyond Boundaries*, 133–72.

Pearson, J., (ed.), *Belief Beyond Boundaries: Wicca, Celtic Spirituality and the New Age* (Aldershot: Ashgate/Open University, 2002).

Pendleton, R., 'Kindred Spirits', in Whittaker (ed.), *beGLAD*, 68–82.

Percy, M., 'A Place at High Table? Assessing the Future of Charismatic Christianity', in Davie *et al.* (eds.), *Predicting Religion*, 95–108.

Perry, M., *Gods Within: A Critical Guide to the New Age* (London: SPCK, 1992).

Pike, S., 'Desert Goddesses and Apocalyptic Art: Making Sacred Space at the Burning Man Festival', in Mazur and McCarthy (eds.), *God in the Details*, 155–76.

—*Earthly Bodies, Magical Selves: Contemporary Pagans and the Search for Community* (Berkeley: University of California Press, 2001).

Pilgrim, G., 'The Quakers: Towards an Alternate Ordering', in Davie *et al.* (eds.), *Predicting Religion*, 147–58.

Playden, Z.-J., 'What You Are, What's To Come: Feminisms, Citizenship and the Divine', in Kaveney (ed.), *Reading the Vampire Slayer*, 120–47.

Plows, A., 'Earth First! Defending Mother Earth, Direct-Style', in McKay, *DIY Culture*, 152–73.

Possamaï, A., 'Alternative Spiritualities and the Cultural Logic of Late Capitalism', *Culture and Religion* 4 (2003), 31–45.

—'Cultural Consumption of History and Popular Culture in Alternative Spiritualities', *Journal of Consumer Culture* 2 (2002), 197–218.

—'Not the New Age: Perennism and Spiritual Knowledges', *Australian Religion Studies Review* 14 (2001), 82–96.

Potash, C. (ed.), *Reggae, Rasta, Revolution: Jamaican Music from Ska to Dub* (London: Books With Attitude, 1997).

Potts, G.H., 'Imagining Gaia: Perspectives and Prospects on Gaia, Science and Religion', *Ecotheology: The Journal of Religion, Nature and the Environment* 8 (2003), 30–49.

Power, M., *David Sylvian: The Last Romantic* (London: Omnibus Press, 2000).

Prendergast, M., *The Ambient Century: From Mahler to Trance – the Evolution of Sound in the Electronic Age* (London: Bloomsbury, 2000).

Radhakrishnan, S., *Eastern Religions and Western Thought* (Oxford: Oxford University Press, 1940).

Rankin-Box, D., *The Nurses' Handbook of Complementary Therapies* (Edinburgh: Bailliere Tindall/Royal College of Nursing, 2001).

RavenWolf, S., *Teen Witch: Wicca for a New Generation* (St Paul: Llewellyn, 1998).

Rawlinson, A., *The Book of Enlightened Masters: Western Teachers in Eastern Traditions* (Chicago: Open Court, 1997).

Reardon, B.M.G., *Religion in the Age of Romanticism* (Cambridge: Cambridge University Press, 1985).

Regardie, I., *The Tree of Life* (Wellingborough: Aquarian, 1969).

Reynolds, S., 'Back to Eden: Innocence, Indolence and Pastoralism in Psychedelic Music, 1966–1996', in Melechi (ed.), *Psychedelia Britannica*, 143–65.

—*Energy Flash: A Journey through Rave Music and Dance Culture* (London: Picador, 1998).

Rice, A., *Interview with the Vampire* (New York: Ballantine Books, 1988).

Richards, G., *Studies in Religion: A Comparative Approach to Theological and Philosophical Themes* (New York: St Martin's Press, 1995).

Richards, G. (ed.), *A Source-Book of Modern Hinduism* (London: Curzon Press, 1985).

Richardson, J.T., 'Studies of Conversion: Secularization or Re-Enchantment?', in Hammond (ed.), *The Sacred in a Secular Age*, 104–21.

Rietveld, H.C., *This is Our House: House Music, Cultural Spaces and Technologies* (Aldershot: Ashgate, 1998).

Rigby, A., and B.S. Turner, 'Findhorn Community, Centre of Light: A Sociological Study of New Forms of Religion', in Hill (ed.), *Sociological Yearbook of Religion in Britain 5*, 72–86.

Ritzer, G., *The McDonaldization of Society*, new century edn (Thousand Oaks, Calif.: Pine Forge Press, 2000).

Robbins, T., and D. Anthony (eds.), *In Gods We Trust: New Patterns of Religious Pluralism in America* (New Brunswick, NY: Transaction Publishers, 1991).

Roberts, R.H., *Religion, Theology and the Human Sciences* (Cambridge: Cambridge University Press, 2002).

Robertson, Roland, 'Antiglobal Religion', in Juergensmeyer (ed.), *Global Religions*, 110–23.

Robertson, Ross, *The Sociological Interpretation of Religion* (Oxford: Blackwell, 1970).

—'Naked on Stilts: Notes from Burning Man', *What is Enlightenment?* 24 (Feb.– Apr. 2004), 25–8.

Roof, W.C., *Spiritual Marketplace: Baby Boomers and the Remaking of American Religion* (Princeton: Princeton University Press, 1999).

Rose, S., 'An Examination of the New Age Movement: Who is Involved and What Constitutes its Spirituality', *Journal of Contemporary Religion* 13 (1998), 5–22.

Roth, G., *Maps to Ecstasy: Teachings of an Urban Shaman* (London: Mandala, 1990).

Ruether, R.R., *Gaia and God: An Ecofeminist Theology of Earth Healing* (London: SCM, 1992).

Rushkoff, D., *Cyberia: Life in the Trenches of Hyperspace*, 2nd edn (Manchester: Clinamen Press, 2002).

—'Foreword', in St John (ed.), *Rave Culture and Religion*, pp. xiii–xv.

Russell, P., *The TM Technique: A Skeptic's Guide to the TM Program* (Boston: Routledge and Kegan Paul, 1976).

Sabin, R., '"I Won't Let That Dago By": Rethinking Punk and Racism', in Sabin (ed.), *Punk Rock*, 199–218.

Sabin, R. (ed.), *Punk Rock: So What?* (London: Routledge, 1999).

St John, G., 'Introduction', in St John (ed.), *Rave Culture and Religion*, 1–15.

St John, G. (ed.), *FreeNRG: Notes from the Edge of the Dance Floor* (Altona, Australia: Common Ground, 2001).

—*Rave Culture and Religion* (London: Routledge, 2003).

Saliba, J., 'Religious Dimensions of UFO Phenomena', in Lewis (ed.), *The Gods Have Landed*, 15–65.

Salomonsen, J., *Enchanted Feminism: The Reclaiming Witches of San Francisco* (London: Routledge, 2002).

Sanders, H., 'Why are the Young Attracted to the Goddess?', <http://homepage.ntlworld.com/sam.levett/witchwords/goddess.htm> (accessed 2 Dec. 2003).

Sanders, J.O., *Heresies and Cults* (London: Lakeland, 1969).

Sandford, J., and R. Reid, *Tomorrow's People* (London: Jerome Publishing, 1974).

Savitra, *Auroville: Sun-Word Rising. A Trust for the Earth* (Auroville, India: Community of Auroville, 1980).

Schleiermacher, F.D.E., *The Christian Faith*, trans. H.R. Mackintosh and J.S. Stewart (Edinburgh: T. and T. Clark, 1928).

—*On Religion: Speeches to its Cultured Despisers*, trans. J. Oman (New York: Harper and Row, 1958).

Schuon, F., *The Transcendent Unity of Religions*, trans. P. Townsend (London: Faber and Faber, 1953).

Scott, K.L. (ed.), *The Dark Shadows Companion* (Los Angeles: Pomegranate, 1990).

Seager, R.H., *The World's Parliament of Religions: The East/West Encounter, Chicago 1893* (Bloomington, Ind.: Indiana University Press, 1995).

Sell, A.P.F., *The Philosophy of Religion 1875–1980* (London: Croom Helm, 1988).

Sharma, C., *A Critical Survey of Indian Philosophy* (London: Rider & Co., 1960).

Sharpe, E.J., *Comparative Religion: A History* (London: Duckworth, 1975).

—*Faith Meets Faith: Some Attitudes to Hinduism in the Nineteenth and Twentieth Centuries* (London: SCM, 1977).

Shields, R. (ed.), *Lifestyle Shopping* (London: Routledge, 1992).

Shiner, L., 'The Concept of Secularisation', *Journal for the Scientific Study of Religion* 6 (1967), 207–20.

Simonelli, F.J., 'Thriving in a Cultic Milieu: The World Union of National Socialists 1962–1992', in Kaplan and Lööw (eds.), *The Cultic Milieu*, 211–24.

Simpson, L., *The Healing Energies of the Earth* (Stroud: Gaia Books, 2000).

Singer, B., and V.A. Benassi, 'Occult Beliefs', in Lehmann and Myers (eds.), *Magic, Witchcraft and Religion*, 384–92; 1st publ. in *American Scientist* 69 (1981), 49–55.

Sjödin, U., 'The Paranormal in Swedish Religiosity', in Davie *et al.* (eds.), *Predicting Religion*, 203–13.

Skippy, R., '*The Door* Theologian of the Year', *The Door Magazine* 183 (2002), <http://www.thedoormagazine.com/archives/buffy.html>.

Smart, N., 'The Global Future of Religion', in Juergensmeyer (ed.), *Global Religions*, 124–31.

Smith, A., 'Burning Man', *Festival Eye*, 2003, 23.

Smith, D.W., *Against the Stream: Christianity and Mission in an Age of Globalization* (Leicester: IVP, 2003).

Smutts, J.C., *Holism and Evolution* (London: Macmillan, 1926).

Spangler, D., 'The New Age: The Movement toward the Divine', in Ferguson (ed.), *New Age Spirituality*, 79–105.

Spencer, W., 'Are the Stars Coming Out? Secularization and the Future of Astrology in the West', in Davie *et al.* (eds.), *Predicting Religion*, 214–28.

Spink, P., *A Christian in the New Age* (London: Darton, Longman and Todd, 1991).

Spretnak, C., 'The Spiritual Dimension of Green Politics', in Spretnak and Capra (eds.), *Green Politics*, 230–58.

Spretnak, C., and F. Capra (eds.), *Green Politics: The Global Promise* (London: Paladin, 1985).

Springhouse Corporation, *Nurse's Handbook of Alternative and Complementary Therapies* (Springhouse, Pa.: Springhouse Corporation, 1999).

Starhawk, *Dreaming the Dark: Magic, Sex and Politics*, 15th anniversary edn (Boston: Beacon Press, 1997).

—*The Spiral Dance: A Rebirth of the Ancient Religion of the Great Goddess* (New York: Harper and Row, 1979).

Stark, R., 'Modernization, Secularization, and Mormon Success', in Robbins and Anthony (eds.), *In Gods We Trust*, 201–18.

—'Rationality', in Braun and McCutcheon (eds.), *Guide to the Study of Religion*, 239–58.

Stark, R., and W.S. Bainbridge, *The Future of Religion: Secularization, Revival, and Cult Formation* (Berkeley: University of California Press, 1985).

Stark, R., and L.R. Iannacconne, 'A Supply-Side Reinterpretation of the "Secularization" of Europe', *Journal of the Scientific Study of Religion* 33 (1994), 230–52.

Starwoman, A., and D. Gray, *How to Turn Your Ex-Boyfriend into a Toad and Other Spells* (London: Thorsons, 1996).

Steenson, M., 'What is Burning Man?', <http://www.tedward.org/WhatIsBM.html> (accessed 9 Aug. 2003).

Stevens, J., *Storming Heaven: LSD and the American Dream* (London: Flamingo, 1993).

Stoker, B., *Dracula* (Oxford: Oxford University Press, 1982).

Straw, W., 'Characterizing Rock Music Culture: The Case of Heavy Metal', in During (ed.), *The Cultural Studies Reader*, 368–81.

Strong, M., *The Great Rock Discography*, 6th edn (Edinburgh: Canongate, 2002).

Stuart, J., 'The Home Counties Witch Project', *Independent on Sunda*, 7 May 2000, 20–2.

Surya Dass, 'What Does Being a Buddhist Mean to You?', *Tricycle: The Buddhist Review* 6.1 (Fall 1996), 43.

Sutcliffe, P., 'Go Forth and Rock', *Q* 140 (May 1998), 68–78.

Sutcliffe, S., 'A Colony of Seekers: Findhorn in the 1990s', *Journal of Contemporary Religion* 15 (2000), 215–32.

—*Children of the New Age: A History of Spiritual Practices* (London: Routledge, 2003).

Sutcliffe, S., and M. Bowman (eds.), *Beyond New Age: Exploring Alternative Spirituality* (Edinburgh: Edinburgh University Press, 2000).

Sutherland, S., and P. Clarke (eds.), *The World's Religions: The Study of Religion, Traditional and New Religions* (London: Routledge, 1988).

Swatos, W., 'Enchantment and Disenchantment in Modernity: The Significance of "Religion" as a Sociological Category', *Sociological Analysis* 44 (1983), 321–38.

Sylvan, R., *Traces of the Spirit: The Religious Dimensions of Popular Music* (New York: New York University Press, 2002).

Tamm, E., *Brian Eno: His Music and the Vertical Color of Sound* (Boston: Da Capo Press, 1995).

Taylor, B., 'Earth and Nature-Based Spirituality (Part 1): From Deep Ecology to Radical Environmentalism', *Religion* 31 (2001), 175–93.

—'Earth and Nature-Based Spirituality (Part 2): From Earth First! and Bioregionalism to Scientific Paganism and the New Age', *Religion* 31 (2001), 225–45.

Taylor, P., 'The Message of the Runes: Divination in the Ancient Germanic World', in Matthews (ed.), *World Atlas of Divination*, 33–44.

Teilhard de Chardin, P., *Le Milieu Divin*, trans. B. Wall (London: Fontana, 1964).

—*The Phenomenon of Man*, trans. B. Wall (London: Fontana, 1965).

Thomas, K., *Religion and the Decline of Magic: Studies in Popular Beliefs in Sixteenth and Seventeenth Century England* (Harmondsworth: Penguin, 1973).

Thomas, O. (ed.), *Attitudes toward Other Religions: Some Christian Interpretations* (London: SCM, 1969).

Thompson, J., and P. Heelas, *The Way of the Heart: The Rajneesh Movement* (Wellingborough: Aquarian, 1986).

Thornton, S., *Club Cultures: Music Media and Subcultural Capital* (Cambridge: Polity, 1995).

Tierney, B., and J.W. Scott (eds.), *Western Societies: A Documentary History*, Vol. 2, 2nd edn (Boston: McGraw Hill, 2000).

Tillich, P., *Christianity and the Encounter of the World Religions* (New York: Columbia University Press, 1963).

—*The Future of Religions* (New York: Harper and Row, 1966).

—*Ultimate Concern: Dialogue with Students*, ed. D.M. Brown (London: SCM, 1965).

Tingay, K., 'Madame Blavatsky's Children: Theosophy and its Heirs', in Sutcliffe and Bowman (eds.), *Beyond New Age*, 37–50; repr. in Pearson (ed.), *Belief Beyond Boundaries*, 239–50.

Tolkien, J.R.R., *The Lord of the Rings* (London: HarperCollins, 1991).

Too, L., *The Complete Illustrated Guide to Feng Shui: How to Apply the Secrets of Chinese Wisdom for Health, Wealth and Happiness* (Shaftesbury: Element, 1999).

Toop, D., *Ocean of Sound: Aether Talk, Ambient Sound and Imaginary Worlds* (London: Serpent's Tail, 1995).

TOPY, 'Occulture', <http://www.uncarved.demon.co.uk/23texts/topywest.html> (accessed 31 Aug. 2003).

—'TOPY London Interviewed by *AntiClockwise Magazine* 1991', <http://www.uncarved.org/23texts/clockwise.html> (accessed 31 Aug. 2003).

—'What is Occulture?', <http://www.uncarved.demon.co.uk/23texts/occulture.html> (accessed 31 Aug. 2003).

Tramacchi, D., 'Chaos Engines: Doofs, Psychedelics and Religious Experience', in St John (ed.), *FreeNRG*, 171–87.

—'Field Tripping: Psychedelic *communitas* and Ritual in the Australian Bush', *Journal of Contemporary Religion* 15 (2000), 201–13.

Traube, E., 'Introduction', in Ohmann (ed.), *Making and Selling Culture*, pp. xi–xxiii.

Trevelyan, G., *Exploration into God: A Personal Quest for Spiritual Unity* (Bath: Gateway, 1991).

Troeltsch, E., *The Social Teaching of the Christian Churches*, trans. O. Wyon, 2 vols (New York: Macmillan, 1931).

Truzzi, M., 'The Occult Revival as Popular Culture: Some Random Observations on the Old and the Nouveau Witch', *Sociological Quarterly* 13 (1972), 16–36.

Tumminia, D., 'When the Archangel Died: From Revelation to Routinisation of Charisma in Unarius', in Partridge (ed.), *UFO Religions*, 62–83.

Urban, H.B., 'The Beast with Two Backs: Aleister Crowley, Sex Magic, and the Exhaustion of Modernity', *Nova Religio: The Journal of Alternative and Emergent Religions* 7 (2004), 7–25.

Valiente, D., *An ABC of Witchcraft Past and Present* (London: Robert Hale, 1984).

Van Rhey, D., 'The Art of Burning Man', <http://www.burningman.com/art_of_burningman/art_of_bm.html> (accessed 9 Aug. 2003).

Wainwright, M., 'Church Fears Modern Beliefs are Undermining Traditional Values', *Guardian*, 7 Sept. 2001, 3.

—'Our Candid Cardinal: Empty Pews in an Age of DIY Spirituality', *Guardian*, 7 Sept. 2001, 19.

Walker, Andrew, *Telling the Story: Gospel, Mission, and Culture* (London: SPCK, 1996).

Walker, Andrew, and K. Aune (eds.), *On Revival: A Critical Examination* (Carlisle: Paternoster Press, 2003).

Walker, Ann, *The Stone and the Plough: The Search for the Secret of Giza* (Shaftesbury: Element, 1995).

Wallace-Murphy, T., and M. Hopkins, *Rosslyn: Guardian of the Secrets of the Holy Grail* (Shaftesbury: Element, 1999).

Wallis, R., *The Elementary Forms of the New Religious Life* (London: Routledge and Kegan Paul, 1984).

—'Ideology, Authority and the Development of Cultic Movements', *Sociological Research* 41 (1974), 299–327.

—*The Road to Total Freedom: A Sociological Analysis of Scientology* (London: Heinemann, 1976).

—'Scientology. Therapeutic Cult to Religious Sect', *Sociology* 9 (1975), 89–100.

Walpole, H., *The Castle of Otranto* (Oxford: Oxford University Press, 1998).

Walter, T., 'Reincarnation, Modernity and Identity', *Sociology* 35 (2001), 21–38.

Walter, T., and H. Waterhouse, 'Lives-Long Learning: The Effects of Reincarnation Belief on Everyday Life in England', *Religion* 5 (2001), 85–101.

—'A Very Private Belief: Reincarnation in Contemporary England', *Sociology of Religion* 60 (1999), 187–97.

Waterhouse, H., 'Reincarnation Belief in Britain: New Age Orientation or Mainstream Option?', *Journal of Contemporary Religion* 14 (1999), 97–110.

Watson, D., 'Beyond Evil', *The Wire* 182 (Apr. 1999), 30–5.

Weatherhead, L., *The Christian Agnostic* (London: Arthur James, 1989).

Weber, E., *Apocalypses: Prophets, Cults and Millennial Beliefs throughout the Ages* (London: Hutchinson, 1999).

—*France Fin de Siècle* (London: Harvard University Press, 1986).

Weber, M., 'The Meaning of Discipline', in Gerth and Mills (trans. and eds.), *From Max Weber*, 253–64.

—*The Protestant Ethic and the Spirit of Capitalism*, trans. T. Parsons (London: Allen and Unwin, 1930).

—'The Protestant Sects and the Spirit of Capitalism', in Gerth and Mills (trans. and eds.), *From Max Weber*, 302–22.

—'The Sociology of Charismatic Authority', in Gerth and Mills (trans. and eds.), *From Max Weber*, 245–52.

West, P., *The Complete Illustrated Guide to Palmistry: The Principles and Practice of Hand Reading Revealed* (Shaftesbury: Element, 1999).

Whale, J.S., *The Christian Answer to the Problem of Evil*, 4th edn (London: SCM, 1957).

White, V., 'Re-Enchanting the World: A Fresh Look at the God of Mystical Theology', *Theology* 103 (2000), 347–55.

Whiteley, S., 'Altered Sounds', in Melechi (ed.), *Psychedelia Britannica*, 120–42.

Whittaker, A. (ed.), *beGLAD: An Incredible String Band Compendium* (London: Helter Skelter, 2003).

Wilcock, D., 'The "Matrix" is a Reality', *New Dawn* 79 (July-Aug. 2003), 55–60.

Wilcox, ' "There Will Never Be a 'Very Special' *Buffy*": *Buffy* and the Monsters of Teen Life', *Journal of Popular Film and Television* 27 (1999), 16–23; reissued on *Slayage: the Online International Journal of Buffy Studies* 2 (Mar. 2001): <http://www.slayage.tv/essays/slayage2/wilcox.htm>.

Wilcox, R.V., and D. Lavery (eds.), *Fighting the Forces: What's at Stake in Buffy the Vampire Slayer* (Lanham, Md.: Rowman and Littlefield, 2003).

Wilding, P., 'Lucifer Rising', *Classic Rock* 31 (Sept. 2001), 52–9.

Williams, D., and K. West, *Born in Albion: The Re-Birth of the Craft* (Runcorn: Pagan Media, 1996).

Williams, Richard, 'The Sound Surprise', in Potash (ed.), *Reggae, Rasta, Revolution*, 145–8.

Williams, Rowan, 'Foreword', in Whittaker (ed.), *beGLAD*, 5–6.

Willin, M.J., 'Music and Paganism', *Pagan Dawn* 146 (Imbolc 2003), 42–3.

Willis, P., *Profane Culture* (London: Routledge and Kegan Paul, 1978).

Wilson, B.R., 'An Analysis of Sect Development', in Wilson (ed.), *Patterns of Sectarianism*, 22–45.

—*Contemporary Transformations of Religion* (Oxford: Oxford University Press, 1976).

—*Religion in Secular Society* (Harmondsworth: Penguin, 1966).

—*Religious Sects* (London: Weidenfeld and Nicolson, 1970).

—'Secularization: The Inherited Model', in Hammond (ed.), *The Sacred in a Secular Age*, 9–20.

—' "Secularization": Religion in the Modern World', in Sutherland and Clarke (eds.), *The World's Religions*, 195–208.

—*Social Change and New Religious Movements* (Los Angeles: Freedom Publishing, n.d.).

—*The Social Dimensions of Sectarianism: Sects and New Religious Movements in Contemporary Society* (Oxford: Oxford University Press, 1990).

—'The Westward Path of Buddhism', in *Buddhism Today: A Collection of Views from Contemporary Scholars* (Tokyo: Institute of Oriental Philosophy, 1990), 49–62.

Wilson, B.R. (ed.), *Patterns of Sectarianism: Organization and Ideology in Social and Religious Movements* (London: Heinemann, 1967).

Wilson, B.R., and J. Cresswell (eds.), *New Religious Movements: Challenge and Response* (London: Routledge, 1999).

Winslade, J.L., 'Teen Witches, Wiccans, and "Wanna-Blessed-Be's": Pop-Culture Magic in *Buffy the Vampire Slayer*', *Slayage: The Online International Journal of Buffy Studies* 1 (Jan. 2001) <http://www.slayage.tv/essays/slayage1/winslade.htm>.

Witherspoon, S., 'The Greening of Britain: Romance and Rationality', in Jowell *et al.* (eds.), *British Social Attitudes: The 11th Report*, 107–39.

Woodhead, L., 'Studying Religion and Modernity', in Woodhead *et al.* (eds.), *Religions in the Modern World*, 1–12.

—'The World's Parliament of Religions and the Rise of Alternative Spirituality', in Woodhead (ed.), *Reinventing Christianity*, 81–96.

Woodhead, L. (ed.), *Reinventing Christianity: Nineteenth-Century Contexts* (Aldershot: Ashgate, 2001).

Woodhead, L., P. Fletcher, H. Kawanami, and D. Smith (eds.), *Religions in the Modern World* (London: Routledge, 2002).

Woodhead, L., and P. Heelas (eds.), *Religion in Modern Times: An Interpretive Anthology* (Oxford: Blackwell, 2000).

Woodhead, L., P. Heelas, and D. Martin (eds.), *Peter Berger and the Study of Religion* (London: Routledge, 2001).

Wright, L., 'Sympathy for the Devil: It's Not Easy Being Evil in a World That's Gone to Hell', in Lehmann and Myers (eds.), *Magic, Witchcraft and Religion*, 393–404; 1st publ. in *Rolling Stone*, 5 Sept. 1991, 63–4, 66–8, 105–6.

Wright, M.A., 'The Great British Ecstasy Revolution', in McKay (ed.), *DIY Culture*, 228–42.

Wright, R., '"I'd Sell You Suicide": Pop Music and Moral Panic in the Age of Marilyn Manson', *Popular Music* 19 (2000), 365–85.

Wrigley, 'TV and Wicca', *Pagan Dawn* 140 (Lammas 2001), 57.

Wuthnow, R., *After Heaven: Spirituality in America since the 1950s* (Berkeley: University of California Press, 1998).

—*The Consciousness Reformation* (Berkeley: University of California Press, 1976).

Wylie, D., *Losing Ground* (London: Fourth Estate, 1998).

Yinger, J.M., *Religion, Society and the Individual* (New York: Macmillan, 1957).

Yip, A.K.T., 'The Self as the Basis of Religious Faith: Spirituality of Gay, Lesbian and Bisexual Christians', in Davie *et al.* (eds.), *Predicting Religion*, 135–46.

York, M., 'Alternative Spirituality in Europe: Amsterdam, Aups and Bath', in Sutcliffe and Bowman (eds.), *Beyond New Age*, 118–34.

—*The Emerging Network: A Sociology of the New Age and Neo-Pagan Movements* (Lanham, Md.: Rowman and Littlefield, 1995).

Zaehner, R.C., *Evolution in Religion: A Study in Sri Aurobindo and Pierre Teilhard de Chardin* (Oxford: Oxford University Press, 1971).

—*Hinduism*, 2nd edn (Oxford: Oxford University Press, 1966).

Zalewski, P., *Golden Dawn Enochian Magic* (St Paul: Llewellyn, 1994).

Zell, O., and M.G. Zell, 'Satanism vs. Neo-Pagan Witchcraft: Confusions and Distinctions', in Zell and Zell (eds.), *The Neo-Pagan Essence*, 29–43.

—'Where on Earth is the Church of All Worlds?', in Zell and Zell (eds.), *The Neo-Pagan Essence*, 44–50.

Zell, O., and M.G. Zell (eds.), *The Neo-Pagan Essence: Selected Papers from the Church of All Worlds* (Chicago: Eschaton, 1994).

Zellner, W.W., and M. Petrowsky (eds.), *Sects, Cults, and Spiritual Communities: A Socio-logical Analysis* (Westport, Conn.: Praeger, 1998).

Zukav, G., *The Dancing Wu Li Masters: An Overview of the New Physics* (London: Fontana, 1980).

DISCOGRAPHY

Aisha Kandisha's Jarring Effects, *Shabeesation* (Barraka el Farnatshi, 1993).

Allen, Mark, *Shamanic Trance: Psiberfunk Mix* (Return to the Source, 1997).

Alpha and Omega, *The Sacred Art of Dub* (AandO Records, 1998).

Ambient Meditations (Return to the Source, 1998).

Autechre, *Anti EP* (Warp, 1994).

Banco de Gaia, *Igizeh* (Disco Gecko, 2002).

The Beatles, *Revolver* (Parlophone, 1966).

—*Sgt. Pepper's Lonely Hearts Club Band* (Apple, 1967; EMI, 1987).

Burzum, *Hlidhskjalf* (Misanthropy, 1999).

Cash, Johnny, *American IV: The Man Comes Around* (American Recordings, 2003).

The Clash, *Sandinista!* (CBS, 1980).

Cope, Julian, *Jehovahkill* (Island, 1992).

Cope, Julian, and Donald Ross Skinner, *Rite* (K.A.K, 1992).

Dayjah and the Disciples, *Storm Clouds* (Third Eye Music, 1994).

Death in Vegas, *Scorpio Rising* (Concrete, 2002).

Deep Trance and Ritual Beats (Return to the Source, n.d.).

Depeche Mode, *Violator* (Mute, 1990).

Disciples Meet The Rootsman, *Rebirth* (Third Eye Music, 1997).

Dread Meets the Rockers Uptown, Social Classics Vol. 2 (EMI/Heavenly, 2001).

Enigma, *MCMXC A.D.* (Virgin, 1990).

Eno, Brian, *Discreet Music* (Editions EG, 1975).

—*Music for Airports* (Editions EG, 1978).

—*Neroli* (All Saints, 1993).

—*On Land* (Editions EG, 1982).

—*The Shutov Assembly* (Opal, 1992).

—*Thursday Afternoon* (EG, 1987).

Eno, Brian, and Harold Budd, *The Plateaux of Mirror* (Editions EG, 1978).

Eno, Brian, and Robert Fripp, *Evening Star* (Editions EG, 1975).

EZ3kiel, *Handle with Care* (Jarring Effects, 2001).

Faithless, *Sunday 8pm* (Cheeky Records, 1998).

Harrison, George, *All Things Must Pass* (Apple, 1970).

Hawkwind, *Space Ritual* (United Artists, 1973; EMI, 2001).

Hazardous Dub Company, *Dangerous Dubs Vol. 2* (Acid Jazz, 1993).

Headz: A Soundtrack of Experimental Hip-Hop Jams (Mo Wax, 1994).

High Tone, *Opus Incertum* (Jarring Effects, 2000).

Hillage, Steve, *Rainbow Dome Musick* (Virgin, 1979).

Incredible String Band, *The 5000 Spirits or the Layers of an Onion* (Elektra, 1967).

Jah Shaka, *Dub Symphony* (Island, 1990).

Leary, Timothy, *Beyond Life with Timothy Leary* (Mercury Records, 1997).

Led Zeppelin, *Houses of the Holy* (Atlantic, 1973).

Little Axe, *Hard Grind* (On-U Sound, 2002).
—*Slow Fuse* (M and G Records, 1996).
—*The Wolf that House Built* (Wired Recordings, 1994).
Mahavishnu Orchestra, *The Inner Mounting Flame* (Columbia, 1972).
Manson, Marilyn, *Antichrist Superstar* (Nothing-Interscope, 1996).
Mayhem, *De Mysteriis Dom Sathanas* (Century Media/Grind Core, 1994).
Moby, *Animal Rights* (Mute, 1996).
Morrison, Van, *Avalon Sunset* (Polydor, 1989).
—*Hymns to the Silence* (Polydor, 1991).
Muslimgauze, *The Inspirational Sounds of Muslimgauze* (Universal Egg, 2000).
Ozric Tentacles, *Afterswish* (Snapper Music, 1998).
—*Erpland* (Snapper Music, 1998).
—*The Hidden Step* (Snapper Music, 2002).
—*Pungent Efulgent* (Snapper Music, 1998).
—*Pyramidion* (Stretchy Records, 2001).
Pablo, Augustus, *Pablo Meets Mr. Bassie: Original Rockers Vol. 2* (Shanachie: 1991).
Pablo, Augustus, and Lee Perry, *Augustus Pablo Meets Lee Perry at the Black Ark* (Rhino Records, 2001).
Peace Not War (Shellshock, 2002).
Porcupine Tree, *Voyage 34: The Complete Trip* (Delerium, 2000).
Roach, Steve, *The Magnificent Void* (Fathom, 1996).
Rolling Stones, *Their Satanic Majesties Request* (Decca, 1967).
The Rootsman, *In Dub We Trust* (Third Eye Music, 1995).
—*Koyaanisqatsi* (Soundclash, 1994).
—*New Testament* (Meteosound, 2002).
—*Realms of the Unseen* (Third Eye Music, 1999).
The Rootsman Meets Celtarabia, *Union of Souls* (Third Eye Music, 1998).
The Rootsman Meets Muslimgauze, *Al Aqsa Intifada* (Third Eye Music, 2002).
Sacred Sites (Return to the Source, 1997).
Satyricon, *Nemesis Divina* (Moonfog, 1999).
The Sex Pistols, *Never Mind the Bollocks* (Virgin, 1977).
The Shamen, *Boss Drum* (One Little Indian Ltd, 1991).
—*The Shamen Collection* (One Little Indian Ltd, 1998).
Singh, Talvin, *Ha* (Universal Island Records, 2001).
Spring Heel Jack, *The Sound of Music EP* (Tugboat Records, 1999).
Suzuki, Tsuyoshi, *Shamanic Trance: Dada Funk Mix* (Return to the Source, 1996).
Sylvian, David, *Camphor* (Virgin, 2002).
—*Dead Bees on a Cake* (Virgin, 1999).
Tribal Futures: The Way Ahead (Yombo/Survival, 2000).
Twinkle Brothers, *Dub with Strings* (Twinkle Records, 1992).
—*Higher Heights (Twinkle Inna Polish Stylee)* (Twinkle Records, 1992).
UB40, *Signing Off* (Graduate, 1980).
Ulramarine, *Companion* (LTM, 2003).
—*Every Man and Woman is a Star* (Rough Trade Records, 1992; LTM, 2002).
Vital Remains, *Dechristianize* (Century Media, 2003).
Zephaniah, Benjamin, and The Hazardous Dub Company, *Back to Roots* (Acid Jazz Roots, 1995).

FILMOGRAPHY

Blade (1998), director Stephen Norrington.
Blade II (2002), director Guillermo del Toro.
Bram Stoker's Dracula (1992), director Francis Ford Coppola.
Buffy the Vampire Slayer (1992), director Fran Rubel Kuzui.
Buffy the Vampire Slayer (1992–2003), series creator Joss Whedon.
Charmed (1998–), series creator Constance Burge.
Close Encounters of the Third Kind (1977), director Steven Spielberg.
The Craft (1996), director Andrew Fleming.
Dracula (1979), director John Badham.
From Dusk Til Dawn (1996), director Robert Rodriguez.
Interview with the Vampire (1994), director Neil Jordan.
Invocation of My Demon Brother (1969), director Kenneth Anger.
Lucifer Rising (1973), director Kenneth Anger.
The Matrix (1999), directors Andy Wachowski and Larry Wachowski.
Nosferatu: Eine Symphonie des Grauens (1922), director F.W. Murnau.
Nosferatu: The Vampyre (1979), director Werner Herzog.
Practical Magic (1998), director Griffin Dunne.
Rosemary's Baby (1968), director Roman Polanski.
Sabrina the Teenage Witch (1996), director Tibor Takáks.
Salem's Lot (1979), director Tobe Hooper.
Scorpio Rising (1964), director Kenneth Anger.
Soul of Britain (2000), producers Gordon Heald (Opinion Research Business) and Graham Judd (BBC).
Star Wars (1977), director George Lucas.
The Wicker Man (1973), director Robin Hardy.
Woodstock: 3 Days of Peace and Music (1994), director Michael Wadleigh.